Springer Texts in Business and Economics

More information about this series at http://www.springer.com/series/10099

Stephen Lynn

Valuation for Accountants

A Short Course Based on IFRS

Springer

Stephen Lynn
NUS Business School
National University of Singapore
Singapore, Singapore

ISSN 2192-4333 ISSN 2192-4341 (electronic)
Springer Texts in Business and Economics
ISBN 978-981-15-0356-6 ISBN 978-981-15-0357-3 (eBook)
https://doi.org/10.1007/978-981-15-0357-3

This Springer imprint is published by the registered company Springer Nature Singapore Pte Ltd.
The registered company address is: 152 Beach Road, #21-01/04 Gateway East, Singapore 189721, Singapore

In memoriam
Prof. F.J. Noronha
Beatus vir

Preface

This book has developed from a single-semester course on valuation that I taught at the National University of Singapore (NUS) for some years to advanced undergraduates in accounting. The course covered valuation techniques for financial instruments, businesses, real estate, intangibles, purchase price allocation, and impairment based on the requirements of Singapore Financial Reporting Standards, which closely conformed to International Financial Reporting Standards (IFRS). The level was introductory but hopefully sufficient to be of practical use in professional settings.

This book is primarily written as a textbook for a similar one-semester course in any jurisdiction using IFRS. It can also be used for self-study by practicing accountants or others who wish to improve their skills in the area.

This book assumes prior knowledge of IFRS financial reporting to the level typically covered in intermediate accounting courses (i.e., single-entity accounting with a basic understanding of group accounting). It also assumes a prior understanding of basic finance topics including present value and the capital asset pricing model (CAPM).

The book requires some prior knowledge of mathematics and particularly statistics. Readers are assumed to be aware of probability, expected value, variance, the concepts of density and distribution functions, and least squares regression. These topics are usually covered in the early part of a typical undergraduate program in accounting or business. In addition, readers are assumed to be familiar with basic financial mathematics, including future and present value calculations under various conventions (including continuous compounding). A brief refresher of basic financial mathematics is provided in Appendix B.

Calculus and matrix algebra are not assumed, though this means that many proofs are omitted or given as brief sketches (e.g., Black-Scholes). We are anyway more concerned with application rather than proofs. Recall of school-level trigonometry is briefly needed in discussing real estate valuation (in calculating distances between locations).

Most financial-instrument models in this book need a computer for their application. Numerical models such as binomial or trinomial lattices are explained using toy models with two or three steps that can be solved manually.

A number of the exercises are programming problems based on a minimal subset of C/C++ that is described in the Appendix. These programming exercises can be ignored if wished, without any loss of continuity.

The sequence of topics puts financial instruments first. Some instructors may prefer to cover business valuation first. If so, I would recommend starting with a brief discussion of the risk-free rate following the initial sections of Chap. 3, after which it should be fine to handle topics in any preferred order with a couple of exceptions as noted below.

Probably, Chaps. 5 and 6 as well as Chaps. 3 and 4 should be read together in that order.

Also, some bond models are extensions of models introduced in the earlier chapter on options, so the sections on these should be read only after the options chapter is covered.

I did not try to be modular in writing this book. But the subject is naturally fairly modular, and so there should not be much problem in varying the order of topics.

Acknowledgments are due to the editorial team at Springer, particularly Stephen Jones who initiated this project, Lucie Bartonek who helped bring it to completion, and Nagarajan Paramasivam. I am also grateful to anonymous reviewers for useful comments and guidance.

Vidhi Killa provided useful research assistance.

I am grateful to NUS Business School and Edmund Keung for giving me time off and reduced workload to work on this book.

Parts of the draft of this book were discussed with Chua Kim Chiu, Lin Yupeng, and Srinivasan Sankaraguruswamy, who provided useful comments.

Chng Chee Kiong suggested the topics to be covered in the NUS valuation course, which are largely the same as the topics in this book.

Li Yan was my co-lecturer in the valuation course for several years. I have benefited from her suggestions and teaching ideas, particularly in the presentation of floating rate note valuation and PPA.

Student feedback over the years has considerably shaped the content and presentation of material in the valuation course and indirectly in this book too.

All errors are my own fault.

Singapore
August 2019

Stephen Lynn

Contents

Overview 1

In this chapter, we introduce the concept of valuation. We discuss different measures of current value required in accounting. These are—fair value, value in use and recoverable amount. We briefly survey the different situations where IFRS requires or allows measuring a current value. These include: PPE under the revaluation model, investment properties under the fair value model, many categories of financial instruments, purchase price allocation in a takeover, and recording asset impairments. We proceed to sketch IFRS 13 *Fair Value Measurement* requirements on fair value. We discuss the fair value hierarchy specified by IFRS 13, and the three approaches to valuation under IFRS 13.

1.1 Learning Outcomes

After completing this chapter, you would be able to:

1. Explain different types of current value in accounting—fair value, value in use and recoverable amount;
2. Explain briefly the fair value hierarchy under IFRS 13 *fair value measurement*;
3. Explain briefly the approaches to valuation in IFRS 13—market, income and cost approaches;

1.2 Introduction

We define valuation as follows for purposes of this book:

> Valuation finds the current value of some item using models from economics.

By value, we mean what the item is worth to some party.

By current, we mean current as of some specific date—this date is called the valuation date.

S. Lynn, *Valuation for Accountants*, Springer Texts in Business and Economics,
https://doi.org/10.1007/978-981-15-0357-3_1

In accounting, the items being valued are usually assets or liabilities on the balance sheet (or bundles of assets or liabilities). The valuation date is usually the balance-sheet date. The viewpoint is that of the organization preparing the balance sheet—the reporting entity.

1.2.1 Brief Comment on Notation

In the sequel, we use the term CU to refer to a unit of an arbitrary currency (We can read CU as an abbreviation of "currency unit".) This mimicks a similar convention in the official examples attached to IFRS standards.

To avoid clutter, we will implicitly assume that "today" or "now" is the valuation date in our examples, unless specifically stated otherwise.

We measure time by default in *years*, as is standard in financial mathematics. For periods given in days, we assume by default 365 days in a year, except when we are discussing some yield conventions that assume otherwise. Thus, 90 days would be treated as $\frac{90}{365}$ years, and the latter fraction would be the time parameter used in our models.

We refer to our valuation date as time 0 (zero years from today). We use the notation V_0 in general to refer to the value at time 0 of the item that we are valuing.

In presenting calculations, I report intermediate numbers usually in a more rounded form than was actually used in the calculation. So there would be some rounding differences if you check calculations by entering numbers exactly as given.

1.3 Current Value Concepts

Three different definitions of current value exist in accounting:

1. Fair value,
2. Value in use, and
3. Recoverable amount.

We briefly discuss each of these below:

1.3.1 Fair Value

The fair value of an asset is the amount of money that the reporting entity could realize if they sold the asset in an orderly market transaction on the valuation date.

The fair value of a liability is the amount of money that the reporting entity would have to pay to transfer the liability to a third party, again in an orderly market transaction on the valuation date.

Fair value is discussed in IFRS 13 *Fair value measurement*. We will sketch some features of this standard later in the chapter.

1.3.2 Value in Use

Value in use and recoverable amount are defined for assets only (or bundles of assets), not liabilities.

The value in use of an asset (or asset bundle) is the present value as of the valuation date of the projected pretax cash flows from using the asset throughout its remaining life.

Thus in contrast to fair value, it is the value from *not* selling the asset.

1.3.3 Recoverable Amount

The recoverable amount of an asset (or asset bundle) is the higher of:

1. the fair value, and
2. the value in use.

Recoverable amount is thus the highest value that can be obtained from the item. If more can be recovered by selling it, then recoverable amount equals fair value. If more can be recovered by not selling it, then recoverable amount equals value in use.

Value in use and recoverable amount arise only in the context of asset impairments under IAS 36.

1.4 Standards Requiring Current Value

In IFRS accounting (IASB 2019), several standards require assets and liabilities to be measured at current values (usually fair value). We briefly outline below the main areas where current value is required or allowed.

1.4.1 PPE and Investment Properties

IAS 16 *Property, Plant and Equipment* (PPE) requires PPE to be initially measured at its acquisition cost. Subsequently, it can be measured using either a historical cost model or a revaluation model. Entities must use the same model for entire classes of PPE. Under the revaluation model, PPE assets are periodically revalued to their fair value and reported at the revalued amount on the balance sheet.

IAS 40 *Investment property* offers a choice between a cost model and a fair value model. The same model must be applied to all investment properties. Under the fair value model, investment properties are reported at their fair value on the balance sheet.

As a consequence of these standards, accountants need some knowledge of how to value properties. The valuation itself would be done by an external valuation professional. But accountants should still know enough to decide whether the valuation is accurate and reasonable.

1.4.2 Financial Instruments

Several standards prescribe financial instrument accounting—IFRS 9 *Financial instruments*, IFRS 7 *Financial instruments: disclosures*, and IAS 32 *Financial instruments: presentation*.

Under IFRS 9 financial assets are classified into two broad types based on how their balance sheet value is measured—fair value and amortized cost. Assets at fair value are further classified into Fair value through profit and loss (FVTPL) and Fair value through other comprehensive income (FVTOCI or FVOCI), depending on whether revaluation gains on these assets are recorded as part of profit for the year or in other comprehensive income respectively. The FVTPL–FVTOCI distinction need not concern us in this book.

In a nutshell, IFRS 9 requires almost all financial assets to be at fair value. The exceptions are debt securities where both the following conditions are true:

1. Under the entity's business model, these items are normally held to maturity,
2. The expected future cash flows from the asset consist only of interest and capital repayments.

Even assets that satisfy both these conditions could be optionally recorded at fair value.

Financial liabilities are usually not at fair value. But one major exception is—derivative contracts (derivatives). Depending on market conditions, these contracts could have a positive fair value—in which case they are recorded as assets; or they could have a negative fair value—in which case they are recorded as liabilities. In either case, they are always recorded at fair value.

Some non-derivative financial liabilities too could potentially be measured at fair value under a fair value option.

In summary, these requirements imply that accountants should have some knowledge of how to value a wide range of financial instruments. Even though the actual valuation could be performed by others, the accountant needs to know enough to assess the accuracy and reasonableness of the valuation.

1.4.3 Employee Stock Options

Related to financial instruments is the issue of accounting for employee stock options (ESOs) under IFRS 2 *Share-based payment*.

When a company compensates an employee by granting her employee stock options, the compensation expense each year is based on the fair value of the employee stock options at the *grant* date. Estimating this requires using specialized valuation models that have little relevance outside accounting. Accountants need to have some understanding of these models.

1.4.4 Purchase Price Allocation, Intangibles and Goodwill

When a company acquires another, the accounting under IFRS 3 *Business combinations* requires extensive fair value measurement. This is in the purchase price allocation or PPA.

Firstly, all the assets and liabilities of the target must be measured at their fair values on the acquisition date.

Secondly, the acquirer must identify unrecorded intangible assets of the target, and then measure these at their fair value on the acquisition date. This requires using specialized models for intangible valuation.

Thirdly, the acquirer must determine the value of non-controlling interest in the target. The preferred method to do so involves estimating its fair value on the acquistion date.

Goodwill emerges as a residual from the purchase price allocation process. Subsequently, it must be tested every year for impairment, which requires estimating its recoverable amount (indirectly).[1]

Acquisition accounting requires a sound knowledge of enterprise valuation, since the acquired company is an enterprise, and NCI and goodwill are parts of that enterprise.

1.4.5 Impairment

PPE and intangibles measured under the cost approach are subject to impairment tests under IAS 36 (depending on the asset, these tests are conducted either every year or only irregularly when some warning sign of impairment is noted). The impairment test requires finding the recoverable amount of the asset. If its balance-sheet carrying amount is higher than the recoverable amount, then the asset must be written down usually to its recoverable amount.

In addition to various fair value models, accountants need a good understanding of what IAS 36 has to say about measuring value in use.

[1] We value goodwill as part of a larger bundle of assets.

1.4.6 Others: Agriculture, Provisions

IAS 41 *Agriculture* requires most agricultural assets to be measured at their fair value on the balance-sheet date.

IAS 37 *Provisions, contingent liabilities and contingent assets* requires provisions (uncertain liabilities) to be measured using a current value definition that resembles fair value.

We will not discuss these somewhat specialized contexts in this book.

1.5 More on IFRS 13

1.5.1 The Fair Value Definition

1.5.1.1 Market

The IFRS 13 definition of fair value requires a market. This should be the principal market for the item, or if there is no principal market, the most advantageous market. By default, the principal or most advantageous market is presumed to be the one in which the entity would usually dispose of the item.

1.5.1.2 Highest and Best Use

In the case of a non-financial asset, the buyer of the asset would presumably require it for some use. This raises the spectre of different would-be buyers offering different prices because they want the item for different uses. IFRS 13 specifies that in estimating fair value, the would-be buyer is assumed to want the asset to put it to its "highest and best use", the one which gives optimal value to the user. By default, this highest and best use is assumed to be the same as the actual current use to which the entity is putting the asset.

1.5.2 The Fair Value Hierarchy

The quality of a valuation depends largely on the quality of the input data. IFRS 13 reflects this by describing a hierarchy of three levels of inputs in descending order of input quality (better quality to worse quality).[2]

1.5.2.1 Level 1

Level 1 inputs are current quoted prices of items that are identical to the item being valued, with the price quotes coming from an active market.

[2] In the language of the standard and elsewhere, Level 1 is a *higher* level than Level 2, which is a *higher* level than Level 3; conversely Level 3 is *lower* than Level 2, which is *lower* than Level 1.

1.5.2.2 Level 2

Level 2 inputs are observable inputs that fall short of Level 1 quality—for example, current quoted prices of similar (but not identical) items, or quoted prices for identical items but from an inactive market.

1.5.2.3 Level 3

Level 3 inputs are unobservable. They reflect assumptions and judgement rather than direct observable evidence of what they purport to measure.

1.5.2.4 Binding Preference

The hierarchy imposes a binding preference in terms of the choice of inputs. If a Level 1 input is available, then it should be used in preference to any lower-level input. Similarly, if no Level 1 input is available, Level 2 inputs should be preferred to Level 3 inputs.

In particular, if a quoted current price for an identical item is available from an active market, that price is the fair value. Valuation models such as those in this book are only applicable when such a price is *not* available.

Even when price quotes are available, there is some room for ambiguity. Should we use the latest bid price (latest price offered by a potential buyer) for an asset, and the latest ask price for a liability (latest price requested by someone willing to take over the liability)? IFRS 13 permits but does not require this treatment. Sometimes, using the latest closing price (price in the last completed transaction) or the midpoint of the latest bid and ask prices may be better.

1.5.2.5 Hierarchy of Items

For disclosure purposes, entities are required to classify fair-valued assets and liabilities too into Level 1, Level 2 and Level 3 depending on what type of inputs predominate in their valuation. To do so requires judgement.

1.6 Valuation Approaches

IFRS 13 lists three main approaches to valuation:

1. The market approach,
2. The income approach, and
3. The cost approach.

1.6.1 The Market Approach

The market approach uses current market prices of identical or similar items to value an item.

1.6.2 The Income Approach

The income approach uses information about the actual or projected income from the item to estimate its fair value.

1.6.3 The Cost Approach

The cost approach values an asset at the amount that an entity would have to pay to replace it—its current replacement cost.

1.6.4 Other Approaches

Two commonly used approaches do not neatly fit into the IFRS 13 classification. These are:

1. The asset approach (to valuing a business)
2. The replicating portfolio approach (to valuing a financial instrument)

1.6.4.1 The Asset Approach

The asset approach is an approach to valuing businesses or business units.

In this approach, we first value the assets and liabilities of the business individually. Then we value the equity in the business as the total asset value (found by adding up the individual asset values) less the total liability value (found by adding up the individual liability values).

Equivalently we can use the total asset value net of working capital liabilities as the estimate of the value of invested capital (debt plus equity).

The asset approach underlies *purchase price allocation* under IFRS 3 *Business Combinations* (See Chap. 7).

1.6.4.2 The Replicating Portfolio Approach

This approach values a financial asset or liability (the target say) by finding some combination of items (a portfolio) that gives the same future payoffs as the target. This portfolio is called a *replicating porfolio*: that is, one that replicates the payoffs from the target.

With well-behaved markets, the price of the replicating portfolio must be the same as the value of the target. Otherwise, *arbitrage* is possible. You could make a riskless, costless, profit by short-selling the more expensive item and then using the funds from the short sale to buy the cheaper item.

So, assuming no arbitrage, we can use the price of the replicating portfolio as the target's fair value.

This concludes our introductory overview of valuation for accountants. In Chap. 2, we begin our discussion of financial instruments. We will start with option valuation.

Reference

IASB. (2019). *International financial reporting standards*. London: IASB.

Forwards and Options

2

In this chapter, we cover forward and option contracts. We introduce generic forward contracts. We move to vanilla options, focusing on options to buy or sell one share, without much loss of generality. We start by briefly defining standard option types—calls vs puts, European vs American vs Bermuda exercise styles, and Asian options. We move to models to value European options when no dividends are due during the option life. Using a simple one-step model of price movements, we explain two approaches to solving option models—the dynamic hedging approach and the risk-neutral probabilities approach. We then introduce the put-call parity relationship. This relationship helps find the price of a European put given that of a similar European call and vice versa. We cover some standard lattice models including the Cox-Ross-Rubinstein binomial model, the equal-probabilities binomial model, and a version of the trinomial model. We introduce the Black-Scholes model as the limit of a binomial model as the number of steps increase. We proceed to adapt the models where possible to the valuation of American options when no dividends are due during the option life. Then we extend the models further where possible to handle fixed dividends that fall due during the option life. We briefly discuss valuation of Bermuda options. We proceed to look at the valuation of employee stock options (ESOs) following the requirements of IFRS 2 *Share based compensation*. We briefly discuss the modified Black-Scholes approach allowed under U.S. GAAP, as well as the Hull-White model of ESO valuation, adapted to comply with IFRS 2. We turn to Asian options, showing how they can be valued by Monte Carlo simulation. We close with how to estimate the volatility parameter for option models using approaches based on historical prices as well as one based on the implied volatility from a traded option.

2.1 Learning Outcomes

After completing this chapter, you would be able to:

S. Lynn, *Valuation for Accountants*, Springer Texts in Business and Economics,
https://doi.org/10.1007/978-981-15-0357-3_2

1. Value a generic forward contract given a quote or estimate for the forward price.
2. Value vanilla European and American call and put options using standard models.
3. Value employee stock options to fulfill IFRS 2 requirements using Black-Scholes and the Hull-White employee stock option model.
4. Value Asian options using Monte Carlo simulation.
5. Estimate historical and implied volatility.

2.2 Forwards

A forward contract (or just forward) is a contract to deliver a fixed amount A units of some item at a fixed future date t, in exchange for an amount of money based on a fixed price per unit K, paid at the same future date. The terms of the contract are fixed in advance when the contract is signed.

We refer to K as the *strike price* or *exercise price* of the contract. We refer to t as the *strike date* or the *exercise date* or the *maturity date* of the contract. We follow the convention of measuring t in years from today (our valuation date).

2.2.1 Fair Value of a Forward

For a freshly-issued forward contract (in an arms-length transaction), the strike price would be set at a level that both sides consider fair. Then neither party would expect to gain or lose at this point. Then the parties would not exchange any money upfront at the time of issue, and both parties would reflect the fair value of the contract on this date as zero.

For a seasoned contract (that is, after the issue date), its fair value depends on the terms and conditions of newly-issued similar contracts in the market.

Suppose that the market currently offers fresh contracts for the same strike date and contract amount as the seasoned forward, but with a strike price of F. We refer to F as the *forward price* corresponding to that strike date.

More formally, we define the forward price F_t corresponding to a date t years from today to be the market strike price for a new forward contract to exchange 1 unit of the item at time t.

Suppose that we hold a seasoned contract maturing at time t years from today with strike price K and quantity A. We are the buyer under the contract, i.e., we have an obligation to buy A units at price CU K per unit at time t. Without much loss of generality, let us fix A to be 1. We are therefore going to model the fair value per unit under the forward contract.

Suppose that the current forward price for date t is F_t.

Then if we wish to transfer our forward contract to someone else today, say Sam Co, the amount that we would get from them (or pay them) would depend on the difference between the K we are locked into under our contract, and the F_t that the market offers.

If F_t is greater than K, Sam Co would benefit to the tune of CU $(F_t - K)$ at time t as compared to entering a new contract today. They should therefore be willing to pay us up to the present value of this difference today to take over this contract (and we should not be willing to take less).

If F_t is less than K, Sam Co would lose money by taking over our contract as compared to entering a new contract today. They would have a gain of CU $(F_t - K)$ at time t as compared to entering a new contract today (a negative gain aka a loss). They would therefore demand that we pay them upfront at least the present value of this loss, if they agree to take over the contract (and we should not be willing to pay more). In this case, the forward is a liability to us, and would be reported under liabilities if today were our reporting date.

Therefore, the fair value of the forward contract from our (buyer) point of view is the present value of CU $(F_t - K)$. Depending on whether this value is positive or negative respectively, the forward would be an asset or a liability on our books.

The relevant discount rate for the present value is the risk-free rate. This is because the transaction is risk-free—there is no uncertainty about how much we have to pay or the current forward price that we are comparing to, and if the other party defaults by not giving us the item, we lose nothing because we don't pay them in that case. Let the continuously compounded risk-free rate be r_c p.a.

Then the fair value of the forward to the buyer is:

$$e^{-r_c t}(F_t - K).$$

Let us consider the valuation from the viewpoint of the *seller* rather than the buyer of the contract.

Suppose that we were the *seller* under the same contract. That is, our contract requires us to *sell* 1 unit of the item at time t for price K. Using similar logic to the buyer case, our contract would have a positive value if F_t is less than K (asset), and a negative value if F_t is greater than K (liability). Sam Co's gain at time t in this case would be $(K - F_t)$.

Thus the fair value of the forward to the seller is:

$$e^{-r_c t}(K - F_t).$$

Notice that the respective values of the forward to buyer and seller always sum to zero. That is, the buyer's asset is always equal to the seller's liability, and vice versa.

2.2.1.1 Example

On Jul 1 2018, Nefertiti enters a forward contract to buy 100 bags of rice on Jan 1 2020 at a strike price of CU 10 per bag. Ramo is the seller under this contract.

The balance-sheet date for both Nefertiti and Ramo is Dec 31 2018. On this date, they both have to record the forward on their respective dates at fair value.

On Dec 31 2018, fresh forward contracts with a maturity of Jan 1 2020 have a strike price of CU 11 (i.e., $F_t = 11$). This date is exactly one year before the strike date (i.e., $t = 1$).

Also on Dec 31 2018 the risk-free rate is 10% continuously compounded (i.e., $r_c = 10\%$).

We wish to find the fair value of the forward to Nefertiti and to Ramo respectively.

To Nefertiti, the value of the contract is:

$$e^{-0.1\times 1}(11 - 10) \times 100 = 90.484.$$

They would record this as an asset.

To Ramo, the value of the contract is:

$$e^{-0.1\times 1}(10 - 11) \times 100 = (90.484).$$

This corresponds to a liability of CU 90.484.

2.2.2 Estimating the Forward Price

A further interesting valuation problem involves estimating the forward price F_t if this is not quoted, based on the spot price (price for immediate delivery) S. Models to solve this problem depend on the nature of the item being bought or sold. We will examine such models for forward interest rates and for forward exchange rates in the next chapter.

2.2.3 Futures

A futures contract is a standardized forward contract that trades on an exchange. In terms of valuation, there is no material difference between a forward and a futures contract. The day-to-day accounting would usually differ between them due to market rules governing futures, which typically require counterparties to settle their gains and losses daily (daily mark to market), but this need not concern us here. In the sequel, we treat forwards and futures as equivalent and use the generic term forwards to refer to both.

2.3 Options

Options, also called *warrants* or *structured warrants*, are contracts that give the holder the right to buy or sell a fixed number of units of some item at a fixed price K at some fixed future dates on or before the contract expiry date t.

Without loss of much generality, let us focus on options to buy or sell one share.

The difference between an option and a forward is that the option holder has a *right* but *no obligation* to exercise the option. For a forward however, the holder has a legally binding obligation to exercise their end of the contract, even if they lose by doing so.

Therefore in contrast to a forward, an option contract would never be a liability to the holder. At worst, its value would be zero. Conversely, to the option issuer, the option is always a liability (or worthless).

Therefore, when the option is issued, the issuer would charge something for it upfront. At a minimum, they would charge the incremental amount that they need to cover their future losses from the option (hedge).

2.3.1 Option Types

2.3.1.1 Calls vs Puts

A *call* is an option to buy the share.
A *put* is an option to sell the share.

2.3.1.2 European vs American vs Bermuda Options

Options can be classified based on their *exercise style* into European, American and Bermuda options.

A *European* option can be exercised only on a single date, which usually corresponds to the expiry date.

An *American* option can be exercised at any time after it is issued until it expires. That is, it can be exercised at any date between the issue date and the expiry date. (But like a European option, it can only be exercised once. Once exercised, the option ceases to exist.)

A *Bermuda* option can be exercised at multiple dates during its life. That is, its life includes both dates when it can be exercised and dates when it cannot be exercised. Like a European or American option, it can only be exercised once. Once exercised, the option ceases to exist.

2.3.1.3 Asian Options

Asian options have strike prices that are not a fixed lumpsum amount, but rather a formula based on the average share price during some part of the option life.

Asian options could have strike dates that follow European, American or Bermuda exercise styles. We could therefore talk of European-style Asian options, American-style Asian options or Bermuda-style Asian options.

2.3.1.4 Vanilla vs Exotic Options

European and American-style puts and calls with fixed strike prices are referred to as vanilla options. All other option types are called exotic options. Exotic options include a wide variety of option types beyond those we introduced here. In this book, we will largely confine ourselves to vanilla options.

2.4 European Options with No Dividends

We start by considering models to value European options, when no dividends are due for the underlying share during the option life (dividends complicate the models as we will see later).

2.4.1 The Single-Step Binomial

We use a simple example to introduce option valuation. Suppose we have a European call option giving us the right to buy the share at CU 6 at a fixed strike date that is 90 days from today.

The current share price is CU 5.

Let us assume that the share price can take on just two values at the 90-day mark. Either it could go up to CU 10, or it could go down to CU 2.

This is of course not realistic at all, but it's just a starting point for a more realistic model.

We can model the price movements using a diagram called a binomial lattice, as shown below:

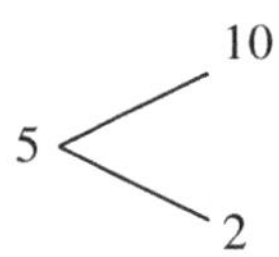

We refer to the price levels as *nodes* and the up and down lines connecting them as *branches*. The start of the lattice is the valuation date, and the end point is the option expiry date.

We can proceed to calculate the option value at the strike date for each of the two possible future prices. If the strike price goes up to CU 10, then we can realize a profit of CU 4 by exercising (we can buy the share for CU 6 and immediately sell it for CU 10). If the expiry-date price is 2, then we would not exercise because we would lose money by doing so. Then the option would just expire unexercised, and we would have no gain no loss or a payoff of zero.

We can record these payoffs in our lattice. Conventionally we record these in square brackets under the share price at the node. These payoffs represent the option value at these nodes.

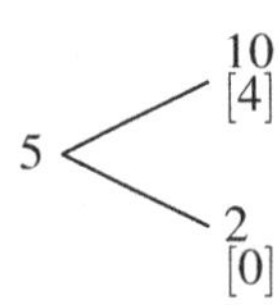

We want to solve for the option value today. We examine two ways to do this below—delta hedging, and risk-neutral probabilities. While the mechanics look different, the two methods are mathematically equivalent. They always give the same answer and can be used to check each other.

We need one further parameter in our model—the risk-free rate. Let us take a risk-free rate of 10% in our example (continuously compounded).

2.4.1.1 Delta Hedging

In the delta hedging approach (also called dynamic hedging), we seek a replicating portfolio consisting of a mix of shares and money that gives us the same payoffs at the expiry date t as the option. That is, the replicating portfolio should give us CU 4 if the share price goes up to CU 10, and should give us CU 0 if the share price goes down to CU 2.

Then the value of the option is simply the value of this replicating portfolio, which is easy to calculate.

Let the number of shares in the portfolio today be Δ (the uppercase Greek letter "delta"). Let the amount of money in the portfolio today be X. These numbers could be positive or negative. A negative value of X implies that we borrow money. A negative value of Δ implies that we acquire a short position in the shares today—we borrow the shares and sell them immediately.

In valuation models for calls, Δ is positive while X is negative. The opposite is true for puts. Recall that the option is a call in our example.

We now solve for Δ and X. Recall that the combination should give us CU 4 if the share price goes up to 10, and CU 0 if the share price goes down to 2.

Also the X that we hold today would grow to $X \times e^{0.1 \times \frac{90}{365}}$ by the exercise date as we can invest it at the risk-free rate (or pay interest at the risk-free rate if it's a liability).

Combining these facts gives us the following two equations:

$$10\Delta + Xe^{0.1 \times \frac{90}{365}} = 4.$$

$$2\Delta + Xe^{0.1 \times \frac{90}{365}} = 0.$$

Solving these simultaneous equations, we get:

$$\Delta = \frac{1}{2}.$$

$$X = -0.9756 \ (4 \ dp.).$$

We can now solve for the value of the replicating portfolio and thence the option value C as follows:

$$C = 5\Delta + X.$$

This gives us $C = \text{CU}1.5244$.

The reason for the term "hedging" in naming this approach is that the option issuer can eliminate their risk (hedge) by buying Δ shares and borrowing (the absolute value of) X when they issue the option. Then their losses from the option would always be perfectly covered by their gains from the replicating portfolio. They would charge the option buyer just the extra amount of cash that they need to set up the replicating portfolio, and this is the fair price of the option. (The issuer borrows CU 0.9756, charges CU 1.5244 for the option, and uses the combined proceeds CU 2.50 to buy half a share.)

Being a perfect hedge, the combination of issuing the option and creating the replicating portfolio is risk-free, which is why the risk-free rate applies.

We can complete our lattice as follows:

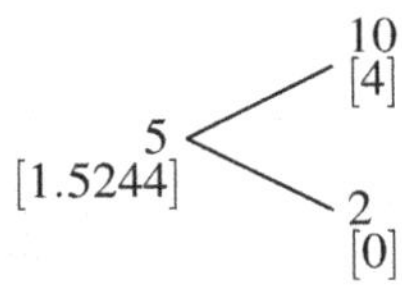

2.4.1.2 Risk-Neutral Probabilities

In this method, we find the option value as the expected present value of the option payoffs, calculated using risk-neutral probabilities.

Risk-neutral probabilities are probabilities under which the current value of an item with uncertain future value (like the share) is exactly equal to the expected present value of its future payoffs, discounted at the risk-free rate.

This is the value that someone who is indifferent to risk would place on the item, as opposed to someone who is risk-averse, who would seek some additional return to compensate for their uncertainty.

In our example, if p_u is the risk-neutral probability of an upward move to CU 10, and p_d is the risk-neutral probability of a downward move to CU 2, we have:

$$C = e^{-0.1\times\frac{90}{365}} \times (p_u \times 4 + p_d \times 0).$$

We need to solve for p_u and p_d which we do by noting that the current share price of CU 5 should be the expected present value of the future share price under these probabilities. So we have:

$$5 = e^{-0.1\times\frac{90}{365}} \times (p_u \times 10 + p_d \times 2).$$

Noting that $p_d = 1 - p_u$, we can solve to get $p_u = 0.3906$ (4 dp).

We can now solve for the option value C, getting $C = 1.5244$.

We have not explained the derivation of this model. A sketch of the logic is given in the chapter appendix.

One point to note here is that the risk-neutral probabilities do not necessarily reflect market assumptions about the future, i.e., they are not the market's imputed probabilities. This is as we cannot assume that investors in the market are risk-neutral. Rather, p_u and p_d should be regarded as just model parameters that it is convenient to interpret as probabilities.

2.4.2 Put-Call Parity

Put-call parity is a relationship between the price of a European call and a European put with the same strike price and strike date. It helps us to price the put given the call price, and vice versa.

Put-call parity can be expressed as follows:

$$P + S - C = Ke^{-r_c t} \tag{2.1}$$

where P, S and C are the current prices of the put, share and call respectively, r_c is the risk-free rate (continuously compounded), and t is the maturity date expressed in years from today.

This formula is true when no dividends are due during the option life. Dividends lead to a modified formula that we consider in a later section. Also put-call parity holds only for European options. It is not true for American options.

To prove the result, consider a strategy where we buy one share and one put option and sell one call (or *write* or *issue* the call, in options jargon).

Now consider the value of this portfolio at time t under three scenarios:

1. The share price has moved to some price $S_U > K$.
2. The share price has moved to be exactly equal to the strike price K.
3. The share price has moved to some price $S_D < K$.

Notice that these three scenarios cover all possible future prices.

In the first scenario, at time t, the put option would expire worthless, the call option would cost us CU $(S_U - K)$, and the share would be worth S_U. Therefore, the value of the portfolio would be CU $[S_U + 0 - (S_U - K)]$ which equals CU K.

In the second scenario, whether exercised or not, the put and call are both worth zero at t, while the share has a value of K at t. Therefore the portfolio will have a value of CU $(0 + 0 + K)$ or CU K.

In the third scenario, the call would not be exercised, costing us nothing, the put would be worth $(K - S_D)$, and the share price would be S_D. Therefore, the portfolio would be worth CU $(S_D + K - S_D)$, which works out to CU K.

In any scenario, the portfolio is exactly equal to K at time t. This means that it should have the same price today as a risk-free bond that pays exactly CU K at time t or $Ke^{-r_c t}$. Equating this to the current price of setting up the portfolio gives us the equation 2.1.

2.4.2.1 Example: Put-Call Parity

We can use put-call parity to derive the price of the put corresponding to the call in our earlier example. Recall that in our example, the share price is CU 5, the strike price is CU 6, the maturity is at 90 days, and that we had derived the call price to be CU 1.5244. Applying put-call parity, we have:

$$P = 6.e^{-0.1\times\frac{90}{365}} - 5 + 1.5244.$$

Solving for P, we get $P = 2.3783$ (4 dp).

We can verify this value by solving for P directly using either risk-neutral probabilities or delta hedging. This is left as an exercise.

2.4.3 Multi-step Lattices

The one-step model is unrealistic. But what if instead of a single step, the binomial lattice was made up of a series of steps, each step constituting a small fraction of the time to maturity?

Such a model is a better fit to reality as it models a large set of possible price paths during the option life, given by the various sequences of possible up and down moves along the branches of the lattice. Then any actual life path is likely to be approximated by one of these sequences. This is illustrated by Fig. 2.1.

Solving a binomial model with reasonable accuracy requires a large number of steps (at least 50). The larger the number of steps, the more accurate the model.

Practical models cannot be solved by hand and need a computer. In this book, we show models with just two or three steps. But this is just so that the computations can be followed by manual calculation, and these are not accurate.

We will focus on some standard models that share some common assumptions and terminology, outlined below.

1. Future share prices at any future date are assumed to have risk-neutral probabilities that are drawn from a *lognormal* distribution. If the share price today is S_0 and the (uncertain) future price at time t (measured in years) is $\tilde{S}_t$, then $\ln(\frac{\tilde{S}_t}{S_0})$ is assumed to have risk-neutral probabilities that follow a normal distribution (a Bell curve or a Gaussian distribution), with mean 0 and standard deviation $\sigma\sqrt{t}$ where σ (the greek letter sigma) is called "volatility".[1] Note that the expression $\ln(\frac{\tilde{S}_t}{S_0})$ can also be interpreted as the continuously compounded returns from

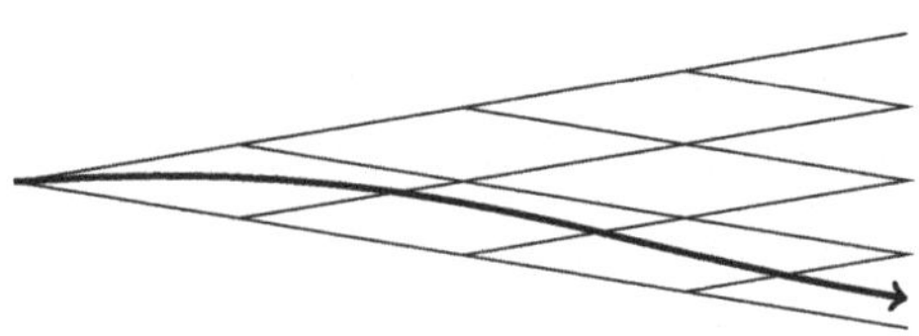

Fig. 2.1 A multi-step lattice showing a potential actual price path in bold

[1]Some alternative models (not considered here) have a non-zero mean called the drift parameter.

buying the share today and holding it to time t. The mathematics captures the following intuition:

- Future prices are as likely to move up as down (so that the current price is the best predictor of the future price),
- Smaller price moves are more likely than larger moves,
- Bigger moves in either direction become more likely for longer periods of time than for shorter periods of time.

Another way to state this assumption is to say that the share price follows a *random walk*.

2. We assume a constant risk-free rate through the option life. In option models this rate is conventionally stated as a continuously compounded rate. We will denote this continuously compounded risk-free rate by r_c.

These assumptions may not be a good fit to reality. We can adapt the models to allow for time-varying interest rates and more complicated volatility structures, but we will not consider such advanced models in our book.

2.4.3.1 Notation

We denote the current share price S as the starting point of the lattice.

Let an upward step at each node be u and a downward step be d. In the standardized models in this chapter, u and d are the same at every step.

The parameters u and d are factors, not increments. So if the price at the current node is S_0, then the price from a single upward step is $S_0 \times u$ or $S_0 u$ (*not* $S_0 + u$), and the price from a single downward step is $S_0 \times d$ or $S_0 d$ (*not* $S_0 + d$ or $S_0 - d$).

In our standardized model, the length of each step is the same. This length is denoted as Δt and is measured in years. Be careful that Δt is a single symbol (*not* $\Delta \times t$). The Δ here is standard mathematical shorthand for "a small change in" some variable. So Δt stands for "a small change in time".

2.4.4 Solving the Model: General Strategy

We solve the multi-step model by starting at the maturity date where the option value is simply the gain from exercising or zero at each ending node. We then move to the immediately prior set of nodes—the prices at the step just before the maturity date. Each node or price here coupled with the up and down branches from it, constitutes a single-step sub-lattice that we can solve using the risk-neutral probabilities approach or delta hedging.

Having solved for the option prices at the second-last set of nodes, we can move to the previous set of nodes, and repeat the same procedure. We can continue this until we reach the initial starting price, where we can solve for the current option value.

For this method to work, the lattice needs to be designed to be *recombining*. That is, the price at a down step from one node should be the same as the price from an up step from the node immediately below it.

2.4.4.1 Risk-Neutral Probabilities General Formula

In our standardized models, the risk-neutral probability approach has the convenient feature that it gives the same risk-neutral probabilities for every single-step component of the multi-step lattice. Therefore, we only need to calculate the risk-neutral probability once.

The risk-neutral probability of an up step is given by:

$$p_u = \frac{e^{r\Delta t} - d}{u - d}. \tag{2.2}$$

See proof in 2.12 to this chapter.

2.4.5 Cox-Ross-Rubinstein (CRR)

In this model (Cox et al. 1979), at each step, the natural logarithm of the share price is assumed to go up or down by a factor corresponding to a one-standard-deviation move. This would be $\sigma\sqrt{\Delta t}$. Thus we have:

$$\ln(Su) = ln(S) + \sigma\sqrt{\Delta t}.$$
$$\ln(Sd) = ln(S) - \sigma\sqrt{\Delta t}.$$

We have the following expressions for u and d:

$$u = e^{\sigma\sqrt{\Delta t}}.$$
$$d = e^{-\sigma\sqrt{\Delta t}}.$$

We illustrate the model with an example of a European call. Suppose that $S = 5$, $K = 6$ (the strike price), $t = \frac{90}{365}$ years (90 days), and the risk-free rate r_c equals 10%.

We will use a three-step model (with a reminder that this is just for illustration, and we need at least 50 steps and a computer for any practical model).

Then each step is 30 days or $\Delta t = \frac{30}{365}$.

The volatility parameter has been estimated to be 30% or 0.30.

We first calculate the up and down steps. These are:

$$u = e^{0.3\sqrt{\frac{30}{365}}} = 1.0898 \ (4 \ dp).$$

$$d = e^{-0.3\sqrt{\frac{30}{365}}} = 0.9176 \ (4 \ dp).$$

Notice that $d = \frac{1}{u}$ in this model. There are other models where this is not true, and we will see one shortly—the equal probabilities model. As a consequence of d being the reciprocal of u in this model, the price returns to the starting point every two steps (i.e., a sequence of an up followed by a down brings us back to the starting point). This can be seen from the lattice in Fig. 2.2.

We first find the option value for the various prices at the exercise date. Except for the top node, all the prices are below the strike price of CU 6. So the option is worth zero at all but the top node. At the top node the option has a value of CU 0.4718 (4 dp). This is reflected in Fig. 2.2.

We now solve for the risk-neutral probability:

$$p_u = \frac{e^{0.1 \times \frac{30}{365}} - 0.9176}{1.0898 - 0.9174} = 0.5264 \ (4 \ dp).$$

We can now solve for the option values at the second-last step. Starting from the bottom, we can see that the option has a value of zero in the bottom two sub-trees.

For the bottom sub-tree:

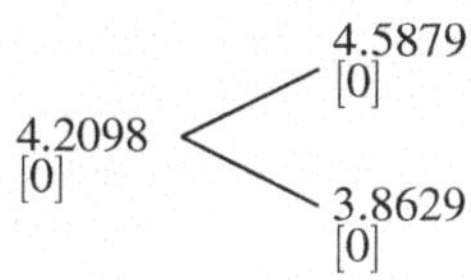

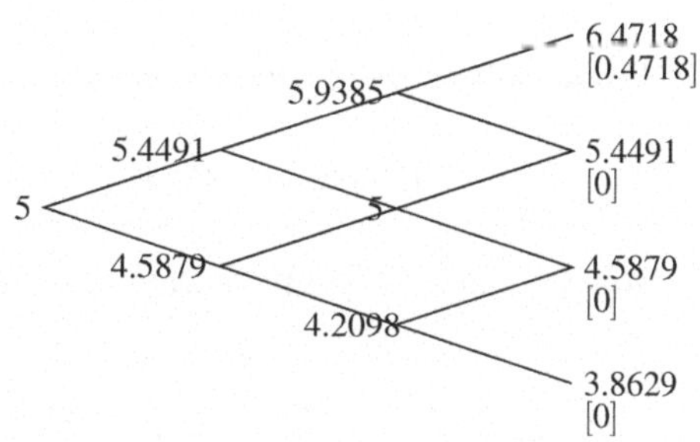

Fig. 2.2 CRR example

For the subtree just higher:

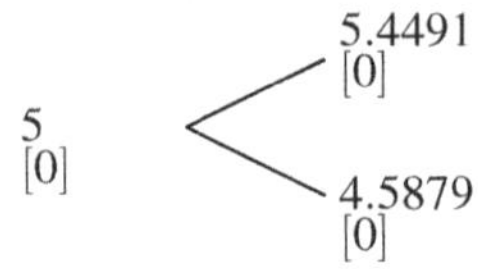

We are left with the top sub-tree:

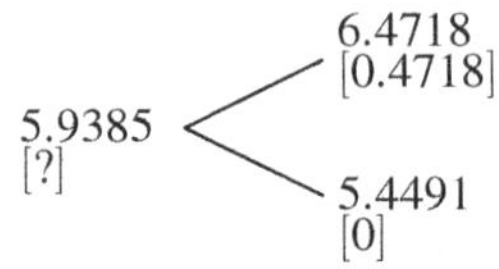

We can use risk-neutral probabilities to work out the option value at this node:

$$0.4718 \times 0.5264e^{-0.1\times\frac{30}{365}} = 0.2464\ (4\ dp).$$

Moving to the preceding set of nodes, we note that the bottom-most node has an option price of zero.

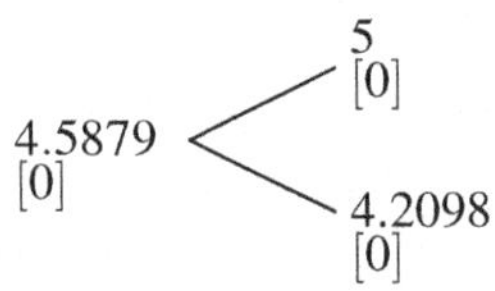

We are left with the top node:

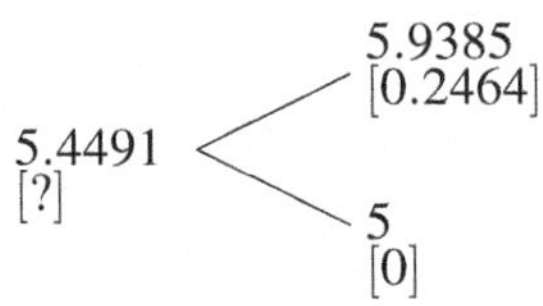

We can solve for the option value at this node as:

$$0.2464 \times 0.5264 \times e^{-0.1\times\frac{30}{365}} = 0.1286\ (4\ dp).$$

Now we can solve for the current option value by solving the initial sub-lattice:

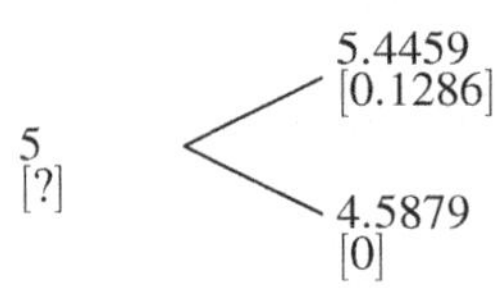

We have:

$$C = 0.1286 \times 0.5264 \times e^{-0.1\times\frac{30}{365}} = 0.0672.$$

2.4.6 The Equal Probabilities Model

It is convenient to construct the lattice so that the risk-neutral probabilities are both always 0.5. Suppose that we seek to do this by multiplying both the up and down steps in CRR by some factor e^X say. Then we have:

$$u = e^{(\sigma\sqrt{\Delta t}+X)}.$$

$$d = e^{(-\sigma\sqrt{\Delta t}+X)}.$$

Plugging these expressions into equation 2.2 and solving for X we get:

$$X = \ln(2) + r_c \Delta t - \ln\left(e^{\sigma\sqrt{\Delta t}} + e^{-\sigma\sqrt{\Delta t}}\right).$$

You can derive or verify this as an exercise.
In practice, we use an approximate measure of X given by:

$$\left(r_c - \frac{\sigma^2}{2}\right)\Delta t.$$

The approximation error is negligible when there are a large number of steps (as there always are in any practical model).

We will use the full expression in our illustrative example so that we get exactly 0.5 as our risk-neutral probabilities. Let us repeat the same facts as in the previous section. To recap, we are valuing a call with $S = 5$, $K = 6$, $r_c = 0.1$, $t = \frac{90}{365}$, $\Delta t = \frac{30}{365}$ (3 steps), and $\sigma = 0.3$.

We compute the up and down steps getting:

$$u = 1.0948\ (4\ dp).$$

$$d = 0.9217\ (4\ dp).$$

We can verify (using equation 2.2) that the risk-neutral probabilities are exactly 0.5.

We can proceed to draw the lattice and solve using either risk-neutral probabilities or delta hedging, as shown in the Fig. 2.3.

In this model $d \neq \frac{1}{u}$, so that prices do not necessarily return to earlier levels.

The equal probabilities model and the CRR model give results that are similar as the number of steps increases.

CRR fails to give proper risk-neutral probabilities in some pathological situations—high risk-free rates and low volatility. For example, suppose $r_c = 60\%$, $\sigma = 1\%$ and $\Delta t = \frac{30}{365}$. Then the CRR formulas for u, d, and p_u are:

$$u = 1.0029.$$

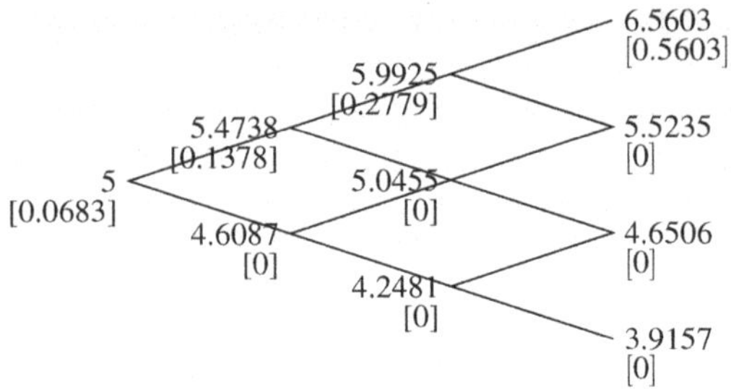

Fig. 2.3 Equal probabilities example

$$d = 0.9971.$$

$$p_u = 932\%.$$

As can be seen, the value of p_u is greater than 100% which does not make sense. The equal probabilities model would always give $p_u = 0.5$ even for these parameters.[2]

Due to its robustness, the equal probabilities model is theoretically better than CRR. But in practice, CRR is common, as it is easier and gives similar results anyway.

2.4.7 Trinomial Model

An alternative to a binomial lattice is a trinomial lattice where there are three branches from each node—up, down and sideways. The sideways branch gives the same price as before.

Let us recall our earlier one-step example with the addition of a sideways step. We are valuing a call option with $K = 6, r_c = 0.1, t = \frac{90}{365}$.

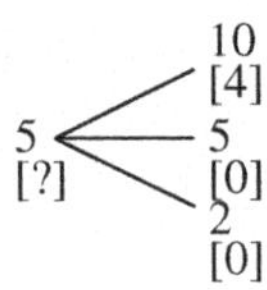

We cannot solve this three-step model using delta hedging. There is no replicating portfolio consisting of Δ shares and X in money. Such a portfolio would have to satisfy all three of the following equations:

$$10\Delta + Xe^{0.1\times\frac{90}{365}} = 4.$$

$$5\Delta + Xe^{0.1\times\frac{90}{365}} = 0.$$

[2]Equal probabilities does have the somewhat strange feature that both the up and down steps are *increases* in this case. You can verify that $u = 1.0536$ and $d = 1.0475$ with these parameters.

$$2\Delta + Xe^{0.1\times\frac{90}{365}} = 0.$$

To satisfy the first two equations we need $\Delta = \frac{4}{5}$, to satisfy the last two, we need $\Delta = 0$, and to satisfy the first and third, we need $\Delta = \frac{1}{2}$. Therefore, all three equations cannot be satisfied simultaneously and there is no solution.

Let us turn to risk-neutral probabilities. There are three probabilities here—p_u,p_m and p_d (the probabilities of the up, middle and down branches respectively). We can set one probability to be one minus the sum of the other two, say $p_d = 1 - p_u - p_m$. Then to solve for the risk-neutral probabilities, we have:

$$e^{0.1\times\frac{90}{365}} \times 5 = 10p_u + 5p_m + 2(1 - p_u - p_m).$$

This single equation has two unknowns. Therefore, there are an infinite number of solutions. We can choose any value of one of the unknowns, and find a value of the other that satisfies the equation.

To get a unique solution, we need to add some additional realistic assumption such as fixing one of the probabilities. One choice could be to set $p_m = \frac{2}{3}$ (Hull 2017). This reflects the idea that a sideways move is more likely than a big up or down move.

If we fix $p_m = \frac{2}{3}$, we can proceed to solve for the other two probabilities, getting $p_u = 0.1406$ (4 dp) and $p_d = 0.1927$ (4 dp).

We can then solve for the call value as:

$$C = e^{-0.1\times\frac{90}{365}} \times 0.1406 \times 4 = 0.5487\ (4\ dp).$$

We turn next to a multi-period model with standard up and down steps. These are:

$$u = e^{\sigma\sqrt{3\Delta t}}.$$

$$d = e^{-\sigma\sqrt{3\Delta t}}.$$

Our up and down steps are bigger jumps than with CRR because we also have the sideways step to model smaller moves.

We fix the middle probability to be $p_m = \frac{2}{3}$. We can then derive the up and down probabilities as follows:

$$p_u = \frac{e^{r_c\Delta t} - \frac{2}{3} - \frac{d}{3}}{u - d}. \tag{2.3}$$

$$p_d = \frac{1}{3} - p_u. \tag{2.4}$$

You can derive or verify this as an exercise. These probabilities will be the same at every sub-lattice.

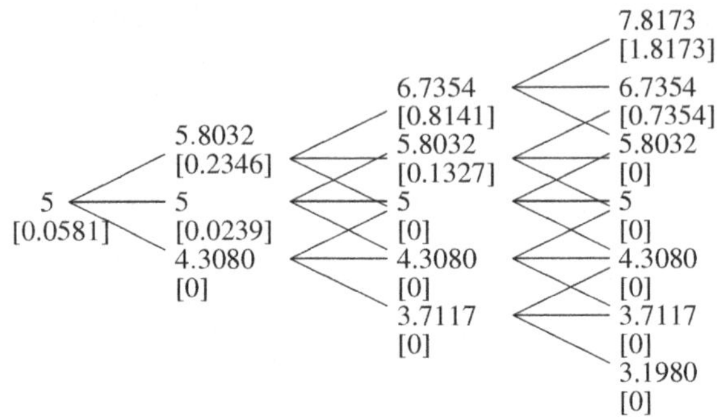

Fig. 2.4 Trinomial lattice example

Let us return to our previous multi-step example. Recall that we are valuing a call with $S = 5$, $K = 6$, $t = \frac{90}{365}$, $\Delta t = \frac{30}{365}$, $r_c = 0.1$ and $\sigma = 0.3$.

We can now get the up and down steps as:

$$u = 1.1606\ (4\ dp).$$

$$d = 0.8616\ (4\ dp).$$

The risk-neutral probabilities are (at every node):

$$p_u = 0.1819\ (4\ dp).$$

$$p_m = \frac{2}{3}.$$

$$p_d = 0.1515\ (4\ dp).$$

We can proceed to draw the lattice and solve as shown in Fig. 2.4.

Here is the calculation at the final step:

$$C = e^{-0.1 \times \frac{30}{365}} \times \left[0.1819 \times 0.2346 + \frac{2}{3} \times 0.0239 + 0.1515 \times 0\right] = 0.0581\ (4\ dp).$$

2.4.7.1 Trinomial Pros and Cons

The trinomial is more computationally expensive than the binomial for the same number of steps. But by modelling a larger set of prices at each step, it increases the realism of the model.

Also, it usually approaches a stable solution in a smaller number of steps compared to the binomial.

The sideways branch allows us to model more extreme up and down movements (with low probabilities). The trinomial can therefore be adapted more easily to volatile markets where large price swings can take place in short periods of time.

2.4.8 Black-Scholes Equation

For very small values of Δt, or equivalently for a very large number of steps, the solution to the CRR model approaches a value that is given by the Black-Scholes equation (Black and Scholes 1973).

For a call option where the current share price is S, the risk-free rate (continuous) is r_c, the volatility is σ, and the maturity date is t in years from today, we have the Black-Scholes equation for the call in equation 2.5.

$$C = S\Phi(d_1) - Ke^{-r_c t}\Phi(d_2). \tag{2.5}$$

$$d_1 = \frac{\ln\left(\frac{S}{K}\right) + \left(r_c + \frac{\sigma^2}{2}\right)t}{\sigma\sqrt{t}}. \tag{2.6}$$

$$d_2 = \frac{\ln\left(\frac{S}{K}\right) + \left(r_c - \frac{\sigma^2}{2}\right)t}{\sigma\sqrt{t}}. \tag{2.7}$$

Here $\Phi(a)$ stands for the probability that some random number $\tilde{z}$ is less than or equal to a, where $\tilde{z}$ is drawn from a standard normal distribution (a Bell curve with mean 0 and standard deviation 1). The function $\Phi(a)$ is referred to as the cumulative distribution function of the standard normal.

We can read the values of $\Phi(a)$ from a table. In Microsoft Excel, the built-in function NORMSDIST(x) gives the value of $\Phi(x)$.

To find the value of a put, we could use put-call parity and the equation for a call in 2.5. But we can also use a direct Black-Scholes equation for a put:

$$P = -S\Phi(-d_1) + Ke^{-rt}\Phi(-d_2), \tag{2.8}$$

where d_1 and d_2 have the same definitions as before (equations 2.6 and 2.7).

We can proceed to use Black-Scholes to solve for the value of the call in our example. Recall that $S = 5$, $K = 6$, $r_c = 0.1$, $t = \frac{90}{365}$ and $\sigma = 0.3$. Using equation 2.5 we get $C = 0.0599$ (4 dp).

2.5 American Options

American options can be exercised anytime. Therefore, they should have a value that is at least as high as that of similar European options (never lower), as they give the holder the same rights as the European option (to exercise at maturity), plus in addition the option to exercise early.

2.5.1 American Call, No Dividends

For an American call option where no dividends are due during the option life, we can prove that it is rational to only exercise it on the expiry date, not before. This is because before the expiry date, it is always better to hold the option rather than to exercise it.

As a result, early exercise has no added value. Therefore, an American call where no dividends occur during the option life should have the same value as a similar European option.[3]

This result does not hold when there are dividends due during the option life.

2.13 sketches the logic behind this result.

2.5.2 American Put, No Dividends

The American put can be exercised anytime before expiry. Unlike an American option with no dividends due in its life, it may be optimal to exercise early with an American put.

Therefore, we need to check at every node prior to expiry whether the value from holding for another step (holding value) is higher than the value from exercising immediately at that node (intrinsic value).

The holding value is the value we calculated before for European options (expected present value of the option at the end of the step using risk-neutral probabilities, or of the replicating portfolio at that node using delta hedging).

The intrinsic value for a put at a node where the price is S_0 is the higher of $K - S_0$ or zero, or:

$$V_I = \max(K - S_0, 0).$$

If the intrinsic value is higher than the holding value at a node, then the option value at that node is the intrinsic value. (We would prefer to exercise at that node rather than hold.) We show this in our lattice diagrams by striking out the holding value and recording the intrinsic value in bold font. The intrinsic value then becomes the value at that node to be used in further computations as we move backwards through the lattice.

Let us consider an American put with the same parameters as our earlier example: $S = 5$, $K = 6$, $r_c = 0.1$, $t = \frac{90}{365}$, $\sigma = 0.3$ and $\Delta t = \frac{30}{365}$.

We will use an equal probability lattice with three steps.

The solution is shown in Fig. 2.5.

As we can see from the figure, the option would be exercised immediately at the start node.

[3]In practice, an unexpected dividend can never be ruled out, so American options do have a slightly higher value than corresponding European options.

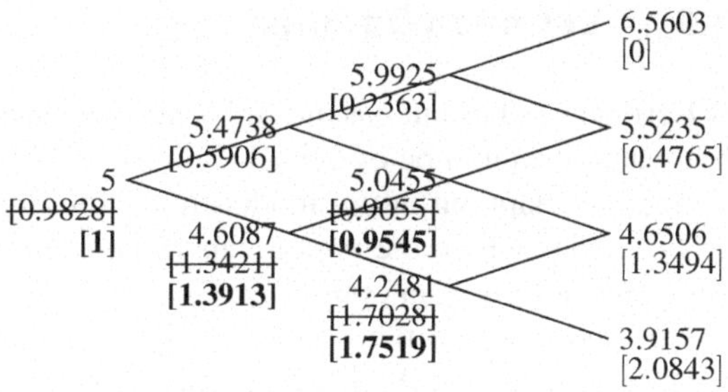

Fig. 2.5 American put example (no dividends)

To illustrate the computations let us consider the bottom price in the second-last step (one step before expiry). The price here is CU 4.2481.

We can estimate the holding value using risk-neutral probabilities to be:

$$V_H = e^{-0.1\times\frac{30}{365}} \times \frac{1}{2}(1.3494 + 2.084) = 1.7028\ (4\ dp).$$

But if we exercise immediately at this node, we get the intrinsic value:

$$V_I = 6 - 4.2481 = 1.7519.$$

This exceeds the holding value.

Therefore we are better off exercising rather than holding at this node.

Therefore we would exercise if we reach this node.

Therefore the option value at this node is the value from exercising (CU 1.7519).

Moving to the preceding step, consider again the bottom node with price CU 4.6087.

Again we can work out the holding value here which is:

$$V_H = e^{-0.1\times\frac{30}{365}} \times \frac{1}{2}(1.7519 + 0.9545) = 1.3421.$$

Note that the values at both the end-nodes are intrinsic values, i.e., we would exercise if we reached either of these nodes.

If we exercise immediately at this node, we get the intrinsic value:

$$V_I = 6 - 4.6087 = 1.3913.$$

Since the intrinsic value exceeds the holding value, we would exercise immediately if we reach this node.

Our American put should have a strictly higher value than the corresponding European put. We can verify this by computing the European put value (we can use put-call parity and the value of the corresponding European call calculated earlier—CU 0.0683), which is CU 0.9222 (4 dp).

2.6 Bermuda Options

A Bermuda call or put has multiple exercise dates during its life, but also parts of its life where it cannot be exercised.

We can adapt our lattice models to handle Bermuda options.

For nodes where the option cannot be exercised, we consider only the holding value, like a European option.

For nodes where the option can be exercised, we check whether the intrinsic value is higher than the holding value, and use the higher of the two, just like an American option.

If there are no dividends during the option life, then a Bermuda call would not be exercised till its maturity date, just like a similar American call. The same proof applies (see sketch in 2.13).

In modelling a Bermuda option, we could ideally choose the step size so that both exercise dates and non-exercise dates are represented in the lattice. For example, if a Bermuda option can be exercised every alternate day during its life, a model with a step size of one day is better than a model with a step size of two days (which may have every node being an exercise date or vice versa).

If an exercise date lies on a branch (i.e., between two nodes), then we consider the decision to exercise at the start node of the branch. We illustrate with a one-step example.

Suppose the current share price is CU 5. This could go up to CU 10 or drop to CU 2 at the end of 90 days. We wish to value a Bermuda put with a strike price of CU 10 and an expiry date of 90 days. It can be exercised either at the expiry date or at a single date which is 45 days from today. The risk-free rate is 10% continuously compounded.

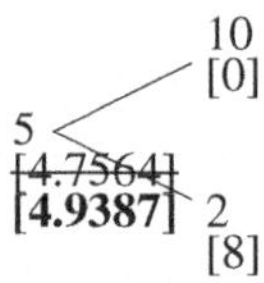

We evaluate whether to exercise at 45 days at the start node with price CU 5.

At this point, if we choose not to exercise till the end of the step (expiry), we would get the holding value, which equals CU 4.7564 (4 dp).

We compare this to the value of exercising early (at 45 days). If we exercise at 45 days, we would get CU 5 at that point (the price doesn't change until the end of the step). The present value of this CU 5 at the start of the step is $e^{-0.1\times\frac{45}{365}} \times 5$ or CU 4.9387 (4 dp).

The expected present value from exercising early at 45 days is higher than the value of holding till the end of the step.

Therefore we would exercise at 45 days.

Therefore the value of the option today is the (present) value from exercising at 45 days, or CU 4.9387.

2.7 Dividends During the Option Life

An option price is affected by a dividend that has an ex-dividend date during the option life.

The ex-dividend date is the cutoff date used to decide who gets the dividend.

People who buy the share on the ex-dividend date or later will not receive the dividend.

People who hold the share just before the ex-dividend date (market closing the previous trading day) will receive the dividend, even if they sell the share the next trading day.

As a result, the share price will fall when trading opens on the ex-dividend date, by approximately the present value of the dividend at that date.

This predictable fall in price would affect the value of a call or put option that has the ex-dividend date during its life.

The call value would be lower than otherwise, while the put value would be higher.

We need to modify our models to reflect this.

2.7.1 European Option with Dividends

Consider a call option with $S = CU\ 5$, $K = CU\ 3.60$, $r_c = 0.1$, $t = \frac{90}{365}$, $\Delta t = \frac{30}{365}$ (3 steps) and $\sigma = 0.3$.

Suppose that a dividend of CU 2 is due during the option life—the ex-dividend date is at 40 days, while the dividend will be paid at 45 days.

We analyze the share as consisting of two components:

1. The claim to receive the dividend: the value of this claim is the present value of the dividend or CU $e^{-0.1 \times \frac{45}{365}} \times 2$ or CU 1.9755 (4 dp).
2. The remaining portion of the share, whose value we shall label $\tilde{S}$. Today (valuation date), $\tilde{S} = 3.0245$ (4 dp).

Only the uncertain portion of the share price $\tilde{S}$ is subject to the up and down swings that we model in the lattice. The claim on the dividend would just grow predictably towards the full value of the dividend and then drop to zero at the ex-dividend date.

Therefore, we can model our lattice using $\tilde{S}$ as a starting point rather than S.

For a European option, we only need to know the share prices at the final nodes. But at this point, $\tilde{S}$ represents the entire share price, since the dividend claim has already expired.

Let us use CRR to construct the lattice. We have:

$$u = 1.0898. \tag{2.9}$$

$$d = 0.9176. \tag{2.10}$$

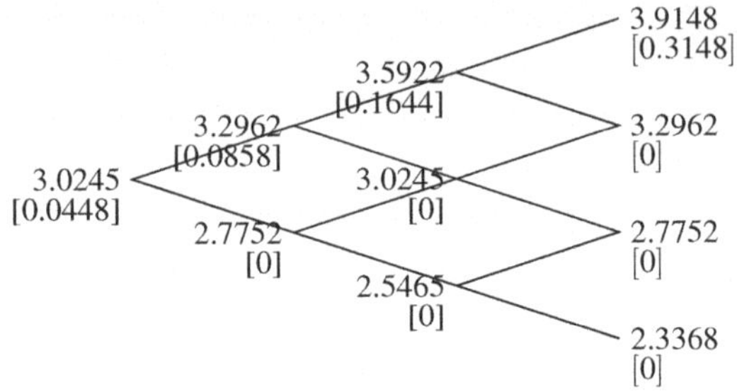

Fig. 2.6 CRR example—European call option with a dividend

$$p_u = 0.5264. \tag{2.11}$$

We can now create our lattice starting with $\tilde{S}$ and proceed to solve. See Fig. 2.6.

2.7.2 Put-Call Parity with Dividends

The put-call parity formula needs modification to reflect a dividend that has an ex-dividend date during the option life.

Recall that the relationship with no dividends was:

$$P + S - C = Ke^{-r_c t}.$$

Recall that our proof strategy was to construct a portfolio of one put, one share and a short position in a call (that is, issue a call). We then showed that this combination always had the value of K at the option expiry date (the exercise date).

If there were a dividend with an ex-dividend date during the option life, the combined prices of the portfolio components would still be K at maturity. But in addition, we would receive the dividend (since we held the share just before the ex-dividend date). Therefore the value of the portfolio would be the present value of K plus in addition the present value of the dividend.

We can express this as:

$$P + S - C = Ke^{-r_c t} + div \times e^{-r_c t_{div}},$$

where div is the amount of the dividend on one share, and t_{div} is the dividend *payment* date (payment date, not ex-dividend date).

An alternative approach is to consider only the dividend-free uncertain portion of the share price $\tilde{S}$ and to use the original formula.

2.7.2.1 Example

We can use put-call parity to find the value of the put in the previous example given the value of the call. Recall that $S = 5$, $K = 3.60$, $r_c = 0.1$, $t = \frac{90}{365}$ (90 days), $t_{div} = \frac{45}{365}$ (45 days). We had estimated C to be CU 0.0448 (4 dp).

We can proceed to solve for the corresponding put price P:

$$P = 3.6 \times e^{-0.1 \times \frac{90}{365}} + 2e^{-0.1 \times \frac{45}{365}} - 5 + 0.0448 = CU\ 0.5326\ (4\ dp).$$

Alternatively, ignoring the dividend and using $\tilde{S}$ rather than S in the original put-call parity formula without dividends, we get:

$$P = 3.6 \times e^{-0.1 \times \frac{90}{365}} - 3.0245 + 0.0448 = CU\ 0.5326\ (4\ dp).$$

2.7.3 Black-Scholes Equation with Dividends

Recall that the Black-Scholes equation is derived as the limiting value from a CRR model with a large number of steps approaching infinity.

For a European option with an ex-dividend date in its life, we can use a CRR lattice whose only difference from the non-dividend case is that the lattice with a dividend starts with $\tilde{S}$ rather than S.

Combining these two facts, the limiting value of a CRR model for a European option with an ex-dividend date in its life would be a Black-Scholes equation in which S is replaced by $\tilde{S}$ everywhere. We can state this as follows:

$$C = \tilde{S}\Phi(d_1) - Ke^{-r_c t}\Phi(d_2).$$

$$P = -\tilde{S}\Phi(-d_1) + Ke^{-r_c t}\Phi(-d_2).$$

$$d_1 = \frac{\ln \frac{\tilde{S}}{K} + \left(r_c + \frac{\sigma^2}{2}\right)t}{\sigma\sqrt{t}}.$$

$$d_2 = \frac{\ln \frac{\tilde{S}}{K} + \left(r_c - \frac{\sigma^2}{2}\right)t}{\sigma\sqrt{t}}.$$

$$\tilde{S} = S - div \times e^{-r_c t_{div}}.$$

We can use this modification of the Black-Scholes equation to estimate the value of the call in our earlier example: $S = 5$, $K = 3.6$, $r_c = 0.1$, $t = \frac{90}{365}$, $\sigma = 0.3$, $div = 2$ and $t_{div} = \frac{45}{365}$. We get $C = 0.0401$ (4 dp).

2.7.4 American Options with Dividends

Consider an American call option with $S = 5$, $K = 3.6$, $r_c = 0.1$, $t = \frac{90}{365}$ (90 days), $\Delta t = \frac{30}{365}$ (three steps) and $\sigma = 0.3$. We will use CRR.

A dividend of CU 2 has its ex-dividend date at 40 days and its dividend payment date at 80 days.

We first construct the lattice starting with $\tilde{S}$ as before. We will label this Lattice 1, since as we will see we need a different lattice later.

For Lattice 1, we have:

$$u = 1.0898.$$

$$d = 0.9176.$$

$$p_u = 0.5264.$$

We find the price of the uncertain non-dividend portion of the share to be:

$$\tilde{S} = 5 - 2 \times e^{-0.1 \times \frac{80}{365}} = 3.0434 \ (4\ dp).$$

We can proceed to construct Lattice 1. See Fig. 2.7.

But we cannot solve this lattice directly. For an American option, we need to find the intrinsic value at every node, not just at the end nodes. To do so, we need to compare the strike price with the *full* share price at every node, not with the notional price of the uncertain portion of the share.

Therefore, before we solve, we need to add back the present value of the dividend to nodes before the ex-dividend date. (After the ex-dividend date, the dividend claim is no longer part of the share.) This gives us another lattice that we can call lattice 2.

Before we construct Lattice 2, we note that the risk-neutral probabilities are derived from Lattice 1, not Lattice 2. This is because these probabilities only refer to the uncertain portion of the share price. The dividend claim is assumed to be certain and has no up and down probabilities.

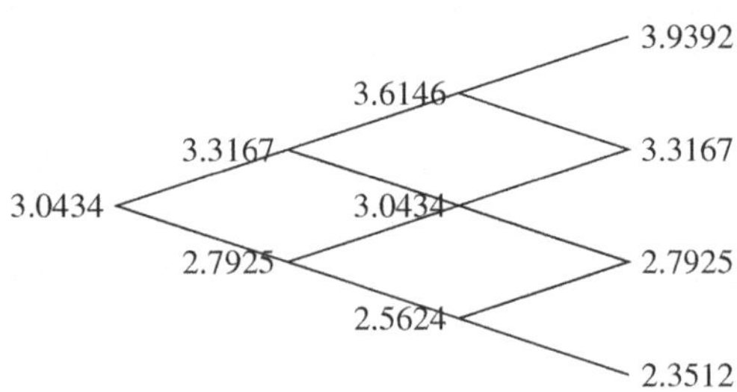

Fig. 2.7 American call option with a dividend—Lattice 1

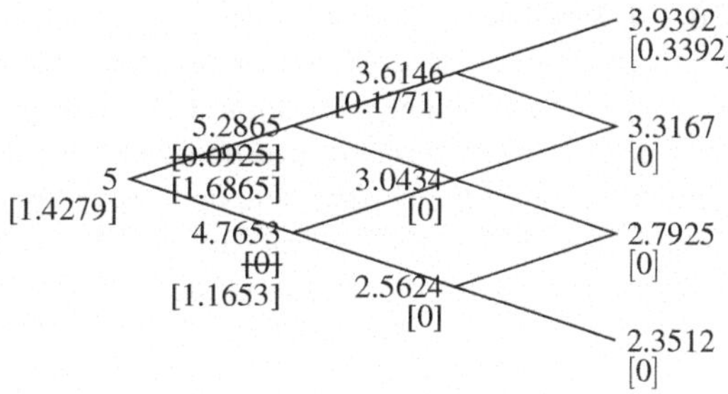

Fig. 2.8 American call option with a dividend—Lattice 2

At the start of the option life, we add back the present value of the dividend at that point which is $2 \times e^{-0.1 \times \frac{80}{365}}$ or CU 1.9566 (4 dp). This gives us the full starting price of CU 5 in Lattice 2.

At the end of the first step, we are at 30 days. This is still before the ex-dividend date. At this point, the dividend is payable in another 50 days. So the present value of the dividend claim at this point is $2 \times e^{-0.1 \times \frac{50}{365}}$ or CU 1.9728 (4 dp). We add this to the lattice price getting prices of CU 5.2895 and CU 4.7653 respectively at the upper and lower nodes.

At the next step and thereafter, we are past the ex-dividend date, so the dividend claim is no longer part of the share price, which equals its uncertain portion as in Lattice 1.

Lattice 2 is shown in Fig. 2.8.

We can proceed to solve Lattice 2 as usual as shown in Fig. 2.8. When there are dividends, it is no longer always optimal for the option holder to wait for the last minute before exercising. This is demonstrated in our example. The option holder would exercise at the end of the first step, to avoid the predictable drop in price after the ex-dividend date.

2.8 Employee Stock Options (ESOs)

Employee stock options (ESOs) are call options that are issued by a company to its employees allowing them to buy the company's own shares at a low strike price.

They are a device to align the interests of top managers with shareholders, since they make the managers potential shareholders themselves and moreover give the managers a personal reason to want the share price to go up.

Accounting for ESOs is governed by IFRS 2 *Share-based compensation*.

2.8.1 Features of Employee Stock Options

Most employee stock options have the following standard features which we will assume throughout our discussion.

2.8.1.1 Vesting

Typically employee stock options cannot be exercised until the employee has worked for the company for some minimum period of time after the option grant date, and/or fulfilled other specified conditions. The date when the conditions are fulfilled is called the *vesting* date and the options are said to *vest* at this point. The conditions required for vesting are called *vesting conditions*. We can refer to the period starting with the option grant date and ending with the vesting date as the *pre-vesting period* or the *vesting period*.

If the employee leaves the company before the options vest, or other vesting conditions are not fulfilled by the vesting date, the options expire automatically at the vesting date.

If the options vest, there is usually a further extended period before the option expiry during which they can be exercised at any date.

Therefore the option is similar to a Bermuda call which cannot be exercised for the first part of its life (pre-vesting) and can be exercised at any time during the second part of its life (post-vesting). It is like a European call pre-vesting, and like an American call post-vesting.

Vesting conditions can be directly based on the employee's performance (performance-based), such as the requirement that the employee stay with the company pre-vesting. They could also be based on a market-based condition, such as a requirement that the share price should hit some minimum level at the vesting date.

The distinction between performance-based vesting conditions and market-based vesting conditions is important for both the accounting and the ESO valuation under IFRS 2.

2.8.1.2 ESOs Cannot Be Traded

Employee stock options are typically non-transferable. In particular, they cannot be bought and sold in a market.

The options that we modelled earlier could be traded. Thus, even for a European option, the option holder could cash in their option at any point in the option life by selling the option. The option values that we calculated at intermediate nodes in a lattice represent the value the holder would get at that node if they sold the option at that node.

An ESO holder can only cash in their options by exercising them, not by selling them. This non-tradeability should lead to a reduced value for ESOs versus regular traded options.

2.8.1.3 Post-vesting Exits

Typical ESO contracts stipulate that the employee cannot retain their options if they leave the company, even after these options have vested. That is, if an employee with vested but unexercised options leaves the company, they must either exercise the options before leaving, or else lose the options.

This would reduce the value of these options compared to regular options that do not disappear before maturity.

2.8.1.4 Dilution

The typical options that we modelled earlier were issued by some arbitrary third party rather than by the company whose shares are the underlying asset for the option contracts.

When the options are issued by the company of the underlying share, it would typically issue new shares when the options are exercised. This would lead to dilution. This potential dilution would reduce the value of the share (and therefore also the value of the option) compared to options issued by a third party.

2.8.2 Relevant IFRS 2 Guidance

We explain the valuation-relevant guidance in IFRS 2 using a simple example.

Suppose that a company grants employee stock options to 10 employees, granting each employee the right to buy one share at the grant-date share price of CU 5.

The options can only be exercised after three years, provided that the employees stay with the company throughout that period. That is, the vesting date is at three years.

Subsequently, there is a further two years before expiry during which the options can be exercised any time.

The company anticipates that one employee will leave each year during the vesting period, so that a total of three employees will leave during the vesting period.

The company's independent valuation expert estimates that the grant-date fair value of each ESO (to buy one share) is CU 1.5, assuming that no employees leave pre-vesting.

Under IFRS 2, we treat the ESOs as compensation to the employees for work done pre-vesting. Therefore, the employees earn the option value over the pre-vesting period. Conversely, the company incurs its related employee compensation expense over the same period.

The total compensation expense to be recorded over the pre-vesting period is given by the fair value of the option at the grant date less an allowance for employees who leave before vesting.

In our example this is (amounts in CU):

Fair value of options granted (1.5 × 10)	15.0
Less: allowance for exits (3 × 1.5)	4.5
	10.5

We spread this cost over the three years of the vesting period usually on a straight-line basis (equal instalments of CU 3.5 each year).

At the end of the first year of our vesting period, the adjusting journal entry to record the employee stock option expense would be something like:

Dr	Employee compensation expense	3.5
Cr	Employee stock options granted [equity account]	3.5

The credit entry is (usually) to an equity account that is (usually) presented as part of shareholders' equity on the balance-sheet.

The allowance for exits may be adjusted each year to reflect differences between actual and anticipated exits. But that need not concern us in this book.

In our example, there are no vesting conditions beyond the bare requirement to stay employed with the company till vesting. Let us extend the example to illustrate more complicated vesting conditions.

Suppose that the same company granted options to another 10 employees on the same date as the ESOs granted earlier. Each of these employees receives an option to buy one share. Let us call these options Batch B, to distinguish them from the options mentioned earlier.

Batch B has the same vesting conditions as before, viz., a vesting period of 3 years followed by an exercise period of another 2 years. But they also carry two other vesting conditions:

- that the employees receive a "satisfactory" grade in their annual performance appraisal for every year of the pre-vesting period.
- that the share price should close at CU 6 or higher the day before the vesting date.

The first of these conditions is a performance-based condition.

The second of these conditions is a market-based condition.

Under IFRS 2, market-based vesting conditions should be reflected in the fair value at the grant date. Non-market-based conditions (that is performance-based conditions) are not reflected in the fair value. Rather they are reflected in the separate allowance for options that will expire unvested.

In our example, suppose that we modify our model to reflect the market-based conditions. This gives us a grant-date fair value of CU1.2 per option.

We further estimate that 4 employees are expected to either leave the company or get an unsatisfactory annual performance appraisal during the pre-vesting period. We can now estimate the total employee compensation cost for the Batch B options over the entire vesting period.

Fair value of Batch B options granted (1.2×10)	12.0
Less: allowance for exits (4×1.2)	4.8
	7.2

The main valuation implications of IFRS 2 are as follows:

1. We need to calculate the fair value of the ESO at the grant date.
2. The fair-value calculation must reflect market-based vesting conditions.
3. The fair-value calculation *should not* reflect performance-based vesting conditions. These are handled separately.

2.8.3 Black-Scholes for ESO Valuation

Black-Scholes is commonly used to value an ESO, though it is not an appropriate model since an ESO is not a European call. But if we can assume no dividends during the post-vesting period, it follows theoretically that the employee would prefer to hold the options till just before they expire. In that case, we can treat them like a European call, in which case Black-Scholes can be used.

Setting the parameter t to the ESO expiry date in a Black-Scholes model may overstate the value of the ESO. This is because in practice, ESO holders do exercise early, before the expiry date, even when it is theoretically not optimal to do so. They may need money for personal reasons, and exercising the option may be the only way to get the money, since they can't sell the options.

As an alternative, we could consider setting t to the vesting date. But again, this would not accurately reflect the option value, since it is usually theoretically better to hold on to the option at this date, and many holders do so, unless they have some compelling personal reasons to exercise.

Therefore, the Black-Scholes parameter t should be set somewhere between the vesting date and the ESO expiry date, with no clear reason to prefer any date within this range. In order to avoid too much discretion in this regard, the Securities and Exchange Commission (SEC) of the USA issued guidance via Staff Accounting Bulletins SAB 107 and SAB 110.

The guidance in SAB 107 and SAB 110 is that if Black-Scholes is used to value an ESO, the parameter t (assumed strike date) should be set to exactly halfway between the ESO vesting date and the ESO expiry date.

While SAB 107 and SAB 110 are not mandatory outside the USA and under IFRS, we can treat the guidance as a best practice recommendation.

2.8.3.1 Example of SAB 107/110

On July 1 2018. X company grants an ESO. The ESO vests on January 1 2019 (0.5 years later) and expires on January 1 2020 (1.5 years later). X Company uses Black-Scholes to value the ESO. They follow the guidance in SAB 107 and SAB 110 and set the parameter t to be $\frac{0.5+1.5}{2}$ years or $t = 1$.

2.8.4 The Hull-White ESO Model

A lattice model can be better adapted than Black-Scholes to the special features of ESOs.

The Hull-White ESO model (Hull and White 2004) is a specialized lattice model for ESO valuation. It can be implemented using a standard binomial or trinomial lattice of share prices. A trinomial lattice is preferred as it is more efficient and flexible. We will describe the model using a trinomial lattice.

We discuss below how the model handles some special features of employee stock options.

2.8.4.1 Dilution

To handle potential dilution, the model sets the starting share price in the lattice to be the share price *just after* the option grant is publicly announced. Then the market reaction to the announcement would reflect the impact of potential dilution on the share price.

This is possible when the announcement is made on the grant date or just after. If the announcement were made much later, then the grant-date share price would be used and some alternative approach would be used to estimate the impact of dilution. If the announcement were made before the grant-date, then we can use the grant-date price which would already reflect the impact of dilution.

2.8.4.2 Early Exercise

To reflect the fact that employees often exercise options early, the model assumes that the option will always be exercised when the price reaches a high enough level. This level is expressed as $M \times K$ where K is the strike price and M is an assumed multiple of the strike price, where M is greater than or equal to 1.

2.8.4.3 Exits After Vesting

The model factors in an exit rate of say x per year or $x \times \Delta t$ per lattice step, where Δt is assumed to be the step size in years. Employees who leave at a particular step exercise their options at that step if the node price is higher than the strike price, or abandon them otherwise.

Exits before vesting are not reflected in the model, to comply with IFRS 2. This is similar to assuming no exits before vesting, and an exit rate of x per year thereafter.

2.8.4.4 Lattice Regions

The lattice has three distinct regions as in Fig. 2.9.

Region A is the portion of the lattice where the share price has hit the trigger price for automatic exercise (equal to $K \times M$). In this region, the option value is given by the value of exercising, or intrinsic value.

Region B is the pre-vesting period. In this region, the option cannot be exercised. The value at each node is then just the holding value.

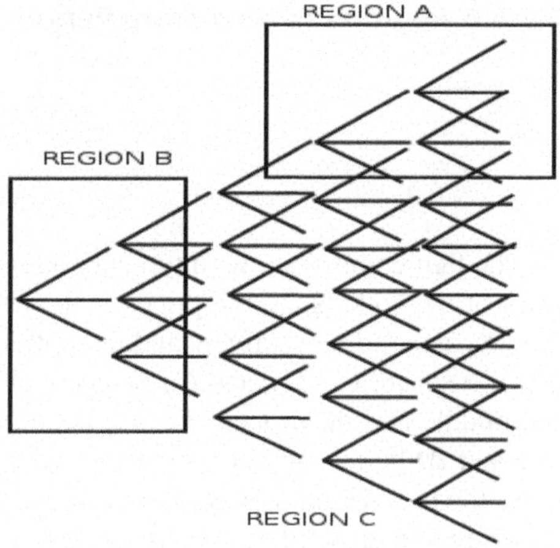

Fig. 2.9 The Hull-White model

In Region C (the open area in the diagram) employees who exit the firm would exercise on exit (or abandon their options, whichever is better). Other employees would compare the holding and intrinsic values and choose the action which gives them the higher of the two. If there are no dividends during the option life, this would always be the holding value.

We illustrate the computations in each of the regions below:

2.8.4.5 Region A: Automatic Exercise

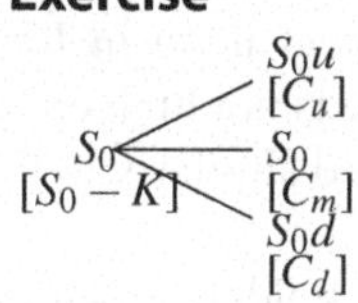

In the automatic exercise region, where prices are equal to or higher than $K \times M$, the value of the option is simply the value from exercising or the intrinsic value. If the price at a node in the region is S_0, then the option value at that node is simply given by the intrinsic value:

$$V_I = S_0 - K.$$

This is always greater than zero because $S_0 \geq K \times M \geq K$.[4]

[4]Weakly greater, in that it could theoretically be zero.

2.8.4.6 Region B: Pre-vesting Period

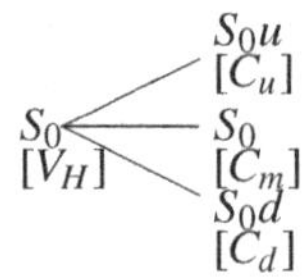

The figure above shows a typical node in Region B (the pre-vesting period). The price at the node is S_0, the prices at the ends of the up, middle and down steps are S_0u, S_0 and S_0d respectively and the option values at the ends of the up, middle and down steps are C_u, C_m and C_d respectively. Let the risk-neutral probabilities of the up, middle and down steps be p_u, p_m and p_d respectively. Let r_c be the risk-free rate and Δt be the step-size in years.

In the pre-vesting period, the option cannot be exercised. Its value at each node in this region is simply the holding value computed using risk-neutral probabilities:

$$V_H = e^{-r_c \Delta t} \left(p_u C_u + p_m C_m + p_d C_d \right).$$

2.8.4.7 Region C: Post-vesting, Price < $K \times M$

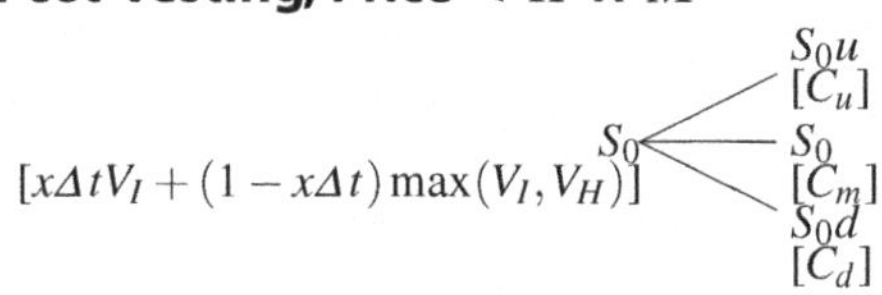

The figure above shows a typical node in Region C, which falls in the post-vesting period, and where the price is not high enough to trigger automatic exercise. Prices and option values are labelled similarly to the diagrams for the earlier regions covered.

Here, some proportion of ESO holders given by $x\Delta t$ will leave the company at the node, and either exercise their options or abandon them, whichever is better. They will receive the intrinsic value, the higher of $S_0 - K$ or zero:

$$V_I = \max(S_0 - K, 0).$$

For the remaining proportion of ESO holders given by $(1 - x\Delta t)$, the option is valued like an American call at this node. They compare the intrinsic value V_I and the holding value V_H, and choose the action that gives the higher value. Therefore, these ESO holders receive:

$$\max(V_I, V_H).$$

The holding value is given by:

$$V_H = e^{-r_c \Delta t} \left(p_u C_u + p_m C_m + p_d C_d \right).$$

Combining holders who exit and those who don't, the expected option value at the node C_0 say is given by:

$$C_0 = x\Delta t V_I + (1 - x\Delta t)\max(V_H, V_I).$$

2.8.4.8 Example: Hull-White ESO Model

We illustrate the model using a four-step trinomial lattice.

The parameters are as follows:

$$S = \text{CU } 4.9$$
$$K = \text{CU } 5$$
$$r_c = 0.10$$
$$t = 2$$
$$\sigma = 0.3$$
$$t_{vest} = 1.4986$$
$$M = 2.6$$
$$x = 0.10$$

Here t_{vest} is the vesting date, measured in years from the grant date. Other parameters follow the notation introduced earlier. The lattice and solution are shown in Fig. 2.10.

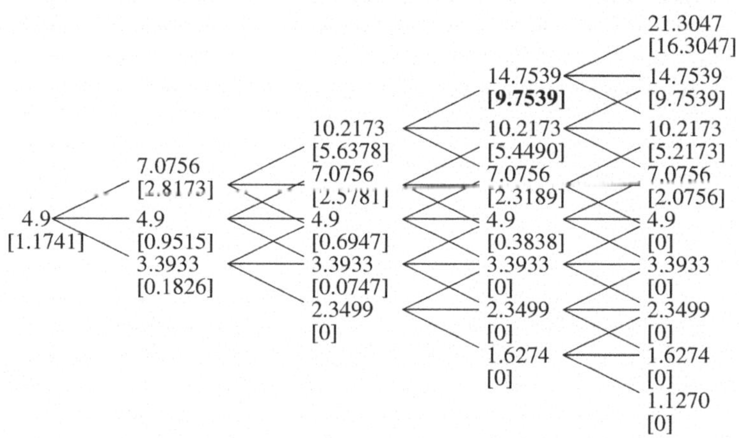

Fig. 2.10 Hull-White ESO model example

2.9 Asian Options: Monte Carlo Simulation

Asian options have a strike price that is based on some function of the share price history before exercise, as opposed to being a fixed number.[5] Asian options could be European, American or Bermuda in terms of their exercise style. We focus on Asian options with European-style exercise. That is, they can be exercised only on the expiry date.

Suppose that we have a European-style Asian call option on a share with the following parameters: the current share price $S = 5$, the continuously compounded risk-free rate $r_c = 0.05$, assumed constant, the time to maturity is $t = \frac{3}{365}$ (3 days), and the volatility is $\sigma = 0.4$.

The strike price is the arithmetic average of the closing share price on each of the three days before expiry.

We model the price movements in the three days until expiry using a 3-step CRR lattice ($\Delta t = \frac{1}{365}$). (Of course, this is just for illustration, and we would need a lattice with many more steps to give a realistic valuation).

We have $u = 1.0212$ and $d = 0.9793$. The three-step lattice is as shown in Fig. 2.11.

We can find the risk-neutral probabilities. The probability of an up-step is $p_u = 0.4980$ and the probability of a down-step is $p_d = 0.502$.

Suppose that we attempt to solve this lattice by working backwards from the last step as we did before.

Starting at the top node in the last step, we can work out that the option strike price at that node must be CU 5.2146 (average of the last three prices). Therefore, the option payoff at that node is CU 0.1096 (5.3241 − 5.2146).

But moving down one node to the ending node marked (A), with price CU 5.1058, we run into a problem. This node can be reached in three different ways, and each of those ways leads to a different strike price K. If we use the shorthand "U" to refer to an up movement at a step and we use "D" to refer to a down movement

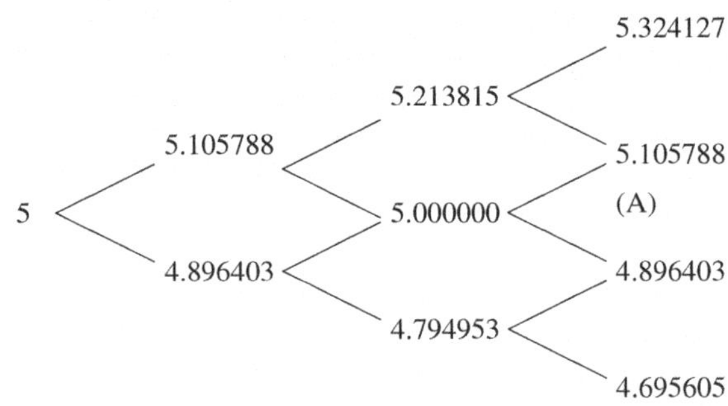

Fig. 2.11 Three-step lattice for Asian call example .

[5]An alternative type of Asian option has a fixed strike price, but compares this to the average share price over some period to compute the payoff on settlement. Such fixed strike price Asian options can be valued similarly to those with a variable strike price.

at a step, then the three ways we can reach (A) are: UUD, UDU and DUU. Each of these gives us a different strike price:

$$\text{UUD: } K = 5.141797$$

$$\text{UDU: } K = 5.070526$$

$$\text{DUU: } K = 5.000731$$

Therefore, the option can have multiple values at this node. Similar issues arise with the end-nodes below it (except for the bottom-most node).

This makes our usual solution strategy a non-starter. We need an alternative.

In this simple three-step lattice, we can actually enumerate all the possible paths, and find the option payoffs for each of these. There are just eight possible paths (2^3 paths). For each path, we can compute the payoff at the end of that path, and we can also compute the risk-neutral probability that prices would follow that path. Putting these together, we can find the expected value of the payoff from all possible paths, where the expected value is calculated based on risk-neutral probabilities. This calculation is illustrated in Table 2.1.

To illustrate the calculations in the table, consider the UUD line. The strike price K is the average of the three prices on the UUD path: CU 5.105788, CU 5.213815, and CU 5.105788. This strike price equals CU 5.141797. Since this is higher than the option price at the expiry date (CU 5.105788), the option expires without being exercised, giving a payoff of zero. The risk-neutral probability of this path being followed is given by $p_u \times p_u \times p_d$, which works out to 0.1235. Therefore the probability-weighted payoff for this path is 0.1235×0 or zero.

We can calculate the probability-weighted payoff for every path and add them all up to get the expected payoff. We get a value of CU 0.03525.

The option value is the present value of this expected payoff. This would be:

$$e^{-0.05\times\frac{3}{365}} \times 0.03525 \approx 0.03523.$$

Table 2.1 Table of payoffs in Asian call example

Path	K	Payoff	Probability	Probability × Payoff
UUU	5.214577	0.10955033	0.1235338	0.013533
UUD	5.141797	0	0.1245074	0
UDU	5.070526	0.03526279	0.1245074	0.004390479
UDD	5.000731	0	0.1254887	0
DUU	5.000731	0.10505774	0.1245074	0.013080468
DUD	4.930936	0	0.1254887	0
DDU	4.862587	0.03381669	0.1254887	0.004243613
DDD	4.795654	0	0.1264778	0
Total		1.0000000		0.03524772

The impact of discounting is minimal in this case due to the short period.

The approach shown above is impractical when we have a large lattice, say one with 50 steps or more (and recall that we need a large lattice for accuracy. Three steps is for illustration only).

For a lattice with 50 steps, the number of paths is 2^{50} paths. This is a very large number, and even a very fast super-computer would have difficulty enumerating and performing calculations over so many paths.

One practical solution could be to use what we commonly do in statistics-based research when we need to draw general conclusions about a large population—we take a random sample. The sample average can then be viewed as an approximate estimate of the true population average. The bigger the sample, the better the approximation is likely to be.

This approach is known as Monte Carlo simulation. It was first introduced by Boyle (1977).

When we take a random sample of the paths in our lattice, we would set the sampling probability to match the risk-neutral probabilities. That is, the probability of a path being chosen in our sample should match the risk-neutral probability for that path.

We can use a random-number generator to ensure this. For example, we have $p_u = 0.4980$ in our example. We choose a random number (a decimal) between 0 and 1, say using the `=RAND()` function in Excel. If this number is less than or equal to 0.4980, we move up. Otherwise, we move down. We repeat the procedure for every step until we have a complete path. Then, we start again to generate another random path, and keep going until we have a large enough sample of random paths. We can then compute the average payoff for all these paths. The present value of this average payoff is our estimate of the option value.

Let us illustrate this by running a tiny simulation of just 10 paths using our example above (the lattice in Fig. 2.11). This is of course just to demonstrate the procedure. Simulation is not needed in this toy example, and a simulation of just 10 paths is far too small anyway. The 10-path simulation is shown in Table 2.2.

Table 2.2 Simulation of example from Fig. 2.11

Sampled path	Random numbers	Path	Payoff
1	(0.73, 0.78, 0.37)	DDU	0.03381669
2	(0.87, 0.54, 0.02)	DDU	0.03381669
3	(0.28, 0.74, 0.78)	UDD	0
4	(0.85, 0.34, 0.53)	DUD	0
5	(0.03, 0.59, 0.30)	UDU	0.03526279
6	(0.02, 0.41, 0.54)	UUD	0
7	(0.33, 0.57, 0.45)	UDU	0.03526279
8	(0.57, 0.91, 0.60)	DDD	0
9	(0.27, 0.39, 0.80)	UUD	0
10	(0.87, 0.80, 0.17)	DDU	0.03381669
	PV of average payoff		0.0172

To explain the logic, let us look at the first simulated path (path 1). Here we draw the random numbers 0.73, 0.78 and 0.37. Recall that our rule is to go up if the random number is less than or equal to 0.4980, and to go down otherwise. Therefore: corresponding to the first number 0.73 (greater than 0.4980), we go down for the first step, corresponding to the second number 0.78 (greater than 0.4980), we go down for the second step, and corresponding to the third number 0.37 (less than 0.4980), we go up for the third step. So the path chosen is DDU. As calculated previously in Table 2.1, the payoff for this path is 0.03381669.

We take the present value of the sample average payoff as our estimate of the option value, getting 0.0172. As we can see by comparing to the true answer of 0.03523, this is materially wrong, due to the small size of our sample. As mentioned earlier, a very large sample is needed for simulation to be reasonably accurate.

Rather than use a lattice, we can simulate a price history by directly drawing a random sample of prices based on some assumed risk-neutral distribution. For example, under the assumptions that underly the Black-Scholes model, prices $S_{\Delta t}$ at some future time Δt years from today (or the start of a step with step size Δt) are assumed to follow a risk-neutral distribution that satisfies the following property:

$$\Delta s = \ln\left(\frac{S_{\Delta t}}{S_0}\right) = (\ln S_{\Delta t} - \ln S_0) \sim N\left(\left(r_c - \frac{\sigma^2}{2}\right)\Delta t, \sigma\sqrt{\Delta t}\right) \tag{2.12}$$

where S_0 is the price today (or the start of a step), r_c is the continuously compounded risk-free rate, σ is the volatility parameter. Equation 2.12 tells us that the natural logarithm of the ratio of the price after Δt years to the price today (or start of the step) follows a distribution (the math symbol $\sim$) that is normal (the notation $N(mean, standard\,deviation)$) with mean $\left(r_c - \frac{\sigma^2}{2}\right)\Delta t$ and standard deviation $\sigma \times \sqrt{\Delta t}$.

We illustrate by running a simulation using the parameters for our earlier example ($S_0 = 5$, $r_c = 0.05$, $\sigma = 0.4$, $K =$ the average closing price on the last three days, time to maturity is three days).

Let us see how this works by manually going through the steps to simulate a single path. To start off with, we find the mean and standard deviation for the normal distribution used to simulate Δs. The mean is given by:

$$\left(r_c - \frac{\sigma^2}{2}\right) \times \Delta t = \left(0.05 - \frac{0.4^2}{2}\right) \times \frac{1}{365} \approx -0.00008.$$

The standard deviation is given by:

$$\left(\sigma \times \sqrt{\Delta t}\right) = 0.4 \times \sqrt{\frac{1}{365}} \approx 0.0209.$$

We use a random number generator to draw a random number from a normal distribution with mean -0.00008 and standard deviation 0.0209. This is our simulated Δs for the first day. We get $\Delta s = -0.02526755$. From this we can calculate our price at the end of the first day as:

$$S_{\frac{1}{365}} = S_0 \times e^{\Delta s} = 5 \times e^{-0.02526755} = 4.875245.$$

Again, we use the random number generator to get another draw from the normal distribution to simulate Δs for the second day. We get $\Delta s = 0.006716101$. From this we can calculate our price at the end of day 2 as:

$$S_{\frac{2}{365}} = S_{\frac{1}{365}} \times e^{\Delta s} = 4.875245 \times e^{0.006716101} = 4.908098.$$

We repeat the process to get the price for day 3. This time our simulated Δs is 0.002827862. The resulting simulated price is:

$$S_{\frac{3}{365}} = 4.908098 \times e^{0.002827862} = 4.921997.$$

Using a computer program, we simulate a million paths to enable sufficient accuracy (see the C++ program in 2.15). We take the present value of the sample average payoff to get an estimated value for the option of around CU 0.0313.

The Asian option that we modelled here is known as a "floating-strike" Asian option. Also classified as an Asian option is a contract where the strike price K is fixed, but the payoff is calculated by comparing K to the average price over several days rather than just the price on the exercise data. (The payoff would usually be settled in cash rather than by issuing shares). Such an option is called a "fixed-strike" Asian option. The Monte Carlo approach easily extends to such fixed-strike Asian options.

The inefficiency of Monte Carlo simulation can be reduced by adopting advanced techniques that we do not have space to go into here in detail. In these methods, rather than simulating just the option by itself, we simulate a portfolio that includes the option together with some combination of instruments that partially hedge it. We should be able to value those other instruments using some separate technique such as a lattice or a formula like Black-Scholes.

Simulating the portfolio requires fewer runs than simulating the Asian option on its own. This is because the portfolio has less variability than the option on its own (the portfolio is partially hedged), so we can simulate a greater portion of that variability with fewer runs.

We can take the sample average portfolio value, and then use it to work out the imputed value of the option on its own, by removing the value of the other items in the portfolio.

For valuing European-style Asian options, a standard improved approach is given by Kemna and Vorst (1990).

2.10 Measuring Volatility

Recall that volatility is the standard deviation of the natural logarithm of the uncertain future share price after one year.

Volatility can be estimated in two different ways:

1. *Historical volatility* uses the past price history to work out what the actual standard deviation of the natural logarithm of prices was in the recent past.
2. *Implied volatility* uses the known current price of a traded option to work out the volatility level that is consistent with that price.

Under IFRS 13, we regard implied volatility as a Level 2 input, while historical volatility is a Level 3 input.

We discuss historical and implied volatility below.

2.10.1 Historical Volatility

We discuss three different ways to estimate historical volatity:

1. *Close-close volatility* estimates volatility based on the closing prices at the end of each day (or other period).
2. *Parkinson High-Low volatility* estimates volatility based on a series of the highest and lowest prices observed during each day (or other period). This measure was introduced by Parkinson (1980)
3. *Garman-Klass volatility* estimates volatility based on a series of the opening, closing, highest and lowest prices observed during each day (or other period). This measure was introduced by Garman and Klass (1980).

In estimating volatility using historical data, it is usually more convenient to look at a series of daily prices (or weekly or monthly) rather than yearly prices. We can then calculate a daily volatility (or weekly or monthly) and convert this to an annualized volatility by multiplying by the square root of the number of days in a year (or weeks or months as appropriate). In our examples, we take this to be 365 days. But in practice, it is standard to take the number of trading days in the year for the specific market (days when the market is open, i.e., excluding weekends and public holidays). The number of trading days is typically around 250 days.

When we count trading days only, we reflect the fact that prices do not move on days when the market is closed. Taking 365 days on the other hand assumes that even when markets are closed, price-sensitive news could enter the market, with its cumulative effect hitting the opening price as soon as the market reopens.

Before discussing each measure of historical volatility with examples, we briefly review some technical background on the definition of volatility.

Recall that volatility is defined as the standard deviation of the natural logarithm of the uncertain future price one year after the valuation date.

We can also define this as the standard deviation of the natural logarithm of the *relative* price at the end of a year, where the relative price is the ratio of the future price after one year to the price today $\left(\frac{\tilde{S}_1}{S_0}\right)$, where $\tilde{S}_1$ is the (uncertain) price after one year, and S_0 is the (known) price today.

To see this, recall first that the standard deviation is the square root of the variance $V(.)$ defined as $V(x) = E(x - Ex)^2$ where E stands for expected value and V stands for variance.

Then we have (using elementary results from mathematical statistics):

$$\begin{aligned} V\left(\ln\left(\frac{\tilde{S}_1}{S_0}\right)\right) &= V(\ln \tilde{S}_1 - \ln S_0) \\ &= V(\ln \tilde{S}_1) + V(\ln S_0) - 2 \times cov(\ln \tilde{S}_1, \ln S_0) \\ &= V(\ln \tilde{S}_1). \end{aligned}$$

Here $cov(x, y)$ stands for the covariance of x and y defined as $E((x - Ex) \times (y - Ey))$. The variance of $\ln S_0$ is zero, since S_0 is a known number, and does not vary at all. Similarly the covariance of $\ln S_1$ with $\ln S_0$ is zero, because S_0 is known and does not vary.

We can therefore define volatility σ as follows:

$$\sigma^2 = V\left(\ln\left(\frac{\tilde{S}_1}{S_0}\right)\right).$$

An underlying assumption of the Black-Scholes model is that the variance of the natural logarithm of the relative prices (price ratios) at any future date say Δt years, is proportional to the squared volatility σ^2 (variance over a year). That is:

$$V\left(\ln\left(\frac{\tilde{S}_{\Delta t}}{S_0}\right)\right) = \Delta t \times V\left(\ln\left(\frac{\tilde{S}_1}{S_0}\right)\right) = \sigma^2 \Delta t.$$

If we refer to the standard deviation of $\ln\left(\frac{\tilde{S}_{\Delta t}}{S_0}\right)$ as the Δt-volatility, $\sigma_{\Delta t}$ say, and recall that this is given by the square root of $V\left(\ln\left(\frac{\tilde{S}_{\Delta t}}{S_0}\right)\right)$, then we have:

$$\sigma_{\Delta t} = \sqrt{V\left(\ln\left(\frac{\tilde{S}_{\Delta t}}{S_0}\right)\right)} = \sqrt{\sigma^2 \Delta t} = \sigma\sqrt{\Delta t}.$$

We will use the term daily volatility to refer to $\sigma_{\Delta t}$ where Δt equals one day.

It is worthwhile to note that the natural logarithm of the relative price also represents a continuously compounded return on investment over the period Δt. Say we buy the share today at S_0 and sell it after Δt years at $S_{\Delta t}$. Let our return on investment as a continuously compounded rate be X (this is a rate per Δt years, not per year).

Then we have:

$$S_{\Delta t} = S_0 \times e^X.$$
$$\Rightarrow X = \ln\left(\frac{S_{\Delta t}}{S_0}\right).$$

We now proceed to discuss the various historical estimates of volatility.

2.10.1.1 Close-Close Volatility

To estimate close-close volatility, we collect a history of daily closing prices usually for the latest year to date. We also keep track of ex-dividend dates during the period, and the amount of the dividend that is removed from the share price on the ex-dividend date. The share price reduces by the amount of the dividend on the ex-dividend date, while the dividend is included in the price on the previous day. So when we are taking the ratio of the two prices, we add back the dividend to the ex-dividend date price, so that we are comparing apples with apples. Before going ex-dividend, the share is a single instrument, whose value gets split the next day into *two* assets—a receivable for the amount of the dividend, and the ex-dividend share. We should compare the share before going ex-dividend to the portfolio of two assets after going ex-dividend. The portfolio value is the ex-dividend share price plus the dividend amount.

Another way to look at this is that if we buy the share at the close of today (the day before the ex-dividend date) paying S_0 and hold it till the end of tomorrow (the ex-dividend date) selling it at the closing price $S_{\Delta t}$ say, we would also receive the dividend amount say div. Therefore our continuously compounded return should include the dividend amount, i.e., if our continuously compounded return is X, we have:[6]

$$S_{\Delta t} + div = S_0 \times e^X.$$
$$\Rightarrow \quad X = \ln\left(\frac{S_{\Delta t} + div}{S_0}\right).$$

Similarly to dividends, we should account for events like stock splits, bonus shares, etc. that occur during a period by adjusting the price comparisons. For example, if we purchased the shares at the close of today for S_0, and a two-for-

[6] Strictly speaking, this should be the present value of the dividend as of the ex-dividend date, but in practice, this is often taken to be the entire dividend unless the effect of discounting is clearly material.

one stock split took place before the market closed the next day, we would treat S_0 as the price of two post-split shares in our calculation, giving:

$$S_{\Delta t} \times 2 = S_0 \times e^X.$$
$$\Rightarrow \quad X = \ln\left(\frac{S_{\Delta t} \times 2}{S_0}\right).$$

where as before, $S_{\Delta t}$ is the closing price on the next day when we hypothetically sell the shares, and X is the continuously compounded one-day return.

We illustrate the procedure with an example. We use a small sample here of just 20 days' data, purely for convenient exposition. In practice, we would usually use the latest full year series of daily prices. The data for our example is in Table 2.3. Price and dividend amounts are in CU.

Let us go through a couple of lines in Table 2.3. For day 1, the closing price is 5.0177. This is not an ex-dividend date, so there is no dividend to be considered in the price ratio. The returns column refers to the natural logarithm of the relative price (plus dividends or any other adjustments needed). In this line it is $\ln \frac{5.0177}{5.0000}$ or around 0.003534. Day 11 is an ex-dividend date, with a dividend of CU 1 being removed from the share. As we see, the share price has dropped on Day 11 by more than CU

Table 2.3 Data for close-close volatility example

Day	Closing price	Dividend	Returns
0	5.0000		
1	5.0177		0.00353375
2	5.0448		0.00538635
3	4.9021		−0.0286943
4	4.8275		−0.0153349
5	4.8767		0.01014
6	4.9512		0.0151612
7	4.9606		0.00189673
8	5.0113		0.0101687
9	4.9867		−0.00492099
10	5.0906		0.0206213
11	4.0664	1.0000	−0.0047652
12	3.8988		−0.0420893
13	3.8987		−2.56492e-05
14	3.8771		−0.00555571
15	3.8269		−0.0130324
16	3.8538		0.0070046
17	3.8211		−0.00852134
18	3.8959		0.0193864
19	3.9843		0.0224369
20	3.9471		−0.00938051

1, from CU 5.0906 to CU 4.0664. To correctly reflect the returns, we must include the dividend in the calculation, giving $\ln \frac{4.0664+1.0000}{5.0906}$ or approximately -0.0048.

To calculate the volatility, we first find the *daily* volatility, by taking the standard deviation of the returns. This works out to 0.01632. To get the annualized volatility, we multiply this number by $\sqrt{365}$, or alternatively by the square root of the number of trading days in a year. Using the square root of 365, we get an annualized volatility of 0.3118 (or around 31%).

2.10.1.2 Parkinson High-Low Volatility

Close-close volatility ignores intra-day price swings, and therefore may understate the true volatility. An alternative calculation developed by Parkinson (1980) is calculated using data on the highest and lowest prices observed during the day. If on day i, H_i is the highest price that day, L_i is the lowest price that day, and n is the sample size, then the Parkinson High-Low (HL) Δt-volatility measure, $\hat{\sigma}_{\Delta t,HL}$ say, is as in Equation 2.13:

$$\hat{\sigma}_{\Delta t,HL} = \sqrt{\frac{1}{4n \ln 2} \sum_{i=1}^{n} \left(\ln \frac{H_i}{L_i} \right)^2}. \tag{2.13}$$

The derivation is beyond our scope. The mathematically adept reader may refer to Parkinson (1980).

For this calculation, we usually do not worry about dividends, splits, etc. at least when using daily data. This is because these events typically occur when the market is closed, i.e., between trading days, and not during a trading day. (If we are using a series of weekly or monthly rather than daily prices, then we may need to adjust for dividends and splits).

We illustrate using an example. As before, we use just 20 days of data purely for convenience of exposition. A longer time-series would be preferred in practice. Our data is in Table 2.4. Each row gives the opening, high, low, and closing price followed by the calculation of $(\ln \frac{H_i}{L_i})^2$.

We calculate $\sum(\ln \frac{H_i}{L_i})^2$ to be 0.01997463.

We can now calculate the daily volatility. This is:

$$\hat{\sigma}_{\Delta t,HL} = \sqrt{\frac{1}{4 \times 20 \times \ln(2)} \times 0.01997463} = 0.018979.$$

To get our annualized volatility estimate, we multiply by $\sqrt{365}$. We get an annualized volatility estimate of approximately 0.3626 (36.26%).

2.10.1.3 Garman-Klass Volatility

Our price data in the previous example included opening and closing prices as well as high and low prices. Garman and Klass (1980) proposed a volatility estimate that takes into account all four prices. Their estimate of Δt-volatility, $\hat{\sigma}_{\Delta t,OHLC}$ say, is as given in equation 2.14

$$\hat{\sigma}_{\Delta t,OHLC} = \sqrt{\frac{1}{n}\sum_{i=1}^{n}\left[\frac{1}{2}\left(\ln\frac{H_i}{L_i}\right)^2 - (2\ln 2 - 1)\times\left(\ln\frac{C_i}{O_i}\right)^2\right]} \tag{2.14}$$

where n is the sample size, and O_i, H_i, L_i, C_i are respectively the opening, high, low, and closing prices on day i.

The derivation of this formula is outside our scope. The mathematically adept reader may refer to Garman and Klass (1980).

We can demonstrate the calculation using the data in Table 2.4. We compute the expression $\frac{1}{2}(\ln\frac{H_i}{L_i})^2 - (2\ln 2 - 1)(\ln\frac{C_i}{O_i})^2$ for each row i, and add them all up to get 0.008283656.

Then our Garman-Klass estimate of daily volatility is as follows:

$$\sqrt{\frac{1}{20}\times 0.008283656} = 0.02035148.$$

We multiply by $\sqrt{365}$ to get our annualized volatility. This works out to around 0.3888 (38.88%).

Table 2.4 Example for Parkinson and Garman-Klass volatility

Day	Open	High	Low	Close	$(\ln\frac{H_i}{L_i})^2$	$\frac{1}{2}(\ln\frac{H_i}{L_i})^2$ $-(2\ln 2 - 1)(\ln\frac{C_i}{O_i})^2$
1	5.0156	5.0480	4.8003	4.8448	0.0025314693	0.0008020189
2	4.8134	4.9947	4.8103	4.9364	0.0014151063	0.0004616051
3	4.9228	4.9847	4.7983	4.8958	0.0014524889	0.0007145600
4	4.7147	4.7152	4.5711	4.6363	0.0009633237	0.0003730406
5	4.5902	4.6351	4.5166	4.5396	0.0006707207	0.0002878962
6	4.5255	4.5989	4.4919	4.5710	0.0005541961	0.0002384382
7	4.5434	4.5859	4.4541	4.4956	0.0008503848	0.0003819807
8	4.4859	4.5490	4.4294	4.4976	0.0007098651	0.0003523116
9	4.4530	4.4552	4.3659	4.3849	0.0004099653	0.0001132357
10	4.3261	4.4824	4.2894	4.3463	0.0019370345	0.0009601342
11	4.3866	4.4624	4.3282	4.3475	0.0009323854	0.0004352255
12	4.3706	4.3738	4.2652	4.2959	0.0006321766	0.0002012852
13	4.2047	4.2243	4.1048	4.1650	0.0008234918	0.0003769806
14	4.1470	4.2010	4.0761	4.1023	0.0009109497	0.0004101050
15	4.1375	4.2158	4.0940	4.1822	0.0008594797	0.0003851346
16	4.1211	4.2125	4.0943	4.1193	0.0008100019	0.0004049272
17	4.2595	4.4118	4.2534	4.3812	0.0013369339	0.0003619044
18	4.3907	4.4360	4.3157	4.4139	0.0007558944	0.0003672187
19	4.5241	4.5846	4.4650	4.4985	0.0006987377	0.0003369295
20	4.4918	4.5021	4.3829	4.4456	0.0007200286	0.0003187240
Total					0.01997463	0.008283656

2.10.2 Implied Volatility

For implied volatility, we estimate the volatility by comparing the actual current price of a traded option to a valuation model such as Black-Scholes with all the parameters except volatility plugged in, and solving for the volatility that would make the value from the model equal to the actual option price. This volatility is the level *implied* by the current price, or the *implied volatility*.

For example, suppose that we are valuing an ESO on the grant date. We have estimated all the parameters except the volatility. We notice that a traded call option on the same date with $S = 5$, $K = 6$, $r_c = 0.1$, $t = \frac{90}{365}$ has a current (grant-date) price of CU 0.06. Solving for the volatility that makes the Black-Scholes value of the option equal to CU 0.06, we get an implied volatility of around 30%. We can use this as the measure of volatility in our Hull-White model.

The process of finding the implied volatility usually needs numerical search techniques and a computer. It cannot be done by hand. The "goal-seek" tool in Microsoft Excel or similar spreadsheet software can be used to find implied volatility.

2.10.2.1 Why Is Implied Volatility Better?

It may not be immediately clear why IFRS 13 regards implied volatility as a Level 2 input, but historical volatility as Level 3. After all, both measures are derived from quoted share prices, which are observable inputs.

The reason is that the volatility parameter reflects *future* price volatility, not past volatility. Using historical volatility to estimate this parameter requires the assumption that history repeats itself, or that the past volatility will continue in future. This assumption is often proved wrong in practice, as periods of relative market calm could be followed by periods of turbulence.

Implied volatility does not require this assumption. Rather it can be interpreted as an estimate of the market's best guess about future volatility, which is exactly what we are trying to measure.

This concludes our discussion of options. In Chap. 3, we will discuss government bonds, from where we get the risk-free rate. Remaining sections in this chapter contain ancillary material referred to earlier in the chapter, and can be treated as chapter appendices.

2.11 Logic Behind the Risk-Neutral Probabilities Approach

Consider the one-step binomial model for a call option that we introduced in the chapter.

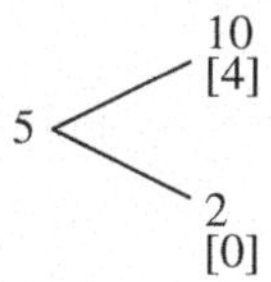

Recall that the strike date is at 90 days, the strike price is CU 6, and the risk-free rate is 10%.

Consider an instrument called an Arrow security. This instrument pays CU 1 if some event occurs and CU 0 otherwise. In other words, it is a simple gamble with a payoff of CU 1.

Now consider two types of Arrow securities—U and D say.

Security U pays CU 1 at 90 days if the share price goes up to CU 10 at that date. It pays zero otherwise.

Security D pays CU 1 at 90 days if the share price goes down to CU 2 at that date. It pays zero otherwise.

Let P_u and P_d be the prices today of the securities U and D respectively.

Consider a portfolio that consists of one security U and one security D.

The value of this portfolio at 90 days will be exactly CU 1. This is because exactly one of the component securities will pay off.

So its value today is the present value of CU 1, discounted at the risk-free rate (since it is guaranteed to give CU 1 in future). This gives us:

$$P_u + P_d = e^{-0.1\times\frac{90}{365}} \times 1.$$

We can use the U and D Arrow securities to create a replicating portfolio for our option. The option gives us CU 4 when the price is CU 10, and nothing when the price is CU 2. A portfolio of four U securities and zero D securities gives the same payoffs today. So we have:

$$C = 4P_u + 0P_d.$$

Also we can create a replicating portfolio for the share itself using U and D securities. The payoffs from the share itself are CU 10 if the price goes up to CU 10, and CU 2 if the price goes down to CU 2. A portfolio of ten U securities and two D securities gives exactly the same payoffs. Therefore, this portfolio should have exactly the same price today as the share itself, or CU 5. This gives us:

$$5 = 10P_u + 2P_d.$$

We can now solve directly for C, but our purpose is rather to explain the risk-neutral probabilities approach. Let us choose two numbers p_u and p_d (lowercase) such that:

$$P_u = e^{-0.1\times\frac{90}{365}} p_u.$$

$$P_d = e^{-0.1\times\frac{90}{365}} p_d.$$

Rewriting our equations in terms of p_u and p_d, we have:

$$p_u + p_d = 1.$$

$$e^{-0.1\times\frac{90}{365}}(10p_u + 2p_d) = 5.$$

$$C = e^{-0.1\times\frac{90}{365}}(4p_u + 0p_d).$$

These are the same as the equations for risk-neutral probabilities.

Our derivation did not use probabilities at all. But we note that p_u and p_d behave like probabilities—they lie between zero and one, they sum up to one, and the share price and call value can be interpreted as the expected present value under these "probabilities".

Therefore it is convenient to treat them as probabilities.

We further observe that these probabilities correspond to those that a risk-neutral person would assign if they valued the share at its current price.

2.12 Derivation of the Risk-Neutral Probability Formula in the Standard Multi-step Binomial Lattice

Consider an arbitrary single-step sub-lattice with starting price S_0.

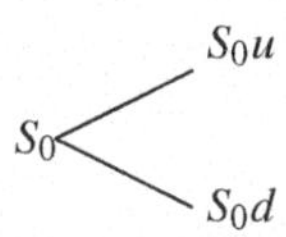

Let the risk-neutral probability of an up step be p_u in this sub-lattice.

Then

$$e^{r\Delta t}S_0 = p_u S_0 u + (1 - p_u)S_0 d.$$

We can divide both sides by S_0 giving:

$$e^{r\Delta t} = p_u u + (1 - p_u)d.$$

Solving for p_u we get:

$$p_u = \frac{e^{r\Delta t} - d}{u - d}.$$

We note that this is true for any arbitrary sub-lattice. It is also independent of the starting price S_0 at the node. So the same value of p_u holds at any node.

2.13 Why an American Call (No Dividends) Is Not Exercised Early

Let us use an equal probability binomial lattice with two steps to demonstrate the logic. The lattice is shown in Fig. 2.12. Using an equal probability lattice is just to reduce clutter in the algebra. The logic can be extended to a lattice with any risk-neutral probabilities, left as an exercise.

The lattice starting price is S, K is the strike price, r_c is the risk-free rate, σ the volatility, t the maturity date in years from today, and Δt the step-size in years. The up and down steps are u and d respectively.

Without loss of much generality let us assume that K is low enough so that the option has a non-zero value at all the ending nodes. The logic extends immediately to a case where the option has zero value at some end-nodes.

Now suppose that at the end of the first step, the price has moved up to Su, i.e., we are at the node marked (A) in the diagram with price Su. If we do not exercise at this point, the option value to us is given by the holding value:

$$V_H = e^{-r_c \Delta t} \times \frac{1}{2} [(Suu - K) + (Sud - K)]$$

Rearranging,

$$V_H = e^{-r_c \Delta t} \times \frac{1}{2} (Suu + Sud) - e^{-r_c \Delta t} K.$$

Substituting $e^{-r_c \Delta t} \times \frac{1}{2}(Suu + Sud) = Su$, we get

$$V_H = Su - e^{-r_c \Delta t} K. \tag{2.15}$$

Suppose that instead we exercise the option immediately at this point. Then the value from exercising (the intrinsic value) is:

$$V_I = (Su - K). \tag{2.16}$$

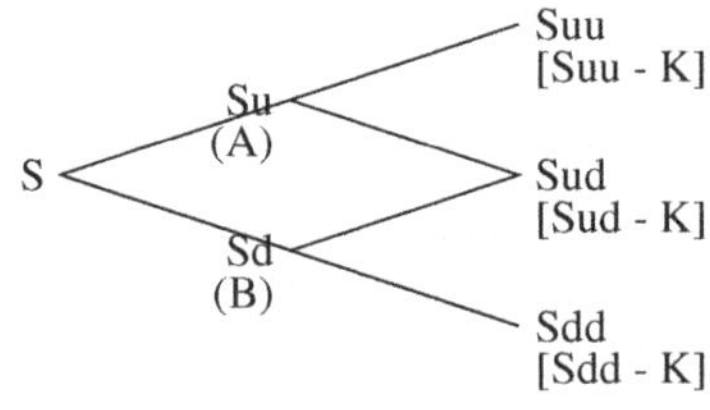

Fig. 2.12 Equal probability lattice for American call no dividends

Comparing equations 2.15 and 2.16 we get

$$V_H - V_I = \left(1 - e^{-r_c \Delta t}\right) K. \tag{2.17}$$

This is greater than zero because $e^{-r_c \Delta t}$ is less than 1 (it is a discount factor). Therefore, V_H is greater than V_I.

Therefore, we are better off holding rather than exercising at this node.

Similarly if the price had moved down to Sd after one step (the node labelled (B) in the diagram), we would have:

$$V_H = Sd - e^{-r_c \Delta t} K.$$

$$V_I = Sd - K.$$

This gives us at this node

$$V_H - V_I = (1 - e^{-r_c \Delta t} K). \tag{2.18}$$

Again at the node labelled (B), holding is better than exercising.

If the bottom end-node were to have an option value of 0 rather than $Sdd - K$, then $Sdd - K$ is less than zero. Then the holding value at (B) is *greater* than the expression above for V_H while the intrinsic value is the same V_I. So holding would still be better than exercising.

We turn next to the start of the lattice. Here the value from exercising is:

$$V_I = S - K. \tag{2.19}$$

The holding value is given by:

$$\begin{aligned} V_H &= e^{-r_c \Delta t} \left[\frac{1}{2} \left(Su - e^{-r_c \Delta t} K \right) + \frac{1}{2} \left(Sd - e^{-r_c \Delta t} K \right) \right] \\ &= e^{-r_c \Delta t} \left(\frac{1}{2} (Su + Sd) - e^{-2 r_c \Delta t} K \right). \end{aligned}$$

Substituting $e^{-r_c \Delta t} \left(\frac{1}{2} (Su + Sd) \right) = S$, we get

$$V_H = S - e^{-2 r_c \Delta t} K. \tag{2.20}$$

Comparing equations 2.19 and 2.20, we have at the start node

$$V_H - V_I = \left(1 - e^{-2 r_c \Delta t}\right) K.$$

This is greater than 0.
Therefore $V_H > V_I$ at the start node.
Therefore we will prefer not to exercise at this node.
Proved that we will not exercise at any node before the expiry date.

2.14 C++ Program for a Binomial Model

This is a C++ program to value a put or call option using an equal-probabilities binomial model.

```
#include <iostream>
#include <math.h>

double eqprob (double myS, double myK, double myt, double myrc,
               double mysigma, int mynumsteps, int myisPut){

  /* declare the return value */

  double retval;

  /* declare variables for supporting calculations */

  double deltat, up, down, pu, pd, pm, discfac ,myX;
  double price[mynumsteps+5],optionvalue[mynumsteps+5];
  int ctr, ctrl;

  /* calculate delta t */

  deltat = myt / ( (double) mynumsteps);

  /* calculate discount factor */

  /* It is efficient to run the model without discounting till
   the very last step when we multiply
   by (e^{-r deltat})^mynumsteps or e^{-r myt} */

  discfac = exp (-myrc*myt);

  /* calculate up and down steps */

  myX = log(2) + myrc*deltat - log( exp(mysigma*sqrt(deltat))
                                   +exp(-mysigma*sqrt(deltat)) );

  up = exp(sqrt(deltat)*mysigma + myX);
  down = exp(-mysigma*sqrt(deltat) + myX);

  /* risk-neutral probabilities are both equal to 0.5 */

  pu = 0.5;
  pd = 0.5;
```

```
/* compute prices at the expiry date */
/* top price */

price[0]=myS*pow(up, mynumsteps);

/* rest of prices (lower price is upper price / up * down) */
for (ctr = 1; ctr <= mynumsteps+1; ctr++){
  price[ctr]=(price[ctr-1] / up) * down;
}

/* compute option values at last node */

if (myisPut == 1){
  for (ctr = 0; ctr <= mynumsteps+1; ctr++ ){
    optionvalue[ctr] = myK - price[ctr];
    if (optionvalue[ctr]< 0){
      optionvalue[ctr]=0;
    } /* put option */
  }
} else {
  for (ctr = 0; ctr <= mynumsteps+1; ctr++){
    optionvalue[ctr] = price[ctr]-myK;
    if (optionvalue[ctr]< 0){
      optionvalue[ctr]=0;
    } /* call option */
  }
}

/* go backwards, solving prior option values
 using risk-neutral probabilities */

for (ctr = mynumsteps-1; ctr >= 0; ctr--){
  for (ctr1 = 0; ctr1 <= ctr+1; ctr1++ ){
    optionvalue[ctr1]=
      (optionvalue[ctr1]*pu + optionvalue[ctr1+1]*pd);
  }
}

retval = optionvalue[0]*discfac;
return retval;
}

int main (){
  double retval;
  double myS, myK, mydays, myt, myrc, mysigma;
  int mynumsteps, myisPut;

  std::cout << "Input starting price: ";
  std::cin >> myS;
  std::cout << "Input strike price: ";
  std::cin >> myK;
  std::cout << "Input days to maturity: ";
  std::cin >> mydays;
```

```
  std::cout << "Input risk-free rate (continuous) as a decimal: ";
  std::cin >> myrc;
  std::cout << "Input volatility as a decimal: ";
  std::cin >> mysigma;
  std::cout << "Input number of steps: ";
  std::cin >>  mynumsteps;
  std::cout << "If the option is a put, type 1. Otherwise type
                                              anything else:";
  std::cin >> myisPut;

  myt = (mydays / 365.0);

  retval = eqprob (myS,myK,myt,myrc,mysigma,mynumsteps,myisPut);

  std::cout << "The option value is: " << retval << std::endl;
}
```

2.15 C++ Program to Perform Monte Carlo Simulation to Value a European-Style Asian Option

This program uses the helper function `simdeltas(.)` which can be found in the programming appendix to the book (Appendix A), The program below assumes that the helper function is in the included file "myfunctions.cpp".

```
/* asianoptionsim.cpp --- Monte Carlo simulation of an
                                        Asian call option
(European exercise style) */

#include <iostream>
#include <math.h>
#include "myfunctions.cpp"

int main(){
  int seed,ctr0,ctr1,tdays,kdays;
  double mynormsim[1000], rc, sigma, S0, K, retval;

  std::cout << "input random number seed: ";
  std::cin >> seed;
  std::cout << "input risk-free rate (rc): ";
  std::cin >> rc;
  std::cout << "input starting share price (S0): ";
  std::cin >> S0;
  std::cout << "input volatility (sigma): ";
  std::cin >> sigma;
  std::cout << "input time to maturity in days (tdays < 1000): ";
  std::cin >> tdays;
  std::cout << "K is calculated over how many days before expiry?
                                              (kdays <= tdays): ";
  std::cin >> kdays;

  srand(seed);
```

```
    retval=0.0;
    for (ctr0=0; ctr0<=1000000; ctr0++){
      mynormsim[0]=S0;
      K=0.0;
      for (ctr1=1; ctr1<=tdays; ctr1++){
        mynormsim[ctr1]=mynormsim[ctr1-1]*exp(simdeltas(rc, sigma,
                                                        1.0/365.0));
        if (ctr1 > tdays - kdays){
          K = K + (mynormsim[ctr1]/kdays);
        }
      }

      if (mynormsim[tdays] > K){
        retval = retval + ((mynormsim[tdays]-K)/1000000.0);
      }
    }
    std::cout << "call value = " << exp(-rc*tdays/365.0)* retval
                                        << std::endl;
}
```

Exercises

(Monetary units are in CU unless otherwise mentioned).

2.1. Forward

On Aug 1 2019, George Inc enters a forward contract to sell 23,000 barrels of oil on Nov 1 2021 at a strike price of CU 60 per barrel.

George Inc needs to fair value the forward on their balance-sheet date, January 31, 2020. On this date, fresh forward contracts with a maturity of Nov 1 2021 have a strike price of CU 80.

Also on Jan 31 2020 the risk-free rate is 3% continuously compounded.

Find the fair value of the forward to George Inc.

2.2. European Put

Consider a European put option maturing in 83 days with $S = 8$, $K = 6$, $r_c = 0.01$, $\sigma = 0.6$.

Value the option using:

(a) A CRR model with three steps,
(b) An equal-probabilities model with three steps,
(c) A trinomial model with three steps,
(d) Black-Scholes.

2.3. European Call

Consider a European call option maturing in 47 days with $S = 9.3$, $K = 9.5$, $r_c = 0.03$, $\sigma = 0.2$.

Value the option using:

(a) A CRR model with three steps,
(b) An equal-probabilities model with three steps,
(c) A trinomial model with three steps,
(d) Black-Scholes.

2.4. American Put
Consider an American put option maturing in 83 days with $S = 8$, $K = 6$, $r_c = 0.01$, $\sigma = 0.6$.
Value the option using:

(a) A CRR model with three steps,
(b) An equal-probabilities model with three steps,
(c) A trinomial model with three steps

2.5. American Call with Dividends
Consider an American call option maturing in 68 days with $S = 3.8$, $K = 2.3$, $r_c = 0.02$, $\sigma = 0.3$. A dividend equal to CU 0.8 is due in 37 days (ex-dividend date as well as dividend payment date).
Value the option using:

(a) A CRR model with three steps,
(b) An equal-probabilities model with three steps,
(c) A trinomial model with three steps,

2.6. Hull-White ESO Model
A company issues an ESO on January 1, 2019, vesting on January 1, 2021. The share price at grant date (after the announcement) is 30. The option strike price is 30.50. The options expire on January 1, 2022, and if the holder leaves the company's employment. 1% of the receiving employees are expected to exit the company year. The risk-free rate is 3%. The volatility of the company's share price is 34%. Assume that the automatic exercise multiple is 1.8.
Value the option using:

(a) Black-Scholes
(b) The Hull-White ESO model (four steps)

2.7. Hull-White ESO Model
Use a Hull-White ESO model (four steps) to value the following ESO:

$$S = CU4.6$$

$$K = CU4.8$$
$$r_c = 0.08$$
$$t = 2$$
$$\sigma = 0.4$$
$$t_{vest} = 1$$
$$M = 2$$
$$x = 0.08$$

2.8. Hull-White ESO Model
Use a Hull-White ESO model (four steps) to value the following ESO:

$$S = CU8.6$$
$$K = CU8.7$$
$$r_c = 0.06$$
$$t = 2$$
$$\sigma = 0.3$$
$$t_{vest} = 1$$
$$M = 2$$
$$x = 0.06$$

2.9. Volatility
Compute close-close volatility using the following data:

Day	Closing Price	Dividend
0	8.32	
1	8.67	
2	8.85	
3	9.42	
4	8.78	
5	8.66	0.5
6	7.87	
7	7.96	
8	7.63	
9	7.68	
10	8.05	
11	8.60	

2.10. Volatility

Compute close-close volatility using the following data:

Day	Closing Price	Dividend
0	3.27	
1	3.67	
2	2.85	
3	3.42	
4	3.78	0.03
5	3.60	
6	3.20	
7	3.13	
8	3.44	
9	3.62	
10	3.05	
11	3.34	

2.11. Volatility

Day	Open	High	Low	Close
1	15.02	15.04	14.82	14.84
2	14.83	14.94	14.31	14.64
3	14.62	14.98	14.38	14.58
4	14.47	14.72	14.35	14.63
5	14.59	14.65	14.36	14.56
6	14.55	14.59	14.49	14.57
7	14.54	14.69	14.41	14.49
8	14.48	14.90	14.24	14.49
9	14.45	14.52	14.36	14.49
10	14.46	14.48	14.28	14.34
11	14.36	14.56	14.22	14.35
12	14.37	14.73	14.26	14.29
13	14.27	14.43	14.10	14.16
14	14.14	14.20	14.07	14.10
15	14.13	14.38	14.09	14.18
16	14.21	14.42	14.04	14.19
17	14.21	14.41	14.03	14.12
18	14.13	14.60	14.10	14.43
19	14.41	14.58	14.23	14.45
20	14.46	14.52	14.29	14.44

Using the price data above, compute:

(a) Parkinson High-Low volatility
(b) Garman-Klass volatility

2.12. Programming
Write a C/C++ function `double crr(...)` that implements a CRR model for a European call or put with starting price S, strike price K, continuous risk-free rate rc, time to maturity t, volatility parameter $sigma$, and number of steps n. Assume no dividends. (Hint: Use the example in 2.14 as a guide.)

2.13. Programming
Write a C/C++ function `double trinomial(...)` that implements a trinomial model for a European call or put with starting price S, strike price K, continuous risk-free rate rc, time to maturity t, volatility parameter $sigma$, and number of steps n. Assume no dividends. (Hint: Use the example in 2.14 as a guide. For a trinomial, the number of nodes at each step increases by 2, thus we have 1 node at the start, 3 nodes at step 1, 5 nodes at step 2, ... Also the only new prices at each step are the new top and bottom prices.)

2.14. Programming
Write a C/C++ function to value a European-style Asian option with a *fixed strike*. That is, the strike price is fixed, but the payoff is based on comparing the strike price to the average closing price over some number of days before expiry. Assume no dividends. (Hint: Use the example in 2.15 as a guide.)

2.15. Programming
Write C/C++ functions `bscall` and `bsput` to value a European call and put respectively using Black-Scholes.

References

Black, F., & Scholes, M. (1973). The pricing of options and corporate liabilities. *Journal of Political Economy, 81*, 637–657.
Boyle, P. (1977). Options: A Monte Carlo approach. *Journal of Financial Economics, 4*, 323–338.
Cox, J., Ross, S., & Rubinstein, M. (1979). Option pricing: A simplified approach. *Journal of Financial Economics, 7*, 229–263.
Garman, M., & Klass, M. (1980). On the estimation of security price volatilities from historical data. *Journal of Business, 53*, 67–78.
Hull, J. (2017). *Options, futures and other derivatives* (10th ed.). New York: Pearson.
Hull, J., & White, A. (2004). How to value employee stock options. *Financial Analysts Journal, 60*, 114–119.
Kemna, A., & Vorst, A. (1990). A pricing method for options based on average asset values. *Journal of Banking and Finance, 14*, 113–129.
Parkinson, M. (1980). The extreme value method for estimating the variance of the rate of return. *Journal of Business, 53*, 61–65.

Government Bonds 3

Valuing government-issued debt gives us the risk-free rate, a key parameter in valuation models. We focus on government bonds for this chapter. We start by discussing yields on zero-coupon debt. This leads to concepts of spot and forward interest rates and discount factors for various maturities (risk-free rates and discount factors). We discuss different yield conventions and how to convert between them. We turn next to coupon bonds—bonds with periodic fixed interest payments. We explain how to value them in terms of a portfolio of zero coupon bonds. In practice, for longer maturities, only coupon bonds exist. We discuss how to use the relationship between coupon bonds and zero-coupon bonds to estimate zero-coupon prices and yields for these maturities—a procedure known as bootstrapping. We further discuss how to use the Svensson model to fit a non-linear curve that matches actual government bond prices. The Svensson model is used by the European Central Bank and the German Bundesbank to report their interest rates. Then we discuss two lattice models of risk-free rates—the Black-Derman-Toy model and the Ho-Lee model. These models can be used to value interest-rate derivatives. Finally we discuss how we can use estimated risk-free rates for different currencies to estimate the forward exchange rate between them, using a model known as covered interest rate parity (CIRP).

3.1 Learning Outcomes

After completing this chapter, you would be able to:

1. Measure risk-free spot and forward interest rates for different maturities using different conventions.
2. Apply bootstrapping or the Svensson model to estimate the risk-free interest rates for different maturities (the term structure) given the prices or yields of actual government bonds of various types (the yield curve).

S. Lynn, *Valuation for Accountants*, Springer Texts in Business and Economics,
https://doi.org/10.1007/978-981-15-0357-3_3

3. Build lattice models of the term structure that can be used to price interest-rate derivatives.
4. Estimate forward currency exchange rates given spot or forward interest rates from different countries.

In this chapter, we discuss government-issued bonds. These are used to determine the risk-free rate in different currencies. We will introduce other bonds in the next chapter.

3.2 Zero-Coupon Bonds

A zero-coupon bond pays a fixed lumpsum amount (the principal or the face value) at its maturity (due date), with no other payments in between. This is a common form for shorter-maturity government bonds, often called Treasury Bills or T-bills or treasuries. Zero-coupon bonds in general are also called *zeroes* or *strips*.

Zeroes usually trade at a price that is lower than the principal. For example, a zero with a principal amount of CU 100 may have a price of CU 99. Then the difference between the principal amount and the price is called the *discount*. In the above example, the discount is CU 1.

$$Discount = Principal - Price.$$

3.2.1 Discount Factors

A spot discount factor for a particular maturity date is the price today in CU of a zero-coupon bond that pays CU 1 principal on that maturity date. We will usually drop the word "spot" and refer to this as just a discount factor.

Equivalently, a discount factor for a particular maturity is the ratio of the current price to the amount due at maturity (principal) for a zero-coupon bond with that maturity.

Consistent with this second definition, a discount factor is expressed units-free, i.e., as a simple percentage or decimal rather than a currency amount.

A discount factor is always as of a particular date (the current date or valuation date), and for a particular maturity. Thus, if a zero-coupon bond that pays $principal$ at a time t years from today, has a price equal to $price$ today, and today is the valuation date, then the discount factor at the valuation date for a maturity of t years from the valuation date is given by the expression:

$$d_t = \frac{price}{principal}.$$

Time is usually measured in years in valuation models. We will follow this convention by default in this book.

3.2.1.1 Example: Discount Factor

A zero-coupon bond pays CU 100 at a time that is 90 days from today (today is the valuation date). Today's price for the zero is CU 99. What is the discount factor for 90 days? (Let's for now treat this as 0.25 years.)

$$d_{0.25} = \frac{99}{100} = 0.99.$$

3.2.2 Yield to Maturity

The yield to maturity for a zero is the rate of return per year that one would get if one bought the zero at its current price and then held it right until it matures and pays the principal.

"Rate of return" can be defined in an infinite variety of ways. The particular rule used to define the rate is called the *yield convention*. We discuss a few common yield conventions below. These are:

1. Bank discount rate,
2. Continuously compounded rates, and
3. Semi-annually compounded annual percentage rates (APR).

3.2.2.1 Bank Discount Rate

This is a simple measure that is widely used in calculating the yield from short-maturity instruments. Official quoted yields for short-maturity zeroes are in this form in many jurisdictions.

The bank discount rate simply takes the difference between the principal and the price (the discount) and treats that as the return over the remaining time to maturity.

For example, for a zero currently priced at CU 99 and paying CU 100 after 90 days,the 90-day return is 1%:

$$\left(\frac{100 - 99}{100}\right).$$

We need to express this return as a rate per year. To do that, we first calculate a rate per day by dividing by the days left to maturity. We then calculate a rate per year by multiplying by 365 days. A standard convention is to assume 365 days in a year (even if it's a leap year).

In our example, the bank discount rate works out to be:

$$1\% \times \frac{365}{90} = 4.056\%(3dp.)$$

To express this calculation as a standard formula, the bank discount rate $r_{t,b}$ say for maturity t is given by:

$$r_{t,b} = \frac{principal - price}{principal} \times \frac{365}{ndays}$$

where

- $principal$ is the principal amount due at maturity,
- $price$ is the price on the valuation date,
- $ndays$ is the number of days from the valuation date to the maturity date,
- t is the time in years from the valuation date to the maturity date.

3.2.2.2 Continuous Compounding

The continuously compounded rate of return $r_{t,c}$ for a maturity t in years can be derived from the expression:

$$price = e^{-r_{t,c}t} \times principal.$$

where $price$ is the price on the valuation date, $principal$ is the amount due on maturity and t is the time from the valuation date to the maturity date measured in years.

Rearranging and taking natural logarithms, we get

$$r_{t,c} = \frac{\ln(price) - \ln(principal)}{-t}.$$

Recalling that the discount factor is equal to the price corresponding to a principal of CU 1, and noting that $\ln(1) = 0$, we have:

$$r_{t,c} = -\frac{\ln(d_t)}{t}.$$

Example: Continuous Rate

The price of a zero paying CU 100 in three months is CU 99. Let's assume for now that three months equal 0.25 years.

Then we have:

$$r_{0.25,c} = \frac{\ln(99) - \ln(100)}{-0.25} = 4.020\%\ (3dp.)$$

or

$$r_{0.25,c} = -\frac{\ln(0.99)}{0.25} = 4.020\%\ (3dp.)$$

3.2.2.3 Semi-annual Compounding

This is a common convention in the bond markets. The reason is that longer-maturity bonds typically pay interest every half-year, so that half-yearly compounding is a good match to the cash flows.

For a zero that pays *principal* at maturity t years from the valuation date, and has a price equal to *price* on the valuation date, the semi-annually compounded "annual percentage rate" (APR) rate $r_{t,2}$ is given by the formula:

$$price = \frac{principal}{\left(1 + \frac{r_{t,2}}{2}\right)^{t \times 2}}.$$

This is a special case of the general APR formula for an interest rate based on k notionally equal compounding periods every year (with k equal to 2 in the semi-annual case):

$$price = \frac{principal}{\left(1 + \frac{r_{t,k}}{k}\right)^{t \times k}}.$$

For example with quarterly compounding, k would equal 4, and with monthly compounding, k would equal 12.

Example: Semi-annual Compounding

If the price is CU 99 for a zero that pays CU 100 after 3 months (0.25 years), find the semi-annually compounded yield.

$$\left(1 + \frac{r_{0.25,2}}{2}\right)^{0.5} = \frac{100}{99}.$$

Square both sides to give:

$$\left(1 + \frac{r_{0.25,2}}{2}\right) = \left(\frac{100}{99}\right)^2 = 1.0203.$$

From this, we can get $r_{0.25,2} = 4.061\%$ ($3dp.$).

3.2.3 Spot and Forward Interest Rates

3.2.3.1 Spot Interest Rates

The spot interest rate for a maturity t is the yield to maturity on a zero with maturity t.

This can of course be defined using different conventions. In practice, the yields are often quoted using the bank discount rate for short maturities and semi-annual compounding for longer maturities.

The spot interest rates represent the closest approximation to a *risk-free* rate of return. A risk-free rate is a key building block of many valuation models.

The particular convention used in a valuation model can vary. In option pricing models and other derivative valuation models, the rate should be a continuously compounded rate. In enterprise valuation models, the rate used is usually based on annual compounding.

3.2.3.2 Forward Discount Factors

A forward contract is a contract requiring the holder to buy (or sell) some item at a future date at a fixed price that is determined in the contract. This fixed price can be termed the *exercise price* or *strike price* under the contract.

Consider a forward contract issued today (the valuation date) to buy a zero-coupon bond at a future date $t1$ years from today, where the zero-coupon bond pays a principal of CU 1 at a maturity date $t2$ years from today. The maturity date $t2$ should be later than $t1$, or $t2 > t1$.

The strike price of this forward contract is called the forward discount factor from $t1$ to $t2$, which we write as ${}_{t1}d_{t2}$.

Equivalently, the forward discount factor is the ratio of the strike price to the principal amount in a freshly-issued forward contract to buy a zero with any given principal amount. Consistent with this definition, the forward discount factor is expressed unit-free, as a pure percentage or decimal, not in currency units.

It is important to remember that forward discount factors are *not* present values. They are future values—values as of the future date $t1$ not as of today (or the valuation date).

Spot discount factors d_t are special cases of forward discount factors ${}_{t1}d_{t2}$, where $t1 = 0$ and $t2 = t$. That is, they reflect the prices for a transaction that takes place immediately—on the spot—rather than at some future date.

3.2.3.3 Forward Interest Rates

The forward interest rate ${}_{t1}r_{t2}$ is the yield to maturity from time $t1$ to time $t2$ (both expressed in years from the valuation date) corresponding to a forward discount factor ${}_{t1}d_{t2}$.

In other words, it is the rate of return per year that one would get between $t1$ and $t2$ with the following actions:

- Buy a zero-coupon bond at $t1$ that matures at $t2$, paying a price corresponding to ${}_{t1}d_{t2}$ per currency unit of principal.
- Hold the zero-coupon bond to maturity $t2$ and collect the principal.

As with spot interest rates, forward interest rates can be defined using a variety of conventions. Similar to spot interest rates, we prefer continuous rates in option pricing models and annually compounded rates in enterprise valuation.

It is important to remember that forward interest rates reflect the return between two future dates $t1$ and $t2$, not the return from today (or the valuation date) to $t2$.

Spot interest rates r_t are special cases of forward interest rates where $t1 = 0$ and $t2 = t$. That is, they reflect interest rates where the starting date is today (or the valuation date).

3.2.3.4 Deriving Forward Interest Rates

In practice, forward discount factors and interest rates are not directly quoted. We can however estimate them from spot discount factors or interest rates.

We use a replicating portfolio argument to drive the logic.

Consider a forward discount factor ${}_{t1}d_{t2}$. This represents the strike price of a forward contract to buy a zero at $t1$ that will pay CU 1 at $t2$. Let this unknown strike price be X.

Consider two investment strategies A and B say.

Under strategy A, we buy a zero-coupon bond today that pays CU X at $t1$. We simultaneously enter into a freshly-issued forward contract to buy a zero-coupon bond at $t1$ that pays CU 1 at $t2$. Recall that the strike price under this contract is X, so we are committed to pay X at $t1$. We proceed to hold the zero to maturity.

The payoff from this strategy is that we collect CU 1 at $t2$. We collect CU X at $t1$, immediately use it to buy the zero-coupon bond, and then hold the zero to $t2$ when we collect CU 1.

Under strategy B, we buy a zero-coupon bond today that pays CU 1 at $t2$, and then hold it to maturity. This strategy too gives us a payoff of CU 1 at $t2$.

Since both strategies A and B give exactly the same payoffs, they should have the same price today. Otherwise, investors would rush to invest in the cheaper strategy and short-sell the more expensive one, and the prices would adjust to compensate till they are the same.

The price of strategy B is d_{t2}.

The price of strategy A is $d_{t1}X$.

Equating these, we have:

$$d_{t2} = d_{t1}X.$$

From this, we can derive

$$X = \frac{d_{t2}}{d_{t1}}.$$

Noting that X is the forward discount factor from $t1$ to $t2$, we get:

$${}_{t1}d_{t2} = \frac{d_{t2}}{d_{t1}}.$$

In other words, we can derive the forward discount factor from $t1$ to $t2$ by taking the ratio of the spot discount factor for the longer maturity $t2$ to that for the shorter maturity $t1$.

Having derived the forward discount factor, we can use it to derive the corresponding forward interest rate under any yield convention.

3.3 Coupon Bonds

Government bonds with a maturity greater than a year are usually coupon bonds rather than zeroes. A coupon bond pays a periodic interest amount in addition to paying the principal or face value at maturity. This periodic payment is called the *coupon* payment or just *coupon*.

The coupon payment could be either a fixed lumpsum amount every year (fixed rate), or could vary using a standard formula based on some quoted reference rate (floating rate). In this chapter, we only consider fixed-rate coupon bonds.

Government coupon bonds typically have half-yearly (semi-annual) coupons with a fixed rate. The annual coupon is typically paid in two equal instalments every half-year.

3.3.1 Coupon Bond Terminology

The *principal* or *face value* of the coupon bond is the lumpsum amount paid at maturity. For example a bond with a face value of CU 5000 will pay CU 5000 at maturity.

The *coupon* is an annual fixed payment that is paid in regular fixed instalments, typically every half-year. Suppose that a bond has a face value of CU 5000 and in addition pays an annual coupon of CU 50 with equal half-yearly payments. Then the bond pays CU 25 every half-year until the maturity date.

The *coupon rate* is given by the annual coupon divided by the face value.

$$coupon\ rate = \frac{annual\ coupon}{face\ value}$$

A bond with a coupon rate of 5% is usually described as a 5% bond.

The *current price* of a coupon bond is the amount that a buyer is currently willing to pay for it.

The price is typically quoted either per CU 100 of face value or per CU 1 of face value, depending on the currency and the bond market convention. For example bonds denominated in US$ typically have prices quoted per $100. Bonds denominated in Japanese Yen typically have prices quoted per ¥ 1. In our generic examples, we will follow the first convention, that is, we will quote prices per CU 100 of face value.

The *yield to maturity* of a coupon bond (or just yield) is the rate of return per year that an investor would receive if they bought the bond at its current price and held it to maturity.

Equivalently, the *yield to maturity* is the discount rate per year that makes the present value of the bond cash flows exactly equal to the current price.

Like interest rates in general, the yield can be calculated in myriad ways. Usually quoted yields for coupon bonds are based on semi-annual compounding. This reflects the fact that coupon payments are usually half-yearly.

3.3.2 Valuing a Coupon Bond

We do not find the price of a bond by applying the yield to find the present value of the cash flows. This is because the yield is derived from the price. We need to know the price in the first place in order to estimate the yield.

We can value a coupon bond (with price unknown) by using a replicating portfolio of zero-coupon bonds whose prices we know. We illustrate this with an example.

Consider a 10% coupon bond with a face value of CU 5000, a maturity of 1.5 years and three equal half-yearly coupon payments. We are valuing the bond on its issue date (today say).

Then the cash flows from the bond are CU 5 at 0.5 years from today, CU 5 at 1.0 years from today, and CU 105 at 1.5 years from today.

Suppose that the discount factors for maturities of 0.5, 1 and 1.5 years are 0.99, 0.98 and 0.97 respectively (the maturities correspond to the remaining coupon payment dates).

Consider a portfolio of three zero-coupon bonds with maturities of 0.5, 1 and 1.5 years respectively, and face values of CU 5, CU 5 and CU 105 respectively.

Notice that the cash flows from this portfolio are exactly the same as those from the coupon bond.

Therefore, the portfolio is a *replicating portfolio* for the coupon bond.

Therefore, the portfolio and the coupon bond should both have the same price today.

The price of the replicating portfolio today is (in CU):

$$0.99 \times 5 + 0.98 \times 5 + 0.97 \times 105 = 111.7.$$

This should also be the price of the coupon bond.

3.4 Seasoned Bonds

So far we have looked at bonds on their issue date or exactly on a coupon date, so that the remaining cash flows occur at a date that represents an exact number of interest payment periods (coupon periods). But the valuation date is more likely to fall between coupon dates. This raises a number of practical issues.

We refer to a bond that is past its issue date as a *seasoned* bond. In this section, we will consider the case of a seasoned bond that is being valued between coupon dates.

3.4.1 Seasoned Bond Example

Consider an 8% bond with three remaining semi-annual coupons and a face value of CU 100. We are valuing it in the middle of the current coupon period.

The bond has coupons of CU 4 each period. Then the next coupon payment is due in 0.25 years, the second-last payment is due in 0.75 years, and the last payment (maturity) is due in 1.25 years.

Suppose that the corresponding discount factors are as follows:

$$d_{0.25} = 0.975$$
$$d_{0.50} = 0.962$$
$$d_{0.75} = 0.957$$

Then we can value the bond as a replicating portfolio of zeroes as before:

$$0.975 \times 4 + 0.962 \times 4 + 0.957 \times 104 = CU107.276.$$

This valuation is called the *dirty price* as we will explain a little later in this section. For now, we will note that the valuation is not different from that of a newly issued bond except for the less convenient maturities.

3.4.2 Practical Issues with Seasoned Bonds

We will discuss three practical issues that arise when valuing seasoned bonds. These are:

1. Counting days (measuring maturities);
2. Accrued interest (how much to pay the previous holder as their share of the next coupon); and
3. Clean vs dirty prices (prices net of or gross of the accrued interest).

3.4.2.1 Counting Days

Coupon dates and maturity dates are calendar dates, not convenient fractions of a year. In computing the period in years, we have to deal with vagaries such as leap years, months of unequal length, and so on. These make the computation of time in years potentially ambiguous. Various market conventions have developed that set rules to fix the calculation. We discuss two of these in the next subsection—the ICMA and the ISDA conventions.

3.4.2.2 Accrued Interest

When we purchase a bond between coupon dates, we have to pay a pro-rated share of the next coupon upfront to the previous holder. This reflects their share of the interest for the period. This payment is called accrued interest. Accrued interest is calculated according to specific formulas built into the bond contract or the particular bond market rules. The formula is based on a precise rule for computing the fraction of a coupon period. This rule is called the *day count convention*. There are several day count conventions in use. We will discuss two of them below—the 30/360 and the Actual/Actual conventions.

Accrued interest can be negative. This happens when the bond is purchased after the *ex-interest date*. The ex-interest date is the cutoff date for paying the next coupon. A holder who purchased the bond on or after the ex-interest date will not receive the next coupon—instead, it goes to the previous holder. In this situation, the previous holder has to pay the buyer the latter's share of the coupon—the interest for the remaining fraction of the period.

3.4.2.3 Clean and Dirty Prices

There are two ways to quote the price of a seasoned bond—either gross of or net of the accrued interest. The *dirty price* is a price that includes the accrued interest. The *clean price* is a price that is net of the accrued interest, i.e., the accrued interest is not included. The buyer pays the clean price plus in addition the accrued interest.

IFRS allows either the clean price or dirty price to be used. But the clean price may be considered better practice as it more precisely isolates the value of the bond. Also using the clean price improves the calculation of hedge effectiveness for instruments like interest rate swaps. We will therefore always use the clean price in the remainder of this book.

3.4.3 ICMA and ISDA Conventions

The ICMA convention is set by the International Capital Markets Association (ICMA), an international association of capital market regulators and investors. The ISDA convention is set by the International Swaps and Derivatives Authority (ISDA), another international association of market participants.

The two conventions can best be explained using an example.

Consider a 6% coupon bond with face value CU 100 issued on Jun 1 2019. The bond pays equal semi-annual coupons. The coupon dates are every Jan 1 and Jun 1 until the maturity date of Jun 1 2021.

We purchase the bond on Nov 15 2019 (the valuation date).

To be more precise, Nov 15 2019 is the *settlement date* for our bond purchase. This is the date when the trade is officially confirmed. It could be a day or two after the transaction, depending on the particular bond market. The settlement date is the date from which we officially own the bond and start earning interest.

As of the valuation date, there are three remaining payment dates for this bond—Jan 1 2020, Jul 1 2020 and Jan 1 2021. The particular convention tells us how to measure these dates in terms of time in years from the valuation date.

In counting days for a given period, the market convention is to include the first day of the period and exclude the last day. This is equivalent to counting from the *beginning* of the first day to the *beginning* of the last day in the period. Thus the period Dec 15 2019 to Jan 1 2020 includes Dec 15 2019 but not Jan 1 2019 (giving 17 days).

We need to be cautious when our valuation date is the balance-sheet date. This reflects the end of the day, not the beginning. For calculating interest periods using market conventions, we would start counting from the *next* day.

Thus if Dec 15 were our balance-sheet date in the above example, we would count only 16 days to Jan 1—i.e., starting from Dec 16.

3.4.3.1 ISDA Convention

Under this convention, we compute the time in years by counting the days in a period and dividing by 365 for a non-leap year and 366 for a leap year. The time to maturity in years is:

$$\frac{nonleapdays}{365} + \frac{leapdays}{366}$$

where

- t_{ISDA} is the time in years computed using the ISDA convention.
- $nonleapdays$ is the number of days in the period that fall during a non-leap year.
- $leapdays$ is the number of days in the period that fall during a leap year.

We illustrate using our example above.

For the time to the first payment on Jan 1 2020 (the period from Nov 15 2019 to Jan 1 2020), there are 47 days all of which fall in the non-leap year 2019. Therefore the time to maturity in years is:

$$\frac{47}{365} = 0.1288 \text{ (4 } dp.\text{)}.$$

For the time to the second payment on Jul 1 2020 (the period from Nov 15 2019 to Jul 1 2020), there are 47 days in the non-leap year 2019 followed by 182 days in 2020 (a leap year). Therefore the time to maturity in years is:

$$\frac{47}{365} + \frac{182}{366} = 0.6260 \text{ (4 } dp.\text{)}.$$

For the time to the last payment on Jan 1 2021, we note that the period from Jan 1 2020 to Jan 1 2021 constitutes a full year. So we can count one full year plus the fraction of the year from Nov 15 2019 to Jan 1 2020 (47 days, all in the non-leap year 2019).

Therefore the time to maturity is:

$$1+\frac{47}{365}=1.1288\ (4\ dp.).$$

Suppose the spot interest rates for maturities corresponding to the three coupon dates are 1%, 2% and 3% respectively, these rates being semi-annually compounded rates based on the ISDA convention. Also suppose that the accrued interest amount due is CU 2.2521.

Then the clean price of the bond is given as:

$$\frac{3}{\left(1+\frac{1\%}{2}\right)^{\frac{47}{365}\times 2}}+\frac{3}{\left(1+\frac{2\%}{2}\right)^{\left(\frac{47}{365}+\frac{182}{366}\right)\times 2}}+$$

$$\frac{103}{\left(1+\frac{3\%}{2}\right)^{\left(1+\frac{47}{365}\right)\times 2}}-2.2521=103.3025.$$

3.4.3.2 ICMA Convention

Under the ICMA convention, we directly measure the maturity in terms of the number of compounding periods rather than the number of years. So with semi-annual compounding, we measure time in half-years.

To apply the convention, we first count complete half-years in the period by counting *backwards* from the last day. We are then left with the initial fraction of a half-year to measure. We measure this as follows:

$$frac=\frac{days\ to\ next\ coupon}{days\ in\ current\ coupon\ period}.$$

For the first cash flow on Jan 1 2020, the time from the valuation date to the next coupon date Jan 1 2020 is 47 days. The total number of days in the current coupon period (Jul 1 2020 to Jan 1 2020) is 184 days. We can compute the initial fraction of a half-year as:

$$\frac{47}{184}=0.2554.$$

We turn next to the second coupon payment date Jul 1 2020. Counting full half-years backwards from the end of the period, we have the period from Jan 1 2020 to Jul 1 2020 as one half year. To this we add the initial fraction of a half-year which is the same as before to get:

$$1+\frac{47}{184}=1.2554.$$

For the last maturity of Jul 1 2021, we count two half-years from Jan 1 2020 to Jan 1 2021. To this, we add the initial fraction of a half-year to get:

$$2 + \frac{47}{184} = 2.2554.$$

Suppose that the spot interest rates for maturities corresponding to the three coupon dates are 2.2%, 4.4% and 6.6% respectively, where these rates are semi-annually compounded rates based on the ICMA convention. These rates are just chosen for illustration and are not consistent with the ISDA rates given previously. Also suppose that the accrued interest under the ICMA convention is CU 2.2337.

Then the clean price of the bond is:

$$\frac{3}{\left(1+\frac{2.2\%}{2}\right)^{\frac{47}{184}}} + \frac{3}{\left(1+\frac{4.4\%}{2}\right)^{1+\frac{47}{184}}} + \frac{103}{\left(1+\frac{6.6\%}{2}\right)^{2+\frac{47}{184}}} - 2.2337 = 99.4042.$$

3.4.3.3 ICMA and ISDA Effect on Cash Flows

The choice of ICMA vs ISDA convention is not just a modelling choice. It could be written into the bond contract and affect the cash flows. For example, the accrued interest calculation would be different under the two conventions. Also, when the ISDA convention is prescribed, the coupon payments are often not equal. Rather the longer half-year receives a correspondingly higher share of the annual coupon.

3.4.4 Accrued Interest

In computing accrued interest, we find the fraction of the coupon period during which the previous bondholder held the bond. We then multiply that by the next coupon amount to get the amount of accrued interest that we owe (assuming purchase before the ex-interest date).

The accrued interest fraction is computed based on standard conventions that are written into the bond contract or the market rules. The conventions are called *day count conventions*, as they are rules for counting days. The conventions are typically stated in the form x/y where x denotes the rule for counting days in a month, and y denotes the rule for counting days in a year.

There are several conventions used in practice. We will discuss two common ones.

3.4.4.1 The 30/360 Convention

This is a common convention in bond markets, though not so much for government bonds.

In this convention, we treat each completed month in the accrued interest period as equal to 30 days. We also count 360 days in a full year.

In our earlier example, we owe the previous bondholder interest for the period from Jul 1 2019 to Nov 15 2019.

The period includes four whole months (July through October) plus 14 days in November.

We count this as $4 \times 30 + 14$ or 134 days.

To get the fraction of a year, we divide this by the convention's number of days in a year, which is 360.

To get the amount of accrued interest that we owe, we multiply this fraction of a year by the *annual* coupon.

In our example, the annual coupon is CU 6, so we have an accrued interest amount equal to

$$\frac{134}{360} \times 6 = 2.2333 \ (4 \ dp.).$$

3.4.4.2 The Actual/Actual (Act/Act) Convention

In this convention, we count the actual number of days in a month, as well as the actual number of days in the year. The convention has numerous variations. For example, it differs depending on whether we follow the ICMA or the ISDA convention.

ISDA Version

Here we compute the accrued interest fraction of a year as follows:

$$yearfrac = \frac{nonleapdays}{365} + \frac{leapdays}{366}$$

where

- $yearfrac$ is the fraction of a year corresponding to the portion of the coupon period that the previous bondholder held the bond (the accrued interest period),
- $nonleapdays$ is the number of days in the accrued interest period falling in a non leap year,
- $leapdays$ is the number of days in the accrued interest period falling in a leap year.

Returning to our earlier example, the previous bondholder held the bond for 137 days in the coupon period (Jul 1 2019 to Nov 15 2019). Since the entire period falls in a non-leap year, we divide by 365 to get $yearfrac$ and multiply by the *annual* coupon (CU 6) to get the amount of accrued interest we owe under this convention:

$$\frac{137}{365} \times 6 = 2.2521 \ (4 \ dp.).$$

ICMA Version

In this convention, we calculate the fraction of a coupon period rather than of a year, as follow:

$$frac = \frac{accruedInterestDays}{couponPeriodDays}$$

where

- $frac$ is the accrued interest period as a fraction of the entire coupon period (the fraction of the coupon period during which the previous bondholder held the bond),
- $accruedInterestDays$ is the number of days that the previous bondholder held the bond during the coupon period,
- $couponPeriodDays$ is the total number of days in the coupon period.

In our earlier example, $accruedInterestDays$ is 137 days (Jul 1 2019 to Nov 15 2019). The total number of days in the coupon period is 184 (Jul 1 2019 to Jan 1 2020).

The accrued interest fraction of the period is 137/184.

The accrued interest that we owe under this convention is:

$$\frac{137}{184} \times 3 = 2.2337 \ (4 \ dp.).$$

3.5 Bootstrapping

In estimating the fair value of a coupon bond, we used a replicating portfolio of zero-coupon bonds. This approach required us to know the prices of zero-coupon bonds for all the needed maturities.

But in practice, zero-coupon bonds are only available for a few maturities, usually short (one year or less). For longer maturities, governments issue coupon bonds instead.

How then do we find the zero-coupon prices or yields for maturities that do not match any actual zero with a quoted price? Bootstrapping is one solution to this problem.

Bootstrapping uses two techniques:

1. *Linear interpolation* to find the discount factor or yield for a maturity that lies between two maturities with known discount factors.
2. *Solving a linear equation:* We know the market prices of coupon bonds with various maturity dates. We can use the fact that these can be expressed as a portfolio of zero-coupon bonds to solve for zero prices that we don't know.

These two techniques are applied in a step-by-step manner moving *forward* along the yield curve. That is, we start by estimating shorter maturities and use these estimates as inputs in estimating longer maturities.

3.5.1 Bootstrapping Example

On Jun 30 2018, the last bid prices are as follows for government bonds (prices in CU based on a face value of CU 100):

Zero with maturity Aug 1 2018	99
Zero with maturity Jul 1 2019	98
2% coupon bond maturing on Jan 1 2020	100

The coupon bond has half-yearly coupon payments (of CU 1 each).

These prices reflect settlement on Jul 1 2018.

We will use bootstrapping to estimate the discount factors for Jan 1 2019 (6 months) and Jan 1 2020 (1.5 years).

To solve for the Jan 1 2019 discount factor, we interpolate between the discount factors for Aug 1 2018 and Jul 1 2019. We can use the nearer discount factor as the starting point (Aug 1 2018), then find the change in discount factor per day, and then multiply that change by the number of days between Aug 1 2018 and our desired maturity of Jan 1 2019.

The discount factor for Aug 1 2018 is 0.99.

The discount factor for Jul 1 2019 is 0.98.

So the change in discount factor per day over that period (334 days) is:

$$\frac{0.98 - 0.99}{334}.$$

The number of days between Aug 1 2018 and Jan 1 2019 is 153.

Therefore, our estimate of the discount factor for a maturity of Jan 1 2019 is:

$$0.99 + \frac{0.98 - 0.99}{334} \times 153 = 0.9854.$$

To solve for the Jan 1 2020 maturity, we use the fact that the coupon bond maturing on that date has the same value as a portfolio of zeroes with maturities coinciding with the coupon dates, where the last of these zeroes has the Jan 1 2020 maturity. Let X be the discount factor corresponding to this zero.

Then we have:

$$100 = 1 \times 0.9854 + 1 \times 0.98 + 101 \times X.$$

Solving for X, we get $X = 0.9706$.

3.5.2 Bootstrapping: Practical Issues

1. Linear interpolation could be between discount factors as demonstrated above. It could also be between spot interest rates defined using any convention (of course there should be consistency in this case—both ends of the interpolation as well as the interpolated yield should be based on the same convention). It could also be between the natural logarithms of the discount factor. It could also be between two forward discount factors ${}_{t1}d_{t2}$ and ${}_{t1}d_{t3}$ or two forward interest rates ${}_{t1}r_{t2}$ and ${}_{t1}r_{t3}$ (notice that $t1$ should be the same at both ends).

   There is no theoretical reason to prefer any of these bases for interpolation over any other. The choice is driven by judgement and practical convenience.
2. Although there are multiple equally good approaches to bootstrapping (giving different but equally reasonable answers), we must arrive at a unique estimate of the term structure and use it consistently in all our related valuations. Otherwise, inconsistencies would arise.
3. Linear interpolation should not be extended to *extrapolation*—estimating a point that is before the start point or after the end point. For very short maturities shorter than the shortest quoted bond maturity, we can interpolate between a discount factor of 1 (today or no discounting) and the shortest maturity for which a price is available. For very long maturities, longer than the longest maturity of a government bond, the convention is to assume that the spot rate corresponding to the longest actual bond maturity would continue for all later maturities, i.e., the term structure is assumed to be flat after this point, or the risk-free rate is assumed to be constant after this point.
4. Linear interpolation is an approximation. The approximation is better when the start and end-points are close together. Therefore when solving for a particular rate using linear interpolation, we should use the prices of zeroes that are as close to that date as possible.
5. Bond markets are not very liquid, and in bootstrapping, one must be wary of using price quotes that could be stale or unrepresentative. Particular caution should be exercised when using the prices of off-the-run bonds.

3.6 The Svensson Model

Bootstrapping models the term structure as a series of straight-line segments. More sophisticated models are available that fit the term structure to a smooth non-linear curve. Of these, the Svensson model (Svensson 1995) is particularly important, as it has regulatory backing, especially in Europe. The German Central Bank (*Bundesbank*) and the European Central Bank report daily estimates of their respective term structures that are based on this model.

In the model, the continuously compounded spot rate for a maturity t in years $r_{t,c}$ is given by the formula[1]:

$$r_{t,c} = \beta_0 + \beta_1 \times \left(\frac{1 - e^{-\left(\frac{t}{\tau_1}\right)}}{\left(\frac{t}{\tau_1}\right)} \right) + \beta_2 \times \left(\frac{1 - e^{-\left(\frac{t}{\tau_1}\right)}}{\left(\frac{t}{\tau_1}\right)} - e^{-\left(\frac{t}{\tau_1}\right)} \right) + \beta_3 \times \left(\frac{1 - e^{-\left(\frac{t}{\tau_2}\right)}}{\left(\frac{t}{\tau_2}\right)} - e^{-\left(\frac{t}{\tau_2}\right)} \right). \quad (3.1)$$

In equation 3.1 the symbols β_0, β_1, β_2, β_3, τ_1 and τ_2 refer to parameters that need to be estimated. The parameters β_0, τ_1 and τ_2 must be greater than zero. The other parameters can be greater or less than zero.

The parameter β_0 can be interpreted as the long-run stable interest rate. Then the other parts of the expression 3.1 represent shorter-term deviations from this rate.

If we fix β_3 to be zero, the last term drops out of equation 3.1. The resulting model is the older Nelson-Siegel model (Nelson and Siegel 1987). Here is the Nelson-Siegel equation:

$$r_{t,c} = \beta_0 + \beta_1 \times \left(\frac{1 - e^{-\left(\frac{t}{\tau_1}\right)}}{\left(\frac{t}{\tau_1}\right)} \right) + \beta_2 \times \left(\frac{1 - e^{-\left(\frac{t}{\tau_1}\right)}}{\left(\frac{t}{\tau_1}\right)} - e^{-\left(\frac{t}{\tau_1}\right)} \right). \quad (3.2)$$

Fitting the Svensson model requires advanced statistical procedures. These procedures would find the values of the parameters that give the best fit to the actual spot rates on the valuation date. We will not go into technical details of these estimation procedures. But we can use readily available tools to implement them. For example, we can use the Solver tool in Microsoft Excel and other spreadsheet software.

To illustrate how to estimate spot rates using the model, here are the parameters reported by the *Bundesbank* for 21 Dec 2018: $\beta_0 = 1.29935$, $\beta_1 = -2.29899$, $\beta_2 = -2.21330$, $\beta_3 = 0.85662$, $\tau_1 = 2.55517$, and $\tau_2 = 0.50126$.

Using these parameters in equation 3.1, we can estimate the one-year-ahead spot rate on 21 Dec 2018 to be -0.68% (2 dp). The parameters are scaled to give an output in percentage points from equation 3.1, thus the output is -0.68, not -0.0068.

We illustrate how to estimate the model parameters using Singapore government bond data for the same date 21 Dec 2018. To keep our explanation concise, we include only benchmark bonds in our analysis, not off-the-run. The data is in Table 3.1.

[1]Be careful that t is not the same symbol as τ. The latter is a Greek lowercase letter pronounced "tau".

Table 3.1 Singapore government bond data 21 Dec 2018

Coupon	Maturity	Price (S$)
Zero	31 Oct 2019	98.26
3.25%	1 Sep 2020	102.10
2.75%	1 Jul 2023	103.21
2.625%	1 May 2028	104.21
3.375%	1 Sep 2033	112.40
2.25%	1 Aug 2036	97.59
2.75%	1 Mar 2046	103.96

Table 3.2 Spreadsheet entries for the bond due 1 Sep 2020

Cashflow (S$)	Maturity (years)	DCF (S$)
1.625	0.19178	1.62396
1.625	0.69589	1.61953
1.625	1.19452	1.61475
101.625	1.69863	100.6669

Coupons are paid semi-annually in arrears. Reported prices are clean prices of S$100 face value. The ICMA Act/Act day count convention is used to calculate accrued interest.

We will use the Solver in the LibreOffice Calc spreadsheet application (version 6.0.4).

To apply the model, we first set up the spreadsheet by inputting our starting trial set of parameters. These can be anything. To reflect the model intuition, we choose the trial level for β_0 to be 2.5%, which is approximately equal to the YTM for the longest bond. For the other parameters, we use the German Central Bank parameters, though we do not expect these to give a good fit. They just serve as an arbitrary starting point.

The next step is to input the bond cashflows for each bond. We can then write spreadsheet formulae to calculate the discounted cash flows based on the rates derived from Equation 3.1. We can in turn use this to compute the clean price of the bond as predicted by the Svensson model.

To illustrate, the values for the bond due 1 Sep 2020 are in Table 3.2 above.

Adding up the discounted cash flows we get a predicted dirty price of S$105.5251. The accrued interest is S$0.9965 (based on the ICMA Act/Act convention). So the predicted clean price is S$104.5286. We can compare this to the actual clean price of S$102.10. There is an error of 104.5286 − 102.10 or 2.4286. It is interesting to consider the square of this error, as squaring treats negative and positive deviations as equivalent. This square is 5.898.

We will estimate the model parameters by trying to minimize the sum of the squared errors for all the bonds. For each bond, we compute the squared error. We then record the sum of squared errors in a particular cell. This will be the "target cell" that Solver tries to minimize.

Table 3.3 Svensson model parameters with best fit

β_0	2.85788594796494
β_1	−1.58758656100673
β_2	−1253.35558575193
β_3	1253.17577117588
τ_1	1.54300096064338
τ_2	1.53952603084514

Table 3.4 Actual vs predicted clean prices

Coupon rate (%)	Maturity date	Actual price (S$)	Predicted price (S$)
Zero	31 Oct 2019	98.26	98.3278566998714
3.25%	1 Sep 2020	102.10	101.865381117125
2.75%	1 Jul 2023	103.21	103.283651492525
2.625%	1 May 2028	104.21	104.00766942599
3.375%	1 Sep 2033	112.40	112.673080344568
2.25%	1 Aug 2036	97.59	97.4018562617236
2.75%	1 Mar 2046	103.96	103.930003434208

In the Solver dialog, we enter the reference to this cell as the target, and choose "minimize" as our objective. We enter the range where we entered the parameters $\beta_0, \beta_1, \beta_2, \beta_3, \tau_1, \tau_2$ in the dialog field that asks which cells need to be changed by trial and error to achieve the objective of minimizing the target.

Finally we enter the constraints in the dialog boxes for that purpose: $\beta_0 \geq 0$, $\tau_1 \geq 0$, $\tau_2 \geq 0$.

We can use the default Solver algorithm in LibreOffice Calc. This is the DEPS algorithm (Zhang and Xie 2003), which is a hybrid of a differential evolution (DE) algorithm and a particle swarm (PS) algorithm. Both these mimic biological processes, evolution in the case of DE, and swarming behavior by animals (ants, birds) in the case of PS.

Since DEPS works by trial and error, it cannot be guaranteed to give the true optimum solution. We therefore run it several times with different starting points. After numerous trials with different starting points, the best solution obtained had a sum of squared errors equal to 0.2169 (4 dp). The parameter levels that achieve this are in Table 3.3.

These parameters give a good fit to the actual prices as shown in Table 3.4.

The predicted term structure is graphed in Fig. 3.1.

3.7 Lattice Models of the Term Structure

We can use a binomial or trinomial lattice to model future spot rates. We can in turn use such a lattice to price a variety of interest-rate derivatives.

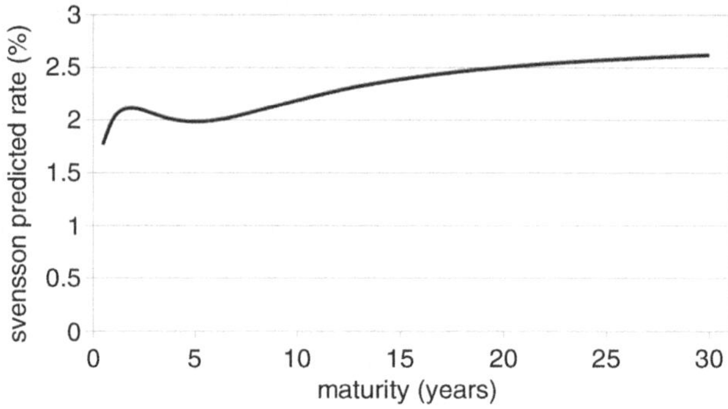

Fig. 3.1 Svensson curve for Singapore 21 Dec 2018

Table 3.5 Term structure for BDT example

Maturity (t)	Spot interest rate ($r_{t,c}$)	BDT volatility
0.5	0.020	30%
1	0.021	28%
1.5	0.025	25%
2	0.028	20%

We discuss two such lattice models here—the Black-Derman-Toy model and the Ho-Lee model.

The Black-Derman-Toy model (BDT) (Black et al. 1990) assumes that future spot rates follow a lognormal distribution. That is, the natural logarithm of the spot rate has a normal distribution.

The Ho-Lee model (HL) (Ho and Lee 1986) assumes that future spot rates follow a normal distribution.

Both models are designed to be consistent with the current term structure. That is, the predicted price of a government bond from the lattice should equal its actual current price.

3.7.1 The Black-Derman-Toy Model (BDT)

We can use an example to illustrate how to construct the BDT lattice. Suppose that the term structure is as in Table 3.5 on our valuation date.

In Table 3.5, the maturity t is in years from the valuation date, and the spot interest rate $r_{t,c}$ is the continuously compounded spot interest rate for maturity t. The volatility in the BDT model is the standard deviation of the natural logarithm of the future one-year spot rate at time t. In Table 3.5, the natural logarithm of the one-year spot interest rate six months from today is assumed to follow a normal probability distribution with standard deviation 30%. Therefore, the standard deviation of the natural logarithm of the six-month-ahead spot interest rate at the same date would be $30\% \times \sqrt{0.5}$ or 21.2132%.

Volatility can be estimated using either historical volatility or implied volatility, as we discussed earlier with option models.

In our example, volatility is less for longer maturities. This is a common pattern in the BDT model, reflecting that yields over a longer horizon fluctuate less than shorter-term yields.

To build the lattice, we start with the first step. The rates in the lattice are spot interest rates for a maturity equal to the step size. Let us set the step size to be 0.5 or half a year. Then at the first step, we have say:

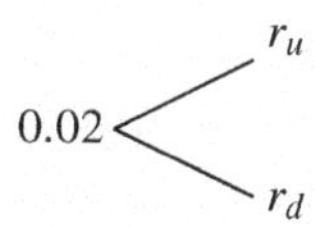

Here 0.02 is the starting rate—the valuation-date rate. Let r_u and r_d be the rates at the up and down nodes respectively after one step, i.e., after 0.5 years. They represent two possible levels of the future half-year spot rate on a date that is 0.5 years later than today.

We fix the risk-neutral probabilities of up and down to be $\frac{1}{2}$ and find the r_u and r_d that are consistent with these probabilities. We start by using a guess for r_d, say 1.8%.

The standard deviation of two equally probable numbers a and b is given by the formula:

$$\sigma(a, b) = \frac{|a - b|}{2} \tag{3.3}$$

From equation 3.3, and noting that $r_u > r_d$, we have:

$$30\% \times \sqrt{0.5} = \frac{|\ln(r_u) - \ln(0.018)|}{2}$$

$$\Rightarrow r_u = 0.018e^{0.3 \times 2 \times \sqrt{0.5}} = 2.7512\%.$$

We can now price a 1-year zero using this rate and a two-step lattice. If our lattice is consistent with the term structure, the 1-year zero should have a price equal to CU 97.9219 calculated as follows:

$$100 \times e^{-0.021} = 97.9219.$$

Our lattice of spot interest rates is:

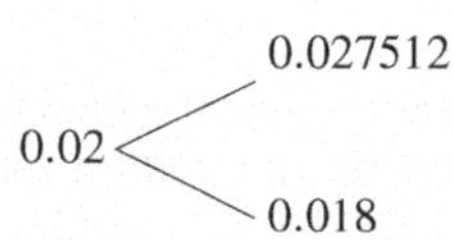

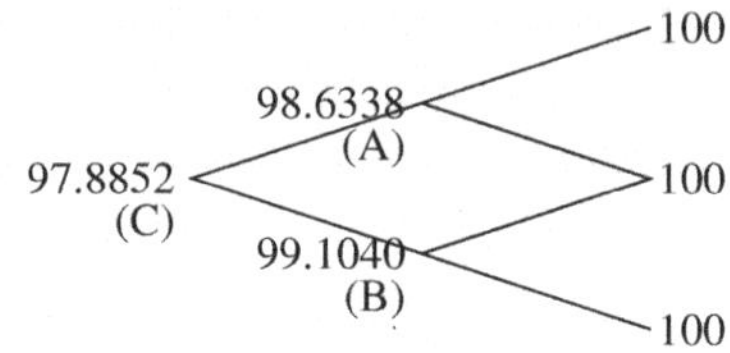

Fig. 3.2 BDT example: Trial lattice for one-year zero

Corresponding to this, we can construct a lattice of prices for the 1-year zero (Fig. 3.2).

The prices at the end-nodes are all equal to the bond payoff of 100. Moving backwards to the node labelled (A), we can calculate the bond value at that node as the expected present value of the next-step price discounted by r_u or 2.7512%. That is:

$$98.6338 = e^{-0.027512\times 0.5} \times \left(\frac{1}{2} \times 100 + \frac{1}{2} \times 100\right).$$

Similarly, at Node B, we have:

$$99.1040 = e^{-0.018\times 0.5} \times \left(\frac{1}{2} \times 100 + \frac{1}{2} \times 100\right).$$

Coming to the initial node (C), we can use the same logic to get:

$$97.8852 = e^{-0.02\times 0.5} \times \left(\frac{1}{2} \times 98.6338 + \frac{1}{2} \times 99.1040\right).$$

This is *not* the same as the actual zero-coupon price of CU 97.9219. So our lattice is *not* term-structure consistent.

We use trial and error to find a level of r_d that leads to the correct bond price. We use the solver tool in LibreOffice Calc. This gives us a value for r_d of CU 0.01741. Our corrected lattice of spot interest rates is as follows:

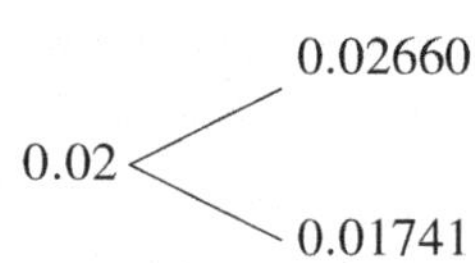

Based on this corrected lattice of spot interest rates, the corrected lattice for the one-year-zero price is as in Fig. 3.3.

We can proceed to add another step to the lattice of spot interest rates. As before, let us use an initial guess for the bottom rate, say r_{dd} at the next step, say $r_{dd} = 1.5\%$. Then we can solve for the rates at higher levels by using the volatility parameter of 0.28. We get Fig. 3.4.

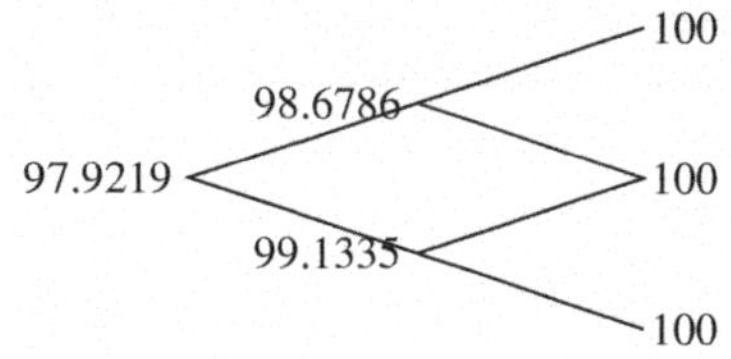

Fig. 3.3 BDT example: Corrected lattice for one-year zero

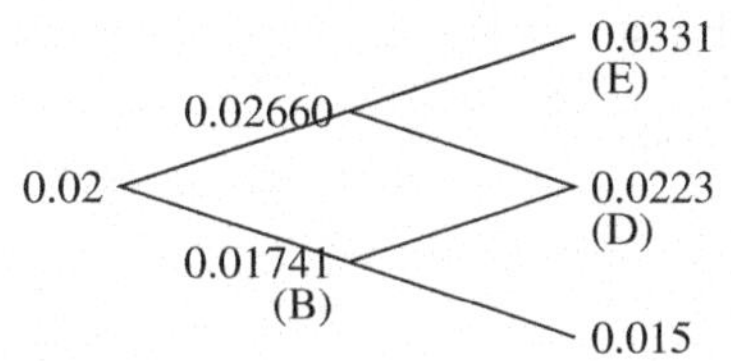

Fig. 3.4 BDT example: Start lattice for rates upto 1 year

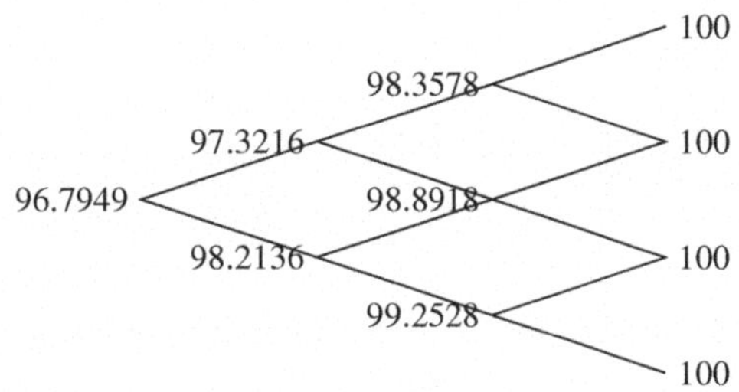

Fig. 3.5 BDT Example: Trial lattice for 1.5-year bond price

To calculate the rate at the node labelled (D) in Fig. 3.4 say r_m, we note that:

$$0.28 \times \sqrt{0.5} = \frac{\ln(r_m) - \ln(0.015)}{2}$$

$$\Rightarrow r_m = 0.015 \times e^{0.28 \times 2\sqrt{0.5}} = 0.0223.$$

We can proceed to calculate the rate at the node labelled (E) in Fig. 3.4:

$$0.0331 = 0.0223 \times e^{0.28 \times 2 \times \sqrt{0.5}}.$$

If our resulting lattice is term-structure-consistent, it should correctly price the 1.5-year zero. The correct price of this zero is:

$$96.3194 = 100 \times e^{-0.025 \times 1.5}.$$

Computing the bond price using our three-step lattice, we have Fig. 3.5.

The lattice in Fig. 3.5 gives us an incorrect price—CU 96.7949, instead of the correct price of CU 96.3194. As before, we use trial and error to find the rates that lead to the correct price. We use Solver in LibreOffice Calc to find the correct level of r_{dd}. We get $r_{dd} = 0.0214$. This leads to the corrected lattice of spot interest rates in Fig. 3.6.

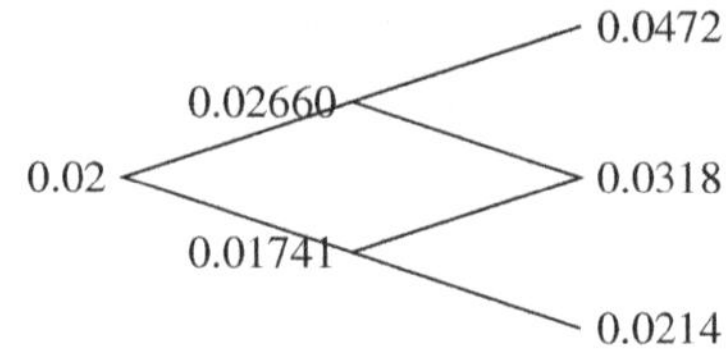

Fig. 3.6 BDT example: Corrected lattice for rates upto 1 year

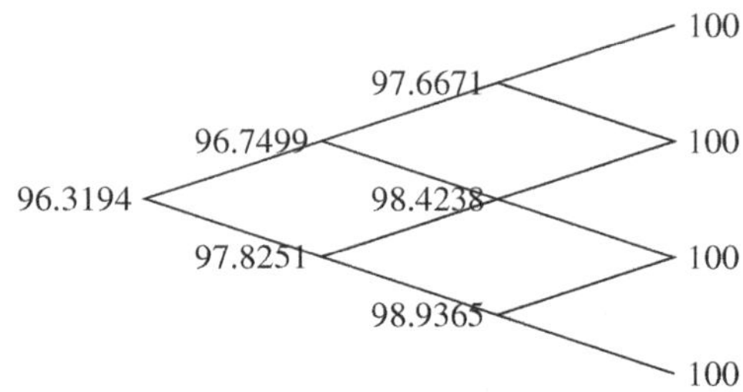

Fig. 3.7 BDT Example: Corrected lattice for 1.5-year bond price

Table 3.6 Term structure for HL example

Maturity (t)	Spot rate ($r_{t,c}$)
0.5	3%
1	3.5%
1.5	4%
2	4.1%

Corresponding to Fig. 3.6, we have the corrected lattice of prices for the 1.5-year zero in Fig. 3.7.

We can proceed to use the same approach to find the spot interest rates at 1.5 years, 2 years, and so on.

Since we need to use trial and error to find the rates at each step, the procedure can be computationally expensive when we have a large number of steps. Recall that in any practical application, we need a large number of steps.

One approach is to first use a coarser lattice to estimate rates and then use it to derive a finer lattice to use in valuation. The coarser lattice is built using trial and error to derive the term-structure-consistent spot rates. To build a finer lattice, we start with the coarser lattice, and then use linear interpolation to fill in the gaps.

3.7.2 The Ho-Lee Model (HL)

For the Ho-Lee model (HL), we can build the lattice similarly to what we did for BDT. The difference is that in HL, future rates follow normal distributions, not lognormal.

We use an example to illustrate the procedure.

Suppose that the term structure is as given in Table 3.6.

In Table 3.6, the maturity t is in years from today, and $r_{t,c}$ is the spot interest rate for maturity t based on continuous compounding.

We assume that volatility is constant at 5%. In this model, volatility is defined as the standard deviation of the one-year spot interest rate. Then the standard deviation of the half-year spot interest rate is $5\% \times \sqrt{0.5}$ or 3.5355%.

We will build the lattice using a step size of 0.5 years. Then the rates in our lattice are the future half-year-ahead spot interest rates at each date that is a countable number of half-years from today (the valuation date).

We start by constructing the first step.

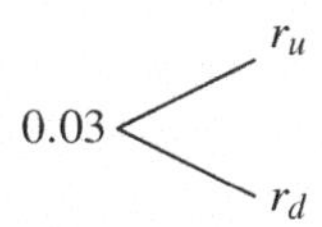

Our starting node is 0.03. This could go up to r_u say or go down to r_d say. We fix the risk-neutral probability of up to be $\frac{1}{2}$. We start by placing a guess for r_d, say 1%.

Now we can use the fact that the standard deviation of two equally probable numbers a and b equals $\frac{1}{2} \times |a - b|$ to solve for r_u.

We have:

$$\frac{r_u - 0.01}{2} = 0.05\sqrt{0.5}.$$

Therefore,

$$r_u = 0.05 \times \sqrt{0.5} \times 2 + 0.01 = 0.0807.$$

We can proceed to check if our lattice matches the term structure by valuing a one-year zero using our lattice. The value of this zero should equal

$$100 \times e^{-0.035} = 96.5605.$$

Using a two-step lattice to price a one-year zero, we get Fig. 3.8.

The zero prices at the end-nodes (the one-year mark) are equal to the payoffs of CU 100. To find the prices at earlier nodes, we use the risk-neutral expected present values, with the discount rates based on our HL lattice of rates. So at the node labelled (A) in Fig. 3.8, we have:

$$96.0448 = (0.5 \times 100 + 0.5 \times 100) \times e^{-0.0807 \times 0.5}.$$

Similarly at the node labelled (B) in Fig. 3.8, we have:

$$99.5012 = (0.5 \times 100 + 0.5 \times 100) \times e^{-0.01 \times 0.5}.$$

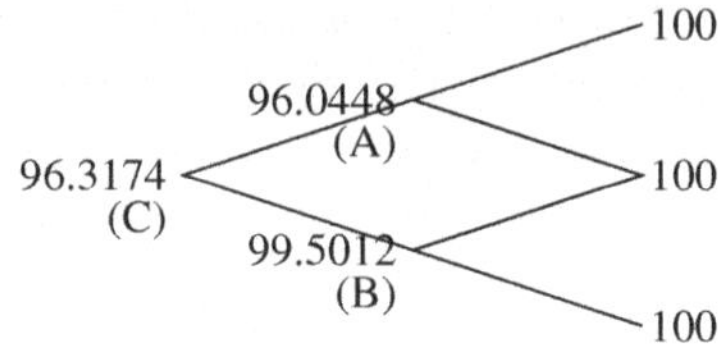

Fig. 3.8 HL example: Trial lattice for one-year zero

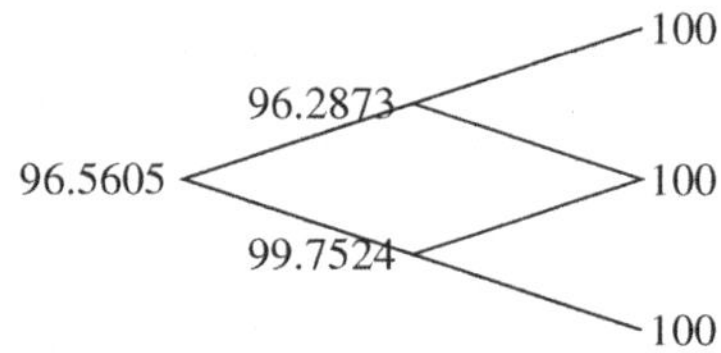

Fig. 3.9 HL example: Corrected lattice for one-year zero

Similarly, at the start node (C) in Fig. 3.8, we have:

$$96.3174 = (0.5 \times 96.0448 + 0.5 \times 99.5012) \times e^{-0.03 \times 0.5}.$$

This value of CU 96.3174 is wrong. It does not equal the correct price of CU 96.5605. So our initial guess of 1% for r_d was wrong. We use trial and error to find the approximately correct level of r_d. Using the Solver tool in LibreOffice Calc, we get $r_d = 0.0050$ (4 dp).

Then our one-step lattice becomes:

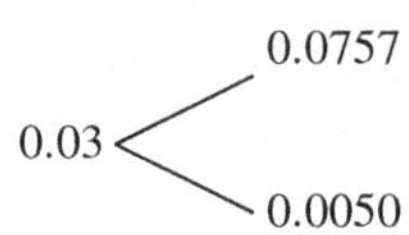

Our corrected lattice of prices for the one-year zero is in Fig. 3.9.

We can proceed to extend our lattice of spot interest rates to a second step. As before, we start with a guess for the rate at the bottom node of the second step, r_{dd} say. Suppose we guess 0% at this node. Then we can solve for the middle node r_m say using the fact that the standard deviation should be $5\% \times \sqrt{0.5}$.

$$\frac{r_m - 0}{2} = 5\% \times \sqrt{0.5}$$

$$\Rightarrow r_m = 5\% \times \sqrt{0.5} \times 2 = 0.0707.$$

Similarly the rate at the top node r_{uu} say would be given by:

$$\frac{r_{uu} - 0.0707}{2} = 5\% \times \sqrt{0.5}$$

$$\Rightarrow r_{uu} = 5\% \times \sqrt{0.5} \times 2 + 0.0707 = 0.1414.$$

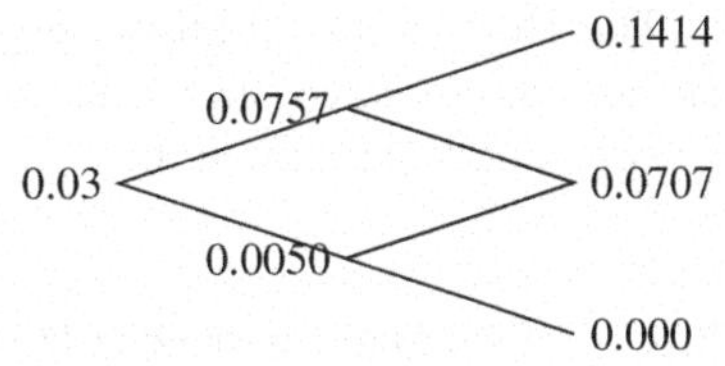

Fig. 3.10 HL example: Trial lattice for rates upto 1 year

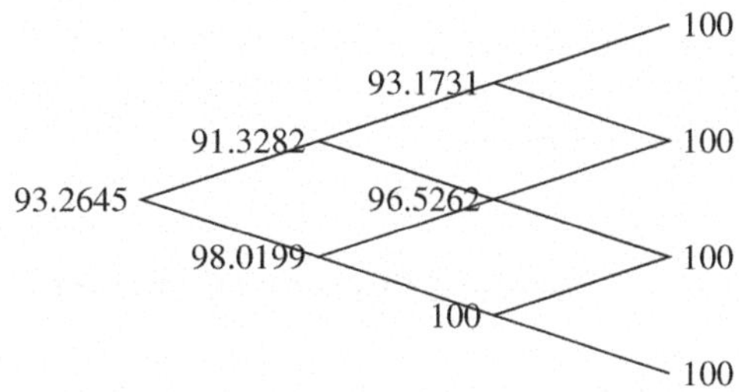

Fig. 3.11 HL Example: Trial lattice for 1.5-year bond price

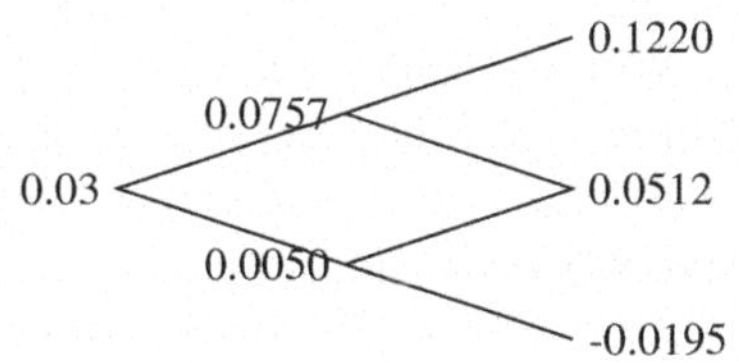

Fig. 3.12 HL example: Corrected lattice for rates upto 1 year

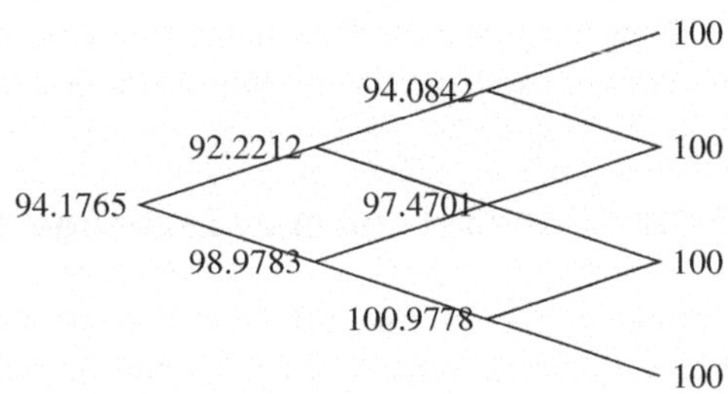

Fig. 3.13 HL Example: Corrected lattice for 1.5-year bond price

Then the two-step lattice of spot interest rates is in Fig. 3.10.

We proceed to check if this lattice (Fig. 3.10) gives us the correct price for the 1.5-year zero. Its price should equal:

$$100 \times e^{-0.04 \times 1.5} = 94.1765.$$

Constructing a three-step lattice of prices for the 1.5-year zero, we get Fig. 3.11.

The lattice in Fig. 3.11 gives us a wrong bond price of CU 93.2645. So we made a wrong starting guess for r_{dd}. We use Solver in LibreOffice Calc to search for an approximately correct r_{dd}. This gives us a value of r_{dd} equal to -0.0195 (a negative interest rate). Our corrected lattice of spot interest rates is in Fig. 3.12.

Then our corrected three-step lattice of prices for the 1.5-year zero is in Fig. 3.13.

The Ho-Lee model allows negative interest rates, unlike BDT. We could view this as a model flaw. But it does allow the model to handle real-life negative interest rates, which BDT cannot do.

3.8 Covered Interest Rate Parity (CIRP)

Covered interest rate parity (CIRP) is a model that helps us to estimate forward exchange rates between two currencies given the term structures (spot interest rates) for each currency.

3.8.1 Forward Currency Contract

A forward currency contract is a contract to exchange a given number of units of one currency for a given number of units of another at a fixed date in the future.

Without losing generality, let us designate one of the currencies the *local* currency, and the other one as the *foreign* currency, where exchange rates are stated in terms of numbers of units of the local currency (LCU say) per unit of the foreign currency (FCU say).

Then we view the local currency as "money" while the other currency is viewed as an item to be bought or sold with its price given in LCU.

Now we can define a forward currency contract as a contract to buy or sell a fixed number of FCU at a fixed future date, for a fixed price, called the forward price.

3.8.2 Forward Currency Exchange Rate

We can define the forward exchange rate for a particular future date t years from today to be the price in LCU to buy or sell one FCU at time t under a forward currency contract issued today. We denote this rate as F_t.

3.8.3 Spot Currency Exchange Rate

The spot exchange rate refers to the price in LCU of one unit of FCU in an immediate (spot) transaction. We denote this as S.

3.8.4 The CIRP Model

We can use a "no free lunch" argument (no arbitrage) to derive a relationship between forward exchange rates and the term structures of the two countries.

Suppose that you borrow LCU S today at the risk-free rate (spot interest rate) to be repaid at maturity t. Recall that S is the spot exchange rate.

The total amount to be repaid at t is LCU $\frac{S}{d_t^{LC}}$ where d_t^{LC} is the local-currency discount factor for maturity t.

Suppose that you use the LCU S that you borrowed to buy FCU 1 at the spot exchange rate S. You invest this FCU 1 in a foreign-currency zero that matures at t. You simultaneously enter a forward currency contract to sell the proceeds from this investment at t at the forward exchange rate F_t.

Then your proceeds in FCU at t are $\frac{1}{d_t^{FC}}$ where d_t^{FC} is the foreign currency discount factor for maturity t. When you convert this to LCU at the forward exchange rate, you would get LCU $F_t \times \frac{1}{d_t^{FC}}$.

In a properly-functioning market, you should not be able to make any profit or loss from this transaction since it cost you nothing and entails no risk. If it were possible to make money from this transaction (or the other side), everybody would rush to do so, and the various rates would quickly adjust by the laws of demand and supply till the opportunity has disappeared.

Therefore, if the strategy nets no profit or loss, the LCU proceeds from your investment should exactly equal the amount you have to repay:

$$\frac{S}{d_t^{LC}} = \frac{F_t}{d_t^{FC}}.$$

This relationship is known as covered interest rate parity (CIRP). We can use it to estimate the forward exchange rate:

$$F_t = \frac{S}{d_t^{LC}} \times d_t^{FC}.$$

This concludes our discussion of government bonds. In Chap. 4, we will discuss non-government bonds and vanilla interest rate swaps.

Exercises

(Monetary units are in CU unless otherwise mentioned).

3.1. Bootstrapping

Refer to the Singapore government bond data in Table 3.1. Use bootstrapping to estimate the spot rates (semi-annually compounded, ICMA) for the following maturities:

(a) June 21, 2019
(b) Dec 21, 2019
(c) June 21, 2020
(d) Dec 21, 2020

Your valuation date is Dec 21, 2018 (i.e., the date when the rates in the table were current).

3.2. Bootstrapping

Suppose that on Aug 12, 2019, you collect the following clean prices of government bonds in country X. Currency units are CU. Accrued interest is based on the Act/Act ICMA convention.

Coupon	Maturity	Price (S$)
Zero	1 Feb 2019	99.5
3.65%	1 Oct 2020	103.20
5.20%	1 Jul 2022	102.21
7.00%	1 Jul 2030	103.00

Use bootstrapping to estimate the spot rates (semi-annually compounded, ICMA) for the following maturities:

(a) Feb 12, 2019
(b) Aug 12, 2020
(c) Feb 12, 2021
(d) Aug 12, 2021

3.3. Svensson Model

Collect current data online on current prices of government bonds in your jurisdiction (if conveniently available online, otherwise you can find the data for another jurisdiction, such as the USA or Singapore). Fit a Svensson model to your data.

3.4. BDT Model

Construct a BDT lattice for the following data. Rates are continuously compounded.

Maturity (t)	Spot interest rate ($r_{t,c}$)	BDT volatility
0.5	0.019	35%
1	0.023	26%
1.5	0.027	24%
2	0.030	19%

3.5. Ho-Lee Model

Construct a Ho-Lee lattice for the following data. Rates are continuously compounded. Volatility is 5% which is constant.

Maturity (t)	Spot rate ($r_{t,c}$)
0.5	5%
1	5.5%
1.5	6%
2	6.2%

3.6. Covered Interest Rate Parity

The spot interest rate in country X for maturities of 3 months is 3.1% (APR semi-annual compounding). The spot interest rate in country Y for maturities of 3 months is 2.6% (APR semi-annual compounding). The currency in country X is XCU, while that in country Y is YCU. The spot currency exchange rate is 0.89 XCU per YCU. Estimate the forward currency exchange rate for 3 months ahead.

References

Black, F., Derman, E., & Toy, W. (1990). A one-factor model of interest rates and its application to treasury bond options. *Financial Analysts' Journal, 46*, 33–39.

Ho, T., & Lee, S. (1986). Term structure movements and pricing interest rate contingent claims. *The Journal of Finance, 41*, 1011–1029.

Nelson, C., & Siegel, A. (1987). Parsimonious modeling of yield curves. *Journal of Business, 60*, 473–489.

Svensson, L. (1995). Estimating forward interest rates with the extended Nelson and Siegel method. *Sveriges Riksbank Quarterly Review, 3*, 13–26.

Zhang, W., & Xie, X. (2003). DEPSO: Hybrid particle swarm with differential evolution operator. In: *SMC'03 Conference Proceedings. 2003 IEEE International Conference on Systems, Man and Cybernetics. Conference Theme – System Security and Assurance (Cat. No.03CH37483)* (Vol. 4, pp. 3816–3821). https://doi.org/10.1109/ICSMC.2003.1244483

Risky Bonds, Floaters and Swaps

4

We turn from risk-free government debt to the more general case of risky bonds. These are usually valued using discount rates that are based on the risk-free rate plus some spread to reflect the higher risk. We start by discussing the concept of duration, a necessary input to our analysis. We discuss two types of spread: First, the Z-spread—a fixed spread above the zero curve or the term structure of spot interest rates; Second, the nominal spread—a fixed premium above the yield to maturity of a government coupon bond that is approximately similar to the bond being valued. We then turn to estimating the spread for a particular bond using a market approach—finding the spread for quoted bonds with a similar credit rating. This leads us to estimating a credit rating when not available—a synthetic credit rating, by comparing standard financial ratios for an issuer, with published averages for issuers with various ratings. We discuss how to use the Jarrow-Lando-Turnbull model to handle future changes in credit rating based on a transition matrix. We turn next to the valuation of floating-rate notes or floaters. We show that a floater with discount rates matching its coupon rates has a value at par. We use this fact to derive floater values under more general conditions. We turn next to a vanilla interest rate swap—an instrument where a fixed rate is exchanged for a floating rate, or vice-versa. We show how a vanilla interest rate swap can be valued using a replicating portfolio that includes a long position in a fixed-rate instrument paired with a short position in a floating-rate instrument, or vice-versa. Finally, we discuss complex instruments that have embedded options—convertible bonds, callable bonds, and puttable bonds. We discuss the Goldman-Sachs lattice model to value convertible bonds. We discuss how to use the Black-Derman-Toy lattice to value callable and puttable bonds.

S. Lynn, *Valuation for Accountants*, Springer Texts in Business and Economics,
https://doi.org/10.1007/978-981-15-0357-3_4

4.1 Learning Outcomes

After completing this chapter, you would be able to:

1. Value a risky fixed-rate bond by applying a spread to a risk-free rate, including being able to:
   a. Calculate duration to use in matching risky with non-risky bonds,
   b. Estimate a synthetic credit rating, and
   c. Use a transition matrix to handle projected future changes in risk.
2. Value floating-rate notes (floaters).
3. Value a vanilla interest-rate swap.
4. Value bonds with embedded derivative features—convertible bonds, callable bonds and puttable bonds.

4.2 Duration

In valuing risky bonds, we typically compare them to similar risk-free bonds as benchmarks. Duration is a metric that we can use to assess how similar two bonds are.[1]

We consider two definitions of duration—Macaulay duration, and modified duration.

Macaulay duration is the weighted average of the various payment dates in the instrument's remaining life (measured in number of compounding periods from today), where the weights at each date are the present values as of today of that date's payments, discounted using the yield to maturity as of today, i.e., the effective interest rate in accounting terms.

Modified duration is the Macaulay duration divided by $1 + \frac{y}{k}$ where y is the yield to maturity as of today expressed as an APR rate per year and k is the compounding frequency (compounding is every $\frac{1}{k}$ of a year).

To illustrate duration, let us consider two instruments A and B say. They both have the same maturity date—1.5 years from today. They also both have the same yield to maturity or effective interest rate—3% APR semi-annually compounded. They also both have the same face value, CU 100 say.

But instrument A is a 3% coupon bond with three semi-annual coupons at exactly the 6-month, 1-year and 1.5-year marks, while B is a mortgage bond with three remaining equal semi-annual payments. We can calculate that each of these payments is CU 34.3383.

[1] In bond portfolio management (and in hedge accounting), duration also serves as a measure of how sensitive an instrument is to changes in interest rates. This use is not important for our purpose of valuation and we will not consider it further in this book.

$$34.3383 = 100 \bigg/ \left(\frac{1}{0.015} - \frac{\frac{1}{0.015}}{1.015^3} \right).$$

Both bonds have a present value of CU 100 today.

We can now compute the Macaulay duration for each bond. For instrument A, the Macaulay duration is given by:

$$\left(\frac{1.5}{1.015} \times 1 + \frac{1.5}{1.015^2} \times 2 + \frac{101.5}{1.015^3} \times 3 \right) \div 100 = 2.9559.$$

The Macaulay duration of instrument A is 2.9559 half-years, or 1.4779 years.

For instrument B, the Macaulay duration is given by:

$$\left(\frac{34.3383}{1.015} \times 1 + \frac{34.3383}{1.015^2} \times 2 + \frac{34.3383}{1.015^3} \times 3 \right) \div 100 = 1.9901.$$

The Macaulay duration of instrument B is 1.9901 half-years, or 0.9950 years.

The higher duration for instrument A indicates that more of the bond payments are made later in its life.

We can now compute the modified duration for each instrument. For instrument A this is:

$$2.9122 = \frac{2.9559}{1 + 0.015}.$$

For instrument B this is:

$$1.9607 = \frac{1.9901}{1 + 0.015}.$$

4.3 Spreads

A risky bond is often discounted using a rate that is the sum of (i) a risk-free rate, and (ii) a markup to reflect risk. We call this markup the *risk premium* or *spread*. We discuss two types of spread, classified by the particular risk-free rate definition that they are based on:

1. The *Z-spread* or zero-volatility spread—this is a constant spread above the spot risk-free rates or rates on zero-coupon government debt for various maturities (usually based on semi-annual APR spot rates).
2. The *nominal spread* or point spread—for a particular risky bond, this is a constant spread above the yield to maturity of the government coupon bond that is most similar in terms of duration.

Spreads are usually expressed in basis points (bps) where 1 basis point represents 0.0001 or $\frac{1}{100} \times \frac{1}{100}$. Thus 100 bps equals 1%.

4.3.1 Z-Spread

We consider two examples—one where the Z-spread is computed as a spread above semi-annually compounded risk-free rates, and the other where the Z-spread is a spread above continuously compounded rates. The first approach reflects how Z-spreads are often quoted in practice, e.g., by Bloomberg. The second approach has the advantage that it allows us to continue using the convenient arithmetic of discount factors rather than the more tedious computations with rates. It also allows us to base the Z-spread on spot rates computed from the Svensson model.

4.3.1.1 Example A: Z-Spread Above Semi-annually Compounded Rates

Suppose the spot interest rates for maturities of 6 months, 1 year and 1.5 years are 1%, 2% and 3% respectively (all semi-annually compounded APR rates).

Consider a risky 2% coupon bond with remaining semi-annual coupons due at exactly the 6-month, 1-year and 1.5-year marks, and a time to maturity of 1.5 years. The bond has a price of CU 97.1353.

We need to solve for Z in the following equation:

$$\frac{CU\ 1}{1+\frac{0.01+Z}{2}} + \frac{CU\ 1}{\left(1+\frac{0.02+Z}{2}\right)^2} + \frac{CU\ 101}{\left(1+\frac{0.03+Z}{2}\right)^3} = CU\ 97.1353.$$

Solving (using a computer and a brute-force trial-and-error approach), we get $Z = 100$ bps.

4.3.1.2 Example B: Z-Spread Above Continuously Compounded Rates

Suppose that the discount factors for maturities of 6 months, 1 year and 1.5 years respectively are 0.99, 0.98, and 0.97.

Consider a risky 2% coupon bond with remaining semi-annual coupons due at exactly the 6-month, 1-year and 1.5-year marks, and a time to maturity of 1.5 years.

The bond price is CU 95.5202.

If Z is the constant spread above continuously compounded spot rates, define $X = e^{-Z}$. Then we have:

$$\begin{aligned} 95.5202 = 0.99 \times 1 \times X^{0.5} \\ +0.98 \times 1 \times X^{1} \\ +0.97 \times 101 \times X^{1.5} \end{aligned}$$

Solving (with a computer and a brute-force approach) we get $X \approx 0.97$.

4.3.1.3 Z-Spread and Valuation

In the above two examples, the spread is not useful for valuation, as we know the price of the risky bond (and indeed use it to derive the spread). But we can also use the spread on a priced bond to value a similar bond whose price we do not know, i.e., we can use the Z-spread on a quoted instrument as a Level 2 input in valuing an unquoted instrument.

Suppose for example that the issuer of the bond in our example B above also has a seasoned loan on their books, with two remaining interest payments at 7 months and 13 months from today respectively. The stated interest rate (coupon rate) is 3%. The estimated discount factors for 7 months and 13 months are 0.995 and 0.985. We can apply the spread computed earlier ($X = 0.97$) to value the loan as follows:

$$0.995 \times 1.5 \times 0.97^{\frac{7}{12}} + 0.985 \times 101.5 \times 0.97^{\frac{13}{12}} \approx 98.1985.$$

In making this calculation, we assume (reasonably) that the unpriced loan carries the same risk as the priced bond, since they come from the same issuer. Since both instruments carry the same risk, they should have the same Z-spread.

4.3.2 Nominal Spread

Consider a risky 2% coupon bond with three cash flows at 6 months, 1 year and 1.5 years respectively. The bond carries a price of CU 94.3428.

We can verify that the YTM is 6% (APR semi-annual):

$$94.3428 = \frac{1}{1.03} + \frac{1}{1.03^2} + \frac{101}{1.03^3}.$$

Serendipitously, there is a government bond with exactly the same coupons, coupon dates and maturity. In other words, the duration matches perfectly. This bond is priced at CU 101.4851. We can verify that its YTM is 1% (APR semi-annual):

$$101.4851 = \frac{1}{1.005} + \frac{1}{1.005^2} + \frac{101}{1.005^3}.$$

The nominal spread is simply the difference between these two yields to maturity, expressed in basis points. In our example, the spread is 500 bps (6–1%).

The spread is not needed for valuation here, as we already know the price of the risky bond. But we can apply it as a Level 2 input in valuing an unpriced bond from the same issuer, or carrying the same risk.

The nominal spread is inaccurate unless a comparable government coupon bond exists that closely matches the risky bond in terms of the timing and amount of cashflows (or has a similar duration). Since this is unlikely, the nominal spread is at best a reasonable approximation in most situations. Despite this, it is widely used.

4.3.3 Deriving the Spread

To derive the spread for an unpriced bond, we can use the spread for a priced instrument of similar risk. But what is "similar risk"? We could look for an instrument for the same issuer. If this is unavailable, we could look for an instrument with the same *credit rating*.

A credit rating is a grade assigned by a credit-rating agency such as Moodys, Standard and Poors, or Fitch. They derive these grades from proprietary models that use the issuer's fundamentals to predict their chances of default. The better the grade, the lower the predicted chance of default.

4.3.3.1 Example: Deriving the Spread

Consider a 6% bond with three remaining semi-annual coupons due at exactly 6 months, 1 year and 1.5 years from today (the valuation date). The maturity date is 1.5 years from today. Let us label this bond Bond A. We wish to value Bond A.

Suppose that Bond A has been assigned a "High Investment" or "HI" grade by a credit rating agency.

We find another HI-grade bond, Bond B say, that has a quoted market price of CU 94.7901. Bond B is a 2% coupon bond that has semi-annual coupons at 6 months, 1 year and 1.5 years from today, just like Bond A, and also matures at 1.5 years just like Bond A.

Suppose that the estimated discount factors for government zero-coupon bonds maturing at 6 months, 1 year and 1.5 years are 0.99, 0.98, and 0.97 respectively.

We can now derive the Z-spread for Bond B. For convenience, let us use a spread above continuous risk-free rates. Then we seek some X such that:

$$94.7901 = 1 \times 0.99 \times X^{0.5} + 1 \times 0.98 \times X^{1} + 101 \times 0.97 \times X^{1.5}.$$

Solving (trial and error with a computer), we get $X = 0.965$ (3 dp.).

Since Bond A has the same credit rating as Bond B, we can infer that it has the same risk. Therefore, it should have the same Z-spread. Therefore, we can use this Z-spread to value Bond A. If the price of Bond A is V_0, we get:

$$3 \times 0.99 \times 0.965^{0.5} + 3 \times 0.98 \times 0.965^{1} + 103 \times 0.97 \times 0.965^{1.5} = 100.4656.$$

4.3.3.2 Synthetic Credit Rating

What if the bond that we are valuing does not have a credit rating? In that case, we can attempt to assign a credit rating ourselves (a "synthetic credit rating"), by comparing the issuer's fundamentals with recent published statistics for issuers of different known credit ratings.

4.3.3.3 Example: Synthetic Credit Rating

A credit rating agency has published the following statistics for issuers of bonds that it rates high investment grade (HI), low investment grade (LI), and junk (J) respectively.

	HI	*LI*	*J*
EBIT interest coverage ratio (times)	5	2	0.9
Operating return on assets (%)	10	6	Negative

We wish to find a synthetic credit rating for an unrated issuer. Analyzing the latest financial statements, we get the following numbers for the issuer:

EBIT interest coverage ratio (times)	2.1
Operating return on assets (%)	3.2

Applying our judgement, we conclude that the issuer is most similar to the LI group. We therefore assign a credit rating of LI (low investment grade) to the issuer. We use this LI credit rating to find the spread.

Judgement is required in this approach, particularly if the ratios give conflicting signals. In that case, we should evaluate their relative importance to the issuer's business model and financing ability, and also the extent to which particular ratios may be influenced by one-off items.

4.3.4 Transition Matrices: The Jarrow-Lando-Turnbull Model

Over time, the credit rating of a bond may degrade (or improve). We need to factor this into our valuation, especially for a longer-maturity bond. To do so, we can use evidence provided by a transition matrix. This is a table giving the recent historical rate at which bonds have changed to a different credit rating during a fixed period, say one year. Transition matrices are available from the credit rating agencies for varying periods such as a year, 5 years or 10 years.

We discuss here how to use a one-year transition matrix to value a risky bond. We do this using a simplified version of the Jarrow-Lando-Turnbull model (Jarrow et al. 1997) with discrete time-steps. This means that we make the simplifying assumption that credit rating changes occur at fixed time steps of one year.

An example of a one-year transition matrix is in Table 4.1. We will use this example matrix to illustrate how to apply the Jarrow-Lando-Turnbull model.

In the table, the row headings represent the credit ratings at the start of the year. These could be one of "HI" or "High Investment Grade", "LI" or "Low Investment Grade", "Junk" or "Below Investment Grade", and "Default" which means that the bond is actually in default. We assume that "Default" is an irreversible condition—

Table 4.1 One-year transition matrix

	→HI (1)	→LI (2)	→Junk (3)	→Default (4)
HI (1)→	99%	0.8%	0.1%	0.1%
LI (2)→	1%	97%	1.5%	0.5%
Junk (3)→	0.1%	3%	95%	1.9%
Default (4)→	0	0	0	100%

i.e., once in default, the bond will never recover. In mathematical language, default is an "absorbing state".

The column headings reflect the credit ratings at the end of the year. Then the entries in each cell reflect the recent historical rate at which bonds have changed their status within a year. Thus the number 3% in the cell with row-heading "Junk→" and column-heading "→LI" reflects that 3% of bonds that started a year as "Junk" were upgraded to "LI" status by year-end.

Consistent with default being an absorbing state, 100% of bonds that go into default stay in default. In practice, this need not be true. There are variants of the model that can handle transition from default to non-default, but we will not consider them here.

Although default is an absorbing state, the model reflects that even in default, the bondholder will recover something, say CU 0.20 per CU 1 of face value. This amount is modelled as a sure thing. That is, whatever happens, the bondholder will get a payoff of CU 0.20 equal to the recovery amount. In other words, the recovery amount is risk-free.

Our example table is hypothetical, but it reflects reality in that the one-year transition rates are small. Most bonds remain in the same credit rating as they started off with.

We can view transition rates as conditional probabilities. For example, we can view the 3% rate of change from "Junk" to "LI" as the probability of a bond being "LI" at the end of 1 year, conditional on its starting the year as "Junk". We can write this as $P(LI_t|Junk_{t-1})$, or the probability of a bond being "LI" at time t when it was "Junk" at time $t-1$ where t is in years.

We adopt a more convenient notation by numbering the credit rating states from best to worst—thus HI is 1, LI is 2, Junk is 3 and Default is 4. Then we use the notation p_{ij} to denote the probability of moving from state i to state j. In this notation we would write $P(LI_t|Junk_{t-1})$ as simply p_{23}. We ignore the subscript t as the transition matrix is stable in our model.

The Jarrow-Lando-Turnbull model requires the following inputs:

1. A one-year *transition matrix* as in Table 4.1,
2. An estimate of the *recovery rate*, or the amount that can be recovered if an instrument goes into default—for example say CU 0.20 recovered for every CU 1 of face value,
3. The current average *spreads* for different credit ratings, and

4. The *risk-free* rates or discount factors corresponding to maturities equal to the various payment dates for the bond being valued.

It is convenient if the spreads are expressed as Z-spreads over continuous risk-free rates. We assume this in our example.

The model assumes that the one-year transition matrix is the same for any starting and ending year, i.e., the same transition probabilities for year 1 to year 2, year 2 to year 3, year 3 to year 4, and so on. Then we say that the transition matrix is time-independent or satisfies the *Markov* or memoryless property. It conveniently follows that we can ignore the prior credit-rating history of the bond when predicting future ratings changes.

Convenience of course does not equate with realism. We discuss later how we can test if this assumption is approximately valid. We do this by using the one-year transition matrix to predict transition probabilities for some longer period say 10 years. We can compare our prediction to actual data for that period, say a 10-year transition matrix.

To apply the model, we first compute *risk-neutral* transition probabilities for each relevant time-step, i.e., Year 0 to Year 1, Year 1 to Year 2, Year 2 to Year 3, ... We express these as a function of the actual transition probabilities.

A risk-neutral probability is the probability that market prices would reflect in an imaginary world where everybody is risk-neutral, but assets have the same prices as they do in the real world. To a risk-neutral person, the value of an uncertain cash flow is simply its expected present value discounted at the risk-free rate.

Let us use the notation $\tilde{p}_{ij}(t, t+1)$ to refer to the risk-neutral probability of a move from state i to state j between time t and $t+1$. We model the risk-neutral probabilities as being in the form:

$$\tilde{p}_{ij}(t, t+1) = \begin{cases} \pi_j(t) p_{ij} & j \neq i \\ 1 - \sum_{i \neq j} \tilde{p}_{ij}(t, t+1) & j = i \end{cases}$$

Here $\pi_j(t)$ is a model parameter, and should be a positive real number. We solve for the risk neutral transition probabilities of moving out of the current state i to some other state $j \neq i$ as some constant $\pi_j(t)$ times the actual transition probability p_{ij}. We solve for the risk-neutral probability of staying in the current state i as simply the remaining probability (1 minus the sum of all the probabilities of moving out of state i).

Let s_i be the Z-spread for credit rating i over continuously compounded risk-free rates, where s_i is expressed as a decimal. Let δ be the recovery rate in case of default, i.e., in default, you would receive δ for every CU 1 of face value. Then we have, for a credit rating i at time t:

$$_{t}d_{t+1} e^{-s_i} = {}_{t}d_{t+1} \left(\tilde{p}_{i4}(t, t+1) \times \delta + \sum_{j<4} \tilde{p}_{ij} \right) \tag{4.1}$$

The left-hand side of this equation (Equation 4.1) is the actual forward price in a risky forward interest rate contract with credit rating i that promises to pay CU 1 at time $t + 1$. The right hand side reflects the expected present value (as of time t) of the same contract in an imaginary risk-neutral world, i.e., with the discount rate being the actual risk-free forward interest rate and the expectation derived under the risk-neutral probabilities. The expected present value reflects that we would get CU 1 in any state except default, where we would get CU δ.

We can cancel ${}_t d_{t+1}$ from both sides. Then the expression is the same for any starting time, so that we can rewrite $\tilde{p}_{ij}(t, t+1)$ as simply $\tilde{p}_{ij}$. Thus, in our formulation, the risk-neutral transition matrix satisfies the memoryless Markov property, just like the actual transition matrix. We can then express Equation 4.1 as follows:

$$e^{-s_i} = \tilde{p}_{i4} \times \delta + \sum_{j<4} (\tilde{p}_{ij} \times 1) \tag{4.2}$$

Having derived the risk-neutral transition matrix, we can use it to derive the risk-neutral probabilities of being in a particular credit rating at any future date. Suppose that we are valuing a bond that has credit rating LI at time 0. If we write $\tilde{p}_{ij}$ as a conditional probability using the notation $\tilde{P}(.|.)$, then using the standard logic of conditional probabilities we get:

$$\begin{aligned}\tilde{P}(HI_2|LI_0) = \tilde{P}(HI_2|HI_1).\tilde{P}(HI_1|LI_0) + \tilde{P}(HI_2|LI_1).\tilde{P}(LI_1|LI_0) \\ +\tilde{P}(HI_2|Junk_1).\tilde{P}(Junk_1|LI_0).\end{aligned}$$

When we have derived the two-year risk-neutral probabilities starting from LI at 0, we can use them to get the 3-year risk-neutral probabilities starting from LI at 0. For example:

$$\begin{aligned}\tilde{P}(HI_3|LI_0) = \tilde{P}(HI_3|HI_2).\tilde{P}(HI_2|LI_0) + \tilde{P}(HI_3|LI_2).\tilde{P}(LI_2|LI_0) \\ +\tilde{P}(HI_3|Junk_2).\tilde{P}(Junk_2|LI_0).\end{aligned}$$

We can proceed to use the same logic to derive the risk-neutral transition probabilities starting from LI at time 0 for any future number of years 4,5,6, ...[2]

Having derived the risk-neutral probabilities for the bond cashflow dates, we can proceed to value the bond. We do this by computing the expected present value of each bond cash flow with the expectation computed using the risk-neutral probabilities and the present value computed by discounting at the risk-free rate.

[2]In matrix notation, this procedure is equivalent to multiplying the risk-neutral transition matrix by itself repeatedly. Thus, if we denote the one-year risk-neutral transition matrix as $\tilde{P}$, and the n-year risk-neutral transition matrix starting from time 0 as $\tilde{P}(0, n)$, we have $\tilde{P}(0, n) = \tilde{P}^n$.

This is the current value of that cashflow in the imaginary risk-neutral world, which by definition should be the same as that in the real world.

We demonstrate the model using an example. Say we are valuing a 3-year 5% risky bond with semi-annual coupons. The valuation date is the issue date. The issuer has credit risk LI on the issue date (time 0). The actual transition probabilities are based on Table 4.1. The Z-spreads over continuously compounded risk-free spot interest rates are 7 bps for HI, 20 bps for LI and 120 bps for Junk. The recovery rate in default is CU 0.20 per CU 1 of face value.

Risk-free discount factors are as follows:

$t =$	0.5	1	1.5	2	2.5	3
$d_t =$	0.99	0.98	0.97	0.96	0.955	0.95

We compute the risk-neutral transition matrix. We start by estimating the parameters π_1, π_2 and π_3 (we can drop t as an argument for π_j since in our formulation, $\pi_j(t)$ is the same for all t).

Applying Equation 4.1, we have:

$$\begin{aligned} e^{-0.0007} &= \tilde{p}_{11}.1 + \tilde{p}_{12}.1 + \tilde{p}_{13}.1 + \tilde{p}_{14}.0.2 \\ &= (1 - 0.01\pi_1) + 0.008\pi_1 + 0.001\pi_1 + 0.001\pi_1 \times 0.2 \\ &= 1 - 0.0008\pi_1 \\ \Rightarrow \pi_1 &= \frac{1 - e^{-0.0007}}{0.0008} = 0.8747. \end{aligned}$$

$$\begin{aligned} e^{-0.002} &= 0.01\pi_2 + (1 - 0.03\pi_2) + 0.015\pi_2 + 0.005 \times 0.2 \times \pi_2 \\ &= 1 - 0.004\pi_2 \\ \Rightarrow \pi_2 &= \frac{1 - e^{-0.002}}{0.004} = 0.4995. \end{aligned}$$

$$\begin{aligned} e^{-0.012} &= 0.001\pi_3 + 0.03\pi_3 + (1 - 0.05\pi_3) + 0.019 \times 0.2 \times \pi_3 \\ &= 1 - 0.0152\pi_3 \\ \Rightarrow \pi_3 &= \frac{1 - e^{-0.012}}{0.0152} = 0.7848. \end{aligned}$$

Based on these parameters, we derive the risk-neutral transition matrix shown in Table 4.2.

Table 4.2 One-year risk-neutral transition matrix

	→HI (1)	→LI (2)	→Junk (3)	→Default (4)
HI (1)→	99.1253%	0.6998%	0.0875%	0.0875%
LI (2)→	0.4995%	98.5015%	0.7493%	0.2498%
Junk (3)→	0.0785%	2.3543%	96.0762%	1.4910%
Default (4)→	0	0	0	100%

We can use the LI row to find the 2-year and 3-year risk-neutral probabilities starting from LI.

$$\tilde{P}(HI_2|LI_0) = 0.991253 \times 0.004995 + 0.004995 \times 0.985015 + 0.000784755 \times 0.007493 = 0.9877\%.$$

$$\tilde{P}(LI_2|LI_0) = 0.006998 \times 0.004995 + 0.985015 \times 0.985015 + 0.023543 \times 0.007493 = 97.0471\%.$$

$$\tilde{P}(Junk_2|LI_0) = 0.000875 \times 0.004995 + 0.007493 \times 0.985015 + 0.960762 \times 0.007493 = 1.4583\%.$$

$$\tilde{P}(Default_2|LI_0) = 0.000875 \times 0.004995 + 0.002498 \times 0.985015 + 0.014910 \times 0.007493 + 1 \times 0.002498 = 0.5074\%.$$

We can proceed to calculate the 3-year risk-neutral transition probabilities starting from LI at time 0. Since we do not need to calculate transition probabilities for year 4, it is sufficient to just calculate the risk-neutral probability of default in year 3 starting from LI in year 0, i.e., $\tilde{P}(Default_3|LI_0)$.

$$\tilde{P}(Default_3|LI_0) = 0.000875 \times 0.009877 + 0.002498 \times 0.970471 + 0.014910 \times 0.014573 + 1 \times 0.005074 = 0.7723\%.$$

This implies that the risk-neutral probability of not being in default after 3 years starting from LI at time 0, say $\tilde{P}(\neg Default_t|LI_0)$, is 99.2277%. The symbol $\neg$ stands for negation, thus $\tilde{P}(\neg Default|X)$ stands for the risk-neutral probability of *not* being in default conditional on event X.

We now turn to valuing the bond. As usual, we can value it as a replicating portfolio of zero-coupon bonds with maturities that match the respective coupon dates, and face values that match the bond cashflows on those dates.

We value each of these zeroes as the risk-neutral expected present value of the bond cashflows. These cashflows equal the full amount in any state except default, and are CU 0.20 per CU 1 of face value in the event of default. Therefore for a cashflow of CU C at time t, we have:

$$C \times d_t \times \left(\tilde{P}(\neg Default_t|LI_0) \times 1 + \tilde{P}(Default_t|LI_0) \times 0.20\right).$$

Since our ratings changes occur only once a year, the predicted credit rating at mid-year is the same as that at the beginning of the year.

We proceed to value the bond. If its value today is V_0, we have:

$$\begin{aligned} V_0 &= 2.5 \times [0.99 + (0.98 + 0.97) \times (1 \times 0.997502 + 0.2 \times 0.002498) + \\ &\quad (0.96 + 0.955) \times (1 \times 0.99493 + 0.2 \times 0.005074)] + \\ &\quad 102.5 \times 0.95 \times (1 \times 0.99228 + 0.2 \times 0.007723) \\ &= 108.8817. \end{aligned}$$

We get a bond value of CU 108.8817. We can compare to the value from just directly applying the LI Z-spread of 20 bps, without considering the transition matrix. This value is CU 108.8939.

4.3.4.1 Practical Issues

When estimating the risk-neutral probabilities, we may get negative values or numbers that exceed 100%. This may indicate that the market anticipates a higher future default rate than that indicated by the actual historical transition matrix. We can consider re-calibrating the model using additional forward looking data on default risk. We could use a bankruptcy prediction model such as Altman's Z-score or the Ohlson bankruptcy prediction model.

The model is driven by the assumption that the actual transition matrix satisfies the Markov property. If we have data on actual longer-term transition probabilities, we can test this critical assumption. To do so, we use the actual (i.e., not risk-neutral) one-year transition probabilities to estimate (actual not risk-neutral) two-year, three-year, etc., transition probabilities. We can then compare these predictions to the actual data. If the actual longer-term transition rates do not match our predictions, then the model is unreliable.

4.4 Floaters

A floating-rate note (FRN) or floater is a coupon bond whose coupon is not an equal lumpsum amount each period. Rather, the coupon is determined based on a published reference rate such as LIBOR (London inter-bank offer rate). For example, the coupon rate could be stated as LIBOR + 10, which means that the coupon would be 10 basis points above the quoted LIBOR rate for a maturity at the coupon due date, where the quote is as of the date when the coupon is set or reset. That date is called the coupon *reset date*. It is typically one period prior to the coupon payment date. The margin of 10 points is called the *reset margin*.

4.4.1 Conventions with Reference Rates

Reference rates like LIBOR are typically simple interest rates quoted daily for short-term maturities ranging up to 1 year.

They typically use the Act/360 day count convention or less commonly the Act/365 convention. We will use the Act/360 convention in our examples. Under this convention, we calculate a fractional part of a year by counting the actual number of days in the fractional period and dividing by 360 days.

So for example, if a 3-month period works out to 90 days, and 3-month LIBOR is 2%, the period in years would be $\frac{90}{360} = 0.25$ years. Then the actual LIBOR interest due at 90 days would be (for CU 100 face value):

$$2\% \times 100 \times \frac{90}{360} = \text{CU}\,0.50.$$

If the convention were Act/365, the period in years would be $\frac{90}{365} = 0.2466$. The interest would be:

$$2\% \times 100 \times \frac{90}{365} = \text{CU}\,0.4932.$$

In this chapter's examples, we will use as our reference rate LIBOR for some currency labelled CU. We will assume the Act/360 convention. We will use the notation L + 10 to signify 10 bps above LIBOR.

4.4.1.1 Example: Floater Basics

A LIBOR + 20 coupon bond is issued on 1 Jan 2018. The bond pays quarterly coupons in arrears on April 1st, July 1st, Oct 1st and Jan 1st each year until it matures on Jan 1 2020 (2 years).

The coupon rate for a particular coupon payment is set at the previous coupon payment date (the reset date), or the bond issue date in the case of the first coupon.

On Jan 1 2018, 3-month LIBOR for CU instruments is 2% p.a. LIBOR quotes are based on simple interest.

From this, the coupon rate for the first coupon, due on Apr 1 2018 is 2.2% p.a. (2% + 20 basis points). Since the payment frequency is quarterly, the actual coupon amount is based on $\frac{1}{4}$ of this, or CU 0.55 for a face value of CU 100.

On Apr 1 2018, 3-month LIBOR is 1.8%. So the coupon rate for the next coupon, due on Jul 1 2018 is 2% (1.8% + 20 basis points). So the actual coupon due on Jul 1 2018 is CU 0.5056 for a face value of CU 100 (91/360 × 2).

4.4.2 Discount Margin

For floaters as with fixed-rate bonds, the market interest rate on the valuation date may not equal the coupon rate. In that case, the value of the floater will deviate from par (face value).

In valuing floaters, it is convenient to express the discount rate similarly to the coupon rate, i.e., as the reference rate plus some spread. The reference rate is the same one used in the coupon rate. Then the *discount margin* is the spread used to express the discount rate.

4.4.2.1 Example: Discount Margin

An issuer has issued a coupon bond with coupon based on LIBOR + 20. But based on the issuer's credit rating and market data, the valuer determines that the market would expect an interest rate of LIBOR + 40 from this issuer.

Then the discount margin is 40 basis points. The discount rate would be based on LIBOR + 40, where the particular LIBOR reference rate would be the same as that used to calculate the coupon.

4.4.3 Valuation of Floaters

When valuing floaters, we do not attempt to project the uncertain future coupon payments. A better approach springs from the fact that when the discount margin and the reset margin are the same, the floater should be at par (at least on coupon reset dates).

Then floaters where the discount margin does not equal the reset margin can be analyzed as a combination of a hypothetical floater with reset margin chosen to be equal to the discount margin, plus or minus some fixed amount each period.

We illustrate this approach by presenting a series of examples.

First, in Case 1, we present the benchmark situation of a floater with discount margin equal to its reset margin, when valued at a reset date. This floater would be at par.

In Case 2, we consider a floater where the reset margin equals the discount margin as in Case 1, but the valuation date lies between two reset dates. In this case, the floater will not be at par, since the fixed next coupon would be discounted using a valuation-date LIBOR that differs from that used earlier to fix the coupon.

In Case 3, we value a floater where the reset margin differs from the discount margin, with valuation on a reset date.

Finally, in Case 4, we consider the general case where the reset margin differs from the discount margin, and the valuation date lies between reset dates.

4.4.3.1 Case 1: Valuation on Reset Date, Reset Margin Equals Discount Margin

Consider a L + 20 floater issued on 1 Jan 2018 with quarterly coupons. The bond has a maturity of one year, that is, 1 Jan 2019. The reset dates are three months prior to the coupon due date. We are valuing the floater on 1 Jan 2018 (the issue date). On this date, 3-month LIBOR is at 2%.

This helps us to fix the first coupon at CU 0.55, due on 1 Apr 2018. We do not know the remaining bond cash flows, but it's sufficient to know that they are discounted at a rate that exactly matches their coupon rate. Thus on 1 Apr 2018, the bond would be at par, or the remaining cash flows are worth exactly 100 on that date.

Therefore we can value the floater as the present value today of CU 100 plus the first coupon on 1 Apr 2018. This gives us:

$$V_0 = \frac{100.55}{\left(1 + 0.022 \times \frac{90}{360}\right)} = 100.$$

4.4.3.2 Case 2: Valuation Between Reset Dates, Reset Margin Equals Discount Margin

Consider a LIBOR + 20 floater issued on 1 Jan 2018 with quarterly coupons. It matures on 1 Jan 2019. The reset dates are three months before each coupon due date.

On the issue date 1 Jan 2018 3-month LIBOR is 2%. Therefore the first coupon is fixed at CU 0.55 [$= 2.2 \times \frac{90}{360}$].

We are valuing the floater on 1 Feb 2018. On this date, 3-month LIBOR is 2% and 1-month LIBOR is 1.8%. The 3-month LIBOR corresponds to a maturity of 1 May 2018 (89 days) while the 1-month LIBOR corresponds to a maturity of 1 Mar 2018 (28 days).

We can use linear interpolation to estimate the rate corresponding to 1 Apr 2018 (59 days):

$$0.018 + \frac{0.02 - 0.018}{61} \times 31 = 1.9016\%.$$

We add 20 bps to get the discount rate of 2.1016%.

The present value as at 1 Apr 2018 of the remaining cashflows as of that date is CU 100, using the same logic presented for Case 1.

Therefore the value of the floater would be the present value today of CU 100 plus the first coupon (CU 0.55) at 1 Apr 2018. To get the clean price we would subtract the accrued interest which works out to:

$$AI = 2.2 \times \frac{31}{360} = 0.1894.$$

Therefore the bond value (clean price of CU 100) is:

$$V_0 = \frac{100.55}{\left(1 + 0.021016 \times \frac{59}{360}\right)} - 0.1894 = 100.0155.$$

The bond value is slightly higher than par because the discount rate has fallen relative to the rate used to fix the coupon.

4.4.3.3 Case 3: Valuation on Reset Date, Reset Margin Different from Discount Margin

Consider a 1-year L + 30 bond issued on 1 Jan 2018 with quarterly coupons due on 1 Apr 2018, 1 Jul 2018, 1 Oct 2018 and 1 Jan 2019.

We are valuing the bond on the issue date 1 Jan 2018. We assess that the appropriate discount margin is 20 bps.

To value this bond, we observe that its cashflows can be replicated by a combination of:

1. A L + 20 bond with the same face value and coupon dates, and
2. A fixed payment on each coupon date given by the bond face value times the difference between $(L + 30) \times \frac{X}{360}$ and $(L + 20) \times \frac{X}{360}$ where X is the number of days in the coupon period.

Then the fair value of the L + 20 bond would be CU 100. To discount the fixed payments, we use LIBOR for maturities corresponding to the coupon dates. On our valuation date, 3-month LIBOR is 2%, 6-month LIBOR is 3%, 9-month LIBOR is 4% and 12-month LIBOR is 5%, corresponding to the maturity dates respectively of 1 Apr 2018 (90 days), 1 Jul 2018 (181 days), 1 Oct 2018 (273 days) and 1 Jan 2018 (1 year). These dates are the same as the coupon dates for our bond.

We add the discount margin of 20 bps to these rates to get the discount rates for the corresponding dates. We get 2.2%, 3.2%, 4.2% and 5.2% respectively.

The fixed payment each coupon date is given by $0.10 \times \frac{X}{360}$ where X is the number of days in the coupon period.

We proceed to calculate the present value of the stream of fixed payments.

$$\frac{0.10 \times \frac{90}{360}}{1 + 0.022 \times \frac{90}{360}} + \frac{0.10 \times \frac{91}{360}}{1 + 0.032 \times \frac{181}{360}} + \frac{0.10 \times \frac{92}{360}}{1 + 0.042 \times \frac{273}{360}} + \frac{0.10 \times \frac{92}{360}}{1 + 0.052} = 0.099.$$

Therefore, the value of the floater is CU 100.099.

4.4.3.4 Case 4: Valuation on Non-reset Date, Reset Margin Different from Discount Margin

Consider an L + 20 floater issued on 1 Jan 2018, with quarterly coupons due on 1 Apr 2018, 1 Jul 2018, 1 Oct 2018 and 1 Jan 2019 respectively. The 3-month LIBOR on 1 Jan 2018 is 2%, used to fix the first coupon.

We are valuing the floater on 1 Feb 2018. On this date, 1-month LIBOR is 1.8% (maturity of 1 Mar 2018 or 28 days), 3-month LIBOR is 2% (maturity of 1 May 2018 or 89 days), 6-month LIBOR is 3.1% (maturity of 1 Aug 2018 or 181 days), 9-month LIBOR is 4.1% (1 Nov 2018, 273 days), and 1-year LIBOR is 5.1% (1 Feb 2019, 1 year).

The discount margin is L + 30. Similarly to Case 3, we can analyse this floater as a combination of a L + 30 floater and a fixed amount each coupon date. In this case, the fixed amount will be negative.

We use linear interpolation to estimate LIBOR for the coupon dates. We get 1.9016% for 1 Apr 2018, 2.7293% for 1 Jul 2018, 3.7630% for 1 Oct 2018, and 4.7630% for 1 Jan 2019. We add 30 bps to these LIBOR rates to get the discount rates for each coupon date.

The dirty price of the L + 30 floater is given by:

$$\frac{100.575}{1 + 0.022016 \times \frac{59}{360}} = 100.2134.$$

The present value of the series of fixed payments is given by:

$$-\frac{0.1 \times \frac{90}{360}}{1 + 0.022016 \times \frac{59}{360}} - \frac{0.1 \times \frac{91}{360}}{1 + 0.03029 \times \frac{150}{360}} - \frac{0.1 \times \frac{92}{360}}{1 + 0.04063 \times \frac{242}{360}} - \frac{0.1 \times \frac{92}{360}}{1 + 0.05063 \times \frac{334}{360}} = -0.099.$$

The accrued interest (on the actual bond) is given by:

$$AI = 2.2 \times \frac{31}{360} = 0.1894.$$

Therefore, the floater value (clean price) is given by:

$$V_0 = 100.2134 - 0.099 - 0.1894 = 99.925.$$

4.5 Vanilla Interest Rate Swaps

A vanilla interest rate swap is a contract that leads to an exchange of a stream of fixed-rate interest payments for a stream of floating-rate interest, or vice-versa.

Take an example. Suppose that we enter a swap on 1 Jan 2018 where we receive a 3% pa fixed interest rate with semi-annual payments (1.5% each half-year), until 1 Jan 2019, in exchange for paying a floating interest rate of L + 10, with quarterly payments and the same expiry date of 1 Jan 2019. The interest payments exchanged are calculated based on the same *notional principal* of say CU 100. The term "notional" here means that the principal amount is just a reference figure used to calculate the interest payments. No principal actually changes hands.

Since we are paying the floating rate, we are called the *floating rate payer*. Our counterparty on the other side of the swap receives the floating rate and pays the fixed rate. They are called the *fixed rate payer*.

4.5.1 Replicating Portfolio

To value the swap, we use a hypothetical replicating portfolio that consists of a long position in a 3% coupon bond with semi-annual coupons and a short position in an L + 10 floater with quarterly coupons, both with principal CU 100 and maturity date 1 Jan 2019. That is, the replicating portfolio includes a fixed-rate bond as an asset and a floater as a liability.

The cash flows from this replicating portfolio exactly match those from the swap. We can therefore value the swap by calculating the value of the replicating portfolio. This is simply the value of the fixed-rate bond (asset) minus the value of the floater (liability).

We refer to the fixed-rate bond as the *fixed leg* of the swap. We refer to the floater as the *floating leg* of the swap.

From the counterparty's point of view (the fixed rate payer) their position can be valued by a replicating portfolio that is exactly the opposite of ours—with the floating leg as an asset, and the fixed leg as a liability.

4.5.2 Valuation

We assume that both counterparties carry the same credit risk. Since they both have the same risk, the same discount rate can be used to value both legs of the swap. We typically use the rates corresponding to the floating leg.

In valuing a swap between coupon dates (for either leg), we may choose to calculate either the clean price or the dirty price—both are allowed under IFRS 9. Clean price may be considered better practice, as it improves the estimation of hedge effectiveness. Swaps are often used as hedging instruments. We will use clean price throughout in our examples.

Let us now value the swap in our example. Suppose that we are valuing the swap on 1 Feb 2018. On this date, 1-month LIBOR is 1.8% (1 Mar 2018 or 28 days), 3-month LIBOR is 2% (1 May 2018, 88 days), 6-month LIBOR is 3.1% (1 Aug 2018, 180 days), 9-month LIBOR is 4.1% (1 Nov 2018) and 1-year LIBOR is 5.1% (1 Feb 2019, 1 year).

Also 3-month LIBOR on 1 Jan 2018 is 2%. This date is the reset date for the floating leg.

The discount margin for the floating leg is assessed as 10 bps (so discount margin equals reset margin in this example).

Using linear interpolation, we can compute LIBOR for maturities of the various coupon dates to be 1.9016% for 1 Apr 2018, 2.7293% for 1 Jul 2018, 3.763% for 1 Oct 2018, and 4.763% for 1 Jan 2019. Adding 10 bps, we get the respective discount rates—2.0016%, 2.8293%, 3.863%, and 4.863%.

Accrued interest for both legs is based on Act/360.

The value of the fixed leg (asset) is given by:

$$\frac{1.5}{1+0.028293\times\frac{150}{360}}+\frac{101.5}{1+0.04863\times\frac{334}{360}}-3\times\frac{31}{360}=98.3424.$$

The value of the floating leg (liability) is given by:

$$\frac{100.525}{1+0.020016\times\frac{59}{360}}-2.1\times\frac{31}{360}=100.0155.$$

Therefore, the value of our swap V_0 say is:

$$V_0=98.3424-100.0155=-1.6731.$$

The swap has a negative value, which means that it is a liability worth CU 1.6731. Our counterparty, the fixed rate payer, would record an asset of exactly the same value, if their valuation is consistent with ours.

4.6 Convertible Bonds

Convertible bonds are bonds that can be converted into the issuing entity's ordinary shares at some point in their life, typically at the bondholder's option. We will assume here that the holder has the option to convert.

Under IFRS 9, an investment in a convertible bond (i.e., as an asset) should be treated as a single item and measured usually at fair value with fair value changes flowing through the income statement (FVTPL).

The accounting for the issuer is different. Under IAS 32, issuers are usually required to analyze convertible bonds into two items—the straight debt component (an equivalent non-convertible bond), and the conversion option. The option would be recorded separately, either as an equity item or as a liability depending on whether the number of shares on conversion is fixed in advance (leading to equity), or variable (leading to a liability). If the conversion option is a liability, then as a derivative liability under IFRS 9, it is measured at fair value through profit and loss.

In valuing the two components initially, IAS 32 requires the issuer to estimate the fair value of the debt component first and then calculate the fair value of the option component as a residual (total proceeds minus straight debt).

4.6.1 The Goldman-Sachs Model

We consider the valuation of a convertible bond as a single item. We have already discussed bond and option models that will be applied to value two separate components when they are recorded and measured separately. We will not discuss this split accounting further in this section.

The Goldman-Sachs model (Goldman Sachs 1994) uses a lattice of share prices to value the convertible bond. These could be constructed using any suitable lattice model such as CRR, equal-probabilities or the trinomial model.

Then we follow the following strategy to solve for the convertible bond value.

We start at the last step in the lattice where the bond can be converted. We evaluate whether the bond would be converted at each node in this step, by checking if the share price at this node is higher than the value of not converting (the present value of the remaining straight-bond cashflows—interest and principal payments—discounted at the risk-adjusted discount rate for the issuer).

If the share price is higher at a node in this last step, then we assume that the bond will be converted at that node. We then use the share price at that node to calculate the convertible bond value at that node.

If the share price is lower at a node in this last step, then the bond will not be converted. Then its value at the node is the present value of the remaining bond cash flows, discounted at the bond's risk-adjusted discount rate (the dirty price of the bond at that node).

Having established the bond values at each node in the last step, we can move backwards in the lattice and use risk-neutral probabilities to work out the bond value at each node in the previous step if the bond is not converted at that node. We call this the holding value and denote it by V_H.

At each node where the bond can be converted, we also calculate the bond value on conversion, based on the share price at that node. We can call this the conversion value and denote it by V_C.

Then the value of the bond at any node where conversion is allowed is given by the higher of the two numbers or $\max(V_H, V_C)$. If conversion is not allowed at a node, then the bond value there is just the holding value.

We can move backwards through the lattice to the starting point to get the convertible bond value on the valuation date.

But the model has a complication—the discount rate used at each node to discount the expected values at the succeeding nodes. This rate can vary at different nodes.

For example, if we are at a node where the bond has been converted to shares at both the succeeding nodes, then the discount rate is the risk-free rate r_c say. This is because the logic here is similar to that for a one-step share option model.

On the other hand, suppose that we are at a node where no future path leads to conversion of the bond, that is, the bond will surely remain a straight bond for the rest of its life. Then the appropriate discount rate to use at that node is the risk-adjusted straight bond discount rate, let us label it y_a.

In the general situation for any node, the appropriate discount rate would lie between r_c and y_a. To reflect this, we calculate the discount rate for each node as follows.

Suppose that the discount rate at the node one step up from the current node is y_u and the discount rate at the node one step down is y_d. Then the discount rate at the current node is given by y_c say where:

$$y_c = p_u y_u + p_d y_d.$$

Here p_u and p_d are the risk-neutral probabilities of up and down respectively.

We can refer to y_c as the *credit-spread-adjusted* discount rate at the node.

In performing this procedure at any node where the bond is converted, we should use the risk-free rate as the discount rate, not y_c. This is because moving forward from that node, the instrument will be a share, regardless of the bond values that we had previously estimated at succeeding nodes while moving backwards through the lattice.

We can now proceed to demonstrate the model using a simple example[3].

Suppose that the convertible bond can be converted into one share per CU 100 of face value. For simplicity, let us assume a constant risk free rate r_c equal to 1% continuously compounded, and a constant risk-adjusted straight bond discount rate y_a equal to 10% continuously compounded.

We assume that the convertible bond has a life of one year $t = 1$, and has semi-annual coupons at a coupon rate of 10% (i.e., a coupon of CU 5 at 6 months and CU 5 at 1 year per face value of CU 100).

Suppose that the current share price is CU 90. The share price volatility parameter σ equals 30%.

Suppose that the bond can be converted any time during its life. That is, the conversion option is exercised American-style.

We use a 3-step CRR model to value the convertible bond.

Then we have the following model parameters (using the same notation as we used before):

[3] In the example, the holder loses the current coupon if they convert on a coupon date, and loses any accrued interest if they convert between coupon dates.

Fig. 4.1 Goldman-Sachs lattice example (convertible bond)

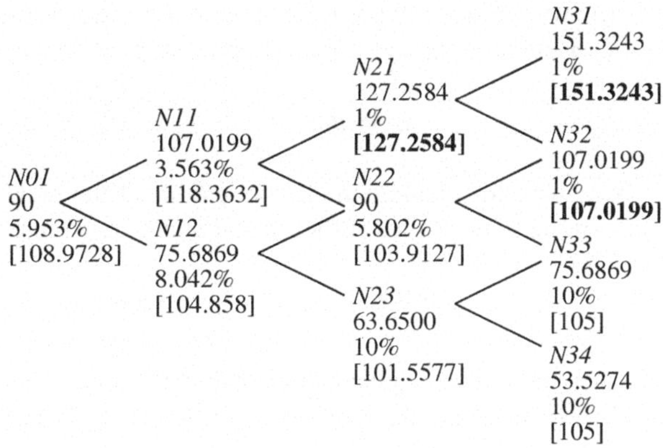

$$\Delta t = \frac{1}{3};$$

$$u = e^{30\% \times \sqrt{\frac{1}{3}}} = 1.1891;$$

$$d = e^{-30\% \times \sqrt{\frac{1}{3}}} = 0.8410;$$

$$p_u = \frac{e^{0.01 \times \frac{1}{3}} - 0.8410}{1.1891 - 0.8410} = 0.4664;$$

$$p_d = 0.5336.$$

The lattice is drawn in Fig. 4.1.

For convenience we label the nodes Nxy where x denotes the step from 0 to 3, where 0 is the starting point, and y denotes the level of the node in a particular step counting from the top downwards. Thus N11 is the top node at the first step, N12 is the bottom node at the first step, and so on.

At each node we record three numbers. The first is the share price at the node. The second is the estimated discount rate at the node y_c. Finally, we have the estimated convertible bond value at the node.

Let us start by considering nodes N31 and N32. At both these nodes, the share price is higher than the straight bond payoff of CU 105. Therefore, the holder will convert at these nodes. Therefore, the appropriate discount rate at both nodes is the risk-free rate r_c or 1%. The bond value at each node is the value from conversion, which is simply the share price at the node.

Moving downwards to N33 and N34, the share price at both nodes is below the value that the holder would get from the straight bond cashflows (CU 105). Therefore, the bond value at these nodes is CU 105. The discount rate at both nodes is the bond discount rate y_a of 10%.

Moving backwards one step, consider N22. The share price here is 90.

First we calculate the discount rate at the node, as the risk-neutral expected value of the discount rates at the up and down steps. This gives us:

$$y_c = p_u \times 1\% + p_d \times 10\% = 5.8024\%.$$

Now we can calculate the holding value at the node as the risk-neutral expected value of the bond values at the up and down steps, discounted at y_c. We have:

$$V_H = e^{-0.058024\times\frac{1}{3}}\,(p_u \times 107.0199 + p_d \times 105) = 103.9127.$$

Since the holding value is higher than the value from converting (the share price of 90), the holder will not convert at this node. The bond value at the node then equals V_H or CU 103.9127.

We can use a similar procedure at the nodes just above (N21) and just below (N23). At N21, y_c equals the risk-free rate r_c and the bond value equals the share price at the node, irrespective of whether we convert at the node. At N23, y_c equals the straight bond discount rate y_a of 10%, and the bond value at the node is simply the present value at that node of the remaining straight-bond cash flows.

Moving back one step, consider N11. At both this node and N12, we must remember to reflect the coupon of CU 5 due during the step, at 0.5 years from time 0 or $\frac{1}{6}$ years from the start of the step.

At N11 we can work out the discount rate at the node y_c to be:

$$p_u \times 1\% + p_d \times 5.8024\% = 3.5626\%.$$

In calculating the holding value, we also add the present value of the coupon due during the step (discounted at y_a).

$$V_H = e^{-0.0356\times\frac{1}{3}} \times (p_u \times 127.2584 + p_d \times 103.9127) + e^{-0.1\times\frac{1}{6}} \times 5 = 118.3632.$$

This is higher than the value from conversion (share price at the node), so the holder will not convert at this node. The bond value at the node equals CU 118.3632.

We perform similar computations at N12, remembering to add the coupon due during the step. The bond value here is CU 104.858.

Finally, we have reached the start node N01.

The discount rate here is given by:

$$y_c = p_u \times 3.5626\% + p_d \times 8.0426\% = 5.9530\%.$$

Then the holding value is given by:

$$V_H = e^{-0.05953\times 13}\,(p_u \times 118.3632 + p_d \times 104.858) = 108.9728.$$

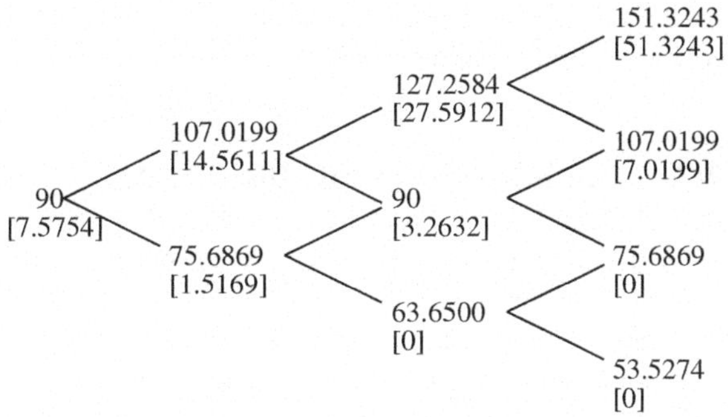

Fig. 4.2 Convertible bond example: CRR lattice for standalone conversion option

Since this is greater than the value from conversion, the holder would not convert at this node. The bond value is the holding value at the node, or CU 108.9728.

Recall that the bond values in the lattice are dirty prices. In this case, the solution is the same as the clean price as we are valuing on the issue date. If our valuation date is between coupon dates, we can get the clean price by subtracting the accrued interest from the value derived from the lattice.

As usual, recall that a 3-step model is for illustration only. For practical use, we need at least 50 steps.

It is interesting to compare the value from the model with that obtained by valuing the straight bond and option components separately.

The value of the equivalent straight bond is:

$$e^{-0.5\times 0.1} \times 5 + e^{-0.1} \times 105 = 99.7641.$$

We calculate the value of the conversion option using the same lattice as we used for the convertible bond. The solved lattice is shown in Fig. 4.2. We get a value for the standalone call option of CU 7.5754.

Adding the estimated values of the standalone straight bond and standalone conversion option, we get CU 107.34, which is different from the value of CU 108.9728 that we calculated earlier. The difference is because a convertible bond cashflows are not replicated by a portfolio that consists of a straight bond and a standalone call option.

If we were doing the accounting for the issuer, we would usually be required under IAS 32 to split the convertible bond into a straight-bond component (liability) and a conversion-option component (usually equity). To do this, we calculate the value of the option component as the issue proceeds minus the fair value of the straight-bond component (with adjustments for transaction costs that we will ignore here).

If for some reason the issue proceeds are not known, say the issue was in exchange for a non-cash asset whose fair value cannot be determined, then we would use CU 108.9728 as the estimated fair value of the entire convertible bond, and then subtract the straight-bond fair value of CU 99.7641 to get the option fair value. We get an option fair value of CU 9.2087.

4.7 Callable and Puttable Bonds

We can value bonds with early redemption options using a lattice of risk-free rates such as the Black-Derman-Toy model (BDT) or the Ho-Lee model. We will illustrate the procedure using a BDT lattice.

A *callable* bond or callable is one where the *issuer* has the right (but not the obligation) to redeem it early at some fixed date or dates by paying a fixed amount. This amount is usually higher than the face value.

A *puttable* bond or puttable is one where the *holder* has the right (but not the obligation) to redeem it early at some fixed date or dates by receiving a fixed amount.

Callable and puttable bonds are derivatives because of the embedded call or put options. From the holder's viewpoint, we can view a callable bond as a combination of a long position in a straight non-callable bond and a short position in a call option to buy the bond. The callable bond would therefore be worth less than its non-callable counterpart.

Similarly, we can view a puttable bond as a combination of a long position in a straight non-callable bond and a long position in a put option to sell the bond early. The puttable bond would therefore be worth more than its non-puttable counterpart.

To illustrate the valuation, let us consider three example cases:

1. *Case B (benchmark)*: A straight 3% non-puttable and non-callable bond with exactly 1.5 years to maturity. The bond pays coupons semi-annually in arrears. Its credit rating leads to a Z-spread of 10 bps above continuously compounded spot interest rate $r_{t,c}$.
2. *Case C (callable)*: This is a bond that is identical to Case B except that the issuer has the right to redeem it anytime before maturity by paying CU 100.6 per CU 100 of face value (that is, the call strike price is CU 100.6).
3. *Case P (puttable)*: this is a bond that is identical to Case B except that the holder has the right to redeem it anytime before maturity, in which case they receive CU 100.2 per CU 100 of face value (that is, the put strike price is CU 100.2).

To value the three cases, we use a lattice of risk-free rates taken from our earlier example of the BDT model (3.7.1). We repeat the salient details here.

The spot interest rates are as in Table 4.3.

Table 4.3 BDT example spot rates

Maturity (t)	Spot interest rate ($r_{t,c}$)
0.5	2%
1	2.1%
1.5	2.5%

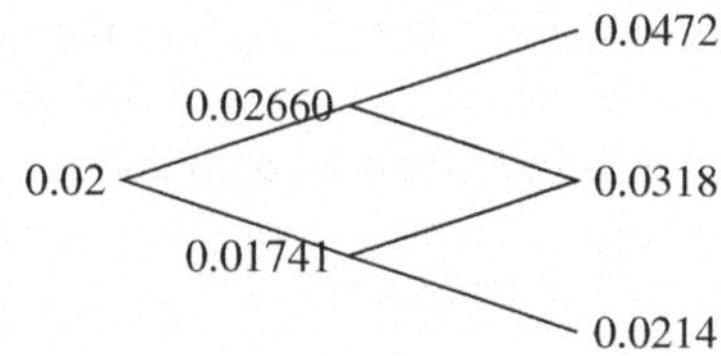

Fig. 4.3 BDT lattice of future 6-month spot interest rates

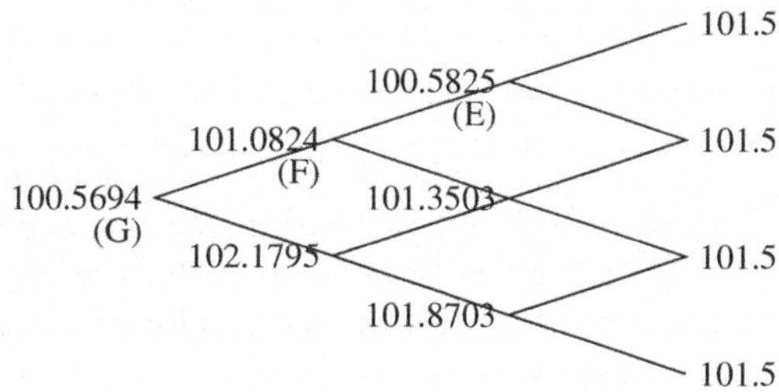

Fig. 4.4 BDT lattice for Case B (benchmark)

The lattice of spot interest rates is in Fig. 4.3. (We derived it earlier. See Fig. 3.6.)

The step size here is 0.5 years which is convenient for our example since the nodes exactly match coupon payment dates.

4.7.1 Case B: Benchmark Example—Straight Bond

For the benchmark bond, we can construct the lattice similarly to the approach we used for a risk-free zero in Sect. 3.7.1. We reflect the Z-spread in the discount rates at each node. We also include the coupon payments at the nodes where they are paid or just before they are paid.

We do not need the lattice to value this bond. We can value it as simply a portfolio of risky zeroes as follows:

$$1.5 \times e^{-0.021 \times 0.5} + 1.5 \times e^{-0.022} + 101.5 \times e^{-0.026 \times 1.5} = 100.5694.$$

The lattice should give us the same bond price since it is term-structure consistent. The solved lattice is shown in Fig. 4.4.

The payoffs of CU 101.5 at the end nodes equal the face value of CU 100 plus the last coupon of CU 1.5.

As usual, we move backwards through the lattice. We solve for the value at each node as the sum of:

1. The expected present value of the values at the next step, discounted using the corresponding rate from the BDT lattice adjusted by the Z-spread of 10 bps; and
2. The coupon payable at that node.

Thus to derive the price in the node labelled (E) in Fig. 4.4, we have:

$$(0.5 \times 101.5 + 0.5 \times 101.5) \times e^{-(0.0472+0.001)\times 0.5} + 1.5 = 100.5825.$$

Similarly for the calculation at the node labelled (F) in Fig. 4.4, we have:

$$(0.5 \times 100.5825 + 0.5 \times 101.3503) \times e^{-(0.0266+0.001)\times 0.5} + 1.5 = 101.0824.$$

And at the initial node (G), we have:

$$(0.5 \times 101.0824 + 0.5 \times 102.1795) \times e^{-(0.02+0.001)\times 0.5} = 100.5694.$$

This equals the bond price we estimated earlier without using the lattice. Verifying the equality is a useful check on our calculations.

In general, the bond prices at each node in our lattice are *dirty* prices. To get the clean price, we subtract the accrued interest from the initial bond price in our lattice (the final calculation).

4.7.2 Case C: Callable Bond Example

For the benchmark bond (case B) we did not need the lattice. But for Case C and Case P, the lattice is essential. As usual, to give a reasonably accurate value, the lattice should have a small step size and a large number of steps. The three-step lattice in our example is for illustration only.

The procedure to price the bond using the lattice is similar to Case B with the following difference:

At nodes where the bond can be called (or just before), the bond clean price cannot be higher than the call price (CU 100.6 in our example). No rational person would pay more than CU 100.6 at this node, since the issuer can immediately take away the bond in exchange for exactly CU 100.6.

If the expected present value of the bond values at the next step is higher than the call price (plus accrued interest) at the node, we would replace this amount by the call price to get the value at this node. Figure 4.5 shows the solved lattice to value Case C.

Consider the node labelled (H) in Fig. 4.5.

The expected present value of the bond values at the next step is given by:

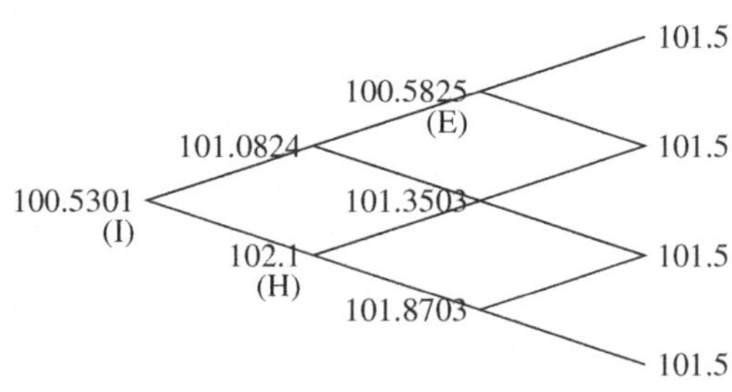

Fig. 4.5 BDT lattice for Case C (callable)

$$(0.5 \times 101.3503 + 0.5 \times 101.8703) \times e^{-(0.0174+0.001)\times 0.5}.$$

This equals CU 100.6795 which exceeds the call price of CU 100.6. (We need not worry about accrued interest in this particular example.)

We therefore replace this value with the call price of CU 100.6 (plus accrued interest, which equals zero in this example). This gives us a value of a dirty price of CU 100.6 plus the coupon of CU 1.5 or a value of CU 102.1 at the node.

We can proceed to find the initial value of the bond as usual. At the start node labelled (I) we have:

$$(0.5 \times 101.0824 + 0.5 \times 102.1) \times e^{-(0.02+0.001)\times 0.5} = 100.5301.$$

Since this is less than CU 100.6, we do not replace this value by the call price.

The bond price is lower than the benchmark bond in Case B by CU 0.0393. This amount can be taken as the estimated value of the issuer's call option. (We remind that the three-step lattice is not accurate, and is for illustration only).

4.7.3 Case P: Puttable Bond Example

The procedure to price the puttable bond using the BDT lattice is similar to the benchmark bond (Case B) with the following difference:

At nodes where the bond can be put (or just before), the bond clean price cannot be *lower* than the put price (CU 100.2 in our example). No rational person will sell the bond for less than CU 100.2 at this node since the buyer can immediately proceed to sell the bond back to the issuer for CU 100.2.

If the expected present value at this node of the next-step payoffs is less than CU 100.2 plus accrued interest, we would replace this value by CU 100.2 (plus accrued interest) in calculating the bond value at this node.

Figure 4.6 shows the solved lattice for Case P.

To illustrate, consider the computations at the node labelled (J) in Fig. 4.6.

The expected present value of the next-step payoffs is given by:

$$(0.5 \times 101.5 + 0.5 \times 101.5) \times e^{-(0.0472+0.001)\times 0.5} = 99.0825.$$

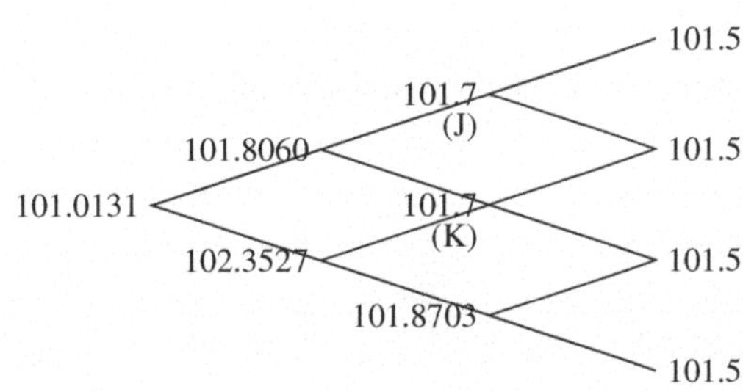

Fig. 4.6 BDT lattice for Case P (puttable)

This is less than CU 100.2, so we replace this value by CU 100.2 (in general plus accrued interest which is zero in our example), giving a value at the node of CU 100.2 plus the coupon payment of CU 1.5 or CU 101.7.

The same thing happens at the node labelled (K) so that the bond there too is worth CU 101.7.

We proceed backwards through the lattice as usual, and obtain an initial bond value of CU 101.0131.

Comparing this to the price of the benchmark Case B, we can infer that the embedded put option is worth CU 0.4437. We remind that the three-step model is for illustration only and not sufficiently accurate.

This concludes our discussion of risky bonds and swaps. In Chap. 5, we move to enterprise valuation.

Exercises

(Monetary units are in CU unless otherwise mentioned).

4.1. Z-Spread

The risk-free rates are 1.3%, 1.4% and 1.5% respectively for maturities of 6 months, 1 year and 1.5 years (semi-annually compounded). A risky 2% coupon bond with a maturity of 1.5 years and half-yearly coupons has a price of CU 97.27. Solve for the Z-spread over semi-annual rates.

4.2. Z-Spread

The discount factors are 0.99, 0.98 and 0.97 respectively for maturities of 6 months, 1 year and 1.5 years. A risky 2% coupon bond with a maturity of 1.5 years and half-yearly coupons has a price of CU 98.4667. Find the Z-spread over continuously compounded rates.

4.3. Jarrow-Lando-Turnbull Model

The one-year transition matrix is as follows (Table 4.4):

The Z-spreads over continuously compounded risk-free spot interest rates are 6 bps for HI, 18 bps for LI and 119 bps for Junk. The recovery rate in default is CU 0.10 per CU 1 of face value.

Table 4.4 One-year transition matrix

	→HI (1)	→LI (2)	→Junk (3)	→Default (4)
HI (1)→	99%	0.7%	0.2%	0.1%
LI (2)→	1.2%	97%	1.3%	0.5%
Junk (3)→	0.1%	2.9%	95%	2%
Default (4)→	0	0	0	100%

Risk-free discount factors are as follows:

$t =$	0.5	1	1.5	2	2.5	3
$d_t =$	0.99	0.985	0.975	0.965	0.955	0.945

Value a 3-year 3% risky bond with semi-annual coupons using the Jarrow-Lando-Turnbull model. The bond is rated LI.

4.4. Synthetic Credit Rating

A credit rating agency has published the following median statistics for issuers of bonds that it rates high investment grade (HI), low investment grade (LI), and junk (J) respectively.

	HI	*LI*	*J*
EBIT interest coverage ratio (times)	6	3	0.9
Operating return on assets (%)	8	3	Negative

We wish to find a synthetic credit rating for an unrated issuer. Analyzing the latest financial statements, we get the following numbers for the issuer:

EBIT interest coverage ratio (times)	3.2
Operating return on assets (%)	5

Decide on the synthetic credit rating. Justify your decision.

4.5. Floater

Consider an L + 10 floater issued on 1 Jan 2019, with quarterly coupons due on 1 Apr 2019, 1 Jul 2019, 1 Oct 2019 and 1 Jan 2020 respectively. The 3-month LIBOR on 1 Jan 2019 is 2.5%, used to fix the first coupon.

We are valuing the floater on 1 Feb 2019. On this date, 1-month LIBOR is 1.9%, 3-month LIBOR is 2.6%, 6-month LIBOR is 3.2%, 9-month LIBOR is 4.0%, and 1-year LIBOR is 4.2%.

The discount margin is L + 8. The accrued interest convention is 30/360.

Value the floater on the valuation date.

4.6. Swap

Suppose that we enter a swap on 1 Jan 2019 where we receive a 5% pa fixed interest rate with semi-annual payments (1.5% each half-year), until 1 Jan 2020, in exchange for paying a floating interest rate of L + 8, with quarterly payments and the same expiry date of 1 Jan 2020. The interest payments exchanged are calculated based on the same *notional principal* of say CU 100.

Suppose that we are valuing the swap on 1 Feb 2019. On this date, 1-month LIBOR is 1.9%, 3-month LIBOR is 2.6%, 6-month LIBOR is 3.2%, 9-month LIBOR is 4.0% and 1-year LIBOR is 4.2%.

Also 3-month LIBOR on 1 Jan 2019 is 2.5%. This date is the reset date for the floating leg.

The discount margin for the floating leg is assessed as 10 bps. The accrued interest convention is 30/360.

Value the swap on the valuation date.

4.7. Goldman-Sachs Convertible Bond Model

We are valuing a convertible bond. Suppose that the bond can be converted into one share per CU 100 of face value. For simplicity, assume a constant risk free rate r_c equal to 1.2% continuously compounded, and a constant risk-adjusted straight bond discount rate y_a equal to 8% continuously compounded.

Assume that the convertible bond has a life of one year $t = 1$, and has semi-annual coupons at a coupon rate of 9%.

Suppose that the current share price is CU 96. The share price volatility parameter σ equals 35%.

Suppose that the bond can be converted any time during its life. That is, the conversion option is exercised American-style.

Value the conversion option using the Goldman-Sachs convertible bond model, using a CRR lattice with 3 steps.

4.8. Callable Bond

Refer to the risk-free rate data in Table 4.3.

Using this data and a BDT lattice, value a 2.8% callable bond with exactly 1.5 years to maturity. The bond pays coupons semi-annually in arrears. Its credit rating leads to a Z-spread of 8 bps above continuously compounded spot interest rate $r_{t,c}$. The issuer has the right to redeem it anytime before maturity by paying CU 100.2 per CU 100 of face value.

4.9. Puttable Bond

Refer to the risk-free rate data in Table 4.3.

Using this data and a BDT lattice, value a 2.8% puttable bond with exactly 1.5 years to maturity. The bond pays coupons semi-annually in arrears. Its credit rating leads to a Z-spread of 8 bps above continuously compounded spot interest rate $r_{t,c}$. The holder has the right to redeem it anytime before maturity and will receive CU 100.1 per CU 100 of face value.

References

Goldman Sachs. (1994). Valuing convertible bonds as derivatives, research note.

Jarrow, R., Lando, D., & Turnbull, S. (1997). A Markov model for the term structure of credit risk spreads. *The Review of Financial Studies, 10*, 481–523.

Business Valuation

5

We start by listing situations when business valuation models are needed in accounting: when valuing shares of a private company in an equity portfolio, in accounting for a takeover, and in performing an impairment test of goodwill. We proceed to discuss the two main approaches to business valuation—the ratio-based approach, and the discounted cash flow (DCF) approach. We discuss a few variations of these approaches, distinguishing between models that value the entire enterprise (enterprise valuation), and those that value just the equity (equity valuation). For DCF models, we distinguish between one-stage, two-stage, three-stage and general multi-stage models. General multi-stage models are based on cashflows projected for a fixed number of years—the planning period—followed by a terminal value, representing the projected value at the end of the planning period. We discuss different approaches to estimating the terminal value. For DCF models of enterprise valuation, we discuss three approaches—WACC, adjusted present value (APV), and residual income valuation. The WACC model discounts projected free cash flows available to both debtholders and shareholders. These cash flows are discounted using a weighted average of the required return demanded by debtholders and shareholders, weighted by their respective proportions in the enterprise's capital structure. The adjusted present value model values the enterprise as a combination of three numbers:

(i) the value of the enterprise if it were 100% equity-owned;
(ii) an adjustment to the value in (i) that reflects the additional value contributed by the interest tax shield due to debt;
(iii) a negative adjustment to the combined value from (i) and (ii) that reflects the risk of bankruptcy due to the company's debt burden.

The residual income valuation model values the enterprise by adding the fair value of operating assets to the present value of excess cashflows generated by these assets, where excess cashflows are total cashflows less a capital charge.

S. Lynn, *Valuation for Accountants*, Springer Texts in Business and Economics,
https://doi.org/10.1007/978-981-15-0357-3_5

5.1 Learning Outcomes

After completing this chapter, you would be able to:

1. Apply ratio-based valuation to value an enterprise or the equity in an enterprise.
2. Apply discounted cash flow models to value an enterprise or the equity in an enterprise.

5.2 Introduction

Business valuation is the valuation of an entire business unit. This could be a company or a division within a decentralized company.

5.2.1 Accountants and Business Valuation

Accountants need business valuation in the following scenarios:

1. A reporting entity has a portfolio of equity investments that are to be measured at fair value under IFRS 9. Some of these shares are investments in private companies for which no share price quote is available. Then we need a business valuation model to value the private-company shares.
2. In a takeover, the acquiring company must complete a purchase price allocation (PPA). In a PPA, the accountant values (at fair value) the assets and liabilities of the acquired company, including previously unrecognized intangible assets, and estimates goodwill as a residual. At various stages in this process, the accountant refers to the target company's estimated fair value as a benchmark. Thus, we need business valuation to provide this benchmark in PPA.
3. Subsequent to a takeover, any goodwill recorded must be tested annually for impairment. Under IFRS, goodwill is not tested directly. Rather it is allocated to business units within the entity, called *cash generating units* (CGU). The entire CGU containing goodwill is tested for impairment by estimating its value in use, fair value, and recoverable amount as the higher of the two. We need business valuation models to find the fair value of a CGU.

We can distinguish between valuing the equity investment in an enterprise (equity valuation) and valuing the entire invested capital of the enterprise (enterprise valuation).

In equity valuation, we seek the value of a single share or of the combined shares outstanding.

In enterprise valuation, we seek the value of both equity and debt capital (as well as other non-standard forms of capital, such as preference shares). This is equivalent to finding the value of total assets less some liabilities that are not included in invested capital.

In the sequel, for convenience, we will refer to the company being valued as the *target* company.

5.2.2 Approaches to Business Valuation

There are two main approaches to business valuation:

1. Ratio-based valuation,
2. Discounted cash flow (DCF) valuation.

Ratio-based valuation is also called the market approach, the method of comparables, or relative valuation. In this approach, we value a company (the target company say) whose price is unknown, by using the value of a similar company or some summary measure of value from a group of similar companies, whose price is publicly quoted. Thus, we rely on Level 2 inputs.

Rather than directly assigning the similar-company value to our target company, we use a valuation ratio. This controls for differences in scale between the two companies.

For example, suppose that the similar company has a market value of equity of CU 2,000,000 and sales of CU 1,000,000. We don't know the market value of equity of the target company, but we do know that its sales are CU 1.3 million.

Rather than directly assigning a value of CU 2,000,000 to our target company, we can use the ratio of market value of equity to sales (price-to-sales or P/S ratio). For the similar company, this is 2 times. We can reasonably assume that our target company should also have a P/S ratio of 2 times. Then its market value of equity should be $2 \times 1{,}300{,}000$ or CU 2.6 million.

The discounted cash flow approach is also called the income approach. In this approach, we value a business by projecting some measure of its cashflows to investors and finding the present value using a suitable discount rate. This discount rate represents the required return that investors demand. This return is called the *cost of capital* (it is a cost from the entity's point of view).

The discounted cash flow approach unavoidably involves subjective judgements and assumptions, or Level 3 inputs. Inspite of this, it may sometimes be preferred to ratio-based valuation. For example, if a company is very unique, it may be impossible to find sufficiently similar companies for ratio-based valuation.

5.3 Ratio-Based Valuation

The general approach to ratio-based valuation is as follows:

1. Identify a group of similar companies known as guideline companies,
2. Compute the level of a valuation ratio for each of the guideline companies,

3. Use the median of the guideline company ratios as the estimate of the valuation ratio for the target company (the mean can be used too if not too distorted by extreme values),
4. Apply the estimated valuation ratios to the target company to estimate its enterprise or equity value.

Valuation ratios have the general form $\frac{x}{y}$, where either x or y is a market-based number (a price or market value), and the other element (y or x) is based on company fundamentals—a non-market-based number usually taken from the financial statements. For example, in the P/S or price to sales ratio, the numerator of equity value or price is a market-based number, while the denominator of sales is a company fundamental.

For most valuation ratios, we can distinguish between *trailing* and *forward* ratios. In the trailing ratio, the fundamental number is its latest reported level. In the forward ratio, the fundamental number is its forecasted level for the next year. Suppose for example that the current equity value of X Inc is CU 2 million. Its latest reported annual sales are CU 1,000,000. Analysts following the company have on average forecasted sales of CU 1.2 million. Then the trailing P/S ratio is $\frac{2,000,000}{1,000,000}$ or 2. The forward P/S ratio is $\frac{2,000,000}{1,200,000}$ or 1.6667.

We turn next to some specific valuation ratios each of which can be constructed as a trailing or forward version. We distinguish between ratios for equity valuation and those for enterprise valuation.

5.3.1 Equity Valuation Ratios

We discuss the following ratios that could be used to value equity:

1. Price-earnings ratio (P/E)
2. PEG ratio (Price-earnings-growth)
3. Price-to-book ratio (P/B)
4. Price to sales ratio (P/S)
5. Dividend yield

5.3.1.1 Price-Earnings Ratio (P/E)

The price-earnings ratio (P/E) of an entity X is given by the formula:

$$\frac{P}{eps}$$

where P starts for the valuation-date share price of entity X ordinary shares, and *eps* is the earnings per share (EPS) for company X—the latest reported 12 months figure (including data from interim reports) in a trailing ratio, or the consensus analyst's forecast of the next year's EPS in a forward ratio.

The numerator and denominator should consistently reflect events like stock splits. We may need to adjust the trailing EPS or the forward EPS for any stock split or other dilutive or anti-dilutive event that took place after the reporting date.

A variant of the ratio avoids this complication by using total rather than per-share numbers. This gives:

$$\text{P/E (Variant)} = \frac{\text{Market capitalization}}{\text{Net income attributable to ordinary shareholders}}.$$

Here the market capitalization is the valuation-date share price multiplied by the valuation-date number of shares outstanding. The denominator is the net income attributable to shareholders of the entity (latest 12 months or consensus forecast for next year). For a group, the denominator would be the net income attributable to shareholders of the parent.

The P/E ratio is only defined when EPS is positive. We cannot compute it when the EPS is negative (i.e., a loss).

P/E Ratio Example

X Inc reported earnings per share of CU 1 on the balance-sheet date of 30 Sep 2018. On 23 Dec 2018 (the valuation date), the share price is CU 0.5. On 1 Nov 2018, X Inc had issued bonus shares in the ratio of 9 bonus shares for every share outstanding. Calculate the trailing P/E ratio.

We first need to adjust the EPS to reflect the post-balance-sheet bonus issue.

The adjusted earnings per share would be CU $1 \times \frac{1}{10}$ or CU 0.10.

Then the P/E ratio is $\frac{0.5}{0.1}$ or 5 times.

5.3.1.2 PEG Ratio (Price-Earnings-Growth)

This is an equity valuation ratio. The PEG ratio is the P/E ratio divided by a measure of the earnings growth rate expressed as a percentage (for example 5% growth is expressed as 5, not 0.05).

Since this ratio has two fundamentals—earnings, and earnings growth, it can be a trailing ratio, a forward ratio or a combination of both, where one of the fundamentals is a forecasted number and the other is a trailing number. Peter Lynch, who popularized the ratio, suggested a trailing P/E divided by a multi-year average annual historical growth rate.

The PEG ratio is only defined when both earnings and earnings growth are positive. It cannot be computed when either number is negative.

PEG Ratio Example

We seek to value Y Inc using a PEG ratio. The guideline companies have a median trailing PEG ratio of 0.8, where earnings growth is based on the arithmetic average annual growth rate of EPS over the last five years. At the valuation date, Y Inc has latest reported 12-month EPS of CU 3. The average annual growth rate of EPS for Y Inc over the last five years is 10%. What is the fair value of a Y Inc share?

Let the fair value be X.

Then we have

$$\frac{(X/3)}{10} = 0.8.$$

Solving for X, we have:

$$X = 0.8 \times 10 \times 3 = CU\ 24.$$

5.3.1.3 P/B Ratio

The P/E and PEG ratios cannot be used to value a company with a loss in the current year (or forecast). The P/B ratio is a more robust ratio that can be calculated as long as the entity does not have negative shareholders' equity.

This ratio is calculated as follows:

$$\text{P/B} = \frac{\text{Market capitalization of equity at valuation date}}{\text{Book value of shareholders' equity}}.$$

Equivalently, we have:

$$\text{P/B} = \frac{\text{Market capitalization of equity at valuation date}}{\text{Book value of net assets}}.$$

The denominator would be as of the latest balance-sheet date (including interim reporting dates) in a trailing ratio, or the forecasted amount for the next financial year-end in a forward ratio.

A trailing P/B ratio is more common, as analysts are less likely to forecast shareholders' equity as opposed to profits.

The ratio could equivalently be defined in terms of per-share numbers.

The ratio is not defined when equity has a negative book value.

An extension of this ratio is the Price to tangible book value ratio. In this extension, goodwill and intangible assets are excluded from the book value in the denominator.

P/B Ratio Example

Z Co has a market capitalization of CU 10 million. Net assets are CU 8 million (latest balance sheet). Total assets include goodwill of CU 6 million and intangibles of CU 3 million. Find the P/B ratio and Price-to-tangible-book ratio.

The P/B ratio is $\frac{10}{8} = 1.25$. Net tangible assets are negative ($8 - 6 - 3 = -1$ million), so the price-to-tangible-book ratio cannot be defined.

5.3.1.4 P/S Ratio

Price-to-sales is estimated as:

$$\text{P/S} = \frac{\text{Market capitalization of equity}}{\text{Sales revenue}},$$

where market capitalization is as of the valuation date and sales revenue could be trailing or forward. The numerator and denominator could equivalently be per-share numbers.

The ratio can be applied even when both earnings and net assets are both negative, though of course in that situation some concern about the entity's viability may be needed. It could be reasonable say for a young company with good prospects whose negative earnings and equity are due to high levels of initial investments in R&D or similar expenses.

The ratio is not useful for some industries where sales revenue is not well-defined, e.g., the financial services industry.

P/S Ratio Example

Company A has sales of CU 10,000,000. Guideline companies have a median P/S ratio of 1.5. Value Company A equity using a P/S ratio.

Estimated fair value of Company A equity

$$= 1.5 \times 10{,}000{,}000$$

$$= CU\ 15{,}000{,}000.$$

5.3.1.5 Dividend Yield

This is an equity valuation ratio. The ratio is defined as follows.

$$\text{Dividend yield} = \frac{\text{Dividend per ordinary share}}{\text{Ordinary share price}}$$

The trailing dividend per share is the last annual dividend (sum of dividends for the last twelve months). The forward dividend per share is the forecasted dividend for the next year.

Dividend yield is particularly applicable in the case of a closely-held entity. Say private company B is 60% owned by a controlling shareholder, and our task is to value the 40% non-controlling interest (NCI). From the viewpoint of the non-controlling shareholder, the value of their interest in B comes from their expected future dividends. Dividends represent what the controlling shareholder chooses to give them.

To value the NCI using dividend yield, we would identify a group of listed guideline companies, all closely-held and dividend-paying. Trading in shares of these companies mainly consists of transactions between current and potential non-controlling shareholders, since the controlling shareholders are unlikely to actively trade their shares on a regular basis.

We can therefore consider the share prices to be a good proxy of the fair value for NCI for these listed guideline companies.

We work out that the guideline-company median trailing dividend yield is 5%. Company B has a trailing dividend per share of CU 0.10. From this, we can work out that the estimated share price of Company B, were it traded, should be:

$$\frac{0.1}{0.05} = \text{CU}\,2.$$

Some further adjustments would be needed to get the fair value of NCI—we would need to estimate a discount for lack of marketability. We will discuss such adjustments in a later chapter.

5.3.2 Enterprise Valuation Ratios

We discuss the following enterprise valuation ratios:

1. EV/EBITDA (Enterprise value to EBITDA)
2. EV/Sales (Enterprise value to Sales)
3. Tobin's Q

5.3.2.1 Enterprise Value (EV) in Ratios

The numerator in all these ratios is Enterprise value (EV). This can be defined as the valuation-date fair value of the *invested capital* in the enterprise.

The invested capital includes both shareholders' equity and debt. The debt amount treated as invested capital is calculated in different ways in practice. One approach is to only consider long-term debt (including its current maturity). Another approach is to include all interest-bearing debt. With both approaches, we would include lease liabilities, and we would exclude provisions and deferred tax liabilities.

In a complex capital structure with preference shares or multiple classes of shares, these different types of shares must also be separately included in the EV calculation. Also, if we are calculating EV for a group, we would add the value of non-controlling interests (NCI) in the group's subsidiaries.

To sum up, if a company has preference shares, ordinary shares, debt capital and NCI in its capital structure with valuation-date market values (fair values) of MVPREF, MVORD, MVDEBT and MVNCI respectively, we have:

$$EV = MVORD + MVPREF + MVDEBT + MVNCI. \tag{5.1}$$

For MVNCI, we usually resort to using the latest reported book value of NCI as the best proxy.

If the company had issued convertible bonds, then we would analyze these as a combination of non-convertible bonds (debt) and a conversion option (usually included in equity). IAS 32 requires companies to perform this analysis anyway, and to present these two components separately, in debt and in equity respectively.

The market value of ordinary equity (MVORD) can be directly measured for a listed guideline company, by simply taking the valuation-date share price and multiplying it by the valuation-date number of shares.

How do we find the market value of debt (MVDEBT)? For publicly traded debt instruments, we can get their market prices directly (Level 2 inputs).

We can also use the fact that IFRS 7 requires entities to report the fair value of various classes of financial instruments. Disclosure of the fair value is required even when these instruments are not carried at fair value. These financial instruments include debt instruments. If the latest financial statements are sufficiently recent, and the debt markets are not very volatile, we can use these reported numbers as estimates of the fair value of debt.

Some elements of debt included in invested capital may not be in the scope of IFRS 7. So their fair value may not be reported in the financial statements. For such items, in the absence of better information, we may assume that their latest reported book value is approximately equal to their fair value.

Summarizing, we can estimate the valuation-date fair value of debt as follows:

$$MVDEBT = MVDEBT1 + MVDEBT2 + BVDEBT3,$$

where:

MVDEBT1 = the valuation-date market value of traded debt instruments for which reliable price quotes are available.

MVDEBT2 = the latest reported fair value of debt items included in invested capital excluding items in MVDEBT1.

BVDEBT3 = the carrying amount (from the latest financial statements) of debt items included in invested capital whose fair value is not reflected in MVDEBT1 or MVDEBT2.

For a convertible bond whose price is available from the market, its fair value can be analyzed into debt or equity portions. But for the purpose of estimating EV, it is fine to just include the full price. This is because EV is an aggregate of both debt and equity. Also, there is no double counting, since MVORD does not reflect the value of the conversion options—it is based on the quoted price of ordinary shares, whose holders do not own these options.

A standard shortcut in practice is to just use the book value of all debt (that is, the entire debt portion of invested capital) in lieu of the market value. So if the book value of debt is BVDEBT, a shortcut formula for EV is:

$$EV \text{ (Variant 1)} = MVORD + MVNCI + MVPREF + BVDEBT. \tag{5.2}$$

Another standard practice is to subtract cash from the expression for EV in either Equation 5.1 or Equation 5.2. Subtracting from Equation 5.1, we would get:

$$EV \text{ (Variant 2)} = MVORD + MVPREF + MVDEBT1 + MVDEBT2 + BVDEBT3 + MVNCI - CASH$$

where CASH refers to the fair value of the entity's cash and cash equivalents at the valuation date (the latest balance-sheet figure).

The logic of subtracting cash is that if an acquirer pays off all equityholders and creditors and takes over the entire invested capital, then the acquirer could immediately use the target's cash to subsidize their takeover cost. This logic assumes that the cash is not needed for some internal purpose or to protect against some operating emergency. In our examples, we will not make this assumption and will not subtract cash.

Example: EV Calculation

We are determining the EV of Company G as of a valuation date of 1 Mar 2018. On that date, Company G has listed bonds with a combined market price of CU 80 million. These include a convertible bond with market price CU 7 million. On the latest balance-sheet date of 1 Jan 2018, Company G reported a fair value of debt equal to CU 89 million, excluding the value of listed bond instruments. The company reported finance lease liabilities worth CU 20 million (book value) at the same date. On the valuation date, Company G has 83 million ordinary shares outstanding trading at a share price of CU 3. In addition, Company G has 23 million 9% cumulative non-redeemable preference shares outstanding, trading at a price of CU 1. NCI in Company G subsidiaries has a reported book value of CU 9 million on the latest balance-sheet date. Calculate the EV.

We have:

		CU (million)
MVORD=	83 m. × CU 3 =	249
MVPREF=	23 m. × CU 1 =	23
MVNCI =	Book value=	9
MVDEBT1=		80
MVDEBT2=		89
BVDEBT3=		20

Therefore:

$$MVDEBT\ \text{(CU millions)} = 80 + 89 + 20 = 189.$$

Therefore, we have (in CU millions):

$$\begin{aligned} EV &= MVORD + MVPREF + NCI + MVDEBT \\ &= 249 + 23 + 9 + 189 \\ &= 470. \end{aligned}$$

5.3.2.2 EV/EBITDA Ratio

This ratio can be calculated as follows:

$$EV/EBITDA = \frac{EV}{EBITDA}$$

where EBITDA stands for annual earnings before interest, taxation, depreciation and amortization. EBITDA can be calculated by taking profits before interest and tax (PBIT or EBIT), a standard income-statement line item, and then adding back any depreciation or amortization expense that was reflected in calculating EBIT. As usual, EBITDA could be on a trailing or a forward basis. (Note that book values included in EV are always latest trailing numbers.)

EV/EBITDA Ratio Example

Company G has an EV of CU 470 million. Its latest reported annual EBIT (latest four quarters total) is CU 50 million. Depreciation expenses of CU 20 million were deducted in arriving at the EBIT figure. Find the EV/EBITDA.

We have:

$$EV/EBITDA = \frac{470}{50 + 20} = 6.71.$$

5.3.2.3 EV/Sales Ratio

This ratio is given by:

$$EV/Sales = \frac{EV}{Sales}$$

where sales represents a year's sales revenue (either trailing or forward).

Like the P/S ratio, EV/Sales is computable even when profits are negative or shareholders' equity is negative, and it is not well-defined for the financial services industry.

EV/Sales Example

We seek the fair value of invested capital for private Company H. The median guideline company EV/Sales ratio is 3.2. Company H has latest reported one-year sales of CU 10 million. What is its enterprise value?

We have as our estimate of EV in CU millions:

$$EV = 3.2 \times 10 = 32.$$

5.3.2.4 Tobin's Q

Tobin's Q is a proposed measure of company performance that seeks to dispense with financial statement numbers. In its ideal form, it can be constructed using only market information.

In its ideal form, Q is defined as:

$$Q = \frac{EV}{RC}$$

where EV is the enterprise value and RC is the replacement cost of the enterprise's total assets (this is a current market value, not the historical cost number). The extent by which the enterprise's value to the market (EV) exceeds the amount that it would need to reassemble all its assets from scratch (RC) gives a measure of how effective the management is in utilizing its assets to generate new value.

In practice, RC is difficult to determine and dependent on subjective judgements. A simplification is to use the book value of total assets rather than RC. This gives us the Perfect-Wiles simple Q (Perfect and Wiles 1994), which we can call q_s, given by:

$$q_s = \frac{EV}{BVTA}$$

where BVTA is the book value of total assets either from the latest balance-sheet (trailing), or as forecasted for next year (forward). A trailing ratio is more common, as analysts do not typically issue forecasts of total assets.

The Perfect-Wiles simple Q is highly correlated with attempts to construct more ideal versions of Q (correlation greater than 90%). It is easier to calculate and less dependent on subjective judgements. We will stick to q_s in our examples.

Tobin's Q (q_s) Example

Company I has total assets (latest book value) equal to CU 84 million. The median q_s for guideline companies is 1.8 times. Estimate the EV of Company I.

Our estimate of the EV in CU millions:

$$84 \times 1.8 = 151.2.$$

5.3.3 Subjective Judgements in the Ratio-Based Approach

The valuation-ratio approach is at first glance a better approach than the discounted cash flow approach, since it relies on Level 2 inputs to a greater degree. But there are at least three ways in which subjective choices affect ratio-based valuation.

Firstly, the choice of guideline companies is partly subjective, though it is largely determined by mechanical considerations such as similar size and industry. The valuer can exercise discretion in the range of allowable sizes, the particular size measure to use, and how broadly to define the industry.

Secondly, the financial-statement numbers used in valuation ratios may require some adjustments before being applied. For example, suppose that we are valuing a private company using a guideline company median P/E of 10 times. The company's

EPS is CU 15 as of the latest reported twelve months. So we could directly estimate a fair price per share of 150 (15 × 10). But suppose, on closer examination, the EPS includes a one-off gain of CU 14, from divesting a subsidiary during the year. Logically, we should exclude this gain to get a more normal EPS of CU 1. Using this to find the fair price per share gives us CU 10, which is clearly more reasonable.

Adjustments such as removing this one-off gain are known as *income normalization* and are often required to get reasonable valuations. Income normalization to some extent involves subjective judgements.

Thirdly, the choice of ratio affects the value estimate. Ideally different ratios should give approximately similar estimates of value. But in practice, there are often significant differences between value estimates produced by different ratios. Given the wide variety of ratios that can be used, this raises the fear that an accountant could shop for a ratio that gives them a desired value.

Given the significant role of subjective judgement, the advantage of ratio-based valuation over the DCF approach is not clear-cut. There could be situations where an accountant may reasonably conclude that a DCF approach is less reliant on Level 3 inputs than a ratio-based valuation.

5.4 Discounted Cash Flow (DCF) Models Introduction

The discounted cash flow (DCF) approach values a business as the present value of a forecasted stream of cash flows to the investor.

Reflecting the assumption that an enterprise is a going concern, this valuation is over an infinite horizon, that is, the cashflows are assumed to continue forever.[1]

The general form of a DCF model to value an enterprise or equity is given in Equation 5.3.

$$V_0 = \sum_{y=1}^{\infty} \frac{CF_y}{(1 + k_y)^{t[y]}} \tag{5.3}$$

where y indexes financial years after the valuation date, CF_y is the projected cash flow to the investor corresponding to financial year y, k_y is the appropriate discount rate for discounting CF_y, and $t[y]$ is the time in years from today when CF_y is assumed to occur (usually the middle of the financial year).

5.4.1 Discounting at a Risk-Free Rate vs a Risk-Adjusted Rate

In DCF models we have two choices:

[1]This may seem unrealistic, but in practice, discounting ensures that the impact of very distant future cash flows will be negligible.

Risk-Free Rate
Firstly, we can adjust the projected cashflows to derive hypothetical risk-free or certainty-equivalent cashflows, and then discount these at the risk-free rate. To arrive at the certainty-equivalent cashflow, we must subtract an estimate of the amount it would cost to insure the cashflow against default.

Risk-Adjusted Rate
Alternatively, we can leave the cashflows unadjusted, and discount them at a risk-adjusted rate (the cost of capital). This is typically estimated by starting with the risk-free rate and adding a spread to reflect risk.

Approach in Our Book
The two methods should give the same valuation if parameters are determined consistently.

The risk-adjusted rate approach is more standard in practice. We will therefore focus on this approach in the remainder of this book.

5.5 One-Stage and Multi-stage DCF Models

We cannot literally keep counting cash flows to infinity. So our summation has to terminate after some finite number of years in an estimate of the value at that point, called the *terminal value*.

This terminal value could use the formula for the present value of a growing perpetuity.

The present value of a stream of annual cash flows growing forever at growth rate g starting from a current level of CF_0, and discounted at a constant discount rate k, where k must be strictly greater than g the growth rate,[2] is given by:

$$V_0 = \frac{CF_0(1+g)}{k-g}.$$

5.5.1 One-Stage Models

A one-stage model is simply the present value of a growing perpetuity. We have:

$$V_0 = \frac{CF_0(1+g)}{k-g}$$

[2]Otherwise the present value is infinite.

where CF_0 is the current level of the relevant cashflow, g is the assumed constant growth rate, and k is the constant discount rate, where k must be strictly greater than g.

The assumed long-run growth rate g should not exceed the long-run growth rate of GDP in a mature economy (as a thumb-rule, not more than 3%). If the growth rate is higher than this, the entity is projected to grow faster than the rest of the economy forever. It logically follows that at some future point, the entity would dominate the whole economy, and if its growth rate persists, that the GDP (dominated by the entity) would also grow at a faster rate. To avoid these unrealistic implications, we must keep g lower than the long-run growth rate of GDP in a mature economy.

5.5.1.1 Example: One-Stage Model

Ho Inc will pay a dividend per ordinary share of CU 1.40 next year. The company faces a cost of equity of 6%. The projected long-run growth rate of dividends per share is 2% per year. Using a one-stage model, find the fair price of an ordinary share of Ho Inc.

We have:

$$V_0 = \frac{1.40}{0.06 - 0.02} = CU\ 35.$$

We do not multiply the numerator by the growth rate, as the number of CU 1.40 is already *next* year's cashflow.

5.5.2 Two-Stage Model

The one-stage model may understate the value of a young growing firm that is (temporarily) growing faster than the long-run GDP growth rate.

An alternative is to assume a higher growth rate for an initial finite period called the high-growth period (first stage), followed by an infinite period of lower growth, called the mature period (second stage). This general form of the model is called a two-stage model.

We have for the general two-stage model.

$$V_0 = \left(\sum_{y=1}^{N} \frac{CF_0(1+g_1)^y}{(1+k_1)^{t[y]}} \right) + \frac{\left(\frac{CF_0(1+g_1)^N(1+g_2)}{k_2-g_2} \right)}{(1+k_1)^{t[N]}}$$

Here CF_0 is the current level of the relevant cashflow, g_1 is the growth rate during the high-growth stage, k_1 is the relevant discount rate during the high-growth stage, N is the number of years during which the high-growth stage continues, y indexes years from 1 to N, $t[y]$ represents the time in years from today when the cashflow for year y is assumed to occur, g_2 is the long-run infinite-horizon growth rate, where

$g_2 < g_1$, k_2 is the long-run discount rate where $k_2 < k_1$ (the entity becomes less risky as it becomes more mature and stable, and correspondingly investors are willing to accept a lower return on investment).

5.5.2.1 Example: Two-Stage Model

Ho Inc will pay a dividend of CU 1.40 per ordinary share next year, projected to grow at 5% per year in the subsequent 2 years (years 2 to 3), and at 2% per year thereafter. The cost of equity in the high-growth stage (years 1 to 3) is 10%, while the cost of equity in the long-run stage is 6%. Find the value of an ordinary share of Ho Inc. using a two-stage model. Assume that cashflows occur at year-end.

We have:

$$V_0 = \frac{1.40}{1.1} + \frac{1.40 \times 1.05}{1.1^2} + \frac{1.40 \times 1.05^2}{1.1^3} + \frac{\left(\frac{1.40 \times 1.05^2 \times 1.02}{0.06-0.02}\right)}{1.1^3} = CU\ 33.2184.$$

5.5.3 Three-Stage Models

The two-stage model can be easily generalized to a larger number of stages. For example, let us consider a three-stage model.

Let g_1, g_2, and g_3 represent the growth rates in the first, second, and third (infinite-horizon) stages respectively.

Let k_1, k_2, and k_3 reflect the forward discount rates during the first, second and third stages respectively.

Let N_1 give the number of years in the first stage. Let N_2 give the number of years in the first and second stages combined, so that the number of years in the second stage is $N_2 - N_1$.

Then we have:

$$V_0 = \left(\sum_{y=1}^{N_1} \frac{CF_0(1+g_1)^y}{(1+k_1)^{t[y]}}\right) + \left(\sum_{a=N_1+1}^{N_2} \frac{CF_0(1+g_1)^{N_1}(1+g_2)^{(a-N_1)}}{(1+k_1)^{t[N_1]}(1+k_2)^{(t[a]-t[N_1])}}\right) + \frac{\left(\frac{CF_0(1+g_1)^{N_1}(1+g_2)^{(N_2-N_1)}(1+g_3)}{k_3-g_3}\right)}{(1+k_1)^{t[N_1]}(1+k_2)^{(t[N_2]-t[N_1])}}.$$

5.5.3.1 Example: Three-Stage Model

Ho Inc has a dividend per ordinary share next year of CU 1.40. The dividend is projected to grow at 10% per year for the subsequent two years (years 2 and 3), and then at 8% for the following two years (years 4 and 5), and then to grow at 2% thereafter. The cost of equity for the first 3 years is 11%, the cost of equity for years

4 and 5 is 10%, and the cost of equity after year 5 is 6%. Find the fair price of a Ho Inc share using a three-stage model.

We have:

$$\begin{aligned} V_0 = {} & \frac{1.40}{1.11} + \frac{1.40 \times 1.1}{1.11^2} + \frac{1.40 \times 1.1^2}{1.11^3} + \\ & \frac{1.40 \times 1.1^2 \times 1.08}{1.10 \times 1.11^3} + \frac{1.40 \times 1.1^2 \times 1.08^2}{1.10^2 \times 1.11^3} + \\ & \frac{\left(\frac{1.40 \times 1.1^2 \times 1.08^2 \times 1.02}{0.06 - 0.02}\right)}{1.10^2 \times 1.11^3} \\ = {} & CU\ 36.6071. \end{aligned}$$

5.5.4 The Fuller-Hsia H-Model

In the two-stage model, the growth rate abruptly falls from the high growth rate g_1 to the low growth rate g_2. The H-model (Fuller and Hsia 1984) is a variant of a two-stage model that allows the growth rate to fall in a linear fashion over the high-growth period. See Fig. 5.1.

In the model $t[y]$ equals y for year y, or cashflows occur at year-end. Also, the discount rate to be used is constant. Let this rate be k.

Then we can use the following approximate formula[3]:

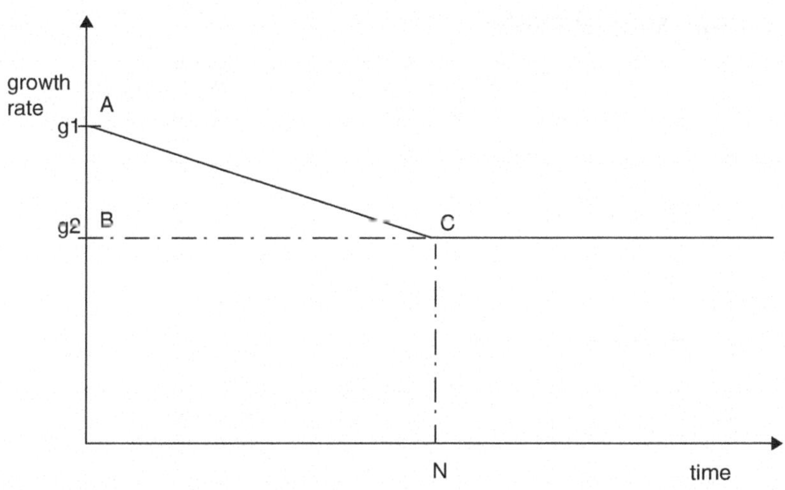

Fig. 5.1 Fuller-Hsia H-model

[3]In the original Fuller and Hsia paper, the parameter H is used to denote our $\frac{N}{2}$. This is why the model is often called the H-model.

$$V_0 = \frac{CF_0(1+g_2)}{k-g_2} + \frac{CF_0 \times \frac{N}{2} \times (g_1 - g_2)}{k-g_2}$$

The model estimates value as the sum of:

1. The value of the cashflows growing forever at growth rate g_2, and
2. An approximate measure of the value added from the initial high-growth period. It is the value that would result if the entire incremental growth represented by the area of triangle ABC ($\triangle ABC$ in geometry notation) were realized in year 1, and were to grow forever thereafter at the stable growth rate g_2. The area of a triangle is given by the formula $\frac{1}{2} \times$ base $\times$ height. For $\triangle ABC$, the base is N or number of years in the high-growth period. The height is $(g_1 - g_2)$, or the difference in growth rates.

Example: H-Model

Da Costa Inc has dividends per ordinary share of CU 1.20 in the current year. These are projected to grow at 10% per year over the next 10 years, and at 2% per year thereafter. The cost of equity is 6%. Value a Da Costa Inc ordinary share using an H-model.

We have:

$$\frac{1.20 \times 1.02}{0.06 - 0.02} + \frac{1.20 \times 5 \times 0.08}{0.06 - 0.02} = CU\ 42.60.$$

5.5.4.1 Three-Stage H-Model

The model can easily be extended to three or more stages. In the three-stage version, cash flows first grow at a high rate g_1 for N_1 years, then decline linearly to a lower rate g_2 in a second stage between N_1 and N_2 years, and finally grow forever after N_2 years at the rate g_2, as shown in Fig. 5.2.

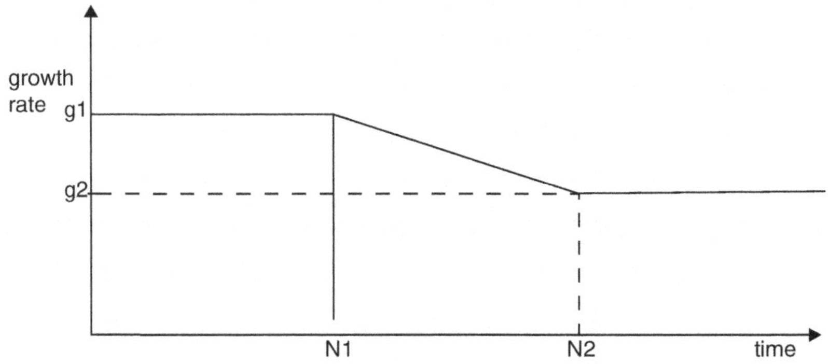

Fig. 5.2 Three-stage H-model

The value is given by:

$$V_0 = \sum_{t=1}^{N_1} \frac{CF_0(1+g_1)^t}{(1+k)^t} + \frac{1}{(1+k)^{N_1}} \times \left(\frac{CF_0(1+g_1)^{N_1}(1+g_2)}{k-g_2} + \frac{CF_0(1+g_1)^{N_1}(g_1-g_2)\frac{N_2-N_1}{2}}{k-g_2} \right)$$

5.5.5 General Multi-stage Model

The models that we discussed earlier all start with a current cash flow and apply a growth rate parameter to project it into the future. A more general procedure is to directly forecast the cash flows each year for an initial number of years known as the *planning period* and then estimate a terminal value at the end of that period. We have:

$$V_0 = \sum_{y=1}^{N} \frac{CF_y}{(1+k_y)^{t[y]}} + \frac{TV}{(1+k_N)^{t[N]}}$$

Here CF_y is the projected cashflow for year y, k_y is the discount rate for year y, $t[y]$ is the time in years from today when CF_y is assumed to occur, N is the number of years in the planning period, and TV is the terminal value—the estimated value of the enterprise (or equity) at the end of the planning period. TV could be determined using any of the models discussed earlier—one-stage, two-stage, three-stage, or H-model. We could also use a ratio-based valuation approach to determine TV.

5.5.5.1 Example: General Multi-stage Model

Kannan Inc has the following projections of free cash flow (FCF_y) for the next 5 years (in CU). The discount rate for discounting free cash flows from time 0 to the end of each year y is shown as k_y.

Year y	*1*	*2*	*3*	*4*	*5*
FCF_y	*100*	*110*	*120*	*125*	*130*
k_y	*0.08*	*0.09*	*0.10*	*0.11*	*0.12*

The discount rate after 5 years will be 12%. The long-run growth rate of free cash flows after year 5 will be 2%. Find the enterprise value of Kannan Inc using a general multi-stage model. Assume cashflows at year-end.

We have:

$$\frac{100}{1.08}+\frac{110}{1.09^2}+\frac{120}{1.1^3}+\frac{125}{1.11^4}+\frac{130}{1.12^5}+\frac{\left(\frac{130\times 1.02}{0.12-0.02}\right)}{1.12^5}=1183.85.$$

5.6 Equity Valuation Models Based on DCF

Two equity valuation models using DCF are:

1. The dividend discount model
2. The flow-to-equity (FTE) model

5.6.1 The Dividend Discount Model (DDM)

In the dividend discount model (DDM), the value of equity is determined as the present value of expected future dividends. The discount rate is the cost of equity, or the rate of return demanded by investors in the entity's equity, usually expressed as an annually compounded rate. We denote this rate as $k_{t,e}$ if it varies with maturity t, or simply as k_e if it is constant for all maturities.

The one-stage form of the DDM is called the Gordon growth model (GGM) (Gordon 1959). We have (Equation 5.4):

$$V_0=\frac{dps_0(1+g)}{k_e-g} \tag{5.4}$$

where V_0 is the fair value of a share, dps_0 is the base dividend, g is the projected growth rate of dividends into the infinite future, and k_e is the cost of equity, assumed constant, and expressed as an annually compounded rate.

Similarly, we can have two-stage models, three-stage models, H-models and general multi-stage models based on dividends.

Dividends often have a fairly predictable pattern over time, since they are a matter of policy. This may enhance the stability of the model relative to alternatives that use more uncertain cashflows.

DDM Example

Png Co currently pays an annual dividend per share of CU 0.50. The company has a history of increasing dividends per share by CU 0.01 every five years. Our valuation date is the ex-dividend date, and the next dividend is expected to be CU 0.01 higher than the current one (i.e., the next dividend is the first one in the next five-year cycle). The cost of equity is 10%. Value the share using a dividend discount model.

We can use the formula for a constant perpetuity of x per period, discounted at k per period, which is $\frac{x}{k}$.

The stream of cashflows can be analyzed as a stream of CU 0.5 per year forever, plus an increment every five years of a perpetuity worth CU 0.01 per year forever. A discount rate of 10% per year is equivalent to a discount rate of $(1.1^5 - 1)$ or 61.051% per five-year period.

Putting these facts together, we have:

$$V_0 = \frac{0.5}{0.1} + \frac{0.01}{0.1} \times \frac{1}{1.1^5 - 1} = CU\ 5.16.$$

5.6.2 The Flow-to-Equity (FTE) Model

The DDM may understate the value of equity in a growing entity where dividend payments have been historically low or zero, as the entity would reinvest most of its profits to maintain its growth. Extrapolating these low dividends into the distant future ignores the fact that dividend payments should increase as growth slows.

Consider the entire cashflow available to shareholders, called the flow to equity or FTE. This entire amount is theoretically controlled by shareholders. They can collectively choose to use it in their best interests. They could either pay themselves a dividend in the current year or they can reinvest the money and use the resulting growth to pay themselves a higher dividend later.

We can therefore view the entire FTE as the cashflow to the shareholders, whether they receive a distribution or not. Therefore, we can use the present value of projected FTE to value the shareholders' interest.

5.6.2.1 Control Perspective

The FTE model reflects a *control perspective*, that is, that the shareholders control the entire cashflow available to them.

This perspective can be unrealistic in practice for several reasons.

Firstly, shareholders' control of cashflows is usually not direct, but through an agent—the management. This agent need not always act in the shareholders' best interest.

Secondly, the control perspective asserts that shareholders control the cashflows *as a unified body*. But that body may be diverse and changing, so that even if the shareholders could decide directly on the use of cashflows, they would likely disagree.

Thirdly, an entity could be controlled by a single controlling interest, in which case the controlling interest has effectively full control, but the other shareholders (the NCI or non-controlling interest) have no control. An FTE model would not be suitable to value NCI without some adjustments for their lack of control.

The FTE model best fits two situations—one where an entity is completely controlled by a single shareholder, and second during a takeover attempt, when the potential acquirer uses a control perspective to decide how much to pay for the shares.

In other situations, such as valuing an entity with diffuse ownership, or valuation of a non-controlling interest, the FTE model is likely to overstate value. The FTE model is sometimes used as a starting point in such situations and then adjusted downwards by applying an estimated discount due to lack of control (DLOC).

5.6.2.2 FTE Computation

The FTE could be computed directly from the cashflow statement, but in practice, a cruder estimate is used, derived from the B/S and I/S. The reason is that the underlying numbers in the cruder calculation usually have a more predictable trend and so these numbers are easier to forecast.

We first explain the cashflow-statement-based number. This is as follows:

$$\begin{aligned} FTE_{CFS} = &\text{ Cash flow from operations (unlevered)} \\ &\underline{\text{Less:}} \text{ Interest paid} \\ &\underline{\text{Less:}} \text{ Net capital expenditure} \\ &\underline{\text{Less:}} \text{ Net repayments of debt} \end{aligned}$$

If interest paid is reflected in the cash flow from operations already (that is, it is a levered number) then there is no need to subtract it separately.

Example: SAP FTE_{CFS} for 2017

From the 2017 annual report of SAP SE, we have (numbers in € million):

Levered cashflow from operations		5,045
Net capital expenditure		(1,112)
(Net cashflows from investing)		
Net debt repayments:		
Debt repayments	(1,391)	
Proceeds from borrowing	27	(1,364)
FTE_{CFS}		2,569

FTE Crude Measure

The FTE based on the B/S and I/S is as follows:

$$\begin{aligned} FTE_{BSIS} = &\text{ Net income} && (1) \\ &\underline{\text{Add:}} \text{ Depreciation and amortization expenses} && (2) \\ &\underline{\text{Less:}} \text{ Net increase in non-cash working capital} && (3) \\ &\underline{\text{Less:}} \text{ Net capital expenditure (CAPEX)} && (4) \\ &\underline{\text{Less:}} \text{ Net repayment of debt} && (5) \end{aligned}$$

Here the first three lines (1) to (3) give a crude measure of the levered cashflow from operations. As usual working capital is defined as net current assets, CAPEX may be defined as the acquisitions net of disposals of PPE during the period, plus the acquisition net of disposals of other noncurrent assets that the valuer identifies as capital in nature, net repayments of debt are repayments less new borrowings, and exclude lease liabilities where repayment is not in cash.

SAP FTE_{BSIS} for 2017

Here is the calculation of the crude FTE measure for SAP SE for 2017, based on their 2017 annual report.[4] Numbers are in € million.

Profit after tax	4,056
Depreciation and amortization	1,272
Increase in non-cash working capital	377
CAPEX	(840)
Less: Net repayment of debt	
(change in financial liabilities)	(1,699)
FTE_{BSIS}	3,166

The CAPEX is calculated as the increase in the combined balances of PPE and intangibles net of depreciation and amortization of €1,272 million.

The net repayment of debt is calculated as the net decrease in financial liabilities (both current and non-current portions) from 2016 to 2017.

This estimation is cruder than FTE_{CFS} and certainly less accurate as a measure of the performance in the current year. But it is easier to project into the future, using proforma balance-sheets and income statements.

5.6.2.3 FTE DCF Model

The general form of the FTE model is as follows:

$$V_0 = \sum_{y=1}^{\infty} \frac{FTE_y}{(1 + k_{y,e})^{t[y]}}.$$

As before, y indexes financial years in the future, $k_{y,e}$ is the cost of equity appropriate to discount the year y cash flow (FTE_y), FTE_y is the flow to equity

[4] I took the depreciation number and the change in working capital number from the indirect-method reconciliation in the cash flow statement. For change in working capital, it is the net change in the following listed items: net trade receivables, other non-cash-item adjustments, other assets, trade payables, and deferred income.

for financial year y, and $t[y]$ is the time in years from today when cash flow FTE_y is assumed to occur.

Example: FTE DCF Model

Amon Inc has a FTE this year of CU 4,000, projected to grow at 2% per year. The company faces a cost of equity of 8%. Find the value of Amon Inc equity based on a one-stage FTE model.

We have:

$$V_0 = \frac{4{,}000 \times (1.02)}{0.08 - 0.02} = CU\ 68{,}000.$$

5.7 DCF Models for Enterprise Valuation

When we value the entire enterprise, we are valuing the *invested capital*. This includes the investment from ordinary shareholders as well as the investment from other types of investors including holders of debt instruments, preference shares or convertible bonds.

In defining invested capital, we exclude pure operating liabilities like accounts payable, unearned revenue, derivative contracts used for hedging, deferred tax liabilities and provisions. If we use the umbrella term "operating liabilities" to refer to these, we have the following balance-sheet equation:

$$\text{Total Assets} - \text{Operating liabilities} = \text{Invested capital.}$$

In DCF-based enterprise valuation, we seek to value the right-hand side of this equation (invested capital), but indirectly, by valuing the left-hand side. To do this, we project the net distributable cashflows generated by the items on the left-hand side, and find their present value.

When valuing an enterprise, we can partition it into different types of operations (business segments) and value each of them separately. This is called sum-of-the-parts valuation. We start by discussing this approach.

We then turn to three different DCF models for enterprise valuation:

1. The weighted average cost of capital (WACC) model
2. The adjusted present value (APV) model
3. The residual income model

5.7.1 Sum-of-the-Parts Valuation

When valuing the entire enterprise, a good practice is to separate out assets that are not directly used in the business operations, and value these separately. For example, the enterprise may hold an investment portfolio that is purely supplementary to its main business activities. Very likely, this investment portfolio value would be reported at fair value under IFRS 9. We can take this investment portfolio out of total assets, and value it separately using its latest reported value. Then we use DCF valuation only for the cashflows generated by the remaining assets.

For example, suppose the value of the investment portfolio was CU 10 million as reported in the latest balance sheet. We project the cashflows generated by the remaining assets and present-value them, getting a present value of CU 100 million. Then the value of the enterprise is (numbers in CU million):

Fair value of operations	100
Fair value of investment portfolio	10
Enterprise value	110

When we separate out assets, we should also take out related income and expense items, and any directly related liabilities. For example, gains on the investment portfolio should not be reflected in the projected financial statements used to project cashflow. Suppose that we have a derivative liability that is classified as a hedging instrument of the investment portfolio. We should exclude that derivative liability from our projected financial statements, and value it together with the investment portfolio.

We can extend this principle to an entity that is diversified and has several different business segments. Consider for example, conglomerates like Siemens (Germany), Cheung Kong Hutchison (Hong Kong), or Keppel (Singapore).

For such companies, we can group assets by business segments, and value each segment separately, then add up the respective segment values to get the enterprise value. We can use the company's own segment disclosure under IFRS 8 *Operating segments* as a starting point for our projections.

Then to value each segment, we would project cash flows separately from that segment, and assess their present value using a cost of capital measure that is specific to that segment.

5.7.1.1 Sum of the Parts Example

Company X has two business segments—one is an oilseeds refining division, and the other is an airconditioner manufacturing division.

The oilseeds division has total assets of CU 100 million. The airconditioner division has total assets of CU 200 million.

The free cash flow from the oilseeds division is projected to be CU 12 million next year, and will grow at 2% each year thereafter. (We get into free cash flow later. For now, sufficient to define it as the cashflow distributable to holders of invested capital). The cost of capital (discount rate) for the oilseeds division is 10%.

The free cash flow from the airconditioner division is projected to be CU 18 million next year, and will grow at 2.5% every year thereafter. The cost of capital (discount rate) for the airconditioner division is 15%.

In addition to the two business segments, Company X has an investment portfolio worth CU 10 million at the latest balance-sheet date.

Now, we can find the enterprise value of Company X by separately valuing the two segments and then adding up their values, plus the value of the investment portfolio.

For the oilseeds division, using a one-stage model, we get (monetary amounts in CU million):

$$\frac{12}{10\% - 2\%} = 150.$$

For the airconditioner division, using a one-stage model, we get (monetary amounts in CU million):

$$\frac{18}{15\% - 2.5\%} = 144.$$

Therefore the enterprise value of Company X is CU 304 million, with the breakdown as follows (numbers in CU million):

Oilseeds division	150
Airconditioner division	144
Investment portfolio	10
Enterprise value	304

We can also apply sum of the parts using ratio-based valuation. Suppose that the current EBITDA of the oilseeds division is CU 13 million, while that for the airconditioner division is CU 20 million.

We have identified a group of oilseeds companies to serve as guidelines for the oilseeds division, and a group of airconditioner companies to serve as guidelines for the airconditioner division.

The median EV/EBITDA ratio for the oilseeds guideline companies is 8 times.

The median EV/EBITDA ratio for the airconditioner guideline companies is 9 times.

Then the estimated enterprise value based on the EV/EBITDA ratio is as follows (monetary amounts in CU million):

Oilseeds division	104	[8 × 13]
Airconditioner division	180	[9 × 20]
Investment portfolio	10	
Enterprise value	294	

5.7.1.2 Sum-of-the-Parts Advantage

Enterprise valuation is conceptually better than equity valuation because of the ability to partition operations into different segments that can be valued separately using separate sets of parameters.

We usually do not have this ability in equity valuation, as net assets are more difficult to partition into segments as opposed to total assets (less operating liabilities). It is less easy to assign non-current liabilities such as debt to different segments than it is for assets, particularly when financing activities are centralized.

In valuing equity, it is therefore often considered better practice to value the enterprise first, and then subtract the fair value of debt to arrive at the value of equity. (If there are other capital structure components such as preferred shares, we subtract their value too).

This indirect valuation of equity as a residual also conforms better to the entity perspective that underlies the IFRS conceptual framework. This is because it values equity as simply the excess of assets over liabilities, rather than as a particular stakeholder's interest.

5.7.2 Cashflows in Enterprise Valuation

We can measure the cashflows for enterprise valuation using the following measures:

1. Cashflow to investors (CFI)
2. Free cash flow (FCF)

Cashflow to investors (CFI) consists of net distributions to holders of invested capital during the year. This extends the logic of the dividend discount model to enterprise valuation.

Free cash flow (FCF) consists of the net cashflow available to distribute to holders of invested capital during the year. This extends the logic of the FTE model to enterprise valuation. Like the FTE model, it reflects a control perspective.

The two cashflow measures are related as follows:

$$FCF = CFI + \Delta Cash.$$

where $\Delta Cash$ is the net increase in cash and cash equivalents during the year.

5.7.2.1 Cashflow to Investors (CFI)

Cashflow to investors is the sum of net distributions to ordinary shareholders and net distributions to other holders of invested capital such as debt, during a particular period, usually a year.

Net distributions to ordinary shareholders are as follows:

	Ordinary-share dividends paid during the year
Add:	Other distributions to ordinary shareholders during the year (buy-backs, etc.)
Less:	Contributions from ordinary shareholders during the year (new issues, etc.)

Net distributions to debtholders during a year are as follows:

	Interest paid during the year
Add:	Debt principal amounts repaid during the year
Less:	New debt raised during the year

The CFI would be the sum of these two figures, plus the net distributions to other types of invested capital such as preference shareholders (preference dividends plus redemption of preference shares less new issues of preference shares) or NCI (dividends paid to NCI plus buyback of NCI shares less increase in NCI holdings).

Cashflow to investors is derived from the liabilities and equity side of the balance sheet. Since this side of the balance sheet cannot be partitioned easily into different operating segments, we cannot use CFI in sum-of-the-parts valuation (where we are partitioning the assets side of the balance sheet).

Example: CFI for SAP (2017)

We calculate the cashflow to investors from the cash flow statement of SAP in their 2017 annual report. Numbers are in € million.

Cashflows to shareholders		
Dividends paid	1,499	
Purchase of treasury shares	500	1,999
Cashflows to debtholders		
Repayment of borrowings	1,391	
Interest paid	200	
Tax shield on interest	(52.8)	
New borrowings	(27)	1,511.2
Cashflows to NCI		
Dividends paid to NCI	45	
Other transactions with NCI	(2)	43
CFI		3,553.2

5.7.2.2 Free Cash Flow (FCF)

This is also referred to as the net cash flow to invested capital or free cash flow to the firm.

Free cash flow (FCF) can be determined from the cashflow statement. But in valuation, we prefer to use a cruder measure derived from the B/S and I/S, as the cruder measure is usually easier to forecast.

This crude measure is as follows:

FCF =		Net operating profit after tax (NOPAT)
	Add back:	Depreciation and amortization expenses included in NOPAT
	Less:	Net increase in non-cash working capital (excluding any items treated as debt)
	Less:	Capital expenditures during the year

Example: SAP Free Cash Flow 2017

We calculate the free cash flow for SAP from the cash flow statement first, so that we can reconcile it to the CFI measure calculated earlier (recall this was €3,553.2 million). Refer to the 2017 annual report for SAP. Numbers are in € million.

Levered cash flow from operations	5,045.0
Add: Interest paid	200.0
Less: Estimated tax savings from interest @ 26.4%	(52.8)
Less: CAPEX (investing outflows)	(1,112.0)
	4,080.2

This reconciles to the CFI as follows (Numbers in € million):

Cashflow to investors (CFI)	3,553.2
Foreign currency adjustments	218.0
Increase in cash	309.0
	4,080.2

The FCF based on the balance sheet and income statement is as follows (numbers in € million):

Operating profit	4,877.0
Less: tax @ 26.4%	1,287.5
NOPAT	3,589.5
Depreciation and amortization	1,272.0
Increase in noncash working capital	377.0
CAPEX	(840)
FCF	4,398.5

5.7.3 The WACC Model

In the WACC model, the projected cashflows are cashflows to invested capital, measured using one of the following metrics:

1. Cash flow to investors (CFI), or the net cash distributed to both ordinary shareholders and debtholders (and other types of investors in a more complex capital structure),
2. Free cash flow (FCF), or the net cash flow available for distribution to all holders of invested capital (that is, before any distribution).

The discount rate is the weighted average cost of capital (WACC). For a capital structure that includes just ordinary shares and debt, this is the weighted average of the after-tax cost of debt and the after-tax cost of equity, where the weights are based on their respective proportions in the capital structure (measured at fair value).

If k_e is the cost of equity, k_d is the pre-tax cost of debt, tx is the corporate income tax rate, $\frac{D}{C}$ is the ratio of debt to total invested capital (both at fair value), $\frac{E}{C}$ is the ratio of equity to total invested capital (both at fair value), then we have in Equation 5.5:

$$WACC = k_e\frac{E}{C} + k_d(1 - tx)\frac{D}{C}. \tag{5.5}$$

The pre-tax cost of debt k_d is partially offset by the tax savings of $k_d \times tx$ due to the usual interest expense deduction, so that the after-tax net cost of debt is $k_d - k_d \times tx$ or $k_d(1 - tx)$.

With more complicated structures, such as with preference shares, the additional components of invested capital are reflected too. For example, suppose that the company has preference shares in their capital structure, where $\frac{P}{C}$ is the ratio of preference share value to total invested capital (both at fair value), and k_p is the required return on preference shares after tax (this can be estimated using the preference-share dividend yield on the valuation date). Then we have:

$$WACC = k_e\frac{E}{C} + k_d(1 - tx)\frac{D}{C} + k_p\frac{P}{C}.$$

Also, if we have convertible bonds or similar instruments in the capital structure, we analyze them into their debt and equity components and allocate these accordingly. (The entity would have already done so in its financial reporting, to comply with IAS 32).

It may be somewhat complex to separately measure and allocate the valuation-date fair value of these convertible instruments. If the impact on the $\frac{D}{C}$ and $\frac{E}{C}$ ratios is unlikely to be material, their latest book values should suffice.

Circular Logic

WACC is based on $\frac{D}{C}$ and $\frac{E}{C}$ which are based on the invested capital (the C in the denominator). But this invested capital is what we are trying to estimate in the first place! So the logic is circular. We need invested capital to measure WACC, which we need to measure invested capital, which we need to measure WACC ...

One standard solution is to fix the values of $\frac{D}{C}$ and $\frac{E}{C}$ outside the model. One standard approach is to fix them to be equal to their assumed long-run target values. These assumed long-run target values are in turn usually assumed to be equal to the average levels in the industry, that is, the enterprise's debt-equity ratio is assumed to converge to the industry average in the long run. (We can also use the median figure from a group of guideline companies to proxy for the industry average).

In calculating the industry average $\frac{D}{E}$ ratios, a common practice is to take the latest reported book value of debt divided by the valuation-date market value of equity. In terms of cost-benefit tradeoffs, it may not be efficient to measure the market value of debt MVDEBT separately for each guideline company using the more cumbersome procedure we outlined earlier (Sect. 5.3.2.1).

Example: WACC with Fixed D/E Ratio

Caesar Inc has the following FCF projections (in CU) for the planning period of 3 years.

Year	*1*	*2*	*3*
FCF	*100*	*110*	*120*

The average industry D/E ratio is 1.5 (ratio based on market values of debt and equity). Caesar Inc faces a corporate income tax rate of 20%. The cost of equity is 10%, and the cost of debt is 8%. The long-run growth rate is assumed to be 2%. Value the enterprise using a WACC model. Assume that cashflows occur at year-end.

We assume that the D/E ratio for calculating WACC is fixed to be the long-run target D/E for Caesar Inc. We further assume that the long-run target D/E would be the same as the industry average D/E ratio of 1.5. Then we can compute the WACC for Caesar Inc as follows:

$$WACC = 10\% \times \frac{1}{2.5} + 8\% \times (1 - 20\%) \times \frac{1.5}{2.5} = 7.84\%.$$

We can proceed to compute the enterprise value:

$$V_0 = \frac{100}{1.0784} + \frac{110}{1.0784^2} + \frac{120}{1.0784^3} + \frac{\left(\frac{120 \times 1.02}{0.0784 - 0.02}\right)}{1.0784^3} = CU\ 1954.20.$$

Iteration

An alternative approach is to use iteration (repeated calculations). First we start off with a trial value of $\frac{D}{C}$, $\frac{E}{C}$, etc. We calculate invested capital based on the trial value to get a first guess of invested capital. Then we plug this first guess into the $\frac{D}{C}$, and $\frac{E}{C}$ ratio formulas to get an updated second guess for these ratios. Then we plug these second guess $\frac{D}{C}$ etc. numbers into our DCF analysis to get a second guess of invested capital. We use this second guess to recalculate $\frac{D}{C}$ etc. giving a third guess, ... and so on, until the repetitive procedure results in measures of WACC and invested capital that are mutually consistent at least up to some pre-decided level of tolerable measurement error (called the tolerance limit).

We can use spreadsheet software to accomplish this, simply by setting up circular formulas in our spreadsheets (the formula for $\frac{D}{C}$ depends on the cell where enterprise value is determined, while the enterprise value calculation depends on the formula for $\frac{D}{C}$). We need to choose a spreadsheet setting that allows circular formulas and iteration.

Example: WACC Model with Iteration

We repeat the facts in the previous example. Caesar Inc has the following FCF projections (in CU) for the planning period of 3 years.

Year	*1*	*2*	*3*
FCF	*100*	*110*	*120*

Caesar Inc has a fair value of debt equal to CU 1500. This is assumed to remain constant in the planning period. Caesar Inc faces a corporate income tax rate of 20%. The cost of equity is 10%, and the cost of debt is 8%. The long-run growth rate is assumed to be 2%. Value the enterprise using a WACC model.

We set up a spreadsheet with circular formulas for WACC and enterprise value (EV). We have:

y	1	2	3	TV
FCF	100	110	120	2,218.5110
DCF	93.1141	95.3155	96.7106	1,787.9460
EV	2,073.0861	2,126.3939	2,175.0108	
WACC	7.40%	7.46%	7.52%	

The EV row gives the enterprise value at the beginning of the respective year. To estimate the fair value we follow an iterative procedure:

1. First, we set the WACC at the beginning of each year to be some guess figure, say $\lambda_1, \lambda_2, \lambda_3$ for years 1, 2 and 3 respectively. These are *forward rates* to discount from the end to the beginning of the respective year.
2. Then we estimate the terminal value TV say, assuming that λ_3 will continue to be the WACC for all years after year 3:

$$TV = \frac{120 \times 1.02}{\lambda_3 - 0.02}.$$

3. Then we can estimate the enterprise value at the beginning of year 3, say EV_3:

$$EV_3 = \frac{120 + TV}{1 + \lambda_3}.$$

4. Similarly, we can move backwards to estimate the enterprise values at the beginning of years 2 and 1 respectively, (say EV_2 and EV_1 respectively).

$$EV_2 = \frac{110 + EV_3}{1 + \lambda_2}.$$

$$EV_1 = \frac{100 + EV_2}{1 + \lambda_1}.$$

5. Now, we can recalculate λ_1, λ_2 and λ_3 to reflect the updated values of EV_1, EV_2 and EV_3. The WACC calculation is based on the beginning enterprise value for the respective year. Thus for year 2, the computation is as follows (using the final numbers in the table, i.e., $EV_2 = 2{,}126.3939$):

$$WACC = \frac{1{,}500}{2{,}126.3939} \times 8\% \times 80\% + \frac{2{,}126.3939 - 1{,}500}{2{,}126.3939} \times 10\% = 7.46\%.$$

6. We repeat steps 1 to 5, and keep repeating until the change in λ_1, λ_2 and λ_3 from the previous iteration is negligible (i.e., within some small tolerance limit). In practice, we can achieve this by setting our spreadsheet program to allow iteration, and entering circular formulas for WACC and EV in the spreadsheet.

The final iteration results are as shown in the table. The enterprise value that we need is given by EV_1, which is CU 2,073.09. We can verify this value by directly computing the discounted cash flows and adding them up, using the final estimate of the WACC each year.

In doing so, we recall that this WACC is a forward rate not a spot rate. For example the WACC for year 2 is a forward rate from year-end 1 to year-end 2 rather than a spot rate from years 0 to 2, as the underlying D/E ratio holds only for year 2. Therefore, when we calculate the discounted cashflow (DCF) for Year 2, we have:

$$DCF = \frac{110}{1.0746 \times 1.0740} = 95.3155.$$

Similarly, the DCF for Year 3 is given by:

$$DCF = \frac{120}{1.0752 \times 1.0746 \times 1.0740} = 96.7106.$$

5.7.4 Adjusted Present Value (APV)

The adjusted present value model (Myers 1974) avoids the circular logic of the WACC model by first valuing the entity as though it had zero debt, and then adjusting for the effects of debt. Debt adds value via the interest tax shield. But debt also reduces value by raising the risk of bankruptcy.

We can state this model as follows (Equation 5.6):

$$V_0 = V_U + V_I - V_B \tag{5.6}$$

where V_U is the value of the unlevered enterprise (that is the hypothetical value that the firm would have if it had zero debt, or if all its debt capital were instead replaced by equity capital), V_I is the value of the interest tax shield due to debt, V_B is the value of the expected cost of bankruptcy.

5.7.4.1 The Unlevered Enterprise V_U

To obtain V_U, we discount either free cash flow or cashflow to investors, using a discount rate that is the hypothetical unlevered cost of equity. This is the cost of equity that the target enterprise would have if it had zero debt, that is, if all the debt in its capital structure were replaced by equity. (Debt tends to increase the cost of equity, as it makes equity more risky).

We can express this formally as follows (Equation 5.7):

$$V_U = \sum_{y=1}^{\infty} \frac{CF_y}{(1 + k_{e,u,y})^{t[y]}} \tag{5.7}$$

where:

y	indexes financial years starting from the next year as year 1 (next year as of the valuation date)
CF_y	is the relevant cash flow for year y. It could be either CFI or FCF.
$t[y]$	is the time when cash flow CF_y is assumed to occur, measured in years after today.
$k_{e,u,y}$	is the cost of equity (for year y) that the firm being valued would have if it were debt-free, that is, the unlevered cost of equity (for year y).

5.7.4.2 The Interest Tax Shield V_I

We can formally express the value of the interest tax shield V_I as in Equation 5.8, subject to some simplifying assumptions:

$$V_I = tx \times D. \tag{5.8}$$

Here tx is the corporate income tax rate, and D is the fair value of debt.

The simplifying assumptions underlying this calculation are as follows:

- The cost of debt is constant, say k_d.
- The debt is maintained at its current level forever.
- The current income tax rate is the best estimate of the future income tax rate for all periods in the future.

Under these assumptions, the present value of the actual stream of interest payments would be equal to that of a constant equal interest payment given by $k_d D$ each year. This gives a tax saving of $tx \times k_d \times D$ every year.

Then we have[5]:

$$\begin{aligned} V_I &= \sum_{y=1}^{\infty} \frac{tx \times k_d \times D}{(1 + k_d)^{t[y]}} \\ &= tx \times D \sum_{y=1}^{\infty} \frac{k_d}{(1 + k_d)^{t[y]}} \\ &= tx \times D(k_d \times \frac{1}{k_d}) \\ &= tx \times D. \end{aligned}$$

An alternative computation of V_I discounts the interest tax savings using the unlevered cost of equity rather than the cost of debt. In that case, V_I can be obtained formally as:

$$\begin{aligned} V_I &= \sum_{y=1}^{\infty} \frac{k_d \times D \times tx}{(1 + k_{e,u,y})^{t[y]}} \\ &= \frac{k_d}{k_{e,u}} tx \times D \quad \text{if } k_{e,u,y} = k_{e,u} \text{ for all } y. \end{aligned}$$

5.7.4.3 Expected Bankruptcy Cost V_B

The last component V_B is difficult to measure, usually requiring more Level 3 inputs. It is often left out in practice with the implicit assumption that it is likely to be negligible. This is not best practice and could be potentially misleading.

We can estimate V_B as follows:

$$V_B = p_B K_B$$

where

[5]Recall that the present value of a perpetuity of CU 1 each year discounted at x each year is $\frac{1}{x}$.

p_B is the probability of bankruptcy over the investment horizon.
K_B equals the estimated losses from bankruptcy, if it occurs.

Over an infinite horizon, the probability of bankruptcy is virtually certain in real life. But what we seek here is a probability that is consistent with the going-concern assumption (zero probability of bankruptcy). More specifically to APV, consider a version of the going-concern assumption where the *unlevered* entity is assumed to never go bankrupt.

Then the risk of bankruptcy arises purely from the addition of debt. As an approximate measure of this additional risk, we could use the default rate for long-term bonds with a credit rating similar to that of the enterprise being valued.

The cost of bankruptcy K_B is estimated to be the amount of value that investors would lose if the enterprise went bankrupt. This is usually expressed as a percentage of the value estimated before considering bankruptcy costs. If this percentage is π_B say then we have:

$$K_B = \pi_B(V_U + V_I).$$

We can then also state the APV enterprise value as follows:

$$V_0 = (1 - p_B\pi_B)(V_U + V_I).$$

5.7.4.4 Example: APV

Caesar Inc has the following FCF projections (in CU) for the planning period of 3 years.

Year	*1*	*2*	*3*
FCF	*100*	*110*	*120*

Caesar Inc has a fair value of debt equal to CU 1500. This is assumed to remain constant in future. Caesar Inc faces a corporate income tax rate of 20%. The unlevered cost of equity is 6%. The long-run growth rate is assumed to be 2%. The probability of bankruptcy is assumed to be 1%. In the event of bankruptcy, an estimated 80% of the enterprise value would be lost (that is, the enterprise value before considering bankruptcy). Value the enterprise using an adjusted present value model. You may assume that cashflows occur at year-end.

We have for the value of the unlevered enterprise:

$$V_U = \frac{100}{1.06} + \frac{110}{1.06^2} + \frac{120}{1.06^3} + \frac{\left(\frac{120\times 1.02}{0.06-0.02}\right)}{1.06^3} = CU\ 2{,}862.2286.$$

We have for the value of the interest tax shield:

$$V_I = 20\% \times 1,500 = CU\ 300.$$

We have $p_B = 1\%$ and $K_B = 80\% \times (V_U + V_D)$. Therefore, we can find the enterprise value as follows:

$$V_0 = (1 - 1\% \times 80\%) \times (2{,}862.2286 + 300) = CU\ 3{,}136.9308.$$

5.7.5 Residual Income Valuation

Consider the following example.

A company has total assets (net of provisions, deferred tax liabilities, and working capital liabilities) with a fair value of CU 100 million.

The company has a relevant cost of capital (WACC) of 10% per year.

Projected cashflows each year (FCF) are a constant CU 12 million every year forever.

Then we can value the enterprise as the present value of the projected cashflows (monetary amounts in CU millions):

$$V_0 = \frac{12}{10\%} = 120.$$

Alternatively, we can separate this value into two parts:

1. The value of the assets (less operating liabilities).
2. Value added, given by the present value of excess cash flows. Excess cash flows are the cash flows each year that are in excess of the cash flow needed to just meet the cost of capital requirement (10% in our example). In our example, the excess cash flow is CU 2 million each year ($12 - 10\% \times 100$).

Using this alternative approach, we have (monetary amounts in CU millions):

$$V_0 = 100 + \frac{2}{10\%} = 120.$$

The alternative approach is called the *residual income* approach. It is useful in situations where the excess cashflows can be directly forecasted. It forms the basis of the multi-period excess earnings model (MPEEM) for intangibles valuation, where we value intangibles as the present value of the value that they add (incremental cash flows) to an existing stock of assets.

Formally, we state the residual income model as follows (Equations 5.9 and 5.10):

$$V_0 = TA_0 + \sum_{y=1}^{\infty} \frac{ECF_y}{(1+k_y)^{t[y]}}. \tag{5.9}$$

$$ECF_y = FCF_y - k_y TA_0. \tag{5.10}$$

where

y	indexes financial years starting from the next year as year 1 (next year as of the valuation date).
TA_0	is the fair value of total assets at year 0 (valuation date).
ECF_y	is the excess cash flow for year y.
FCF_y	is the free cash flow (FCF) for year y.
$t[y]$	is the time when cash flow CF_y is assumed to occur, measured in years after today.
k_y	is the relevant discount rate for year y (usually the WACC).

Example: Residual Income Valuation

Shah Inc has the following FCF projections (in CU) for the planning period of 3 years.

Year	*1*	*2*	*3*
FCF	*100*	*110*	*120*

Shah Inc has a fair value of total assets equal to CU 1,250. Shah Inc faces a constant WACC of 8%. The long-run growth rate is 1%. Find the enterprise value using residual income valuation.

We have the excess cash flows as follows:

Year	1	2	3
ECF	0	10	20

Then we can compute the enterprise value as follows:

$$V_0 = 1,250 + \frac{0}{1.08} + \frac{10}{1.08^2} + \frac{20}{1.08^3} + \frac{\left(\frac{20\times 1.01}{0.08-0.01}\right)}{1.08^3} = CU\ 1{,}503.5273.$$

This concludes our overview of enterprise valuation. In Chap. 6, we continue the topic by discussing the estimation of needed inputs, such as the cost of capital.

Exercises

(Monetary units are in CU unless otherwise mentioned).

5.1. Ratios

Find and download the latest annual reports of the following companies:

- Siemens Group
- SAP Group
- Cheung Kong Hutchison Group
- Singapore Airlines (SIA) Group

For each company, compute the following trailing ratios based on the consolidated statements in the latest annual report (no need to seek interim reports):

(a) P/E/G ratio
(b) Dividend yield
(c) P/B ratio
(d) P/E ratio
(e) EV/EBITDA ratio
(f) EV/Sales ratio
(g) Tobin's Q (q_s)

5.2. Three-Stage Model
Kashmir Inc has a dividend per ordinary share next year of CU 1.30. The dividend is projected to grow at 8% per year for the subsequent two years (years 2 and 3), and then at 3% for the following two years (years 4 and 5), and then to grow at 1% thereafter. The cost of equity for the first 3 years is 16%, the cost of equity for years 4 and 5 is 8%, and the cost of equity after year 5 is 7%. Find the fair price of a Kashmir Inc share using a three-stage model. You may assume that cashflows occur at year-end.

5.3. H-Model
Lim Inc has dividends per ordinary share of CU 0.80 in the current year. These are projected to grow at 3% per year over the next 10 years, and at 0.5% per year thereafter. The cost of equity is 6.2%. Value a Lim Inc ordinary share using an H-model.

5.4. FTE Computation
Find and download the latest annual reports of the following companies:

- Siemens Group
- Royal Dutch Shell Group
- Cheung Kong Hutchison Group
- Singapore Airlines (SIA) Group

For each of these companies, do the following:

(a) Calculate the consolidated FTE from the latest annual report, from the consolidated cash flow statement.
(b) Calculate the consolidated FTE using the cruder calculation from the consolidated balance sheet and income statement.

5.5. FCF Computation
Find and download the latest annual reports of the following companies:

- Siemens Group
- Royal Dutch Shell Group
- Cheung Kong Hutchison Group
- Singapore Airlines (SIA) Group

For each of these companies, do the following:

(a) Calculate the consolidated FCF from the latest annual report, using the consolidated cash flow statement. Reconcile this to the cashflow to investors.
(b) Calculate the FCF using the cruder calculation from the consolidated balance sheet and income statement.

5.6. APV Model
Shah Inc has the following FCF projections (in CU) for the planning period of 3 years.

Year	1	2	3
FCF	90	99	110

Shah Inc has a fair value of debt equal to CU 800. This is assumed to remain constant in future. Shah Inc faces a corporate income tax rate of 20%. The unlevered cost of equity is 8%. The long-run growth rate is assumed to be 1%. The probability of bankruptcy is assumed to be 1%. In the event of bankruptcy, an estimated 90% of the enterprise value would be lost (that is, the enterprise value before considering bankruptcy). Value the enterprise using an adjusted present value model.

References

Fuller, R., & Hsia, C. (1984). A simplified common stock valuation model. *Financial Analysts Journal, 40*, 49–56.
Gordon, M. (1959). Dividends, earnings and stock prices. *Review of Economics and Statistics, 45*, 37–51.
Myers, S. (1974). Interactions of corporate financing and investment decisions—Implications for capital budgeting. *Journal of Finance, 29*, 1–25.
Perfect, S., & Wiles, K. (1994). Alternative constructions of Tobin's Q: An empirical investigation. *Journal of Empirical Finance, 1*, 313–341.

Inputs to Business Valuation

6

We discuss the inputs for enterprise valuation, particularly in a DCF model—the cost of capital, the projected cash flows, and the selection of comparable companies or guideline companies. We first discuss the projection of cashflows. We start by explaining the mid-year convention and the partial-year adjustment, that help align projected cash flow dates to the valuation date. We turn to the construction of proforma income statements and balance sheets, using an example. We discuss how Monte Carlo simulation can be used to model uncertainty in cash flows and parameters. We discuss how to handle multiple-currency cashflows using CIRP. We turn next to the cost of capital. The weighted average cost of capital is built up from the cost of equity and the cost of debt. The cost of equity is usually measured using CAPM (the capital asset pricing model). We discuss how to apply the CAPM to find the cost of equity for a private company by aggregating betas for a set of similar listed guideline companies. We turn to the cost of debt and how to estimate it, for example by constructing a synthetic credit rating. Finally, we discuss how to combine the cost of equity and the cost of debt to arrive at the WACC. For small and/or very specialized enterprises, it may be difficult to find listed similar companies. For such companies, an alternative to using CAPM is to use a build-up model to derive the cost of equity. We briefly discuss this model. We turn next to the choice of guideline companies—listed companies that are similar to the entity being valued. We consider how location, size, industry and strategic positioning are factors in choosing guideline companies.

6.1 Learning Outcomes

After completing this chapter, you would be able to:

1. Prepare projected financial statements and projected cashflows for DCF valuation.

S. Lynn, *Valuation for Accountants*, Springer Texts in Business and Economics,
https://doi.org/10.1007/978-981-15-0357-3_6

2. Compute the cost of capital for different DCF valuation models.
3. Select guideline companies for ratio-based valuation or cost-of-capital computations.

For convenience, we will refer to the company being valued as the *target company*.

6.2 Timing of Cashflows

We first discuss two assumptions on the timing of the cashflows—the mid-year convention, and the partial-year adjustment.

6.2.1 Mid-year Convention

Projected cashflows for a year are by default assumed to occur continuously through the year. One way to approximately model this is to treat them as occurring as a lumpsum at the midpoint of the year. This convention is called the mid-year convention.

6.2.1.1 Example: Mid-year Convention

We are valuing Company Y at the end of the financial year. Projected free cash flows for the next 3 years are as follows (in CU):

Year (y)	*1*	*2*	*3*
FCF (FCF_y)	*100*	*110*	*120*

The WACC is 10%. Calculate the discounted cashflows for the first three years using the mid-year convention.

We assume that the year 1 cashflow occurs at time 0.5, the year 2 cashflow at time 1.5, and the year 3 cashflow at time 2.5.

y	1	2	3
FCF_y	100	110	120
$t[y]$	0.5	1.5	2.5
DCF	95.3463	95.3463	94.5583
	$\frac{100}{1.1^{0.5}}$	$\frac{110}{1.1^{1.5}}$	$\frac{120}{1.1^{2.5}}$

6.2.2 Partial-Year Adjustment

In the previous example, we were valuing the enterprise just before the start of a new financial year. In general, our valuation date is likely to fall sometime during a financial year. The standard practice is to align cashflows to financial years. If we are valuing an entity during a year that is partially completed, we prorate the first year's cashflow to reflect only the portion projected to occur in the remaining portion of the year. We usually round to the start of the nearest month, say the next month if the valuation date is the 15th or later day of the current month, and the current month if the valuation date falls on days 1 to 14 of the current month. Also we count fractions in months, not days, i.e., every month is 1/12 of a year.

6.2.2.1 Example: Partial-Year Adjustment and Mid-year Convention

We are valuing Company A on August 1st, 2018. The company's year-end is December 31st. Projected FCF for the next three years are as follows:

Year ending	*31 Dec 2018*	*31 Dec 2019*	*31 Dec 2020*
FCF	*100*	*110*	*120*

The WACC is 10%. Find the discounted cashflows for these three years. Apply the mid-year convention and the partial-year adjustment.

For the first year, we assume that the remaining part of the year is $\frac{5}{12}$ of the year at the valuation date. We pro-rate the Year 1 cashflow to reflect only $\frac{5}{12}$ of the amount.

Applying the mid-year convention, the cashflow for the first year 2018 is assumed to occur at the middle of the 5-month period, or $\frac{2.5}{12}$ of a year (2.5 months later).

The cashflows for the remaining years are assumed to occur at the middle of the respective years. For year 2, that would be $(0.5 + \frac{5}{12})$ years from today. For year 3, that would be $(1.5 + \frac{5}{12})$ years from today.

We have:

y	1	2	3
FCF_y	$100 \times \frac{5}{12}$	110	120
$t[y]$	$\frac{2.5}{12}$	$\frac{5}{12} + 0.5$	$\frac{5}{12} + 1.5$
DCF	40.8475 $\frac{100 \times \frac{5}{12}}{1.1^{\frac{2.5}{12}}}$	100.7974 $\frac{110}{1.1^{\left(\frac{5}{12}+0.5\right)}}$	99.9644 $\frac{120}{1.1^{\left(\frac{5}{12}+1.5\right)}}$

6.3 Projecting Financial Statements

In projecting cashflows, it is good practice to project the condensed balance sheet and income statement, and to derive the relevant cash flow numbers from these projected financial statements, also called proforma financial statements. This can help us to verify the internal consistency and reasonableness of our projections, as these projected statements are constrained to satisfy the balance-sheet equation.

We can follow these steps:

1. Prepare a record of condensed balance sheets and income statements for the past several years (adjusted to the extent possible for changes in accounting policies and standards over the period).
2. Identify key *value drivers*. Value drivers are *ratios* derived from the past financial statements, whose values are useful in projecting financial numbers into the future. Many value drivers involve dividing by *sales*. These include the growth rate in sales, the ratio of various key expense items to sales, and the ratio of various working capital items to sales. Other value-drivers may not involve sales, e.g., ratios used to project capital expenditure, depreciation, or interest.
3. Perform *income normalization*. This involves preparing a *normalized* income statement for the current year. This involves identifying and excluding one-off items that cannot be projected into the future, e.g., investment gains or losses, gains or losses from divestment of a business, foreign currency translation losses, etc. Such items are typically projected to be zero in future years. For investment or translation gains, this assumption can be interpreted as saying that they are equally likely to be positive or negative in future, and on average would be zero.
4. Using the value drivers and the normalized income statement as a base, we can project the income statement and the balance sheet for the future years in our planning period (that is, period before the terminal value calculation). If we are applying sum-of-the-parts valuation, we would project financial statements separately for each segment.
5. In making our projections, we usually keep one balance-sheet item as a plug figure (residual computed automatically based on the other projections). This is usually either reserves (retained earnings) or cash.
6. In making our projections, we should also consider any forward-looking information provided by the target company management. For example, if management has indicated a major capital expenditure over the next two years, we should reflect that in our projections.
7. We should perform sanity checks on our projections to make sure that they are internally consistent and do not reflect any logical absurdities. Particularly the reasonableness of the plug figure should be checked.
8. We should ensure that our projections include specific amounts for depreciation and amortization, as well as capital expenditure. These amounts are needed to compute free cashflows.

6.3.1 Projecting Cashflows Example

The actual condensed income statements (Table 6.1) and balance sheets (Table 6.2) for Siti Inc are as follows for the years 2001 to 2010 (amounts in CU'000).

We wish to project cashflows to 2011 and beyond based on this past history. We will discuss the projections for 2011.

Table 6.1 Siti Inc condensed income statements (CU'000)

Year	2001	2002	2003	2004	2005	2006	2007	2008	2009	2010
Sales	21,188	22,456	23,812	25,247	26,772	28,371	30,067	31,869	33,796	35,813
COGS	8,460	8,988	9,540	10,115	10,712	11,335	12,019	12,761	13,522	14,327
Gross margin	12,728	13,468	14,272	15,132	16,060	17,036	18,048	19,108	20,274	21,486
Other operating expenses	6,026	6,296	6,541	6,857	7,134	7,460	7,808	8,179	8,561	8,960
Depreciation	1,900	2,043	2,150	2,284	2,411	2,567	2,708	2,896	3,064	3,238
EBIT	4,802	5,129	5,581	5,991	6,515	7,009	7,532	8,033	8,649	9,288
Interest expense	490	518	547	576	617	651	695	736	778	828
Investment gains	(415)	(486)	306	325	(167)	(216)	37	418	479	(402)
Profit before tax	3,897	4,125	5,340	5,740	5,731	6,142	6,874	7,715	8,350	8,058
Income tax	779	825	1,068	1,148	1,146	1,228	1,375	1,543	1,670	1,612
Net profits	3,118	3,300	4,272	4,592	4,585	4,914	5,499	6,172	6,680	6,446

Table 6.2 Siti Inc condensed balance sheets (CU'000)

Year	2001	2002	2003	2004	2005	2006	2007	2008	2009	2010
PPE	20,442	21,533	22,822	24,085	25,678	27,101	28,960	30,621	32,410	34,480
Investments	585	99	405	730	563	347	384	802	1,281	879
Inventory	1,543	1,706	1,795	1,802	1,982	2,096	2,253	2,349	2,490	2,718
A/R	4,241	4,484	4,755	5,064	5,335	5,684	6,021	6,367	6,766	7,154
Cash	1,002	1,003	1,002	1,007	998	997	1,014	986	999	1,000
Total assets	27,813	28,825	30,779	32,688	34,556	36,225	38,632	41,125	43,946	46,231
Shareholders' equity	9,838	9,864	10,738	11,468	11,960	12,362	13,105	14,180	15,464	15,838
A/P	1,633	1,707	1,836	1,946	2,044	2,189	2,334	2,450	2,570	2,758
Debt	16,342	17,254	18,205	19,274	20,552	21,674	23,193	24,495	25,912	27,635
Total equities	27,813	28,825	30,779	32,688	34,556	36,225	38,632	41,125	43,946	46,231

We start by identifying value drivers. We calculate ratios whose trend may tell us what drives particular line items in the balance sheet and income statement.

Our value drivers are as in Table 6.3 for the years 2002 to 2010 (we omit 2001 as some of the ratios cannot be calculated without information from the previous year 2000).

We start by projecting sales growth year on year. This appears to represent a stable growth rate of approximately 6% over the last 10 years. Accordingly, we will use a growth rate of 6% to project sales.

We would expect cost of goods sold and working capital items to vary directly with sales. We therefore calculate COGS as a percentage of sales, and use turnover ratios to analyze the pattern of working capital items. For COGS we notice that it is stable over the years at around 40% of sales. We therefore choose 40% of sales as a reasonable basis to project our 2011 COGS.

Table 6.3 Siti Inc estimated value drivers

Year	2002	2003	2004	2005	2006	2007	2008	2009	2010
Sales growth	5.98%	6.04%	6.03%	6.04%	5.97%	5.98%	5.99%	6.05%	5.97%
COGS/Sales	40.02%	40.06%	40.06%	40.01%	39.95%	39.97%	40.04%	40.01%	40.01%
Other operating expenses/sales	28.04%	27.47%	27.16%	26.65%	26.29%	25.97%	25.66%	25.33%	25.02%
Depreciation/beg.PPE	9.99%	9.98%	10.01%	10.01%	10.00%	9.99%	10.00%	10.01%	9.99%
Interest/beg.debt	3.17%	3.17%	3.16%	3.20%	3.17%	3.21%	3.17%	3.18%	3.20%
PPE growth	5.34%	5.99%	5.53%	6.61%	5.54%	6.86%	5.74%	5.84%	6.39%
Inventory turnover	5.27	5.31	5.61	5.40	5.41	5.33	5.43	5.43	5.27
A/R turnover	5.01	5.01	4.99	5.02	4.99	4.99	5.01	4.99	5.01
Purchases (CU'000)	9,151	9,629	10,122	10,892	11,449	12,176	12,857	13,663	14,555
A/P turnover	5.36	5.24	5.20	5.33	5.23	5.22	5.25	5.32	5.28
Debt/Assets	59.86%	59.15%	58.96%	59.47%	59.83%	60.04%	59.56%	58.96%	59.78%

For the working capital items, we apply standard turnover ratios. One difference is that we compute these ratios based just on the item balance at year-end rather than the average of beginning and year-end balances. The reason is that this makes it easier to apply the ratio to project the working capital levels for 2011.

The A/P turnover is computed as Purchases/ending A/P, where purchases are estimated as COGS *plus* ending inventory *minus* beginning inventory.

We find that A/R turnover has a stable level of approximately 5 times through the years. We therefore find it reasonable to estimate 2011 A/R as $\frac{1}{5}$ of sales.

We find that inventory turnover has a reasonably stable level of approximately 5.4 over the years. We therefore find it reasonable to estimate 2011 inventory as $\frac{1}{5.4}$ times COGS.

We find that A/P turnover has a reasonably stable level of approximately 5.3 over the years. We therefore find it reasonable to project 2011 A/P as $\frac{1}{5.3}$ of 2011 purchases. We estimate 2011 purchases to be CU 15,279 thousand.

Turning to other items, other operating expenses could have a variable and fixed component. We could use linear regression to estimate the variable and fixed components separately. But we calculate the ratio of these expenses to sales each year and find it reasonably stable at around 26.4% (the average level) of sales over the years. We therefore decide to directly apply this percentage of 26.4% to 2011 projected sales to get 2011 projected other operating expenses.

To project PPE, we can look at the direct trend of PPE levels or the trend of changes in PPE net of depreciation expense. In our case, we note that the PPE grows at a fairly stable rate of around 6% year on year. This suggests that Siti Inc regularly expands capacity to keep pace with its sales growth.

We apply a 6% growth rate to 2010 PPE to get our estimate of 2011 PPE.

For depreciation expense, we note that it is approximately 10% of beginning PPE over the years, suggesting an average life of PPE of 10 years. We apply 10% of the 2010 PPE to get our depreciation estimate for 2011.

We can also estimate CAPEX for 2011 as the change in PPE net of depreciation (solve for X in the equation: Beginning PPE + X − depreciation = Ending PPE). This works out to CU 5,517 thousand.

For projecting interest expense, we could use information on effective interest rates from the notes to the financial statements. In our case, we estimate interest expense as a percentage of beginning debt. This ratio is stable at approximately 3.18% (the average level). We therefore use 3.18% of 2010 debt to calculate our interest expense for 2011.

We do not attempt to project investment gains and losses as these are one-off items. We set them to be zero in 2011 consistent with the assumption that gains of some amount are as likely as losses of the same amount.

Similarly, we leave investments (balance-sheet) at the 2010 level. We can choose to exclude them from the balance sheet altogether and value them separately.

To estimate the debt level, we look at the debt to total assets ratio over the years. We note that debt has been stable at around 60% of total assets. We therefore are comfortable projecting 60% of total assets as our debt level for 2011.

We note that cash has been stable at around CU 1 million each year. We therefore project CU 1 million as our cash level for 2011.

We have substantially projected all the items in our condensed income statement and balance sheet for 2011. We use shareholders' equity as a plug figure. This gives us an amount of CU 16,633 thousand for shareholders' equity. This implicitly reflects that dividends of CU 3,761 thousand are projected in 2011 (solve for X in the equation: Beginning Shareholders' Equity + Net income − X = Ending shareholders' equity)

Our projections for 2011 are shown in Table 6.4. Amounts are in CU'000.

We can proceed to estimate our FCF for 2011 and reconcile it to our CFI. The calculation is in Table 6.5.

6.3.2 Modeling Uncertainty with Monte Carlo Simulation

One way to model uncertainty in our cashflows is to allow some numbers in our projections to change randomly. We can do this by using a random number generator to generate the random component in the formulas. We then run our calculations several times allowing the random component to change randomly each time. We record the range and distribution of values that we get.

We can consider two types of random numbers in our models: one drawn from a uniform distribution, and one drawn from a normal distribution. There are of course a wide variety of other distributions that can be modelled, but we will stick to these basics here.

Table 6.4 Siti Inc 2011 projections

	2011F
Sales	37,962
COGS	15,185
Gross margin	22,777
Other operating expenses	10,022
Depreciation	3,448
EBIT	9,307
Interest	879
PBT	8,428
Income tax	1,686
Net profits	6,742
PPE	36,549
Investments	879
Inventory	2,812
A/R	7,592
Cash	1,000
Total assets	48,832
A/P	2,883
Debt	29,299
Equity (plug)	16,650
Total	48,832
Dividends	5,930
CAPEX	5,517

Table 6.5 Siti Inc projected FCF and CFI for 2011

	2011F
EBIT	9,307.0
Income tax	(1,861.4)
NOPAT	7,445.6
Depreciation	3.448.0
ΔNWC	(407.0)
CAPEX	(5,517.0)
FCF	4,969.6
Dividends	5,930.4
Interest	879.0
Tax shield on interest	(175.8)
Debt repayments	(1,664.0)
CFI	4,969.6

To draw a number from a uniform distribution between some lower bound L and some upper bound H means that any number between L and H is equally likely to be drawn.

To draw a number from a normal distribution with mean μ and standard deviation σ means that numbers closer to the mean are more likely to be drawn, and that the variation increases as σ increases.

In MS Excel or similar spreadsheet programs, we can use the following functions to draw a random number.

The function "$= RAND()$" draws a random number between 0 and 1 from a uniform distribution.

The function "$= RANDBETWEEN(lowerbound, upperbound)$" draws a random whole number between lowerbound and upperbound from a uniform distribution.

To draw a number from a normal distribution in MS Excel, we first draw a random number (uniform) between 0 and 1 using "$= RAND()$", and then use the inverse normal function "$= NORMINV(\ldots)$" to find the point on a normal curve whose cumulative probability matches that random number.

This is the Excel function: "$= NORMINV(RAND(), mean, std\_deviation)$".

6.3.2.1 Monte Carlo Simulation Example

To illustrate, let us extend our Siti Inc example from earlier.

We extend our projections to four years, and will calculate the terminal value at the end of the fourth year (mid-point if we use the mid-year convention). We use the same parameters as before. The projections are shown in Table 6.6 before any randomness is introduced. Numbers are in CU'000.

We introduce randomness in our projections as follows:

First, we allow the investment gains and losses to be a random number between −500 and 500 ("$= randbetween(-500, 500)$"). Then the balance-sheet account investments would also change by the amount of the random gain or loss each year.

Second, we allow the growth rate in sales to vary. In a particular year, the growth rate is drawn from a normal distribution with mean 6% and standard deviation 3%.

We have as our Excel formula for sales in a particular year:

$$RC[-1] * (1 + \text{norminv(rand(), 6\%, 3\%)})$$

where $RC[-1]$ is the cell just to the left in the same row.

It is good practice not to introduce random numbers in the last year's figures, which are used to determine the terminal value. Otherwise, we could be assuming that some one-off number such as investment gains continues every year in the same amount forever. Accordingly, we enter the random number calculations only for years 2011 through 2013. In 2014, which is used to determine the terminal value, we have zero investment gains and a growth rate of 6%.

We use a general multi-stage dividend discount model with a planning period up to 2014, and a growth rate of 1% thereafter. Our cost of equity is 10%. We use

Table 6.6 Siti Inc baseline projections (no randomness)

	Parameter	2010A	2011F	2012F	2013F	2014F
Sales	6%	35,813	37,961.78	40,239.49	42,653.86	45,213.09
COGS	40%	14,327	15,184.71	16,095.79	17,061.54	18,085.23
Gross margin		21,486	22,777.07	24,143.69	25,592.31	27,127.85
Other operating expense	26.40%	8,960	10,021.91	10,623.22	11,260.62	11,936.26
Depreciation	10%	3,238	3,448.00	3,654.88	3,874.17	4,106.62
EBIT		9,288	9,307.16	9,865.59	10,457.52	11,084.97
Interest expense	3.18%	828	878.79	931.72	985.47	1,042.45
Investment gains		(402)	0	0	0	0
PBT		8,058	8,428.37	8,933.87	9,472.05	10,042.53
Income tax	20%	1,612	1,685.67	1,786.77	1,894.41	2,008.51
Net profits		6,446	6,742.69	7,147.10	7,577.64	8,034.02
PPE	6%	34,480	36,548.80	38,741.73	41,066.23	43,530.21
Investments		879	879.00	879.00	879.00	879.00
Inventory	5.4	2,718	2,811.98	2,980.70	3,159.54	3,349.12
A/R	5	7,154	7,592.36	8,047.90	8,530.77	9,042.62
Cash		1,000	1,000.00	1,000.00	1,000.00	1,000.00
Total assets		46,231	48,832.14	51,649.33	54,635.55	57,800.94
A/P	5.3	2,758	2,882.77	3,068.78	3,252.90	3,448.08
Debt	60%	27,635	29,299.28	30,989.60	32,781.33	34,680.56
Shareholders equity		15,838	16,650.08	17,590.96	18,601.32	19,672.30
Total		46,231	48,832.14	51,649.33	54,635.55	57,800.94
Dividends			5,930.61	6,206.22	6,567.28	6,963.04
CAPEX			5,516.80	5,847.81	6,198.68	6,570.60
Purchases			15,278.70	16,264.51	17,240.38	18,274.81

the mid-year convention. Without introducing any randomness, we get a baseline present value of CU 78,755,740.

After introducing the random formulas, we run the simulation 1,000 times. We create a histogram of the results (unit is CU'000). This is shown in Fig. 6.1.

The results of our Monte Carlo simulation show that under our assumptions, the equity value could vary between around CU 65 million and CU 95 million, with the expected value being CU 78.779 million (the average of our simulated outcomes, approximately the same as the baseline value without randomness).

6.3.3 Cashflows in Foreign Currencies

Some or all of the cashflows may be denominated in foreign currencies, i.e., not the main reporting currency for the target company.

We have two choices. Firstly, we can translate these cashflows to the target company's domestic currency by using forward foreign exchange rates derived from

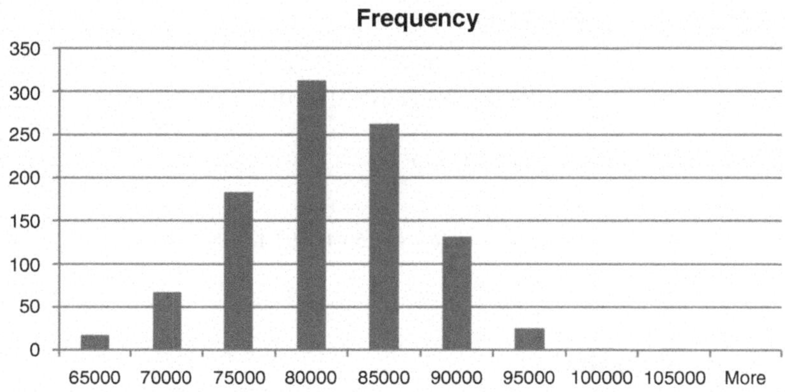

Fig. 6.1 Siti Inc simulated value of equity

CIRP (see Sect. 3.8). Then we can proceed to discount these cashflows using a discount rate for the domestic currency.

Alternatively, we can leave the cashflows in foreign currency units, but discount them using a discount rate for the foreign currency. The risk-free rate would reflect the risk-free rate for the foreign, not the domestic currency (rates on government bonds from the government that issues the foreign currency). Spreads would also reflect those on foreign-currency instruments, and would not be the same as the spreads on the domestic-currency instruments.

6.3.3.1 Example: Foreign Currency Cashflows

We project FCF in a foreign currency (FCU) of FCU 100, FCU 110 and FCU 120 in future years 1, 2 and 3 respectively. These cashflows occur at the end of each year. Our WACC is 10%, based on local-currency (LCU) risk-free rates and spreads. The local currency risk-free rate is 2%, assumed constant. The foreign currency risk-free rate is 5%, assumed constant. The valuation-date spot exchange rate is LCU 5 per FCU. Calculate the discounted cashflows in LCU units.

Let F_t be the forward exchange rate at time t. Then we have (applying CIRP):

$$F_1 = 5 \times \frac{1.02}{1.05} = 4.8571.$$

$$F_2 = 5 \times \frac{1.02^2}{1.05^2} = 4.7184.$$

$$F_3 = 5 \times \frac{1.02^3}{1.05^3} = 4.5836.$$

Then the projected cashflows in LCU are:

y	1	2	3
FCF_y	485.71	519.02	550.03

The discounted cashflows in LCU are:

y	1	2	3
Discounted FCF_y	441.56	428.94	413.24

6.4 Cost of Capital

To estimate the WACC, we need to estimate the following different components:

1. The risk-free rate,
2. The cost of debt,
3. The cost of equity.

We discuss each of these separately.

6.5 Risk-Free Rate

The risk-free rate was already discussed in detail in Chap. 3. It is most accurately given by the term structure of zero coupon spot or forward interest rates. We can directly use these spot or forward interest rates in business valuation, except that we usually express them as annually compounded rates to conform to the usual convention in business valuation.

It is usually convenient to assume a constant risk-free rate throughout the horizon (e.g., as a building-block for a constant WACC). Some standard choices for this constant risk-free rate are as follows:

1. We could use the estimated parameter β_0 from the Svensson model (see Sect. 3.6). This parameter is interpreted as a long-run continuously compounded constant spot interest rate. To convert this rate to an annually compounded rate r_a say, we use:

$$(1 + r_a) = e^{\beta_0} \Rightarrow r_a = e^{\beta_0} - 1.$$

For example, from our earlier examples using the German and Singapore term structures (Sect. 3.6), if our valuation date were 21 Dec 2018, we would use a constant risk-free rate of $(e^{0.0129935} - 1)$ or 1.3078% in Germany, or a constant risk-free rate of $(e^{0.028532} - 1)$ or 2.8943% in Singapore.[1]

2. We could also solve for some constant annually-compounded interest rate y say that gives the same present value as the actual yield curve for an arbitrary annuity, say CU 1 per year. If the term structure of spot interest rates is expressed in terms of annually compounded rates $r_{t,a}$ for maturity t, we have:

$$\sum_{t=1}^{\infty} \frac{1}{(1+y)^t} = \frac{1}{y} = \sum_{t=1}^{\infty} \frac{1}{(1+r_{t,a})^t}.$$

We need to assume that $r_{t,a}$ flattens to a constant rate for some high enough t, usually the maturity of the longest available government bond. Say this point where the yield curve is assumed to flatten is at N years. Then the present value today of the cashflows after this point is given by:

$$\left(\frac{1}{r_N}\right) \Big/ (1+r_N)^N .$$

From this, we can solve for y.

3. **YTM on longest bond**: Another common assumption is to use the yield to maturity on the longest maturity benchmark government bond as an estimate of the constant risk-free rate, expressed as an annually compounded rate.
4. **YTM on 10-year bond**: Another common assumption is to use the yield to maturity on the 10-year benchmark government bond as an estimate of the constant risk-free rate, expressed as an annually compounded rate.

6.5.1 The Risk-Free Rate and Currency

The appropriate risk-free rate for a business valuation is decided not by the country in which the business operates, but rather by the currency used to project cashflows.

For example, suppose that we are valuing a company that is based in Singapore, but reports in US dollars. Then the risk-free rate is determined not by the term structure of Singapore government bonds, but rather the term structure of US government bonds.

6.6 Cost of Debt

The cost of debt reflects the returns demanded by the debtholder of the target company, as of the valuation date.

[1] Strictly speaking, for Germany, we should use the term structure on ECB bonds rather than Bundesbank data, since Germany does not issue its own currency. In practice, however, Bundesbank rates are considered a good enough proxy for risk-free rates in Germany.

The cost of debt could be interpreted as the market yield to maturity on a freshly-issued long-term bond issued by the target company on the valuation date (or the rates given by the Z-spread on such a bond if we allow the cost of debt to vary for different maturities). This cost could be proxied by a number of measures:

6.6.1 Level 1: Yield on Traded Bonds

If the target entity has long-term bonds outstanding that trade in a properly functioning market with quoted prices, then the valuation-date yield to maturity (or Z-spread) on such bonds is a direct Level 1 measure of the cost of debt.

6.6.2 Level 2: Effective Interest Rate on Recently-Issued Debt

If the target company has no traded debt instruments, then a second-best alternative is to use the reported effective interest rate on a recently issued bond or loan, if the issue date is close enough to the valuation date.

6.6.3 Level 2: Spread on Traded Bond of Similar Risk

In the absence of either traded bonds or a recently issued debt instrument, the valuer can refer to the average yield to maturity (or Z-spread) for traded bonds that have the same credit rating as the target company. Then we would determine the cost of debt by taking the risk-free rate plus a spread (Z-spread or nominal spread) as discussed in Sect. 4.3.

6.6.4 Level 3: Spread Based on Synthetic Credit Rating

If we do not have a credit rating for the target company, we can construct a synthetic credit rating as discussed in Sect. 4.3.3.2. This is clearly a Level 3 input, so should only be used if the methods based on Level 1 or Level 2 inputs are not available.

6.7 Cost of Equity

Two commonly used models to estimate the cost of equity are:

1. The capital asset pricing model (CAPM),
2. The build-up model.

The CAPM finds the cost of equity for a target company by starting with the risk-free rate and adding a fixed spread for risk that is obtained by multiplying beta (β) for the target company shares by an equity risk premium.

Beta is a measure of risk for the target company that tracks how sensitive it is to market-wide shocks. Roughly, if beta is 3 for a target company, that means that a market-wide shock that moves the entire market up or down by 1 basis point on average would move the target company shares by 3 basis points on average in the same direction (up or down).

The equity risk premium is the extent by which average returns on a broad market portfolio are higher than the risk-free rate. Equivalently, it is the spread over the risk-free rate that investors in a broad market portfolio demand, to compensate for their additional risk.

The build-up model starts with the risk-free rate and adds separate spreads for market risk, size, and industry. This approach is more commonly used when valuing small enterprises.

6.7.1 The Capital Asset Pricing Model (CAPM)

The capital asset pricing model (CAPM) (Sharpe 1964; Lintner 1965) models the return on any instrument, labelled as instrument i say, as:

$$\tilde{R}_i = R_f + \beta_i (R_m - R_f) + \tilde{\epsilon}_i, \tag{6.1}$$

where

- $\tilde{R}_i$ is the holding return on instrument i over some fixed period say a day, month, year etc. Holding return is the return from buying the instrument at the beginning of the period and holding to the end of the period. It includes both capital appreciation and any income from the instrument over the period (in the case of a share, it includes any dividends with an ex-dividend date during the period). The superscript $\tilde{}$ is a standard mathematical notation indicating that the variable referred to has a random component (R_i in this case).
- R_f is the holding return on a risk-free instrument (government bond) over the same period that $\tilde{R}_i$ is measured.
- R_m is the holding return on a broad diversified market portfolio over the same period that $\tilde{R}_i$ and R_f are measured. In practice, this return is measured using an index such as the Dow Jones Industrial index in the USA.
- β_i or beta for instrument i is a parameter that captures how variable are the returns on instrument i relative to the broader market.
- $\tilde{\epsilon}_i$ is a random term. It could be either positive or negative. It is assumed to be distributed normally (Bell curve) with a mean of zero.

We next discuss the estimation of beta.

6.7.2 Regression Beta

The key measurement issue in CAPM is how to measure beta (β_i).

In our context, we are mainly concerned with the beta for an equity instrument, that is, the ordinary share of an enterprise.

For a listed enterprise i with a history of share prices, we can use linear regression to estimate β_i for ordinary shares of i.

We re-write the model in Equation 6.1 as follows:

$$\tilde{R}_i = R_f(1 - \beta_i) + \beta_i R_m + \tilde{\epsilon}_i. \tag{6.2}$$

Then if we set the term $R_f(1 - \beta_i)$ in Equation 6.2 to be equal to α_i say, we have:

$$\tilde{R}_i = \alpha_i + \beta_i R_m + \tilde{\epsilon}_i. \tag{6.3}$$

We can estimate the parameters α_i and β_i by using linear regression of $\tilde{R}_i$ on R_m, where we measure R_i using a recent time series of periodic returns on shares of i, and we measure R_m using the corresponding returns on a broad market index for the market where shares of i trade.

6.7.2.1 Regression Beta Example: SAP

We collect daily prices from 1 Jan 2018 to 1 Jan 2019 for SAP. We also collect the corresponding levels of the relevant market index for SAP (the DAX index). These prices and index levels are adjusted for dividends and stock splits.[2]

We calculate daily SAP returns based on the daily prices (daily change in price expressed as a percentage). Similarly we calculate daily market returns (daily change in the index expressed as a percentage).

We then run a linear regression of the SAP share price returns on the market returns. We obtain the following equation:

$$\text{SAP returns} = 0.0007 + 1.05 \times \text{Market returns}.$$

Therefore, our estimated regression beta for SAP is 1.05.

The regression output is shown graphically in Fig. 6.2.

6.7.3 Guideline Company Beta

We cannot use regression to find beta for a private company, since such a company does not have a share price history. We estimate the beta for such a company using the median or average regression beta from a group of similar guideline companies.

---

[2] I used Yahoo Finance to collect the data.

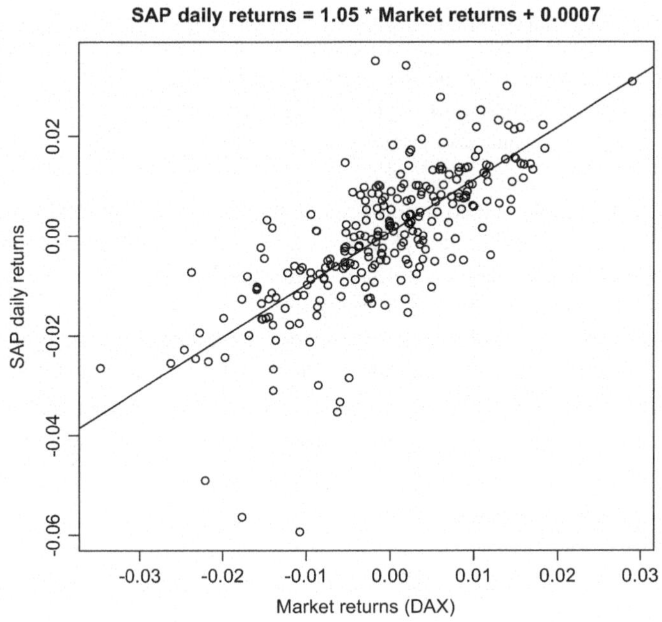

Fig. 6.2 SAP regression beta estimation

The procedure is as follows:

1. Identify the guideline companies.
2. Use linear regression to find the regression beta for the ordinary shares of each of the guideline companies.
3. The guideline companies differ from each other and the target company in terms of leverage or gearing (the D/E ratio). To common-size the guideline companies in terms of leverage, we estimate an *unlevered* beta for each guideline company, with the notation β_U say (we drop the subscript i for conciseness). The unlevered beta is the beta that the company's ordinary shares would have in a hypothetical situation where all the company's debt is completely replaced by ordinary shares—that is, it is a zero-debt firm. To estimate the unlevered beta, we use Hamada's formula (Hamada 1972):

$$\beta_U = \beta_L \Big/ \left(1 + \frac{D}{E}(1 - tx)\right). \tag{6.4}$$

where

β_L is the levered beta (for ordinary shares of some company i. We drop the subscript i for conciseness). This is the actual beta that reflects the company's actual leverage.

β_U is the unlevered beta (for company i ordinary shares.)

$\frac{D}{E}$ is the *fair-value-based* debt-to-equity ratio (for company i).

tx is the corporate income tax rate faced by company i.

Hamada's formula is a commonly-used heuristic to reflect the impact of after-tax leverage on risk and thence β (it does have a theoretical basis too).

4. We take the median guideline company unlevered beta, say $\widehat{\beta_U}$, to be our estimate of the unlevered beta for the target company.
5. We can proceed to estimate the levered beta for the target company by using $\widehat{\beta_U}$, Hamada's formula, and our estimate of the $\frac{D}{E}$ ratio for the target company. This is often assumed to be a long-run target $\frac{D}{E}$. Further, the long-run target $\frac{D}{E}$ is often set to be equal to the average of the industry $\frac{D}{E}$ ratio (or median of the guideline company $\frac{D}{E}$ ratios). If our estimate of the target company's $\frac{D}{E}$ ratio is $\widehat{(D/E)}$, we have, using Hamada's formula:

$$\beta_L = \widehat{\beta_U}\left(1 + \widehat{(D/E)}(1 - tx)\right).$$

Here all the parameters (beta, leverage, tax rate) are specific to the target company. The ratio $\frac{D}{E}$ is based on fair values, not book values.

6.7.3.1 Guideline Company Beta: Example

We are valuing a private company. We have collected information for five guideline companies as shown in Table 6.7.

From the data, we can work out the unlevered beta β_u for the guideline companies, applying Hamada's formula. We get Table 6.8.

The median of the unlevered betas is 1.0275. We assign this as our estimated unlevered beta for the target company.

The target company has a target long-run D/E of 1.5, which we use to calculate the levered beta. The company faces an income tax rate of 20%. Therefore, applying Hamada's formula, we can get the levered beta for our target company:

$$\beta_L = 1.0275 \times (1 + 1.5 \times (1 - 20\%)) = 2.2606.$$

Table 6.7 Guideline company levered betas

Company	Regression beta	D/E ratio	Tax rate
1	2.1	1.5	30%
2	2.8	2.3	25%
3	1.9	0.8	10%
4	1.2	0.2	30%
5	2.5	1.8	20%

Table 6.8 Guideline company unlevered betas

Company	β_U
1	1.0243
2	1.0275
3	1.1046
4	1.0526
5	1.0246

Our estimated beta for the target company is 2.2606.

6.7.4 Estimating k_e and $k_{e,U}$

Having estimated beta using a guideline company approach, we can proceed to estimate k_e for the target company using CAPM.

$$k_e = r_a + \beta_L(r_m - r_a)$$

where

k_e is the cost of equity, expressed as an annually compounded rate per year.
r_a is the risk-free rate, expressed as an annually compounded rate per year.
r_m is the average market return, expressed as an annually compounded rate per year.

In practice, we estimate the term $(r_m - r_a)$ as a fixed parameter called the equity risk premium or ERP. Then we can rewrite the formula for k_e as:

$$k_e = r_a + \beta_L \times ERP.$$

We can similarly obtain the *unlevered* cost of equity $k_{e,U}$, which is needed for the APV, by using β_U instead of β_L in the formula. We have:

$$k_{e,U} = r_a + \beta_U \times ERP.$$

6.7.4.1 Example $k_{e,U}$ Calculation

A company has an unlevered beta of 1.0275 and a levered beta of 2.2606. The risk-free rate is 2%, and the equity risk premium is 5%. Find the levered cost of equity. Find the unlevered cost of equity.

The levered cost of equity is:

$$2\% + 2.2606 \times 5\% = 13.3\%.$$

The unlevered cost of equity is:

$$2\% + 1.0275 \times 5\% = 7.14\%.$$

6.7.5 Estimating the Equity Risk Premium (ERP)

We can follow two different approaches to measure the ERP (Damodaran 2012).

1. We can use historical data on the market index to measure the mean annual market returns over a long period to proxy for r_a. We can use either the geometric or arithmetic mean.
2. We can use a forward-looking procedure that compares the actual current market index with the expected dividends from the index.

Let us use an example to illustrate the calculation of the arithmetic and geometric mean. Suppose that we have compiled data on the level of a market index every year for the last 20 years. The data is as in Table 6.9.[3]

Our estimate of the risk-free rate r_a is 2% per year based on annual compounding.

6.7.5.1 Arithmetic Mean

The arithmetic mean approach estimates the market return R_m for a year by taking the arithmetic average of a past series of annual returns on the relevant market index.

Table 6.9 Market index 20 years data

Year	Index	Returns
1	9748	NA
2	12337	0.26559294
3	11866	−0.03817784
4	12111	0.02064723
5	12987	0.07233094
6	13831	0.06498806
7	12881	−0.06868628
8	14434	0.12056517
9	15296	0.05972011
10	16417	0.07328713
11	17134	0.04367424
12	18467	0.07779853
13	18328	−0.00752694
14	20606	0.12429070
15	21100	0.02397360
16	21751	0.03085308
17	23603	0.08514551
18	24479	0.03711393
19	25020	0.02210058
20	26010	0.03956835

[3]This is simulated data for a fictional market index. It does not represent any actual index.

In our example, we would add up the returns in Table 6.9 and divide by the number of returns in the series (19). This gives us an arithmetic average of 0.0551189 or 5.5119%.

Our estimate of the equity risk premium is (5.5119%–2%) or 3.5119%. This is the number that we would use in the CAPM equation to estimate the cost of equity.

6.7.5.2 Geometric Mean

The geometric mean computes an average by multiplying numbers with each other and then taking the root based on the number of observations N say. Therefore, it finds some number X such that we multiply our starting number repeatedly for N iterations by X, or in other words if we multiply the starting number by X^N, we would get the ending number in the series.

In our context, we seek the geometric mean of one plus the annual return. We can express this as:

$$R_a = \left(\prod_{y=1}^{N} (1 + R_y) \right)^{\left(\frac{1}{N}\right)}.$$

where the symbol $\prod$ is standard mathematical notation for a cumulative *product* over terms indexed y ranging from 1 to N, and R_y is the annual return for the y'th year in the series.

We estimate our geometric mean (over 19 years) as 1.053011 corresponding to an annualized rate of return of 5.3011%. Then our estimate of the market return R_m is 5.3011%, and our estimate of the equity risk premium is $5.3011 - 2\% = 3.3011\%$.

The geometric mean is conceptually better than the arithmetic mean, because it can be interpreted as a compound interest rate. Thus, if we start with the beginning level of our index 9748, and apply the geometric mean as a compound rate of interest for the next 19 years, we would get the ending market index in the series.

$$9748 \times (1 + 5.3011\%)^{19} = 26010.$$

In other words, our calculation shows that the market has returned an annually compounded rate of return of 5.3011% over the last 19 years. The arithmetic mean does not have this interpretation.

Adding a compound interest rate to the risk-free rate is also more internally consistent, since the risk-free rate is an annually compounded interest rate.

The geometric mean has the property that we only need the first and last items in the series to calculate it. (The intermediate terms cancel each other out in the cumulative product expression, if we express each term as a ratio of beginning and ending index levels, as you can verify.)

We have:

$$\left(\frac{26010}{9748}\right)^{\left(\frac{1}{19}\right)} = 1.053011.$$

This property that the geometric mean depends on just two numbers makes it less stable. The number could change significantly if we vary the start and end points of our calculation. Supposing for example, that we started with the year 2 index figure. Then our geometric mean calculation would be:

$$\frac{26010}{12337}^{\left(\frac{1}{18}\right)} = 1.042308.$$

This corresponds to a market return of 4.23% a year, significantly lower than the calculation with just an additional year of data.

This instability and dependence on the choice of start and end points is a practical disadvantage of the geometric mean over the arithmetic mean. When choosing between them, we would trade off between the conceptual superiority of the geometric mean and the practical issues with it. (The arithmetic mean also has practical estimation issues. For example, it could be very sensitive to years with extremely large positive or negative returns. If we have such observations in our sample, the geometric mean may be preferable. Another non-standard alternative could be to use the median.)

6.7.5.3 Implied Equity Premium

The two measures we discussed earlier gave historical market returns. But the number in the CAPM equation is really a forward-looking measure of returns—the expected market return in the future. There is no reason to expect the past rate of return to continue into the future.

An alternative approach is to set the current level of the market index to be the fair value from a standard dividend discount model, and then solve for the rate of return that leads to that fair value. For example, suppose that our current level of the market index is P_0. Suppose also that we have estimated the current forward dividend yield on the market index to be 3%. We expect dividends to grow at a rate of 1% in the long run. We can set P_0 equal to the value from a one-stage dividend discount model (Gordon growth model) as follows:

$$P_0 = \frac{0.03 \times P_0}{R_m - 0.01}.$$

This simplifies to the following expression (P_0 drops out):

$$1 = \frac{0.03}{R_m - 0.01}.$$

Solving, we get $R_m = 0.03 + 0.01 = 4\%$.

If our risk-free rate is 2%, this leads to a measure of the equity premium equal to 0.04–0.02 or 2%.

It is also a standard practice to use the dividend yield on the index directly as a measure of the future market return. This treats the future growth rate of dividends as zero. Conversely, we can use more complex dividend-based models such as the H-model or three-stage models to solve for the market return.

6.7.6 Build-Up Method

The build-up method is an alternative to CAPM. It is often preferred when we are valuing small or medium enterprises (SMEs), where finding comparable guideline listed companies may be difficult. To apply this method, we need regularly published market statistics on the returns from the broad market, as well as from particular industry and size groups.

To apply the build-up method, we start with the risk-free rate and add successive spreads for equity risk (the equity risk premium), size risk, and industry risk. We may also add a firm-specific spread for risks facing the target company, though this is subjective and clearly Level 3. It would need to be carefully justified using risk assessment information for the target company.

We have:

$$k_e = r_a + ERP + SIZEP + INDP.$$

where k_e is the constant cost of equity, r_a is the annually compounded constant risk-free rate, ERP is the equity risk premium, SIZEP is the size premium, and INDP is the industry premium.

We can determine SIZEP as the historical premium that returns from the particular size decile of listed firms to which our SME would belong show over broader market returns (often this is the smallest-size firms).

We can determine INDP as the historical premium that returns from the particular industry that our target company belongs to show over broader market returns. Strictly speaking, this should be controlled for size, i.e., it should reflect the returns for the same industry within the same size decile. But if such detailed information is not available, we assume that the same INDP applies for all size deciles.

6.7.6.1 Example: Build Up Approach

We are valuing Tiny Co, a private SME. The risk-free rate r_a is 2% annually compounded. The equity risk premium estimated using a geometric mean model is 3%. Using historical market data, we estimate that companies in the size decile with the smallest listed firms (by market capitalization) have on average returned a premium of 1.5% over the broader market averages. We do not know the market value of Tiny Co, but we do know that in terms of revenues and total assets, it is smaller than almost all listed companies.

We also estimate that listed companies in the same industry as Tiny Co returned on average 0.8% higher than the broader market average.

What is the cost of equity for Tiny Co based on a build-up approach?

We have:

$$k_e = 0.02 + 0.03 + 0.015 + 0.008 = 7.3\%.$$

6.8 Choosing Guideline Companies

It is difficult to find guideline companies that are very similar to the target company. Companies tend to have unique features, such as the personalities of key management personnel, or the organization culture, or the particular strategic position that the company seeks in an industry.

As such, we seek a group of guideline companies that are similar to the target company in a few key respects. Typical criteria are size, industry, regional location, and strategic position. If we are performing sum-of-the-parts valuation, we identify separate sets of guidelines for each separate business segment.

We briefly discuss each of these criteria below.

6.8.1 Industry

We start our selection of guideline companies by restricting to listed companies that operate in the same industry. Given the diverse nature of business operations, it may sometimes be difficult to define the industry. As a guide, we may use standard industry codes defined by the listing authority or some independent source. These are usually at different levels of specialization. For example, with the Standard Industrial Classification (SIC) codes used by the US government and others, codes in the 1000 to 1999 range refer to the mining sector. Within that sector, codes within the range 1300 to 1399 refer to oil and gas. Within that industry, code 1381 refers to "drilling oil and gas wells", while code 1389 refers to "oil and gas field services".

We can choose how specialized we want to be depending on whether our target company's business can easily be pigeonholed into a specialized code, and also depending on the total number of peer companies available within that code. For example, if our target company is in code 1381, but we cannot find a sufficient number of peers in that group, we may opt to define industry more broadly.

If we are valuing a conglomerate, which operates in many industries, we may choose sum-of-the-parts valuation, in which case we would identify separate sets of guidelines for each business segment. If we want to find guideline companies for the conglomerate as a whole, we can search for conglomerates with a similar mix of businesses and/or a mix of guideline companies from all the industries in which the conglomerate operates.

6.8.2 Location

Simultaneously to the industry restriction, we restrict our choice to companies that operate in the same geographical area as our target. In a globalized world, even a small company may operate in multiple jurisdictions and deal with different currencies, so we may need to define location as a broader geographical region that includes multiple countries and currencies, such as "South-East Asia" or "Europe and the Middle East", or more complicated non-standard groupings ("Brazil and Russia").

If we were searching for peers for SAP for example, the field of operations would be worldwide.

When we include companies from different countries with different reporting currencies and different accounting requirements, we may need to be cautious about comparing valuation ratios, other ratios and even regression betas. We may need to be aware of broader regional differences, and make adjustments if necessary to reflect them.

6.8.3 Size

Due to economies of scale and greater complexity, larger companies are often very different from their smaller counterparts. We therefore seek listed guideline companies that are approximately the same size as our target company in terms of metrics such as total revenues, total assets, or employee strength. For very small target companies, that are far below the size of any listed company, it may be preferable to use DCF valuation with a build-up-method cost of equity as opposed to selecting guideline companies that may not really be comparable.

6.8.4 Strategy

Apple and Dell may both sell computers, but they are very different businesses, and would be poor guidelines for each other. The difference comes from the different strategies that each company pursues to achieve their goals. Apple pursues a policy of "product differentiation" whereby a company attracts a quasi-monopoly power by offering a product that is sufficiently different from competitors so that the competing products are perceived as poor substitutes. Dell on the other hand pursues a policy that leans more to "cost leadership". Dell's products are more generic than those of Apple, but they are able to compete effectively by lowering cost without sacrificing quality, by exploiting lean manufacturing strategies such as just-in-time. This gives Dell pricing power.

We can analyze where a company falls in terms of these different strategies by analyzing their return on assets using Dupont analysis:

$$\text{Return on assets} = \text{Net profit margin} \times \text{Asset turnover.}$$

A company that leans towards product differentiation would have higher margins (because of its quasi-monopoly power) and lower asset turnover (since the focus is not on lean operations). A company that leans towards cost leadership would have thinner margins (because they would seek to exploit their pricing power to grab market share), and a stronger asset turnover (because of their focus on reducing costs).

We therefore look at these ratios for our target company, and seek guideline companies that are similar in terms of the levels of these ratios.

This concludes our discussion of enterprise valuation. In Chap. 7, we discuss intangibles, purchase price allocation in a takeover, and goodwill impairment.

Exercises

(Monetary units are in CU unless otherwise mentioned).

6.1. Projecting Cash Flows
Find and download the latest annual reports of the following companies:

- Siemens Group
- Royal Dutch Shell Group
- Cheung Kong Hutchison Group
- Singapore Airlines (SIA) Group

For each of these companies, do the following:

(a) Project the consolidated balance sheet and income statement for the next five years, in the reporting currency.
(b) Use your projections to compute the FCF for each year for the next five years.
(c) Convert the cashflows to US$ cashflows using CIRP (if the reporting currency is not already US$).

6.2. WACC Computation
You would need to find annual reports and other relevant information for the following companies:

- Siemens Group
- Royal Dutch Shell Group
- Cheung Kong Hutchison Group
- Singapore Airlines (SIA) Group

For each of these companies, do the following, for each of the next five years, based on a reporting currency perspective (not US$):

(a) Calculate the levered cost of equity (It is fine to use the company's own regression beta, computed from a price series, or as reported by Yahoo finance or similar service).
(b) Calculate the unlevered cost of equity.
(c) Estimate the cost of debt.
(d) Calculate the WACC.

6.3. WACC-Based DCF
Refer to your calculations from Exercises 6.1(b) and 6.2. Using these:

(a) Find the DCF-based enterprise value for each of the four companies in their reporting currency. (You may need to find additional inputs, such as the long-term growth rate.)
(b) Based on your answer to (a), find the DCF-based fair value of equity per share for each of the entities.
(c) Compare your prediction to the current price of a share.

6.4. Guideline Companies
Suppose that you are valuing Rolex, a private entity. Based on whatever public information you find available, find 5 guideline companies for Rolex. Justify your choices.

References

Damodaran, A. (2012). *Investment valuation* (3rd ed.). Hoboken: Wiley.
Hamada, R. (1972). The effect of the firm's capital structure on the systematic risk of common stocks. *Journal of Finance, 27*, 435–452.
Lintner, J. (1965). Security prices, risk, and maximal gains from diversification. *Journal of Finance, 20*, 587–615.
Sharpe, W. (1964). Capital asset prices: A theory of market equilibrium under conditions of risk. *The Journal of Finance, 19*, 425–442.

7 Intangibles Valuation, Purchase Price Allocation (PPA) and Goodwill Impairment

We start by outlining the key requirements of IAS 38 *Intangible Assets* in conjunction with relevant aspects of IFRS 3 *Business Combinations*. We proceed to briefly outline the three broad approaches to intangibles valuation—market, income, and cost approaches. We then proceed to examine selected standard intangible valuation techniques in more detail, with examples—the relief from royalty model, the replacement cost model, the with and without model and the multi-period excess earnings model. We then take up lifing—models to estimate the life of intangibles. We show with an example how intangibles life can be determined by fitting a survival curve based on a Weibull distribution. We also briefly discuss Iowa type curves as alternatives to the Weibull survival curve. We turn next to purchase price allocation (PPA) in a takeover. This is the task of apportioning the purchase price of the acquired company among its various assets and goodwill, with the assets including newly-identified intangibles. We turn next to the task of fair-valuing NCI. We consider two approaches to fair-valuing NCI. Firstly, we consider a top-down model that starts with a model of equity based on a control perspective, and then successively applies discounts for lack of control and for lack of marketability. Secondly, we explain a bottom-up model that attempts to directly project the cashflows due to NCI and to discount them at a rate that is specific to NCI. Finally, we discuss the impairment of goodwill with an example. We focus on the calculation of value in use.

7.1 Learning Outcomes

After completing this chapter, you would be able to:

1. Value intangibles using selected standard techniques.
2. Estimate the life of an intangible using survival curve analysis.
3. Perform the main steps in a purchase price allocation (PPA) in a takeover.

S. Lynn, *Valuation for Accountants*, Springer Texts in Business and Economics,
https://doi.org/10.1007/978-981-15-0357-3_7

4. Value non-controlling interest using top-down and bottom-up approaches.
5. Perform an impairment test of goodwill.

7.2 IFRS and Intangibles

An intangible asset under IAS 38 is a non-financial asset that does not have any physical substance—it does not exist physically. Examples are trademarks, brands, or contractual advantages of various kinds.

Intangible assets are typically recognized only when they are acquired from outside the reporting entity, not when they are generated internally within the reporting entity. For example, Coca Cola's balance sheet does not include its own famous brandname "Coca Cola" as an asset. But Coca Cola does recognize various other brandnames that they acquired either through purchase or in a takeover.

There is one exception to this rule of "no internally generated intangibles". This is the development cost asset. This asset is recognized at the late stage of an R&D project, when the project is deemed certain of success and likely to generate future cashflows with high probability. At this stage, subsequent R&D costs on the project are capitalized into an intangible asset called development costs.

In most cases, intangible assets are first recognized during a takeover, as part of purchase price allocation (which we discuss later in this chapter). IFRS 3 *Business Combinations* gives the following non-exhaustive list of types of intangibles that can be recognized:

A. **Marketing:** These are assets that are generated mainly from marketing efforts, e.g., a brandname.
B. **Customer-related:** These are assets that are generated from the entity's customer base, e.g., a customer relationship asset, a CRM database.
C. **Artistic:** These are assets that are a product of artistic efforts, e.g., a proprietary jingle used in advertising, a logo.
D. **Contract-related:** These assets arise from contractual rights, e.g., a franchise, the rights to exclusively use some resource under contract with the owner (use rights).
E. **Technology-related:** These arise from proprietary technology. They include patents, software, in-process research and development.

7.2.1 Identification Criteria

In identifying an asset as an intangible, at least one of the following two criteria must be satisfied (in addition to the usual criteria to identify any asset such as that the entity controls the item and the item is expected to generate future benefits):

1. Separability
2. Legal claim

7.2.1.1 Separability

If an asset satisfies the separability criterion, then the entity controlling the asset is at least hypothetically able to sell the asset as a standalone item. For example, suppose that an online retailer has accumulated a customer relationship management (CRM) database, containing detailed information on their customers and those customers' preferences. There should be a market for this database as a standalone asset, as other external retailers could benefit from the information and be willing to pay for it separately. We can argue that the CRM database satisfies the separability criterion.

7.2.1.2 Legal Claim

A different criterion to identify an asset looks at whether the entity has an exclusive legal claim to control the profits arising from the intangible. For example, if an entity possesses a patent for a particular technology, it can legally challenge any attempt from other parties to use the technology without its permission. Even in the case where the company does not have a document certifying its exclusive control, it may be able to legally challenge attempts to usurp its knowhow, under copyright law or other intellectual property protections that may be available in the jurisdiction where it operates. In that case, it can identify an intangible asset under a legal claim criterion.

7.2.1.3 Two Special Cases

Two special cases that deviate somewhat from the identification criteria are human resource assets, and customer base assets.

In the case of human resources, we typically do not identify or recognize them as intangibles, even if they appear to satisfy the identification criteria. It could be distasteful to account for employees or their services as though they are someone's property.

In the case of a customer base asset, typically called a "customer relationship" asset, we would recognize the asset even if it does not clearly satisfy the identification criteria—we cannot sell our customers, and we cannot usually legally force them to buy from us. But typically a base of loyal customers forms a big part of the value purchased in a takeover, and it would be misleading to exclude it. The standard therefore provides a somewhat more flexible interpretation of the identification criteria in this special case of a customer relationship asset.

7.2.2 Recognition Criteria

Identifying an intangible asset does not mean that it automatically qualifies to be recognized on the balance sheet. In order to be recognized, further criteria must be satisfied. The benefits from the asset must be probable, and the value of those benefits should be reliably measurable.

7.3 Valuation Techniques for Intangibles

Three broad approaches to fair-value intangibles are as follows:

1. The market approach
2. The income approach
3. The cost approach

The market approach values the intangible using the known market value of similar items, if available. The market approach is less applicable for intangibles, as they typically are not traded in markets.

The income approach values the intangible by capitalizing current or expected future income from the intangible.

The cost approach values the intangible by estimating how much it would cost to replace it (i.e., its replacement cost.)

Many techniques used in practice are hybrids of these three approaches. Rather than discuss each of the approaches separately, we will give illustrative examples of a few specific techniques that are in standard use to value particular types of intangibles.

These are:

1. Relief from royalty
2. Replacement cost
3. With and without
4. Multi-period excess earnings model (MPEEM)

7.3.1 Relief from Royalty

The relief from royalty approach is used to value assets such as copyright, trademarks or patents, that we use in our business. If someone else owned the intangible asset, we would have to pay for the right to use it. We therefore value the intangible asset in terms of the amount that we save by owning it. If we considered selling the intangible asset, this is the minimum price that we would accept. Therefore, it would be the price that would be offered by a potential buyer in a well-functioning market. Therefore, it is a reasonable measure of fair value.

We illustrate with an example.

7.3.1.1 Example: Relief from Royalty

Srivastava Inc owns a trademark. Its projected sales under the trademark are as follows for the next five years (amounts in CU):

Year	1	2	3	4	5
Sales	1,000	1,100	1,200	1,300	1,400

Sales are projected to grow after year 5 at 1% per year.

The royalty rate in the industry for similar trademarks is 2%, based on recent transaction data.

To value the trademark, we would estimate the future royalties from the trademark, and obtain their present value by applying an appropriate discount rate.

In choosing a discount rate for an intangible asset, the basic principle is that the intangible asset is *at least as risky* as the business entity as a whole, and likely more risky. So the discount rate for the intangible asset should be at least as high as the WACC for the relevant enterprise (Srivastava Inc in our example). The discount rate is expressed in the form $WACC + X$ where X is some markup.

In the case of a marketing intangible like a trademark, one external benchmark could be the WACC of a young single-product company in the same industry. We note that Startop Co is a young single-product company in the same industry, selling a similar product. Startop Co has a WACC of 12%. From this, we derive our discount rate for the trademark to be 12%, or $WACC + 200$ bps.

We can now proceed to value the intangible. We calculate the royalties for five years and a terminal value equal to the present value of the long-run royalties after Year 5 based on a single-stage model with a 1% growth rate and a 12% discount rate. We follow the *mid-year convention*. We have (amounts in CU):

Year	1	2	3	4	5	Terminal Value (at 4.5 years)
Royalties	20	22	24	26	28	$\frac{28\times1.01}{0.12-0.01}$ CU 257.09.
DCF	18.898	18.561	18.079	17.487	16.814	154.385

Adding up the discounted cashflows gives us a fair value for the trademark of CU 244.22.

7.3.2 Replacement Cost: Software

In the replacement cost approach, we value an intangible asset by the amount that we would have to spend to replace it, were it suddenly unavailable.

We illustrate with an example of software.

7.3.2.1 Example: Replacement Cost for Software

Bolshoi Inc has an accounting software system that it uses for its accounting and management information systems. We are valuing this software as an intangible asset, using a replacement cost approach. That is, we seek to estimate how much it would cost us to recreate the software if it suddenly disappeared along with all its supporting documentation, backups, source programs, etc. We seek the expert advice of a computer systems analyst to obtain our estimates.

The systems analyst verifies that the source programs used to develop the software are 12,000 lines long. The analyst estimates that a programming team could recreate these 12,000 lines at a rate of 12 lines per programmer-hour and a cost of CU 100 per programmer-hour (henceforth just "hour" for conciseness).

This gives us an initial replacement cost estimate of CU 100,000 obtained by multiplying 1,000 estimated hours by CU 100 per hour (1,000 hours = 12,000 lines $\times \frac{1}{12}$ hours per line). We refer to this initial replacement cost estimate as the *duplication cost new*. It is the cost today of exactly duplicating the software system.

The duplication cost new is not however the replacement cost, since if were creating the software today, we may be able to create it more efficiently, say by using a different design.

The systems analyst estimates that we could design new software that exactly replicates the functionality of the existing software, by refactoring the source code so that it fits into just 10,000 lines. This gives us a revised replacement cost estimate of CU 83,333.33 (833.33... hours × CU 100 per hour). We call this the *replacement cost new*. It is the cost of replacing the software with *new* software that provides the same functionality.

The analysis so far does not take into account that the software is not new. The software has lost some value due to age. If the software were a tangible asset like PPE, we would estimate something like depreciation on the replacement cost new to reflect loss of value due to wear and tear over the years. But an intangible asset does not suffer from wear and tear.

An intangible asset does however suffer from *obsolescence*, a loss of value because more advanced technology has made some of its functionality obsolete.

The systems analyst estimates that two modules of the software have been rendered obsolete, because their functions have been taken over by a web-based interface shared with other supply-chain partners. These two modules would contribute 2,000 lines of the refactored 10,000-line source code. Eliminating these two modules would lower costs by CU 16,666.67 (166.67 hour times CU 100 per hour). Subtracting this from the replacement cost new gives us a revised cost estimate of CU 66,666.67.

This is not the end of the story. This is a *pre-tax* estimate. If we actually spent this amount on a new software development project, we would receive a related tax deduction. If our corporate income tax rate is 20%, then the tax savings due to this deduction are CU 13,333.33. Therefore, the after-tax replacement cost estimate is CU 53,333.33. This is our final estimate of the software replacement cost. It is therefore our estimate of the fair value of the software. This is the minimum amount that we would ask for if someone were to buy the software from us.

To summarize the analysis, we have: (amounts in CU)

Duplication cost new	100,000
Adjustment for better design	(16,666.67)
Replacement cost new	83,333.33
Adjustment for obsolescence	(16,666.67)
Replacement cost (pre-tax)	66,666.67
Tax savings	(13,333.33)
Replacement cost (post tax)	53,333.33

7.3.3 Replacement Cost Example: Assembled Workforce

Although human resources are usually not recognized as assets on the balance sheet, we often need to determine their fair value as part of a purchase price allocation. We usually need the fair value of the *assembled workforce* of an acquired company as a supporting calculation in order to apply the multi-period excess earnings model (MPEEM) to value one or more intangible assets. The assembled workforce is the acquisition-date combined employee strength of the acquired company.

Human beings are of course usually tangible. The intangible asset in this case refers to the services that the employees provide, not the employees themselves.

We discuss the replacement cost approach to valuing the assembled workforce using an example.

7.3.3.1 Example: Assembled Workforce

We have taken over Nguyen Co. On the takeover date, the details of Nguyen Co employees are as follows in terms of rank, numbers and compensation:

Rank	Number	Salary (CU per year)	Perks (CU per year)
CEO	1	100,000	100,000
Senior management	10	80,000	20,000
Junior management	50	60,000	1,000
Supervisors	250	40,000	1,000
Workers	1,250	25,000	200

We hire a human resources (HR) consultant to help us estimate the replacement cost of the assembled workforce.

If our workforce suddenly disappeared and we were forced to replace them from scratch, we would need to spend money on these activities:

1. **Search:** to advertise positions and interview applicants
2. **Hiring:** upfront costs of engaging a new employee (administrative costs, commission to headhunters etc.)
3. **Training:** A fresh new employee would not be able to work as efficiently as the current worker without some period of training.

Our HR consultant advises us that search and hiring costs can be approximately measured as one month of basic salary—the standard commission charged by a headhunter. This gives us the following costs for each category of employee (amounts in CU):

Rank	Number	Salary	Hiring cost per head	Total cost
CEO	1	100,000	8,333.33	8,333.33
Senior managers	10	80,000	6,666.67	66,666.67
Junior managers	50	60,000	5,000	250,000
Supervisors	250	40,000	3,333.33	833,333.33
Workers	1,250	25,000	2,083.33	2,604,166.67

For training costs, the HR consultant suggests the following assumptions.

The CEO would need no training.

Senior management would each require 5 days of training under the tutelage of the CEO. The total cost would be 5 days of salary plus perks for the senior managers plus the same time lost for the CEO. If we assume 365 days in a year, we have (monetary amounts in CU):

$$\begin{aligned}\text{Training cost} &= 10 \text{ managers} \times \frac{5}{365} \text{ years} \times (80{,}000 + 20{,}000) \text{ p.a.}\\ &\quad +1 \text{ CEO} \times \frac{5}{365} \text{ years} \times (100{,}000 + 100{,}000) \text{ p.a.}\\ &= 16{,}438.\end{aligned}$$

Junior managers would each require 10 days of training, under the tutelage of a senior manager, with 1 senior manager required to train all the junior managers. Therefore the total training costs in CU for junior managers are as follows:

$$\begin{aligned}\text{Training cost} &= 50 \text{ junior managers} \times \frac{10}{365} \text{ years} \times (60{,}000 + 1{,}000) \text{ p.a.}\\ &\quad +1 \text{ senior managers} \times \frac{10}{365} \text{ years} \times (80{,}000 + 20{,}000) \text{ p.a.}\\ &= 86{,}301.37.\end{aligned}$$

Supervisors would each require one month of training under the tutelage of a junior manager, with one junior manager needed to train all the supervisors. Therefore, the total training costs for supervisors in CU are as follows (assuming a month is 1/12 of a year):

$$\begin{aligned}\text{Training cost} &= 250\text{ supervisors} \times \frac{1}{12}\text{ year} \times (40{,}000 + 1{,}000)\text{ p.a.}\\ &\quad + 1\text{ junior manager} \times \frac{1}{12}\text{ year} \times (60{,}000 + 1{,}000)\text{ p.a.}\\ &= 859{,}250.\end{aligned}$$

Workers would each require 6 months of training under the tutelage of a supervisor, with 5 supervisors required to train all the workers. Therefore the costs of training workers in CU are as follows:

$$\begin{aligned}\text{Training cost} &= 1{,}250\text{ workers} \times \frac{6}{12}\text{ year} \times (25{,}000 + 200)\text{ p.a.}\\ &\quad + 5\text{ supervisor} \times \frac{6}{12}\text{ years} \times (40{,}000 + 1{,}000)\text{ p.a.}\\ &= 15{,}852{,}500.\end{aligned}$$

We can now compile the pre-tax costs of our assembled workforce (amounts in CU).

Rank	Search and hiring	Training	Total
CEO	8,333.33	0	8,333.33
Senior managers	66,666.67	16,438.36	83,105.02
Junior managers	250,000	86,301.37	336,301.37
Supervisors	833,333.33	859,250	1,692,583.33
Workers	2,604,166.67	15,852,500	18,456,666.67
TOTAL	3,762,500	16,814,489.73	20,576,989.73

If Nguyen Co corporate income tax rate is 20%, then the tax savings would be CU 4,115,397.95. The after-tax replacement cost of our assembled workforce would be CU 16,461,591.78.

This value would not be recognized as an intangible asset under IAS 38. It would be treated as part of goodwill.

7.3.4 The With and Without Model

In the "with and without" model, we value an intangible by comparing cashflows *with* the intangible to cashflows *without* the intangible. As usual, we only need to consider items that are different between the two alternatives.

7.3.4.1 Example: With and Without

We illustrate the method with an example. We have just acquired Dinky Inc. At the acquisition date, Dinky possesses a contract with a key supplier. Under the contract Dinky agrees to buy widgets exclusively from the supplier. In exchange, the supplier guarantees Dinky a fixed price of CU 9 per widget for the duration of the contract. The contract has a remaining life of 3 years. Dinky plans to buy 10,000 widgets in Year 1, 10,100 widgets in Year 2, and 10,200 widgets in Year 3.

We estimate that the average open market price of widgets will be as follows in the next three years (amounts in CU):

Year	1	2	3
Price	15	25	23

Therefore the contract gives Dinky an advantageous price and cost savings. We identify this as a contract-related intangible asset, and proceed to value it using the "with and without" method.

If Dinky did not have the contract, the purchase costs for the input would be higher. This would be partially offset by lower taxes.

Dinky Inc faces a corporate income tax rate of 20%.

We calculate the cash outflows *with* the intangible:

Year	1	2	3
Purchase cost	90,000	90,900	91,800
Tax savings	(18,000)	(18,180)	(18,360)
Net relevant cash outflow	72,000	72,720	73,440

We calculate the cash outflows *without* the intangible:

Year	1	2	3
Purchase cost	150,000	252,500	234,600
Tax savings	(30,000)	(50,500)	(46,920)
Net relevant cash outflow	120,000	202,000	187,680

Taking the difference between the with and without cashflows, we have the incremental savings from the intangible as follows:

Year	1	2	3
Incremental savings from intangible	48,000	129,280	114,240

We need to determine the present value of these savings. To decide on an appropriate discount rate, we start with the WACC for Dinky Inc which is 12%, and estimate a suitable spread above this to reflect the higher risk of the intangible. We assess that the spread should be 500 bps. Then the discount rate is 17%.

Discounting the cashflows at 17% under a mid-year convention, we get a present value of CU 223,682.48. This is our estimate of the fair value of the contract-related intangible asset.

7.3.5 The Multi-period Excess Earnings Model (MPEEM)

The multi-period excess earnings model (MPEEM) values an intangible asset as the present value of the incremental benefits that it produces. This is an extension of the residual income valuation approach.

Intangible assets do not produce benefits in isolation. They are productive as part of a combination of assets.

In order to isolate the incremental benefits from the intangible alone, we consider an imaginary situation where we own the intangible only, and have to pay rent to outside parties for all the other supporting assets that we need to produce value. Then the net benefits after subtracting these hypothetical rents gives us an estimate of the value added by the intangible asset on its own.

The hypothetical rents from the various supporting assets are known as *contributory charges*. Contributory charges are measured using a *contributory charge rate* times the fair value of the supporting asset.

Contributory charge rates can be measured in two different ways–rates *on* the supporting asset, and rates *on and of* the supporting asset.

A rate *on* the supporting asset reflects that the supporting asset is maintained at its valuation-date fair value throughout the life of the intangible being valued. Then the contributory charge reflects only payment for the right to use the supporting asset. The charge does not include any compensation for wear and tear or other loss on the supporting asset.

Then the notional "lessee" of the supporting asset is expected to maintain the asset in its original condition throughout the period of its use. The costs required to do so must be reflected as part of the cashflows before considering contributory charges.

A rate *on and of* the supporting asset allows the supporting asset to decline in value over the life of the intangible asset being valued due to wear and tear, obsolescence, etc. Then the hypothetical rental payments reflect not just payments for the right to use the supporting asset, but also compensation for the decline in its value.

We will focus on contributory charge rates *on* the supporting asset in our example. This means that the supporting asset is maintained at its valuation-date fair value throughout the life of the intangible asset being valued. It also means that the projected cashflows before considering contributory charges must be net of costs required to maintain the supporting asset value.

If the supporting asset is one that we have valued using a present value calculation with some discount rate k say, then the contributory charge on that supporting asset should match the discount rate k.

We demonstrate the multi-period excess earnings model using an example.

7.3.5.1 MPEEM Example: Customer Relationship Asset

We have acquired Chuchai Inc. We have identified a customer relationship intangible that we proceed to measure at its fair value using MPEEM.

We use the following case facts:

1. Sales from the existing customers are projected to be CU 100 million next year and to grow at 1% per year thereafter, assuming no attrition.
2. Existing customers are projected to depart at a straight-line rate over the next five years.
3. Operating expenses are projected to be a constant 46% of sales. These include projected depreciation based on tax depreciation rules rather than financial reporting assumptions.
4. Chuchai Inc faces a corporate income tax rate of 20%.
5. Working capital requirements are projected to be 3% of sales.
6. The customer relationship asset depends on the following supporting assets—net working capital, PPE, a trademark, and the assembled workforce.
7. The valuation-date fair value of the PPE is CU 20 million.
8. The valuation-date fair value of the assembled workforce is estimated at CU 15.30 million, using a replacement cost model.
9. The contributory charge rate on the net working capital is 5%, which is an after-tax rate.
10. The contributory charge rate on the PPE is 7%, which is an after-tax rate.
11. The contributory charge rate on the assembled workforce is estimated at 13%. This is computed as the Chuchai Inc after-tax WACC of 10% plus a spread of 300 bps.
12. All the projected sales are of the trademarked product.
13. The market royalty rate for trademarks is 2% of sales.
14. The discount rate applicable to the customer relationship asset is estimated at $WACC + 500\,\text{bps}$ or 15%.

Sales

We first calculate the percentage of sales that will survive at the middle of each year. We will later use the mid-year convention in our discounting. We have (amounts in CU millions):

Year	1	2	3	4	5
Sales	100	101	102.01	103.03	104.06
Survival rate (end of year)	80%	60%	40%	20%	0%
Survival rate (mid-year)	90%	70%	50%	30%	10%
Surviving sales (mid-year)	90	70.70	51.01	30.91	10.41

NOPAT

We next project the net operating profit after tax (NOPAT) based on the surviving sales.

We reflect the cost of the trademark as part of the NOPAT calculation rather than via a separate contributory charge. We do this by recording a hypothetical royalty charge for use of the trademark.

The calculations are as follows (amounts in CU millions):

Year	1	2	3	4	5
Surviving sales	90	70.70	51.01	30.91	10.41
Operating expenses	(41.40)	(32.52)	(23.46)	(14.22)	(4.79)
Royalty for trademark	(1.8)	(1.41)	(1.02)	(0.62)	(0.21)
Pre-tax profit	46.8	36.76	26.52	16.07	5.41
Income tax	(9.36)	(7.35)	(5.30)	(3.21)	(1.08)
NOPAT	37.44	29.41	21.22	12.86	4.33

Contributory Charges

We proceed to project and sum up the contributory charges for the supporting assets. The working capital requirements are estimated at 3% of the surviving sales. For the other supporting assets, i.e., PPE and workforce, the computation is based on assuming that the entire supporting asset is needed to support the entire sales level (based on 100% survival). For a lower survival percentage, we prorate the contributory charge. For example, in year 1, we take 90% of the total contributory charge, based on the projected survival percentage of 90% at mid-year.

Year	1	2	3	4	5
NWC (CU million)	2.70	2.12	1.53	0.93	0.31
Charge on NWC (5%)	0.14	0.11	0.08	0.05	0.02
Charge on PPE (7%)	1.26	0.98	0.70	0.42	0.14
Charge on workforce (13%)	1.79	1.39	0.99	0.60	0.20
TOTAL	3.19	2.48	1.77	1.06	0.35

Cashflows and Present Value

Finally we can proceed to compute our excess cashflows and present value.

For the cashflows, we directly use the NOPAT less the contributory charges. Contributory-charges are on an after-tax basis since we used after-tax rates to compute them.

We conventionally do not add back depreciation or amortization, or subtract relevant CAPEX.

The reason is that we assume that depreciation and amortization are approximately equal to the CAPEX required to maintain the supporting assets at their starting fair value. So the CAPEX and depreciation add-back would cancel each other out.

We also do not conventionally subtract the increase in non-cash working capital. The reason is that our calculations are based on the hypothetical assumption that we do not own any working capital ourselves and rent it from outside, with the cost reflected via a contributory charge.

As a result of these conventions, our projected incremental cashflows are the same as projected incremental accrual accounting profits, with the exception that usually tax depreciation is substituted for book depreciation.

We proceed to show our cashflow calculation and discounting. We discount at WACC+500 or 15%. The discounting follows the mid-year convention. Amounts are in CU million.

Year	1	2	3	4	5
NOPAT	37.44	29.41	21.22	12.86	4.33
Contributory charges	(3.19)	(2.48)	(1.77)	(1.06)	(0.35)
Cashflows	34.25	26.93	19.45	11.80	3.97
DCF	31.94	21.84	13.71	7.23	2.12

The estimated fair value of our customer relationship asset using MPEEM is CU 76.845 million.

7.3.6 Tax Amortization Benefit (TAB)

In our previous examples, we did not consider that an intangible asset may add some additional value in the form of a tax shield. This would happen if the tax rules allow the intangible fair value to be amortized for tax purposes over some period, leading to a related tax deduction. Then the present value of the related tax savings is an additional source of fair value, called the "tax amortization benefit" or TAB for short. We can choose whether or not to estimate the TAB and include it in the fair value of the intangible asset.

To illustrate consider Srivastava Inc who own a trademark valued at CU 244.22 before considering any tax amortization benefit. The discount rate of 12% used to value the trademark is based on the WACC of 10% plus a markup of 200 bps.

The tax rules allow Srivastava Inc to obtain a deduction equal to 20% of the trademark fair value each year for the next five years. Srivastava Inc faces an income tax rate of 20%. The tax savings from these deductions are CU 9.7688 per year for the next 5 years (CU 244.22 × 0.20 × 0.20).

Discounting these tax savings at 12%[1] gives us a present value of 35.215 (using the end-year convention to reflect tax payment at year-end). Adding this to the trademark value before TAB of CU 244.22 gives us an updated fair value for the trademark of CU 279.43 including the TAB.[2]

7.4 Lifing

The life of an intangible is an important parameter in valuation, and also to determine the amortization rate.

For some intangibles, it is straightforward to determine the life. For example, for most contract-related intangibles, the life of the intangible would be based on the contract term.

For some other intangibles, there is no clear deterioration in value due to aging. Examples could be trademarks or brandnames. Such intangibles are called non-wasting assets and assumed to have an indeterminate life. They are not amortized, but are subject to an impairment test each year.

Goodwill too is a non-wasting asset and subject to an annual impairment test. Goodwill is not classified as an intangible asset under IFRS. It fails the identifiability criteria. It is viewed as a residual amount that contains various unidentifiable items.

For some other intangibles, we can use statistical analysis of the past experience to estimate the life (Reilly and Schweihs 1998). We can do this when the asset is an aggregate of numerous units, and when we have data on past starts and endings of individual units. An example could be a customer relationship asset, where the units are individual customer accounts. Another could be a customer deposit intangible for a bank.[3]

When we have detailed data on starts and endings of individual asset items, we can use the *actuarial* method of lifing to determine the life. We will proceed to study this method in more detail. The method employs the following procedure:

[1]There is some variation in practice in the choice of discount rate.

[2]Strictly speaking, the fair value of the TAB used to calculate the TAB should be the final figure which includes the TAB, which means that we need circular logic and iteration to solve. But the sequential method shown here is standard and well-accepted in practice.

[3]Deposits are liabilities to the bank, but there is an associated intangible asset that reflects the benefits to the bank from the lower-than-market interest rates that they typically pay on deposits.

1. We collect data on the past starts and endings of individual asset items going back a number of years. We use the technical terms "placements" and "retirements" to refer to starts and endings of individual items respectively. For example, in a customer relationship asset, a placement would refer to a new customer account being opened, while a retirement would refer to a customer account being closed.
2. We identify an "experience band". This is a recent period of usually between one year and three years. We refer to survivor numbers of different ages in the experience band to compile a table comparing age and survivor numbers.
3. From our table of age and survivor numbers, we can proceed to compute historical survival rates for different ages. The survival rate for a particular age-band would be the number of survivors to that age band divided by the total number of items in the sample. We can plot the data in this table (ages and survival rates) to get a *stub curve*. This curve is called a stub curve because it does not go all the way down to zero survivor rates.
4. Based on our stub curve, we can use statistical techniques like regression to find a standard parametric survival curve that gives the best fit to our data. One standardized survival curve is the Weibull curve, which we will study here.
5. We then calculate the average age of our surviving units at the valuation date.
6. Finally, we determine the average remaining useful life (RUL) of our surviving assets, by analyzing the survivor curve.

7.4.1 Weibull Curve Estimation: Example

We have taken over Kim Inc in early 2010. We identify a customer relationship asset that we will proceed to value. We estimate its life first.

Kim Inc has maintained records of placements and retirements over the last ten years as in Table 7.1.

Each row in Table 7.1 shows the history of placements that started during the year. The top left-hand corner in each cell gives the number of survivors at the beginning of the column year (out of the original placements that started in the row year). The bottom right-hand corner in each cell gives the number of retirements during the column year (out of the original placements that started in the row year).

Thus for example, the numbers in the cell in the row labelled 2001 and the column 2001 track 72 placements that started in 2001. Of these 60 retired during 2001. In other words, 72 customer accounts were opened in 2001, of which 60 were closed in the same year.

Moving right to the cell with row 2001 and column 2002, we see that 12 of the 2001 placements had survived to 2002 (top left-hand corner). Of these, none retired during the year, so that (moving right again), we have 12 survivors at the beginning of 2003, of which 2 retired during the year, so that we have 10 survivors at the start of 2004,. . . . . ., and so on till we are left with 2 survivors from the 2001 placements at our valuation date in early 2010.

Table 7.1 Kim Inc placements and retirements

							Experience band			
Year	2001	2002	2003	2004	2005	2006	2007	2008	2009	2010
2001	72 60	12 0	12 2	10 0	10 1	9 1	8 3	5 2	3 1	2
2002		70 69	1 0	1 0	1 0	1 1	0 0	0 0	0 0	0
2003			71 65	6 0	6 1	5 1	4 2	2 0	2 1	1
2004				75 65	10 4	6 0	6 0	6 1	5 0	5
2005					70 60	10 6	4 0	4 1	3 0	3
2006						60 51	9 3	6 0	6 1	5
2007							90 70	20 10	10 4	6
2008								60 40	20 9	11
2009									120 100	20
2010										20

Similarly, the row labelled 2002 tracks account closings for 70 customer accounts that were opened in 2002 (none survived to 2010). The row labelled 2003 tracks account closings for 71 accounts that started in 2003 (one survived to 2010), and so on.

The sharp fall during the first year is because the company attracts new customers by offering them promotional prices during a trial period that is less than a year. Many customers choose to close their accounts after the trial period is over.

At our valuation date, we have 20 new accounts that were opened in 2010. None of these have been closed so far.

For our experience band, we choose the three years from 2007 to 2009. This gives us data on customer accounts that are in their 1st to 9th year of age.

We proceed to compile this data for our stub curve. The tabulated data is in Table 7.2. The stub curve is plotted in Fig. 7.1.

The column labelled "Exposed" in Table 7.2 tracks the number of items in the experience band that had survived to reach each age. The column labelled "Retired" tracks the number of items that had retired at each age-band, that is, items that did not survive to the next year of age. The column labelled "Survivors" tracks the numbers at each age that survived beyond that age. Finally, the column labelled "Survival rate" gives the ratio of the number of survivors at each age to the total number of exposures (393).

Table 7.2 Kim Inc stub curve data

Age	Exposed	Retired	Survivors	Survivor curve
1	270	210	60	15.2672%
2	49	22	27	6.8702%
3	20	4	16	4.0713%
4	16	2	14	3.5623%
5	13	3	10	2.5445%
6	7	0	7	1.7812%
7	10	4	6	1.5267%
8	5	2	3	0.7634%
9	3	1	2	0.5089%
	393			

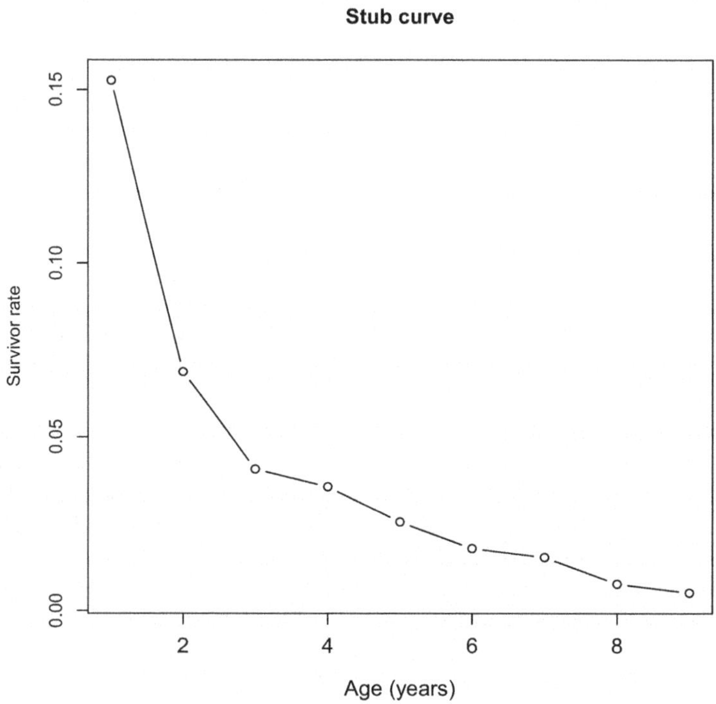

Fig. 7.1 Stub curve

To illustrate, consider the row for the age 5 years. In our experience band (referring to Table 7.1), we have three rows with accounts in their 5th year of age: the 2005 row, since placements started in 2005 are in their 5th year of age in 2009; the 2004 row, since placements started in 2004 are in their 5th year of age in 2008; and the 2003 row, since placements started in 2003 are in their 5th year of age in 2007. Recall that our experience band comprises the three years from 2007 to 2009.

In the exposures column in Table 7.2 for age 5, we count 13 exposures: 3 in their 5th year in 2009 (2005 row in Table 7.1), 6 in their 5th year in 2008 (2004 row in Table 7.1), and 4 in their 5th year in 2007 (2003 row in Table 7.1).

Of these, 3 were retired at age-band 5: 0 in 2009, 1 in 2008, and 2 in 2007.

We therefore have 10 survivors (13 − 3). This gives us a survival rate of $\frac{10}{393}$ or 2.5545%, where 393 is the total of all the exposures in our sample.

Of all the 393 exposures in our sample, 2.5545% survived beyond the 5-year age-band.

We can therefore turn next to estimate the Weibull survival curve (Weibull 1951).

A survival curve is the complement of a cumulative probability distribution function. For a cumulative probability distribution function, $F(x)$ say, over a random variable $\tilde{x}$, we have $F(x) = \Pr(\tilde{x} \leq x)$. The corresponding survival curve $S(x)$ say is defined as $S(x) = \Pr(\tilde{x} > x)$. We can see that $S(x) = 1 - F(x)$. In our case, we are modelling ages, so our random variable is time from placement to retirement (or life) $\tilde{t}$ say, and a survival rate $S(t)$ gives $\Pr(\tilde{t} > t)$, or the probability that the time from placement to retirement (or life) is greater than t. We have:

$$S(t) = \Pr(\tilde{t} > t).$$

The Weibull survival curve follows the equation in Equation 7.1:

$$S(t) = e^{\left[-\left(\left(\frac{t}{x_0}\right)^m\right)\right]} \tag{7.1}$$

where x_0 is referred to as the *scale* parameter, and m is referred to as the *shape* parameter.[4]

To be able to fit the Weibull curve to our stub curve using linear regression, we transform Equation 7.1 to a linear equation as follows.

First, take the natural logarithm of both sides. We have:

$$\ln S(t) = -\left(\left(\frac{t}{x_0}\right)^m\right)$$

$$\Rightarrow -\ln S(t) = t^m \left(\frac{1}{x_0}\right)^m.$$

Define $\left(\frac{1}{x_0}\right)^m = e^c$ say.

Then we have (recalling that $-\ln x = \ln[1/x]$):

[4]Some sources refer to these parameters as α and β or a and B, but not in a mutually consistent way, e.g., α could be the scale parameter for one source, but the shape parameter for another. We reproduce here the notation from the original paper.

Table 7.3 Kim Inc regression data

Age (t)	$\ln\ln\frac{1}{S(t)}$	$\ln t$
1	0.6309872	0
2	0.9850601	0.6931472
3	1.1635323	1.0986123
4	1.2043984	1.3862944
5	1.3005253	1.6094379
6	1.3932450	1.7917595
7	1.4308016	1.9459101
8	1.5841606	2.0794415
9	1.6640516	2.1972246

$$\ln\frac{1}{S(t)} = t^m \times e^c.$$

Take the natural logarithm of both sides. We have:

$$\ln\ln\frac{1}{S(t)} = m\ln t + c.$$

This is a linear equation. We can estimate the parameters m and c by using linear regression, where the dependent variable is $\ln\ln\frac{1}{S(t)}$ and the independent variable is $\ln t$.

In our example, the data for the regression are as in Table 7.3.

We run the regression to estimate x_0 and m, getting results as shown in Fig. 7.2.

Our parameter estimates are $c = 0.6429760$ and $m = 0.4350924$. We can then work out that the corresponding estimate of x_0 is 0.2281409.

A graph of our estimated Weibull survival curve is in Fig. 7.3.

The average age of our customer accounts on the valuation date is 2.054795 years computed as: $(2\times9+0\times8+1\times7\ \ldots\ +20\times0)/73$. We have 73 surviving accounts on our valuation date.

We next need to find the average remaining useful life (RUL) for items with this age. This life will be the time period over which we amortize the intangible. It will also be the horizon over which we calculate cashflows to value the intangible, if we use a DCF approach like MPEEM.

The average remaining useful life is given by the following formula:

$$RUL(t) = \frac{\text{Area under the survival curve to the right of } t}{S(t)}$$

The intuition behind this formula is outlined in the appendix to this chapter.

We can approximately find the area by using the *ordinate approximation approach*. This finds the approximate area by adding up the areas of a series of rectangles that correspond to the points in our data. In other words, this is the area

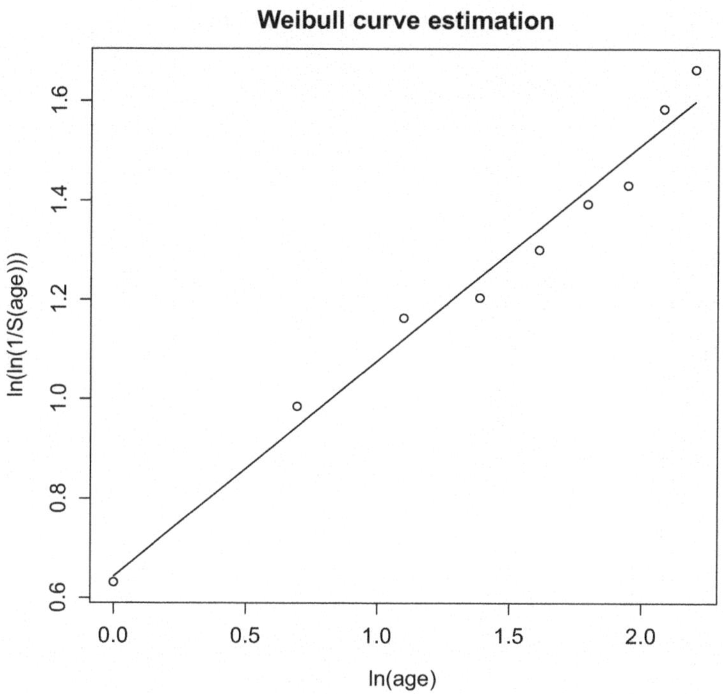

Fig. 7.2 Kim Inc graph of estimated Weibull regression line

of a histogram that approximates the Weibull curve. The height of each rectangle is the average of the heights $S(.)$ at each of its endpoints.

In the Weibull curve, survival rates $S(t)$ never actually hit zero. This is because $S(t)$ is of the form e^X, and there is no X such that $e^X = 0$.

Therefore, we fix some small probability, say 0.005, to be "as good as zero" for our purposes. We stop adding rectangles when we reach the time corresponding to that level.

Let us choose 0.005 to be our lowest survival rate. Then we solve for the age corresponding to that level. Using solver, we can get an age of 10.5326 years.

We proceed to apply the ordinate approximation approach for our example, as shown in Table 7.4.

To get the area of a rectangle, we take the average height of the points at each edge, and multiply by the length of the base (increment in age). We could write this as a formula as follows:

$$\frac{1}{2}\left(S(t_x) + S(t_{x-1})\right) \times (t_x - t_{x-1}) .$$

For example, for the rectangle between age 2.054795 and 3 (x is 2 in the formula above), we have an area equal to:

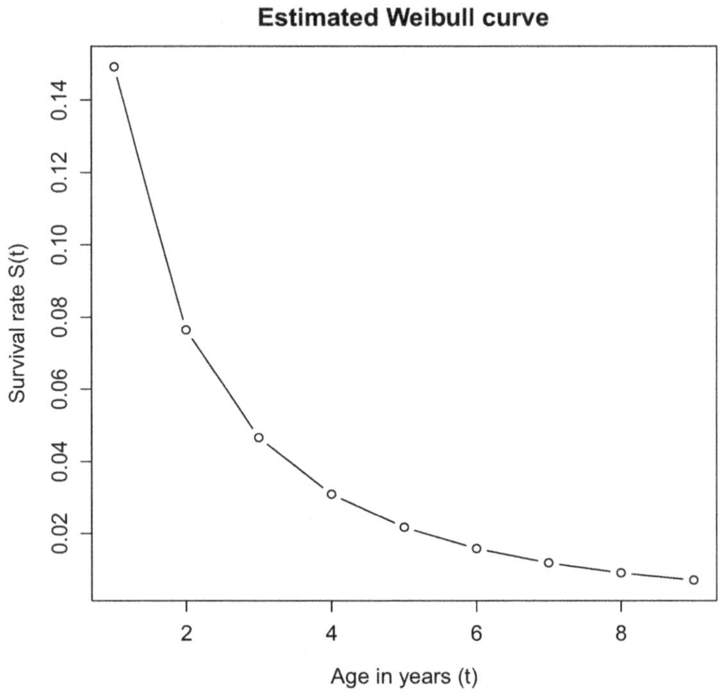

Fig. 7.3 Kim Inc fitted Weibull survival curve

Table 7.4 Kim Inc raw data for ordinate approximation

Index (x)	Age (t_x)	$S(t_x)$	Area of rectangle
1	2.054795	0.074117725	0.000000000
2	3.000000	0.046521515	0.057014435
3	4.000000	0.030902949	0.038712232
4	5.000000	0.021679248	0.026291098
5	6.000000	0.015800521	0.018739884
6	7.000000	0.011849855	0.013825188
7	8.000000	0.009088323	0.010469089
8	9.000000	0.007098001	0.008093162
9	10.000000	0.005627766	0.006362884
10	10.532576	0.005000000	0.002830045

$$0.5 \times (S(3) + S(2.054795)) \times (3 - 2.054795) = 0.05701.$$

When we sum up the areas of all the rectangles, we get a total area of 0.182338. Dividing this by $S(2.054795)$ or 0.0741, we get an approximate RUL of 2.46 years.

7.4.2 Iowa Curves

Iowa type curves (Winfrey 1935) are an alternative to the Weibull curve.

Iowa curves are of four main types.

7.4.2.1 O-Type Curves

These are curves with high “infant mortality”, i.e., new placements retire in the short run at a high rate, but those who survive beyond this may last much longer. Our customer-relationship example would fit this pattern.

7.4.2.2 L-Type Curves

These are curves where older items are more likely to survive. An example could be a brandname or trademark, where brands that have successfully survived to a longer age are more likely to have a long remaining life as tried-and-tested survivors.

7.4.2.3 R-Type Curves

These are assets where older items are *less* likely to survive, due to greater wear and tear or similar effects such as obsolescence. Most tangible physical assets are of this kind. For intangibles, many technology-related intangibles could be of this type, as older technologies face shorter remaining lives due to the higher risks of obsolescence.

7.4.2.4 S-Type Curves

These are curves where both older and newer items have around the same remaining lives. They may be characteristic of intangibles in companies operating in highly competitive industries, where intangible lives may be short due to competitive pressures irrespective of whether the intangible is new or has managed to survive longer than average.

Iowa curves can be estimated using regression approaches. We can also follow an old-fashioned manual approach as follows.

We first draw the stub curve on translucent tracing paper. We then superimpose the drawing on various standard Iowa curves, drawn to the same scale. We decide based on our observation which Iowa curve gives the best fit. We then use this chosen Iowa curve to work out our RUL.

7.5 Purchase Price Allocation (PPA)

We explain PPA using an example.

7.5.1 PPA Example

Ghosh Inc has acquired 65% of the shares of Smith Inc paying a total consideration of CU 20 million. Ghosh Inc thereby acquires control of Smith Inc.

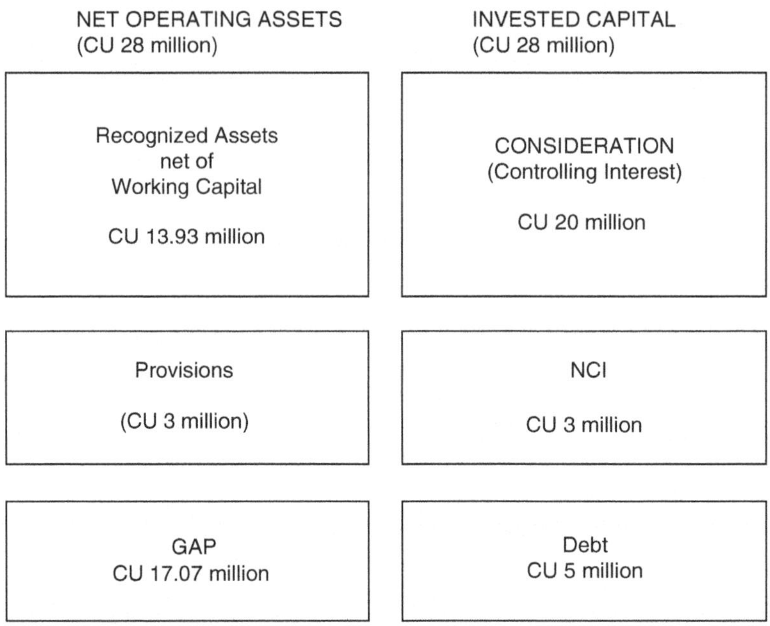

Fig. 7.4 PPA example box analysis I

At the takeover date, the fair values of Smith Inc balance-sheet items are as follows (amounts in CU million):

Net working capital (NWC)	3.43
PPE	10.50
Provisions	(3.00)
Debt	(5.00)

We measure the takeover-date fair value of the 35% non-controlling interest (NCI) to be CU 3 million.

Then the takeover-date fair value of the total equity is CU 23 million (controlling interest CU 20 million plus NCI 3 million).

Then the takeover-date fair value of the invested capital is CU 28 million (equity 23 million plus debt 5 million). This is also the enterprise value.

This should match the fair value of assets less operating liabilities such as provisions and working capital liabilities. But there is a gap of CU 17.07 million. This is illustrated graphically in the box analysis shown in Fig. 7.4.

The enterprise value is supported by a free cash flow model that Ghosh Inc developed before the takeover and refined after the takeover using updated information from Smith Inc internal records. The FCF model gives an enterprise value that is approximately equal to the actual enterprise value of CU 28 million. Verifying this approximate equation serves to validate both the consideration paid as well as the FCF model.

We need not go into details of the FCF model here, but we will keep in mind that the WACC used as the discount rate was a constant 9%.

The gap of CU 17.07 million that we noticed in Fig. 7.4 would partly comprise Smith Inc intangible assets that had not been previously recognized because they were internally generated. They need to be identified and valued now.

We identify two intangible assets for Smith Inc—an assembled workforce, and a customer relationship asset. Under IAS 38 rules, the assembled workforce cannot be recognized and is treated as part of goodwill. But we need to value it anyway as a supporting calculation.

Using a replacement cost model, we value the assembled workforce at CU 5 million. Using MPEEM, we value the customer relationship asset at CU 6 million. The supporting assets for the MPEEM are net working capital, PPE and the assembled workforce, with after-tax contributory charges on these assets as follows:

NWC	1%	
PPE	4%	
Assembled workforce	9.1%	$(WACC + 10\,\text{bps})$

The MPEEM cashflows are discounted at a discount rate of 9.2% $(WACC + 20\,\text{bps})$. This represents the required rate of return for the customer relationship asset.

We next proceed to estimate the net deferred tax liability arising from the takeover. This is CU 3 million. Smith Inc faces a corporate income tax rate of 20%.

We can now refine our box analysis as shown in Fig. 7.5. Goodwill is the residual amount of CU 14.07 million. It includes the assembled workforce of CU 5 million. IFRS (IAS 38:15) does not allow us to treat the assembled workforce as a separate asset.

7.5.2 WACC-WARA Comparison

As a sanity check, we need to verify that the weighted average return on assets for all the items on the left-hand side of Fig. 7.5 are equal to the WACC (the weighted average return on invested capital, or the right-hand side of Fig. 7.5).

The weights for each item are the proportion of the item's fair value to the total enterprise value. The required rate of return for each asset item matches the contributory charge rate of the item used in the MPEEM. The calculations are shown in Table 7.5.

The rate of return for the provisions is the discount rate that was used in estimating the fair value of the provision.

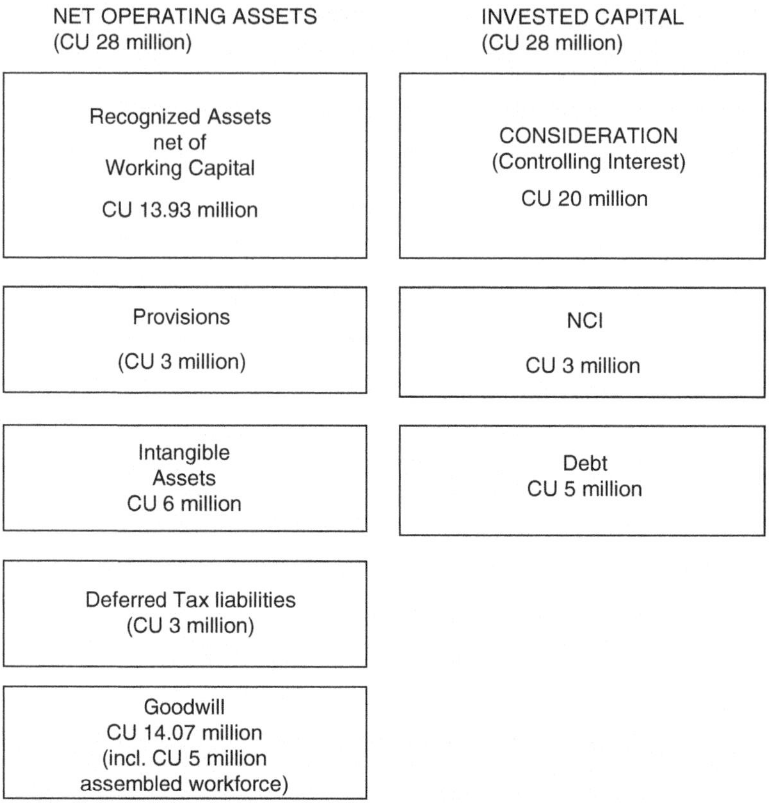

Fig. 7.5 PPA example box analysis II

Table 7.5 PPA example: WACC-WARA sanity check

Item	Fair value	Rate	Weight	Rate × weight
NWC	3.43	1%	3.43/28	0.001225
PPE	10.50	4%	10.50/28	0.015
Provisions	(3)	1%	(3)/28	(0.001071)
Deferred tax	(3)	0%	(3)/28	(0)
Assembled workforce	5	9.1%	5/28	0.01625
Customer relationship	6	9.2%	6/28	0.019714
Other goodwill	9.07	12%	9.07/28	0.03887

We treat deferred tax liabilities as undiscounted, or with a 0% required rate of return, following the conventional accounting treatment.

The required rate of return on other goodwill (goodwill *excluding* the assembled workforce) should be higher than the required rate of return on any other asset. This is to reflect the higher risk associated with goodwill. Goodwill is riskier because it includes uncertain future benefits whose sources do not satisfy even the criteria for identifiability or separate recognition (that is, the benefits may not even be probable or quantifiable). In our example, the required rate of return on goodwill is 12% ($WACC + 200$ bps).

To compute the WARA, we take the weighted average of the rate of return on each item, as shown in the table. We get a WARA of 8.99989%.

To pass a sanity check, the WARA should be reasonably close to the WACC. In our example, the WACC is 9%, so we can justify that the WARA is close enough.

An alternative way to run the sanity check is to leave the rate on other goodwill as an unknown, and then solve for the rate on other goodwill that would make the WARA exactly equal to the WACC. We then check if this estimated rate is higher than the rate of return on all other assets as required. If not, we have failed the sanity check.

If we could not pass the sanity check, we would need to review and re-do our PPA analysis (usually making changes in the valuing of intangibles), until we can pass the sanity check.

As part of our purchase price allocation, we found the fair value of NCI. An alternative calculation is allowed under which NCI is not valued directly, but measured as the NCI share of the identifiable net assets ("identifiable" can be read as "everything except goodwill"). In our example, the NCI computed under this approach would be 35% times the identifiable net assets of CU 8.93 million. This gives us an NCI of CU 3.1255.

We turn next to the valuation of NCI.

7.6 Non-controlling Interest (NCI)

There are two approaches to valuing NCI:

1. The top-down approach
2. The bottom-up approach

7.6.1 The Top-Down Approach

In the top-down approach, we start with a model that values equity reflecting a control perspective. That could be an FTE model. Alternatively we could first calculate enterprise value using an FCF model, and then subtract the fair value of debt.

From our control-perspective starting point, we apply two successive discounts to obtain the fair value of NCI. The first is a discount due to a lack of control (DLOC), and the second is a discount due to lack of marketability (DLOM). We apply the discounts sequentially, that is, the discount applied second would be based on the net amount after the discount applied first (the order doesn't matter). To illustrate, consider the example in Table 7.6. Amounts in the table are in CU million.

Table 7.6 Example: Top-down valuation of NCI

Enterprise value (FCF model)	100
Fair value of debt	(60)
Equity value (with control)	40
NCI share of equity @ 30%	12
DLOM (20%)	(2.40)
	9.60
DLOC (30%)	(2.88)
NCI Fair value	6.72

Note the sequential application of the discounts in Table 7.6. We do not add up the rates (30% + 20%) and then apply this total (50%) to the starting point of CU 12 (which would have given us an NCI of CU 6 million). Sequential application assumes that there is some overlap between the discounts.

We turn next to models for estimating the DLOM and DLOC.

7.6.1.1 DLOM: Amihud-Mendelson Model

The discount due to lack of marketability reflects the fact that shares of the acquired entity usually do not trade after the takeover, i.e., they do not have an active market. Even in cases where the shares continue to be listed separately, the volume of shares actively traded would only be a fraction of the shares outstanding. This is because the controlling shareholder would not dilute their holdings by actively trading their shares. They are likely to enter the market only occasionally.

The Amihud-Mendelson model (1986) values the DLOM as the present value of all the future *transaction costs* from trading a share. Lack of marketability would significantly raise these costs.

The model makes the following assumptions:

1. Share prices (or equity values) follow a random process where future positive returns of some amount are as likely as future negative returns of the same amount, so that the expected future price (or equity value) is the same as the current price (or equity value). Let this current price or equity value be P_0.
2. Transactions occur on average n times per year.
3. The cost of equity is constant, say k_e per year, expressed as an APR rate with compounding frequency n times per year.
4. The transaction cost for each transaction is a fixed proportion of the share price, say c.

Then the present value of the stream of transaction costs is as follows:

$$PV = \frac{cP_0}{(1+\frac{k_e}{n})} + \frac{cP_0}{(1+\frac{k_e}{n})^2} + \frac{cP_0}{(1+\frac{k_e}{n})^3} \cdots$$

$$= \frac{cP_0}{\left(\frac{k_e}{n}\right)}.$$

Then the discount as a proportion of the equity value is given by Equation 7.2

$$DLOM = \frac{c}{\left(\frac{k_e}{n}\right)}. \tag{7.2}$$

7.6.1.2 DLOM Example

We have acquired Fischer Inc. We estimate that the non-controlling shareholders would likely trade their shares (buy or sell) on average once every half-year. Fischer Inc has a cost of equity equal to 11% (semi-annually compounded). The transaction costs are estimated to be 3% of the share price. Find the DLOM.

$$DLOM = \frac{0.03}{\left(\frac{0.11}{2}\right)} = 54.55\%.$$

7.6.1.3 DLOC: Transaction-Based Model

To estimate the discount due to lack of control, we can often refer to transaction information on takeovers of similar companies.

When a takeover is announced, the share price rises to a level that is commensurate with a control perspective, to reflect what the acquirer is willing to pay. Comparing the share prices before and after a takeover announcement gives us an estimated *control premium*—the extent to which the price went up to reflect control. Then the DLOC is the reverse of this—the extent by which a price that reflects control needs to be reduced to reflect a lack of control.

7.6.1.4 DLOC Example

We have acquired Limpopo Inc, a private company. A comparison of similar recent takeovers in the same industry shows that on average the share price went up by 18% between a date 5 days before the takeover announcement and a date 5 days after the takeover announcement (the 10-day window is to allow for early leaks of information on the takeover, and also for the announcement to be confirmed). Find the DLOC.

The control premium is 18%.

We can think of this as an increase of CU 18 from an original price of CU 100 to a new price of CU 118.

Then the discount is the same CU 18 as a proportion of the price after the takeover announcement (price with control) or CU 118.

$$DLOC = \frac{18}{118} = 15.2542\%.$$

7.6.2 The Bottom-Up Approach

In the bottom-up approach, we directly forecast the expected cashflows due to NCI and then discount them using a discount rate attributable to NCI. We typically choose a discount rate that is much higher than the CAPM cost of equity, to reflect the higher risks faced by NCI.

7.6.2.1 The Harper-Lindquist Model

The Harper-Lindquist model (1983) is a simple bottom-up approach. In this model, the projected cashflows to NCI include:

1. Projected dividends on ordinary shares,
2. An opportunity to sell the shares at full control-perspective value at some point in the future.

We illustrate with an example.[5]

7.6.2.2 Example: Harper-Lindquist Model

Joe Inc owns shares of NCI in Harriet Inc, a private company. FTE per share for Harriet Inc is CU 1 in the current year. FTE is expected to grow at 5% per year for the next 5 years and thereafter. We project that there would be a takeover offer for Harriet Inc at the end of 5 years. In the takeover offer, NCI would get the chance to sell their shares at the same price as the controlling shareholders can. Dividends per share are projected to be CU 0.10 per year for the next 5 years. The cost of equity applicable in the FTE model is 10%. The cost of equity relevant to NCI would reflect a substantial markup over this, at 23% (determined based on evidence from published research studies). Find the fair value per share of NCI using the Harper-Lindquist model.

The fair value per share under an FTE model after 5 years would be (in CU):

$$\frac{1 \times 1.05^6}{0.10 - 0.05} = 26.8019.$$

This reflects the sales price after 5 years. Therefore the cashflows are:

Dividend	0.1	0.1	0.1	0.1	0.1
Sales proceeds					26.80
Total	0.1	0.1	0.1	0.1	26.90

[5]The assumptions here are unrealistic in terms of our discussion elsewhere, for example the high terminal growth rate, but this simple example serves to illustrate the basic features of the model like a similar example in Harper and Lindquist (1983). It is easy to modify the model to incorporate more complex assumptions.

The present value of these cashflows at 23% is CU 9.80 per share (applying the end-year convention).

7.6.2.3 Extending Harper-Lindquist

The model can be generalized by using Monte-Carlo simulation to allow for varying dividend patterns and varying times for future takeovers. We will not go into details here.

7.6.2.4 Discount Rate Estimation

To decide on the discount rate for NCI, k_{NCI} say, we can use a heuristic where we start with the usual CAPM cost of equity k_e say and then markup by the DLOM and DLOC as follows:

$$k_{NCI} = k_e \times (1 + DLOM) \times (1 + DLOC).$$

Example: Discount Rate Estimation

The CAPM cost of equity is 10%. We have identified DLOM to be 20% using the Amihud-Mendelsohn model. We have found a DLOC of 30% based on control premiums in recent similar takeover transactions. Find an appropriate discount rate for NCI in a bottom-up model.

$$k_{NCI} = 0.1 \times (1 + 0.2) \times (1 + 0.3) = 15.6\%.$$

7.7 Impairment of Goodwill

Goodwill is a non-wasting asset, so it is not subject to amortization. But instead, it must be tested for impairment every reporting period (including interim reporting periods).

In testing goodwill for impairment, we do not test it alone, but rather as part of a bundle of assets called a cash-generating unit or CGU. Goodwill from a particular acquisition is allocated to CGUs based on the extent to which the acquisition benefited the CGUs, or the extent to which the CGUs reap synergies from the acquisition.

As a simple example, if we have two divisions, say a textile division and an oil-refining division, and we take over an oil refinery that we then merge with our existing operations, then the goodwill would be allocated to the oil-refining division, not the textile division.

A CGU is defined as the smallest group of assets that can produce cashflows independently. The illustrative examples accompanying IAS 36 give some examples that help to flesh out the definition.

For example consider a railway line in a coal mine. The railway line is solely used to transport coal from one part of the line to another, and can only be sold as scrap metal. In this case, the railway line does not produce cashflows by itself. If tested for impairment, the railway line must be tested as part of a larger unit such as the mine. The railway line is not CGU.

For another example, consider a bus company that has obtained a contract with a city to deliver bus service on five different routes. To comply with the contract, the bus company must provide regular service on all five routes. The bus company runs each route independently, with separate assets and personnel for each route. The bus company also tracks revenues, expenses and profits separately for each route. But we cannot classify an individual bus route as a CGU. This is because an individual bus route cannot be operated by itself. The bus company has to run all five routes or they will breach the contract. In this case, the CGU is the group of all five bus routes.

When goodwill is included in a CGU, we must test the entire CGU for impairment every reporting period. To do so, we first determine the value in use (VIU) of the CGU. The value in use is the present value to the entity of the projected cashflows from using the CGU. (We will discuss an example later.)

If the carrying amount of the CGU exceeds the value in use, then we may need to impair. We next proceed to determine the fair value less costs to sell (FVLCS) of the CGU. This starts with the fair value of the CGU computed using enterprise valuation approaches, either ratio-based or DCF-based. A CGU is a business unit, which is why we use enterprise valuation. From the fair value, we get the FVLCS by deducting the various estimated costs that we would incur if we actually sold the CGU (transaction costs, stamp duty, etc.).

The recoverable amount of the CGU is the higher of the VIU and the FVLCS. If the VIU were higher than the FVLCS, we are better off keeping and using the CGU rather than selling it. In that case, the value from use is a better estimate of what the CGU is worth to us. If the FVLCS were higher than the VIU, then we are better off selling the CGU. In that case, the value from selling is a better estimate of what the CGU is worth to us. Note that the calculation does not reflect our actual intention at all, it is purely hypothetical.

There may be some situations where either the VIU or the FVLCS cannot be determined. For example, a CGU may have no external market at all, and hence no fair value. In such cases, we would use the available number as our recoverable amount. For example if FVLCS cannot be computed, then the recoverable amount equals the VIU.

We proceed to compare the recoverable amount to the carrying amount of the CGU. If the carrying amount is too high, i.e., the carrying amount exceeds the recoverable amount, then we record an impairment charge. The assets in the CGU must be marked down till the CGU reflects the recoverable amount.

The impairment charge must be allocated to the individual assets in the CGU. The rule is that we first take as much of the impairment charge as possible to the goodwill in the CGU. We impair other assets only if the goodwill is completely wiped out.

If we impair CGU assets other than goodwill, the remaining impairment charge is spread among these assets in proportion to their relative carrying amounts before impairment. There are some constraints—we cannot impair any asset to a level that is below zero, or below its individual fair value less costs to sell if known, or its individual value in use if known.

Impairment of goodwill cannot be reversed. IFRS does however allow reversing impairment of other assets. (We will not go into details here.)

There are two other complications that we will briefly mention here, without going into details or examples, as they are not directly related to our topic of valuation (there are illustrative examples accompanying the standard).

If goodwill arises from a takeover where NCI was measured as the NCI share of identifiable net assets, then we treat this as though there is an extra off-balance-sheet component of goodwill that represents the NCI share of goodwill. When we test for impairment, we first gross up the carrying amount by this extra goodwill and then compare to the recoverable amount. Impairment if any is taken proportionately to the off-balance-sheet and the recognized components of goodwill.

There may be some assets that are shared by several CGUs, and where the asset values cannot be reasonably allocated among the CGUs. In such cases, we conduct the impairment test at the level of the group of CGUs that share the assets (after testing and impairing as needed the individual CGUs). Any impairment charge from this higher-level impairment test flows down to the individual CGUs, and as usual, is first taken to any remaining goodwill.

In this book, our focus is on valuation, so we will not go beyond the above sketch of the basic mechanics of impairment. The main new valuation issue that we encounter is value in use (VIU). We proceed to discuss this.

7.7.1 Value in Use (VIU)

Unlike fair value, which can be measured in a variety of ways, value in use is always a present value, by definition.

The projected cashflows used to measure value in use (VIU) bear a superficial resemblance to FCF. They are of the approximate form EBITDA less CAPEX less change in non-cash working capital. But the interpretation of the cashflows is different. FCF takes the viewpoint of the capital providers, and reflects the cashflows available to pay them. The VIU cashflows take the viewpoint of the entity, and reflect the net cashflows that the CGU produces for the entity to use as needed.

The projected cashflows must be based on the entity's internal budgets or other management accounting data. The planning period in the VIU projections must match the planning period in the CGU's own plans, and typically should not be allowed to exceed five years. Any cashflows beyond five years should reflect a constant or declining growth rate that is at or below the long-run growth rate of GDP in the country.

Projected cashflows should not include any borrowing costs, that is, they are before interest. They should also consistently reflect the current state of the CGU. Any budgeted costs or benefits arising from planned future improvements or restructuring should not be reflected. In particular, the CAPEX outflow should only include the expenditure required to maintain the existing capital asset base of the

CGU. That is, the CAPEX outflow should only consider replacement of existing assets as they are retired, not an addition to the capital base.

IAS 36 requires VIU to be measured using pre-tax cashflows discounted at a pre-tax discount rate. But in practice, the computations are more complex. This is due to a suggestion in the basis for conclusions (IAS 36:BCZ 85) that the present value obtained by computing pre-tax cashflows at a pre-tax rate should be the same as that obtained by computing after-tax cashflows at an after-tax rate. Also, an after-tax discount rate is easier to determine in practice, using CAPM. So in practice, the VIU is determined by discounting after-tax cashflows at an after-tax rate, and the value obtained is then presented as the present value from discounting pre-tax cashflows at some imputed pre-tax rate that gives the same answer as the after-tax discounting.

The discount rate used to measure VIU should be a CGU-specific rate, such as the WACC for the CGU (based on the CGU-specific costs of equity and debt, and the D/E ratio for the CGU). In practice, the entity WACC is often used, though this requires justification such as that the CGU carries the same risk as the entity as a whole.

We illustrate VIU with an example.

7.7.1.1 VIU Example

We are estimating the VIU of Varthaman Division, a CGU of Mahavir Inc group.

From the internal budgets and management planning documents of Varthaman, projected Varthaman sales for the next five years are as follows (in CU '000):

Year	*1*	*2*	*3*	*4*	*5*
Sales	*300*	*720*	*745*	*781*	*823*

These sales figures include projected sales from Mahavir's plans to take over a related external company and merge its operations with Varthaman Division in Year 2. The projected sales from the external company in year 2 are CU 400,000 projected to grow thereafter at a compound annual growth rate of 5%.

Varthaman's budgets include projected operating expenses (excluding depreciation and amortization) at a budgeted 50% of sales. Projected borrowing costs for Varthaman are as follows (CU '000):

Year	*1*	*2*	*3*	*4*	*5*
Borrowing costs	*10*	*11*	*10*	*10.5*	*11*

Varthaman's projected non-cash working capital requirements are estimated to be 2% of sales. The current actual non-cash working capital level is CU 6,000.

Varthaman's capital budgets include projected outlays of CU 13,000 in year 2 and CU 19,000 in year 3 to acquire new machinery. These machines are strict additions to Varthaman's capital base and will not replace any existing machines. The purchase of the machines would receive a 100% tax depreciation deduction in the year of purchase.

Varthaman's projected tax depreciation for the next five years is as follows:

Year	*1*	*2*	*3*	*4*	*5*
Tax depreciation	*5*	*20*	*25*	*5*	*6*

Tax depreciation arising from the takeover in Year 2 is negligible.

Varthaman Division faces a statutory income tax rate of 20%. The after-tax WACC for the division (CGU-specific) is estimated to be 8%.

The long-run growth rate of GDP is 2%.

Using the above data and making any necessary assumption, find the VIU for Varthaman.

We start by revising the projected sales to exclude projected sales from the future takeover. This gives us the following numbers:

Year	1	2	3	4	5
Sales (excluding takeover)	300	320	325	340	360

We can proceed to obtain EBITDA by subtracting the budgeted operating expenses at 50% of sales:

Year	1	2	3	4	5
Sales	300	320	325	340	360
Operating Expenses	150	160	162.5	170	180
EBITDA	150	160	162.5	170	180

To obtain cashflows we next need to subtract the increase in working capital (ΔNWC say). This is calculated as follows (CU '000):

Year	1	2	3	4	5
NWC	6	6.4	6.5	6.8	7.2
ΔNWC	0	0.4	0.1	0.3	0.4

To arrive at our pre-tax cashflows, we further need to subtract capital expenditures. But these should not include the expenditures to add new machines. As our estimate of the capital expenditure required to maintain the existing machines (maintenance CAPEX), we can use the projected tax depreciation, under the assumption that it is approximately the same as the amounts we would need to spend to reverse wear and tear on existing machines. But in doing so, we should exclude the tax depreciation for the budgeted new machines. This gives us the following estimates of maintenance CAPEX (CU '000):

Year	1	2	3	4	5
Maintenance CAPEX (tax depreciation)	5	7	6	5	6

We can proceed to calculate our pre-tax and post-tax cashflows (CU '000).

Year	1	2	3	4	5
EBITDA	150	160	162.5	170	180
ΔNWC	(0)	(0.4)	(0.1)	(0.3)	(0.4)
Maintenance CAPEX	(5)	(7)	(6)	(5)	(6)
Pre-tax cashflows	145	152.6	156.4	164.7	173.6
Tax	29	30.52	31.28	32.94	34.72
After-tax cashflows	116	122.08	125.12	131.76	138.88

We calculate the after-tax terminal value at year 5, TV say, assuming a conservative growth rate of 1%, after Year 5, less than the GDP growth rate. This gives us (CU '000):

$$TV = \frac{138.88(1.01)}{0.08 - 0.01} = 2003.84.$$

We can proceed to find the present value of the after-tax cashflows discounting at the after-tax WACC of 8%. This present value works out to around CU 1.94 million (with mid-year discounting). This is our VIU.

To complete the analysis, we need to find and report the pre-tax discount rate that gives the same present value. In our calculations, we set the pre-tax terminal value to be the same as the after-tax terminal value (CU 2,003,840), thus extending the logic that the present value based on pre-tax cash flows should match the after-tax present value. This logic should be true for the terminal value as much as the value today, since the terminal value is just the projected present value at the end of the planning period.

Using the goal seek or solver tools in spreadsheet software, we can solve for this rate. We get a pre-tax discount rate of around 9.85% (based on mid-year discounting).

This concludes our discussion of intangibles, PPA and goodwill impairment. In Chap. 8, we will discuss property valuation.

Appendix: Deriving the RUL Formula

In this appendix, we will discuss the logic behind the formula for remaining useful life. This is not a rigorous mathematical proof. Rather it is an informal sketch of the underlying logic, pointing to our customer relationship example to make things more concrete.

Recall that the formula for the average remaining life ("remaining useful life" or RUL) after time t is:

$$RUL(t) = \frac{\text{Area under the survival curve to the right of } t}{S(t)}$$

If $AVGAGE$ is the average age of our items on the valuation date, we can substitute $AVGAGE$ for t in the formula to get:

$$RUL(AVGAGE) = \frac{\text{Area under the survival curve to the right of } AVGAGE}{S(AVGAGE)}$$

Suppose that we ran a simulation of the life history of a very large number of starts $NUMSTARTS$ say (we could take for example $NUMSTARTS = 1{,}000{,}000$). The simulation draws the simulated starts from a Weibull curve that follows the given parameters (recall that in our example these are shape $m = 0.4350924$, and scale $x_0 = 0.2281409$).

We note the number of simulated starts that survive to the average age of our actual items say $AVGAGE$ (recall that $AVGAGE$ is 2.054795 years in our example). This should naturally be approximately equal to $S(AVGAGE) \times NUMSTARTS$, where $S(AVGAGE)$ is the Weibull survival curve probability at $AVGAGE$. Let us call this number X.

$$X \approx S(AVGAGE) \times NUMSTARTS.$$

We continue running our simulation until only a very small percentage of the original simulated starts survive say 0.005% (50 observations if we started with 1,000,000). We stop the simulation at this point.

We record how long each of the items that had reached our $AVGAGE$ lived thereafter.

We rank these in order of their remaining lives and plot their simulated remaining lives on a horizontal bar chart, with those with the shortest remaining lives at the top and those with the longest at the bottom. See Fig. 7.6 (not drawn to scale).

The right edges of this chart approximately trace out the tail of the Weibull survival curve $S(t)$ for ages t greater than AVGAGE, scaled by $NUMSTARTS$, i.e., $S(t) \times NUMSTARTS$. The bigger our simulation, the better the approximation.

Finally, we can obtain the average remaining life in our simulation by adding up all the remaining ages for each of the X survivors in our sample, and then dividing

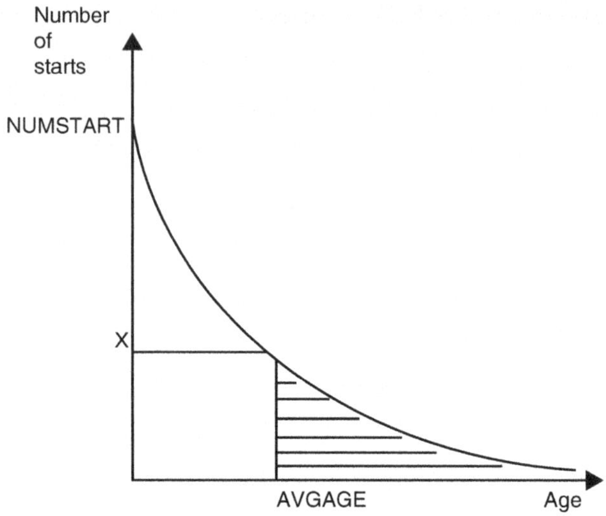

Fig. 7.6 Simulated remaining lives on a horizontal bar chart

by X to get an average. If RL_i is the remaining life after $AVGAGE$ for an item indexed i, we have:

$$\text{Simulated } RUL = \frac{\sum_{i=1}^{X} RL_i}{X}. \tag{7.3}$$

Adding up the remaining lives for each of the X observations is the same as adding up the length of all the horizontal bars in our bar chart.

Notice that adding up the lengths of the bars in the chart is a crude way to estimate the area of the enveloping curve, which, please recall, approximates the tail of the curve $S(t) \times NUMSTARTS$ at $t = AVGAGE$. We can think of this as measuring the area by filling it in with closely packed horizontal lines, and counting the cumulative lengths of these lines.

Now suppose that we changed the scale of our diagram to reflect $NUMSTARTS = 1$. So each simulated start is counted as a fraction equal to $\frac{1}{NUMSTARTS}$ of a unit. The resulting graph approximately describes the tail of our Weibull distribution $S(t)$.

Then Equation 7.3 for our simulated RUL becomes (dividing both numerator and denominator by $NUMSTARTS$):

$$\text{Simulated } RUL = \frac{\frac{1}{NUMSTARTS} \sum_{i=1}^{X} RL_i}{\frac{X}{NUMSTARTS}}. \tag{7.4}$$

Observe that:

$$\frac{X}{NUMSTARTS} \approx S(AVGAGE).$$

Also observe that the numerator in the right-hand-side expression in Equation 7.4 approximately equals the area under the tail of the Weibull survival curve $S(t)$ to the right of $AVGAGE$.

The approximation gets better and better as our simulation gets bigger and bigger. If we could run a perfect simulation, we would get:

$$RUL(AVGAGE) = \frac{\text{Area under the survival curve to the right of } AVGAGE}{S(AVGAGE)}.$$

This is what we set out to establish.

Exercises

(Monetary units are in CU unless otherwise mentioned).

7.1. Relief from Royalty

Mehbooba Inc owns a trademark. Its projected sales under the trademark are as follows for the next five years (amounts in CU):

Year	1	2	3	4	5
Sales	900	1,010	1,100	1,120	1,300

Sales are projected to grow after year 5 at 0.1% per year. The market royalty rate for similar trademarks is 3%.

Value the trademark using a relief in royalty approach, using a discount rate of 10%. Also calculate a TAB, assuming that the trademark cost can be deducted from taxable income on a straight-line basis over 5 years.

7.2. Replacement Cost: Software

Ibrahim Inc has an accounting software system that it uses for its internal accounting.

A systems analyst verifies that the source programs used to develop the software are 10,000 lines long. The analyst estimates that a programming team could recreate these lines at a rate of 22 lines per programmer-hour and a cost of CU 110 per programmer-hour.

The systems analyst estimates that we could design new software that exactly replicates the functionality of the existing software, by refactoring the source code so that it fits into just 9,000 lines.

The systems analyst estimates that two modules of the software have been rendered obsolete. These two modules would contribute 900 lines of the refactored 9,000-line source code.

The income tax rate is 20%.

Value the software.

7.3. Replacement Cost: Assembled Workforce

We have taken over Carrie Co. On the takeover date, the details of Carrie Co employees are as follows in terms of rank, numbers and compensation:

Rank	Number	Salary (CU per year)	Perks (CU per year)
CEO	1	120,000	10,000
Senior management	10	50,000	2,000
Junior management	50	20,000	800
Supervisors	250	12000	100
Workers	1,250	9,600	10

We hire a human resources (HR) consultant to help us estimate the replacement cost of the assembled workforce.

Our HR consultant advises us that search and hiring costs can be approximately measured as one month of basic salary—the standard commission charged by a headhunter.

For training costs, the HR consultant suggests the following assumptions:

The CEO would need no training.

Senior management would each require 2 days of training under the tutelage of the CEO.

Junior management would each require 5 days of training under the supervision of one senior manager (for all the junior managers).

Supervisors would each require 6 days of training under the supervision of one junior manager (for all the supervisors).

Workers would each require 10 days of training under the supervision of one supervisor (for all the workers).

The income tax rate is 20%.

Estimate the fair value of the assembled workforce using a replacement cost approach.

7.4. With and Without

We have just acquired Pinky Inc. At the acquisition date, Pinky possesses a contract with a key supplier. Under the contract Pinky agrees to buy widgets exclusively from the supplier, at a fixed price of CU 8 per widget. The contract has a remaining life of 3 years.

We estimate that the average open market price of widgets will be as follows in the next three years (amounts in CU):

Year	1	2	3
Price	9	7	8.5

Pinky's anticipated demand for widgets is 10,000 per year. Pinky Inc faces a corporate income tax rate of 20%.

The appropriate discount rate for this contract intangible is 13%.

Value the intangible.

7.5. MPEEM We have acquired Valentine Inc. We have identified a customer relationship intangible that we proceed to measure at its fair value using MPEEM.

We use the following case facts:

1. Sales from the existing customers are projected to be CU 90 million next year and to grow at 1.3% per year thereafter, assuming no attrition.
2. Existing customers are projected to depart at a straight-line rate over the next five years.
3. Operating expenses are projected to be a constant 45% of sales. These include projected depreciation based on tax depreciation rules rather than financial reporting assumptions.
4. Valentine Inc faces a corporate income tax rate of 20%.
5. Working capital requirements are projected to be 3% of sales.
6. The customer relationship asset depends on the following supporting assets—net working capital, PPE, a trademark, and the assembled workforce.
7. The valuation-date fair value of the PPE is CU 19 million.
8. The valuation-date fair value of the assembled workforce is estimated at CU 9.30 million, using a replacement cost model.
9. The contributory charge rate on the working capital is 3%.
10. The contributory charge rate on the PPE is 6%, which is an after-tax rate.
11. The contributory charge rate on the assembled workforce is estimated at 10%. This is computed as the after-tax WACC of 7% plus a spread of 300 bps.
12. All the projected sales are of the trademarked product.
13. The market royalty rate for trademarks is 2% of sales.
14. The discount rate applicable to the customer relationship asset is estimated at $WACC + 500$ bps.

Use MPEEM to value the customer relationship asset.

7.6. Lifing

Table 7.7 shows placements and retirements for a customer relationship asset of Ho Inc. Using the data in Table 7.7, apply the actuarial method to estimate the average remaining useful life (RUL) at the start of 2020. Use a Weibull survival curve in your estimation.

7.7. PPA

Barack Inc has acquired 88% of the shares of Lam Inc paying a total consideration of CU 21 million.

At the takeover date, the fair values of Lam Inc balance-sheet items are as follows (amounts in CU million):

Net working capital (NWC)	4.53
PPE	20.50
Provisions	(13.00)
Debt	(5.00)

Table 7.7 Ho Inc placements and retirements

							Experience band			
Year	2011	2012	2013	2014	2015	2016	2017	2018	2019	2020
	70	10	6	4	4	3	2	1	1	
2011	60	4	2	0	1	1	1	0	0	1
		70	5	4	1	1	0	0	0	
2012		65	1	3	0	1	0	0	0	0
			72	6	6	5	4	2	2	
2013			66	0	1	1	2	0	1	1
				70	5	1	1	1	1	
2014				65	4	0	0	0	0	1
					60	10	3	3	2	
2015					50	7	0	1	0	2
						60	8	5	5	
2016						52	3	0	1	4
							60	5	2	
2017							55	3	0	2
								60	10	
2018								50	8	2
									60	
2019									50	10
2020										23

We measure the takeover-date fair value of the 12% non-controlling interest (NCI) to be CU 1 million.

The pre-takeover DCF valuation of Lam Inc used a WACC of 10% (constant).

We identify two intangible assets for Lam Inc—an assembled workforce, and a customer relationship asset.

Using a replacement cost model, we value the assembled workforce at CU 5 million. Using MPEEM, we value the customer relationship asset at CU 8 million. The supporting assets for the MPEEM are net working capital, PPE and the assembled workforce, with after-tax contributory charges on these assets as follows:

NWC	1.2%	
PPE	4.3%	
Assembled workforce	10.1%	$(WACC + 10\,\text{bps})$

The MPEEM cashflows are discounted at a discount rate of 10.2% $(WACC + 20\,\text{bps})$. This represents the required rate of return for the customer relationship asset.

Deferred tax liabiities arising from the takeover are CU 3.2 million. The income tax rate is 20%. The average discount rate for valuing provisions is 1%.

Prepare a box analysis as in Fig. 7.5. Prepare a WACC-WARA reconciliation as in Table 7.5. Does this pass a sanity check? If not, what are the next steps?

7.8. DLOM
We have acquired Mendelsohn Inc. We estimate that the non-controlling shareholders would likely trade their shares (buy or sell) on average once every year. Mendelsohn Inc has a cost of equity equal to 12% (annually compounded). The transaction costs are estimated to be 3.2% of the share price. Find the DLOM.

7.9. DLOC
We have acquired Junius Inc, a private company. A comparison of similar recent takeovers in the same industry shows that on average the share price went up by 13% between a date 5 days before the takeover announcement and a date 5 days after the takeover announcement. Find the DLOC.

7.10. Harper-Lindquist
Gregory Inc owns shares of NCI in Olga Inc, a private company. FTE per share for Olga Inc is CU 1.2 in the current year. FTE is expected to grow at 3% per year for the next 5 years and thereafter. We project that there would be a takeover offer for Olga Inc at the end of 5 years. Dividends per share are projected to be CU 0.03 per year for the next 5 years. The cost of equity applicable in the FTE model is 9%. The cost of equity relevant to NCI would be 30% (determined based on evidence from published research studies). Find the fair value per share of NCI using the Harper-Lindquist model.

7.11. VIU

We are estimating the VIU of Vorty Division, a CGU of Mota Inc group.

From the internal budgets and management planning documents of Vorty, projected Vorty sales for the next five years are as follows (in CU '000):

Year	1	2	3	4	5
Sales	310	335	645	731	723

These sales figures include projected sales from Mota's plans to take over a related external company and merge its operations with Vorty Division in Year 3. The projected sales from the external company in year 3 are CU 400,000 projected to grow thereafter at a compound annual growth rate of 5%.

Vorty's budgets include projected operating expenses (excluding depreciation and amortization) at a budgeted 50% of sales.

Vorty's projected non-cash working capital requirements are estimated to be 3% of sales. The current actual non-cash working capital level is CU 5,000.

Vorty's projected tax depreciation for the next five years is as follows: (excluding tax depreciation arising from the takeover)

Year	1	2	3	4	5
Tax depreciation	5	3	3	4	5

Vorty Division faces a statutory income tax rate of 20%. The after-tax WACC for the division (CGU-specific) is estimated to be 9%.

The long-run growth rate of GDP is 1%.

Using the above data and making any necessary assumption, find the VIU for Vorty.

7.12. Programming

The ordinate approximation approach to finding the RUL as in Table 7.4 can be refined by using thin rectangles say corresponding to a base (incremental age) of 0.001 years rather than 1 year, to get a more accurate estimate of the area in the Weibull curve tail. Write a C/C++ program to find the RUL using thin rectangles.

References

Amihud, Y., & Mendelson, H. (1986). Liquidity and stock returns. *Financial Analysts Journal, 42*, 43–48.

Harper, J. Jr., & Lindquist, J. (1983, April). Quantitative support for large minority discounts in closely held corporations. *The Appraisal Journal, 51*, 270–277.

Reilly, R., & Schweihs, R. (1998). *Valuing intangible assets* (1st ed.). Columbus: McGraw-Hill.

Weibull, W. (1951). A statistical distribution function of wide applicability. *Journal of Applied Mechanics, 18*, 293–297.

Winfrey, R. (1935). *Statistical analysis of industrial property retirements* (Vol. 125). Ames: Iowa State College of Agriculture and Mechanic Arts.

Property

8

We start by reviewing when valuation is needed—when property is measured using the revaluation model under IAS 16 or under the fair value model for investment properties under IAS 40, and for impairment testing. We proceed to discuss the concept of "highest and best use" in the particular context of valuing land. We outline three approaches to property valuation—the market, income and cost approaches. Under the market approach, we discuss the comparable transaction approach and the multiple regression approach. The comparable transactions approach values a property using the adjusted recent sales price of a similar property. In this context, we discuss two rules for measuring similarity between properties—the Euclidean norm, and the Minkowski *p*-norm. Multiple regression analysis values a property using data on the prices and other attributes of a number of other properties in the neighborhood. It seeks the pricing model that best fits actual data on pricing and these attributes from recently sold properties. We study two regression approaches—the standard ordinary least squares (OLS) approach and a spatial regression approach, geographically weighted regression. We turn next to income-based approaches, which derive the fair value of a property by capitalizing rental income from the property. We discuss two broad approaches—direct capitalization, which applies a standard multiple or rate based on the rental income, and yield capitalization, which applies a discounted cash flow methodology. Finally, we discuss the cost approach, which values a property at the replacement cost. This approach starts by estimating the required outlay for a brand-new replacement property ("duplication cost new") and then applying a series of adjustments for the loss of value due to factors such as age.

S. Lynn, *Valuation for Accountants*, Springer Texts in Business and Economics,
https://doi.org/10.1007/978-981-15-0357-3_8

8.1 Learning Outcomes

After completing this chapter, you would be able to:

1. Define property and explain when property valuation is needed under IFRS.
2. Explain the "highest and best use" concept in valuing land.
3. Value properties using prices of similar properties, by simple comparison as well as regression-based approaches including ordinary least squares (OLS) and geographically weighted regression (GWR).
4. Value properties using income-based approaches, including both simple multiple-based approaches (direct capitalization) as well as a DCF approach (yield capitalization).
5. Value properties using a replacement-cost approach.

8.2 Property Valuation and IFRS

8.2.1 Property Definition

For accounting purposes, property could include most tangible non-current assets, with the exception of biological assets. This would cover real estate including land and buildings, both fixed and movable equipment, and items such as vehicles or furniture and fittings.

To focus our discussion, we will limit it to the valuation of real estate (land and buildings). Other property is valued using the same broad approaches, with some differences in details. For example, location is a key factor in valuing real estate, but this would not extend to movable property like vehicles or furniture.

8.2.2 Valuation Requirements in IFRS

Under IAS 16 *Property, plant and equipment*, PPE must be initially recognized at its acquisition cost. Subsequent recognition could follow one of two alternative models—the cost model, and the revaluation model. Under the cost model, PPE continues to be stated at its original cost, less accumulated depreciation and impairment if any. Under the revaluation model, PPE is periodically revalued to its fair value as of the revaluation date. Between revaluations, PPE is depreciated, with the depreciation based on the last revalued amount. Entities must classify their PPE into various classes such as "Land and Buildings", "Machines", etc. They must then apply the same model to all the items in a particular class.

Under IAS 40 *Investment property*, investment property is initially recorded at acquisition cost. Subsequent measurement could follow either the cost model or the fair value model. The cost model is identical to the cost model under IAS 16. Under the fair value model, investment property is recorded at its fair value as of the balance-sheet date, with fair value gains and losses taken to the income statement directly. An entity must use the same model (either cost or fair value) for all its investment properties.

Even when the cost model is followed, impaired properties must be marked down to a current value. The impairment test requires fair value measurement.

Unlike goodwill, property is not automatically tested for impairment every period. Impairment tests are only conducted if there is some prior evidence of impairment. Examples of such triggers are damage to the property, or forced idle capacity over an extended period, which would reduce value in use.

Property under IAS 16 or IAS 40 could be reclassified as "held for sale" under IFRS 5 *Non-current assets held for sale and discontinued operations*. This happens when the entity intends to sell the property and expects the sale to conclude within a year. On reclassification and thereafter, we continue to value the property in accordance with the original standard (IAS 16 or IAS 40) with some differences:

- We stop depreciating the property while it is held for sale.
- We test for impairment just before reclassification and if necessary thereafter (if there is a trigger). In the impairment test:
  - We only consider fair value less costs to sell, not value in use (there is no value in use since the asset is not in use).
  - If the asset is at fair value at the point of reclassification, it is immediately marked down to fair value less costs to sell, with the markdown recorded as an expense.

To sum up, accountants need to be able to prepare or audit fair value measurements of property. This is true even if the cost model is followed.

Of course, valuation is typically carried out by a third party valuation expert. The accountant's role is more one of an intelligent user of the valuation information.

8.3 Valuing Land: Highest and Best Use

In finding the fair value of a piece of land, we would use a recently-quoted price for the land from an active market if this is available (a Level 1 input).

In the absence of an active market, if a non-related party makes an unforced legally-binding offer to buy the land at some price, then that price is the best estimate of fair value. If multiple such offers exist, then the fair value would be based on the best offer, i.e., the offer which would pay the highest price for the land.

8.3.1 Highest and Best Use

If we do not have an actual price, then we need to estimate the best price that we could obtain from a hypothetical transaction. This calculation is affected by the fact that potential buyers could use the land for different purposes. The price that a particular buyer would pay depends on the particular use that they plan for the land.

Then the fair value estimate is given by the highest price potentially offered, which in turn is approximately equal to the highest-value use of the land. We refer to this as the value from the "highest and best use" of the land.

In determining the highest and best use, we consider the standard uses for similar land in nearby locations. We do not speculate on unusual or far-fetched uses of the land, unless there is clear evidence that a potential buyer seeks the land for some such use, and then some reliable estimate of the potential value added from that use.

We usually assume that the "highest and best use" is the same as our current use of the land. If the land is not yet in use, but we have a stated future intended use, then that is the highest and best use.

Example 1 Hakim Inc owns land on which it is currently building a block of residential apartments at a total cost of CU 30 million (present value today). Hakim Inc plans to rent out the apartments, with the expected present value of the estimated profits being CU 32 million. Value the land.

The "highest and best use" is the actual planned use—building apartments and renting them out. The value from this use is the net present value of CU 2 million (the future profits of CU 32 million less the initial investment of CU 30 million). Therefore, the estimated fair value of the land is CU 2 million.

Example 2 Cassandra Inc owns forest land. They are contractually bound not to develop the land, but to maintain it in pristine condition as a nature reserve. This contractual arrangement was part of the terms of the purchase agreement that they had signed with the previous owner when purchasing the property. Cassandra Inc does earn some income from allowing tourists to visit the land. The present value of all future income from this source is estimated to be CU 5 million. Solomon Inc wishes to buy the land in order to clear the forest and develop it as a hotel. Cassandra estimates that the net present value from this project (excluding the land purchase cost) would be CU 28 million. What is the fair value of the land?

In this case, Cassandra's use of the land is not freely chosen, but rather imposed by a contractual constraint. We therefore cannot assume that this is the best possible use of the land (in the sense of highest value added), unless all potential buyers would face the same constraint. This is not the case here, since Solomon Inc is clearly able to develop the land. The highest and best use therefore is Solomon's planned use of developing the land for a hotel (absent any information about other potential uses). Since we estimate that this is worth 28 million to them, they should be willing to offer up to CU 28 million for the land. The fair value is CU 28 million.

Example 3 Leopoldina Inc owns a "chilly crab" seafood restaurant located on the coast. They also own a plot of land between the restaurant and the sea. They do not use this land for any purpose whatsoever, but the open space gives their customers a spectacular view of the sea. Roark Inc has indicated interest in buying up this land in order to build on it. Leopoldina Inc has rejected this offer, as the building would block the view. What is the highest and best use?

In this case, Leopoldina has no use for the land by itself, but the land adds value as part of a bundle of assets—restaurant plus land. We should value the entire bundle as a unit, and not the land by itself.

Example 4 Valentina Inc owns a piece of land. They are considering a project for the land with an estimated expected present value of CU 8 million. Muthusamy Inc has just made a legally binding offer to buy the land for CU 6 million. What is the fair value of the land?

Valentina's proposed use may well be the "highest and best use" in this case. but here we have a Level 1 input in the form of Muthusamy's offer. We therefore take CU 6 million as the best estimate of the fair value.

8.4 Three Valuation Approaches Outlined

As with valuation in general, there are three main approaches to property valuation:

1. The market approach
2. The income approach
3. The cost approach.

We briefly outline each approach below. The remainder of the chapter would be devoted to a detailed discussion of the approaches.

8.4.1 The Market Approach

The market approach values a property using the average price of similar properties. We discuss two methods under this approach:

1. Comparable transactions method
2. Multiple regression analysis (or hedonic valuation).

The comparable transactions approach values a property (the target property) by collecting data on similar properties that sold recently. We can then value the property by taking the price of the most similar property, or a weighted average of the prices of several such similar properties. We may make further adjustments for differences between the target property and the similar property.

The multiple regression approach uses data on several properties that recently sold in a neighborhood to find an equation that links the property price to several attributes of the property (e.g., floor space, location, etc.) We can then use this equation to value our target property.

We discuss two variants of the regression approach:

1. *Ordinary least squares (OLS)*: This is the standard approach to regression and estimates a single equation based on all the data.
2. *Geographically weighted regression (GWR)*: This approach computes a different pricing equation for different locations. In estimating the equation for a particular location, it allows an increased influence from properties that are nearer that location, and a reduced influence for properties that are further away.

In classifying market approaches, we may also distinguish between mass appraisal methods and individual appraisal methods. Mass appraisal methods use data on several properties to develop pricing functions that can be applied to value properties across a neighborhood or wider area. Individual appraisal focuses on a single target property and values it by collecting data on a few neighboring properties. Multiple regression analysis is a standard mass appraisal technique, while the comparable transactions approach is typically individual appraisal.

8.4.2 The Income Approach

In the income approach, we value a property as the value of the rental income that it could provide.

We discuss two broad variants of the income approach:

1. Direct capitalization
2. Yield capitalization.

In *direct capitalization*, we value a property by using a standard multiple of the property price to some income measure (or equivalently a rate where the income measure is the numerator and the property price is the denominator.) These standard multiples or rates are usually based on current property prices in the neighborhood. So in practice, this is a hybrid of the market approach and the income approach.

In *yield capitalization*, we project the rental income and expense cashflows over the expected life of the property. We discount these using a property-specific rate to get the value of the property.

8.4.3 The Cost Approach

In the cost approach, we value a property by estimating how much it would cost to replace it if it disappeared. We typically start by estimating the cost of a brand-new replacement property. We then make a series of adjustments to reflect the loss of value due to age, wear and tear etc.

8.4.4 The Valuation Hierarchy

In terms of the IFRS 13 valuation hierarchy of inputs, the market approach is usually best as it usually relies more on Level 2 inputs.

The market approach may not be available, for example if there are no recent transactions for similar properties. In that case, the income approach is usually the second-best choice.

The cost approach would usually only be undertaken if the other approaches fail. For example, suppose that we are valuing a manufacturing plant that the entity employs in its own manufacturing. The plant is not rented out, and there is no rental market where it could be rented out. There is also no external market to buy the plant, as it is customized to meet the entity's very specific manufacturing requirements and would not be useful to any external party. In this case, replacement cost is the only approach left. It usually requires significant assumptions and Level 3 inputs.

We proceed next to discuss each of the three approaches in more detail.

8.5 The Market Approach

We will first discuss the comparable transactions approach.

8.5.1 Comparable Transactions

Recall that the comparable transactions approach values a property by comparing it to "similar" properties. This raises the question of how we define "similar".

We typically use a dissimilarity score, built up by combining differences between the properties on several attributes of interest. The higher the score, the less similar the two properties are.

In practice, such a score is typically called a "distance" measure. But we will reserve the term "distance" to refer to actual physical distance between two locations. For the dissimilarity score, we will use the equivalent technical term "norm".

A norm can be interpreted as the distance between two points on a graph. If our score is built up of just one, two or three components, we can draw and visualize this graph and physically measure the distance, For four or more attributes, we can no longer draw or visualize the graph, but we can still use algebra to calculate distances in these higher-dimension spaces.

We will consider two norms:

1. The Euclidean norm
2. The Minkowski p-norm.

The Minkowski p-norm is a generalization of the Euclidean norm.

8.5.1.1 The Euclidean Norm

The Euclidean norm measures the distance between two points on a graph using traditional geometry. Consider a two-dimensional graph with dimensions X,Y, where X represents floor-space say, and Y represents number of rooms for a property.

We consider two properties A and B. Property A has floor-space X_A and number of rooms Y_A. Property B has floor-space X_B and number of rooms Y_B. Just to avoid ambiguity in our accompanying figure, let's stipulate that $X_B > X_A$ and $Y_B > Y_A$.

Now we plot the points A or (X_A, Y_A) and B or (X_B, Y_B) on a graph as shown in Fig. 8.1. Our norm would be the length of the line AB.

Recall Pythagoras theorem: In a right-angled triangle (like ABC in Fig. 8.1), the square of the length of the hypotenuse (or diagonal side AB in the diagram) equals the sum of the squared lengths of the other two sides (i.e., BC and AC in Fig. 8.1). From this we have:

$$AB^2 = BC^2 + AC^2 = (Y_B - Y_A)^2 + (X_B - X_A)^2.$$

If we represent the Euclidean norm showing the dissimilarity between A and B as $||AB||_E$, we get:

$$||AB||_E = \sqrt{(X_B - X_A)^2 + (Y_B - Y_A)^2}.$$

This is the Euclidean norm in two dimensions.

We extend to an arbitrary number of dimensions say N dimensions. Let the N dimensions or property attributes be $(x_1, x_2, x_3, \ldots, x_N)$ say. Let $(x_{1A}, x_{2A}, \ldots x_{NA})$ give the values of the attributes for property A. Let $(x_{1B}, x_{2B}, ...x_{NB})$ give the values of the attributes for property B. Then the Euclidean norm $||AB||_E$ is:

$$||AB||_E = \sqrt{\sum_{i=1}^{N} (x_{iB} - x_{iA})^2}.$$

Fig. 8.1 2D Euclidean norm computation

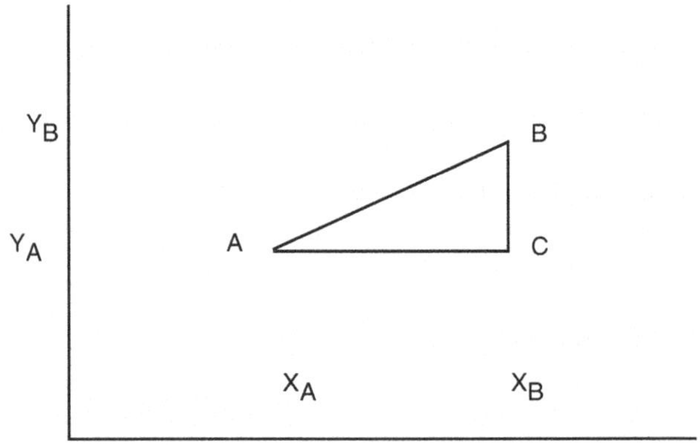

We modify this formula to reflect:

- weighting,
- categorical variables.

Weighting

Consider the two-dimensional case where our variables are X equal to floor space in square metres, and Y equal to number of rooms.

The difference between Y = 2 rooms and Y = 1 room is more material than the difference between X = 120 square metres and X = 121 square metres.

We can reflect this in our norm calculation by *weighting* the differences to give the difference in number of rooms a higher weight than the difference in floor space. Suppose we want that a difference of one unit in number of rooms is 20 times more significant than a difference of 1 unit in floor space. Then we could calculate the norm as:

$$||AB||_E = \sqrt{[1 \times (X_B - X_A)]^2 + [20 \times (Y_B - Y_A)]^2}.$$

We have put a weight of 1 on the difference in X and a weight of 20 on the difference in Y.

In terms of drawing a graph, this means that the length that denotes 1 room on the Y-axis is the same as the length that denotes 20 square metres on the X-axis.

In general, for N items, we have:

$$||AB||_E = \sqrt{\sum_{i=1}^{N} [A_i(x_{iB} - x_{iA})]^2},$$

where A_i is the *weight* on item i.

When we have a large enough sample of properties, we can divide by the sample standard deviation for each dimension i, say $\hat{\sigma}_i$, to get a roughly comparable scale for the different dimensions. This gives us the expanded equation below.

$$||AB||_E = \sqrt{\sum_{i=1}^{N} \left[A_i \left(\frac{x_{iB} - x_{iA}}{\hat{\sigma}_i}\right)\right]^2}.$$

We retain the weights A_i. Now their role is more to indicate our judgement on the relative importance of the various attributes rather than to make their scales comparable.

We illustrate with an example. Table 8.1 lists data on a number of properties in Alphabet City, Manhattan, New York, NY, USA, that sold during a period extending from July 2018 to May 2019. These are all condominium-type residential apartments in apartment buildings with an elevator. This data is publicly reported.

Table 8.1 Property sales in Alphabet City 2018–2019

Record #	Area (sq.ft.)	Year built	Sale price (US$)	Sale date (mm/dd/yy)	Age (years)	eu1	eu2	m1
1	605	1920	847,000	03/27/19	99	2.6556212	2.655621	4.287862
2	481	2014	732,376	07/25/18	5	2.0187012	3.096822	7.108318
3	495	2014	710,000	03/25/19	5	1.9664612	1.966461	2.378466
4	733	2014	1,016,213	10/09/18	5	1.0783820	2.584194	5.970987
5	640	1928	33,159	09/18/18	91	2.4306812	3.379847	8.591813
6	500	1928	975,000	06/04/18	91	2.7695440	3.631188	9.223630
7	933	2005	1,372,500	07/30/18	14	0.3908229	2.380734	5.298691
8	951	2005	1,350,000	09/28/18	14	0.3356229	2.372297	5.217453
9	1124	1910	1,270,000	11/30/18	109	2.4111829	3.365851	7.788807
10	751	1910	780,000	08/13/18	109	2.5867936	3.493802	8.551541
11	528	2008	685,000	10/25/18	11	1.8484352	2.988622	7.049761
12	434	1965	640,000	09/27/18	54	2.4642250	3.404050	8.574552
13	1039	1965	1,549,000	05/03/19	54	1.1235878	1.123588	1.330838
14	1254	2013	2,112,868	08/22/18	6	0.8659934	2.503017	5.739328
$\hat{\sigma}$	267.9941				43.67997			

We wish to value a property in Alphabet City with an area of 1022 square feet and built in 2014. Our valuation date is 31 May 2019.[1]

To compute our Euclidean norm, we will use property area in square feet, and property age in years. We compute the sample standard deviations for these components shown in the last row of Table 8.1.

We compute the Euclidean norm shown in the column labelled "eu1" in Table 8.1. To illustrate the calculation, here is the Euclidean norm for Record #8:

$$\sqrt{\left(\frac{951 - 1022}{267.9941}\right)^2 + \left(\frac{14 - 5}{43.67997}\right)^2} \approx 0.34.$$

To value the target property, we can choose the most similar property. In this case, it is property #8. This sold at a price of US$1,350,000.

Our target property has a larger area. To adjust for the larger area, we find the price per square foot of the most similar property (around US$1,420) and then apply this to our target property's area. This gives us an estimated value of US$1,420 × 1022 square feet or around US$1.45 million.

We could also adjust for the difference in age. Our target property is newer than the most similar property. We can look at the per-square-foot prices of properties #2, 3 and 4, as they are the same age as our property. But their price per square foot

[1]This is an actual property that sold on 31 May 2019 for US$1,440,000.

ranges from $1,386 to $1,522 which can be taken as being in the same ballpark as $1,420. So we don't adjust further for age (though this is a judgement call).

Categorical Variables

When we compare two properties, we are often interested in attributes that are not easy to quantify. We can refer to such attributes as *categorical variables*.

For example, we could have an expert's rating of the construction quality: say, in three grades of "good", "adequate" and "bad". We could also have a True/False variable, for example whether the property sold in 2019 or not.

To incorporate such non-quantitative information in our Euclean norm, we need to express it using numbers. For example, we could represent the grades of "good", "adequate" and "bad" using numerical scores of 3, 2 and 1 respectively.

For a true/false variable such as whether the property sold in 2019, we can assign a value of 1 if true, and 0 if false.

Once they are converted to numbers, we can include categorical variables in our norm calculation by treating them in exactly the same way as we treat regular quantitative variables.

When categorical variables are included, it is less meaningful to interpret the norm as distance on a graph (what is the "distance" between "true" and "false", or "good" and "bad"?) But the norm still works fine in telling us how similar two properties are.

So proceeding to include categorical variables, we end up with our final official formula for the Euclidean norm in Equation 8.1.

If we have $N1$ regular quantitative variables indexed $x_1, x_2, \ldots, x_{N1}$, and $N2$ categorical variables indexed $c_{N1+1}, c_{N1+2}, \ldots c_{N1+N2}$, we have in Equation 8.1:

$$||AB||_E = \sqrt{\sum_{i=1}^{N1}\left[A_i\left(\frac{x_{iB} - x_{iA}}{\hat{\sigma}_i}\right)\right]^2 + \sum_{j=N1+1}^{N1+N2}\left[A_j\left(\frac{c_{jB} - c_{jA}}{\hat{\sigma}_j}\right)\right]^2}. \tag{8.1}$$

As an example, let us take the sale date in our earlier example in Table 8.1. Let us use this to create a True/False variable which equals 1 if the property sold in 2019 and 0 otherwise. (This is not shown in the table, but easy to derive—it is 1 for records #1, 3 and 13, and 0 otherwise). This variable has a sample standard deviation of 0.4258.

Now we will include this variable in our norm calculation in addition to age and area. This gives us the Euclidean norm in the column labelled "eu2" in Table 8.1.

Now, the most similar property is property #13, with a norm of around 1.12. We can verify the calculation as:

$$\sqrt{\left(\frac{1039 - 1022}{267.9941}\right)^2 + \left(\frac{54 - 5}{43.67997}\right)^2 + \left(\frac{1 - 1}{0.4258}\right)^2} \approx 1.12.$$

The price of property #13 implies a price per square foot of US$1,491, Applying this to our target property, we get an estimated fair value of 1491 × 1022 or around US$1.52 million.

8.5.1.2 The Minkowski *p*-Norm

The Minkowski p-norm, say $||AB||_{M,p}$ is a generalization of the Euclidean norm. We have for some parameter p, and otherwise using the same notation as before:

$$||AB||_{M,p} = \left(\sum_{i=1}^{N1} |A_i (x_{iB} - x_{iA})|^p + \sum_{j=N1+1}^{N1+N2} |A_j (c_{jB} - c_{jA})|^p \right)^{\frac{1}{p}}. \quad (8.2)$$

When $p = 2$, Equation 8.2 becomes a variant of the Euclidean norm.

In practice, the most common non-Euclidean version is to set $p = 1$. Let us compute the Minkowski p-norm with $p = 1$ in our earlier example given in Table 8.1. We will set the weights for each variable to be the reciprocal of the mean absolute deviation for the variable. Mean absolute deviation is the mean of the absolute (unsigned) differences between each value and the median value. We can compute the mean absolute deviations (MAD say) as follows:

	MAD
Area (square feet)	221.5714
Age (years)	39.07143
2019 sale (True/False)	0.2142857

The Minkowski 1-norm is as shown in Table 8.1 in the column labelled "m1". The most similar property is #13. We can verify the calculation as follows for #13:

$$\frac{|1039 - 1022|}{221.5714} + \frac{|54 - 5|}{39.0714} + \frac{|1 - 1|}{0.2142857} \approx 1.33.$$

8.5.2 Multiple Regression Analysis (MRA)

Multiple regression analysis (MRA) uses data on a large number of property transactions to estimate a function that treats the property price as a function of several other attributes. Typically the function is *linear*. That is, price is calculated as a score taken by adding up the value of each attribute times some imputed price for that attribute. If we label the attributes $x_1, x_2, \ldots, x_k$ where we have a total of k attributes, we have, for the property indexed i the pricing function P_i as follows:

$$P_i = a_0 + a_1 x_{1i} + a_2 x_{2i} \ldots . + a_k x_{ki}.$$

Such a function is often called a hedonic valuation function, and so this valuation approach is also called "hedonic valuation". This means in our context that the property is analyzed as a bundle of various attributes. We compute the price of the property by adding up the values of all the separate attributes in the bundle. We estimate the price of each attribute from a sample and then use these estimated prices to value the target property.

The attributes $x_1, x_2, \ldots, x_k$ may include a mix of quantitative and categorical variables, as with the norm calculation. They may also include a mix of variables that are intrinsic to the property as well as variables that relate to the neighborhood. Variables intrinsic to the property could include for example floor space, number of rooms, etc. Variables intrinsic to the neighborhood could include for example air quality, crime rate, etc.

The parameters $a_0, a_1, \ldots a_k$ are referred to as "regression coefficients". Specifically we call the parameter a_i the regression coefficient on the variable x_i (the imputed price per unit for variable x_i).

Let us also set our notation to refer to the *estimate* of parameter a_j as $\hat{a}_j$.

To find the parameter estimates $\hat{a}_0, \hat{a}_1, \ldots, \hat{a}_k$, we search for the equation that gives the *best fit* to the observed data. "Best fit" can be defined in many ways. We discuss two approaches here:

1. Ordinary least squares (OLS)
2. Geographically weighted regression (GWR).

8.5.2.1 Ordinary Least Squares (OLS)

In ordinary least squares, we seek to minimize the *sum of squared deviations*. That is, we define "best fit" to be that equation whose predicted values have the property that when subtracted from the actual values (deviations), and then squared (squared deviations), and then added up across the whole sample (sum of squared deviations), the result gives a lower value than any other possible equation could (least squares).

Mathematically, we seek to solve the following program:

$$\min_{\hat{a}_0, \hat{a}_1, \ldots \hat{a}_k} \sum_{i=1}^{N} \left[\left(P_i - (\hat{a}_0 + \hat{a}_1 x_{1i} + \hat{a}_2 x_{2i} + \ldots + \hat{a}_k x_{ki})\right)^2 \right]$$

where P_i is the actual price for property i, N is the number of properties in the sample, and other notation is as before.

For convenience, let us introduce a data attribute x_{0i} that simply equals 1 for every i. Then the constant term a_0 can be thought of as the regression coefficient of x_{0i}.

We can use calculus to derive the solution to the least squares program (the detailed derivation is not addressed here). This solution turns out to be the solution to the following set of $K + 1$ simultaneous equations in $K + 1$ unknowns $(\hat{a}_0, \ldots, \hat{a}_k)$.

$$\hat{a}_0 \sum_{i=1}^{N} x_{0i} x_{0i} + \hat{a}_1 \sum_{i=1}^{N} x_{0i} x_{1i} + \hat{a}_2 \sum_{i=1}^{N} x_{0i} x_{2i} + \ldots + \hat{a}_k \sum_{i=1}^{N} x_{0i} x_{ki} = \sum_{i=1}^{N} x_{0i} P_i.$$

$$\hat{a}_0 \sum_{i=1}^{N} x_{1i} x_{0i} + \hat{a}_1 \sum_{i=1}^{N} x_{1i} x_{1i} + \hat{a}_2 \sum_{i=1}^{N} x_{1i} x_{2i} + \ldots + \hat{a}_k \sum_{i=1}^{N} x_{1i} x_{ki} = \sum_{i=1}^{N} x_{1i} P_i.$$

$$\hat{a}_0 \sum_{i=1}^{N} x_{2i} x_{0i} + \hat{a}_1 \sum_{i=1}^{N} x_{2i} x_{1i} + \hat{a}_2 \sum_{i=1}^{N} x_{2i} x_{2i} + \ldots + \hat{a}_k \sum_{i=1}^{N} x_{2i} x_{ki} = \sum_{i=1}^{N} x_{2i} P_i.$$

$$\ldots$$

$$\ldots$$

$$\hat{a}_0 \sum_{i=1}^{N} x_{ki} x_{0i} + \hat{a}_1 \sum_{i=1}^{N} x_{ki} x_{1i} + \hat{a}_2 \sum_{i=1}^{N} x_{ki} x_{2i} + \ldots + \hat{a}_k \sum_{i=1}^{N} x_{ki} x_{ki} = \sum_{i=1}^{N} x_{ki} P_i.$$

If the solution exists, we can solve these equations by elimination, The solution is tedious by hand, but can easily be automated.

A solution may not exist, for example if one of the equations turns out to be simply a rearrangement of another one, say multiplied by a constant. This pathological situation is unlikely (unless we made the mistake of including two variables that are simply variants of each other e.g., areas in square feet and areas in square meters; or more subtly, number of rooms, number of bedrooms, and number of rooms that are not bedrooms—one of these variables is redundant).

Ordinary least squares is a commonly used technique, and software to do it is readily available, including as part of spreadsheet programs like Excel. We will illustrate OLS by using our earlier example of property prices from Alphabet City, Manhattan (Table 8.1).

Using the data in Table 8.1, we estimate the following regression equation (I used the statistics software R)[2]:

$$\text{Sale Price} = a_0 + a_1 \times \text{Area} + a_2 \times \text{Age} + a_3 \times (\text{Sold in 2019}).$$

This gives us the following parameter estimates:

$\hat{a}_0$ (constant)	−10,800.5
$\hat{a}_1$ (area)	1,528.2***
$\hat{a}_2$ (age)	−3,227.6
$\hat{a}_3$ (sold in 2019)	126,480.6

[2]The results may be somewhat distorted by the anomalous observation #5.

The three stars next to the estimate for area indicate that a standard test for statistical significance supports that the true coefficient is likely to be significantly different from zero with a high probability. The tests do not support any of the other coefficients being different from zero.

The sale price of property i is given by a constant term of \$−10,800.5 plus a value of \$1,528.20 per square foot less an amount of \$3,227.60 for every year of age, plus a premium of \$126,480.6 for properties that sold in 2019 (vs 2018).

Apply this to our target property (recall area of 1022 sq feet, age of 5 years and valued in 2019) we have:

$$\text{Price} = -10,800.5+1,528.20\times 1022-3,227.6\times 5+126,480.6\times 1 = \$1,661,363.$$

We can estimate a simpler model that uses just one variable, area, dropping the non-significant variables for age and sold in 2019.

This gives us the equation:

$$\text{Price} = -134,469.7 + 1,524.2 \times \text{area}.$$

Applying to our target property, we get a value of \$1,423,263.

8.5.2.2 MRA-Based Adjustment

Recall that in the comparable transactions approach, we found the most similar property. Then to find the value of the target property, we took the price of the most similar property and made some adjustments to reflect differences between that property and the target property. These adjustments are somewhat subjective.

If we have a multiple regression analysis equation that applies to both the similar property and the target, we can utilize that to make a non-subjective adjustment. Let $\hat{P}_T$ be the predicted price of the target property from the regression equation. Let $\hat{P}_S$ be the predicted price of the similar property from the regression equation. Let P_S be the actual price of the similar property.

Then P_S is our starting estimate for the price of the target (we are following the comparable transactions approach). For our adjustment, we simply subtract $(\hat{P}_S - \hat{P}_T)$, the amount by which the MRA-predicted price of the similar property exceeds the MRA-predicted price of the target property.

$$\text{Adjusted similar price} = P_S - (\hat{P}_S - \hat{P}_T).$$

Let us apply this to our earlier example from Alphabet City Manhattan (Table 8.1). Recall that using our expanded Euclidean norm eu2 or the Minkowski 1-norm, property #13 was the most similar. This property sold for US\$1,549,000 on May 3, 2019, had an area of 1039 square feet, and had an age of 54 years at our valuation date May 31, 2019.

Recall that our target property had an area of 1022 square feet and an age of 5 years on the valuation date May 31, 2019. Recall that our regression equation is:

$$\text{Price} = -134,469.70 + 1524.20 \times \text{area}.$$

Applying this equation, we get $\hat{P}_T = US\$1{,}423{,}263$, $P_S = US\$1{,}549{,}000$ and $\hat{P}_S = US\$1{,}449{,}174.10$.

This gives us the following fair value calculation for the target using comparable transactions:

$$1{,}549{,}000 - (1{,}449{,}174.1 - 1{,}423{,}263) \approx \text{US\$}1{,}523{,}089.$$

Rather than using a single similar property, we can consider a weighted average of a group of similar properties.

We can choose the weight W_i as follows for similar property i (suggested by Pagourtzi et al. 2003).

Let $||Ti||_X$ be the norm comparing property i and the target (X could be either "EU" for Euclidean norm, or "M,p" for a Minkowski p-norm). Let max $||T||$ be the highest $||Ti||_X$ among the properties for which we are calculating the weighted average.

Let ASP_i be the adjusted sales price for similar property i. Other notation is as defined earlier. Then we have:

$$W_i = \frac{1}{\left(\frac{1}{2}\max||T||\right)^2 + (||Ti||_X)^2 + \left[2(\max||Ti||) \times \frac{|ASP_i - P_i|}{P_i}\right]^2}.$$

These weights are higher for observations with higher similarity measures and a smaller adjustment in ASP.

To illustrate, let us use our earlier example in Table 8.1. We will use the Euclidean norm eu2, and use the *two* most similar properties, given by record #13 (eu2 = 1.12) and record #3 (eu2 = 1.97).

The weight for property #13 is calculated as follows:

$$\frac{1}{(0.5 \times 1.97)^2 + 1.12^2 + \left(2 \times 1.97 \times \frac{|1{,}549{,}000 - 1{,}523{,}089|}{1{,}549{,}000}\right)^2} = 0.45.$$

We can work out that the ASP for property #3 is US\$1,513,253. Then the weight for property #3 is calculated as follows:

$$\frac{1}{(0.5 \times 1.97)^2 + 1.97^2 + \left(2 \times 1.97 \times \frac{|1{,}513{,}253 - 710{,}000|}{710{,}000}\right)^2} = 0.04.$$

Therefore the weighted average ASP from the two properties is:

$$\frac{0.45}{0.49} \times 1,523,089 + \frac{0.04}{0.49} \times 1,513,253 \approx \text{US\$}1.522 \text{ million}.$$

This is the estimated fair value for the target property based on the weighted average of the two most similar properties.

We turn next to geographically weighted regression (GWR).

8.5.2.3 Geographically Weighted Regression (GWR)

In our previous example, we ignored location data except that we chose all our sample properties from the same neighborhood (Alphabet City). But when we model property prices over a larger area, we need to factor in location as a key variable.

While common sense and experience concur that location is important, *how* location affects price is less straightforward. It is not a simple linear relationship. If we plot prices on a map, we would see a pattern, but a complicated and rugged one. Such a pattern cannot be captured by some simple mathematical function.

Geographically weighted regression (GWR) (Brunsdon et al. 1996) seeks to model the effect of location on price without parameterizing it (or trying to explain it as an equation). To do this, GWR estimates a *different* regression equation at different locations. The definition of "best fit" changes at different locations and therefore the regression equation does too. To achieve this, GWR defines "best fit" as one which minimizes the sum of *weighted* least squares.

The weights change from location to location. At each location where we are calculating a regression equation, the weight for each property in the sample depends on the property's physical distance from that location. The further away the sample property is from the location, the lower the weight.

GWR can be viewed as an extension of a technique known as kernel regression. In kernel regression too, we compute a separate regression for different sample observations using weighted least squares, and the weights decrease for observations that are "further away" from the regression's central point. But in kernel regression unlike GWR, "further away" is not based on a literal physical distance. Rather it is determined using a dissimilarity score based on the x variables used in the regression (a Euclidean norm or Minkowski p-norm).

We discuss later several choices of weighting function, as well as how to calculate physical distance between two locations given their latitudes and longitudes in degrees. But first let us formally describe the GWR algorithm.

The GWR program to determine the regression equation at a specific location i is given by:

$$\min_{\hat{a}_{0i}, \hat{a}_{1i}, \ldots \hat{a}_{ki}} \sum_{j=1}^{N} \left[\left(w_{ij} \left(P_j - \left(\hat{a}_{0i} + \hat{a}_{1i} x_{1j} + \hat{a}_{2i} x_{2j} + \ldots + \hat{a}_{ki} x_{kj} \right) \right) \right)^2 \right]$$

where $\hat{a}_{1i}, \hat{a}_{2i}, \ldots, \hat{a}_{ki}$ are the estimated parameters *at location i* (recall that we estimate a different set of parameters for each location); and w_{ij} is the weight on property j which is based on how far it is (physical distance) from location i.

We would re-run this program for different locations in the area to get a map of different regression equations at each location. The locations could be those of the different properties in the sample, or could be a grid of positions.

As with OLS, we can reduce the problem to a set of $K+1$ simultaneous equations in $K + 1$ unknowns (though here we have a different set of simultaneous equations for each location i). These equations are as follows:

$$\hat{a}_{0i}\sum_{j=1}^{N}x_{0j}w_{ij}x_{0j} + \hat{a}_{1i}\sum_{j=1}^{N}x_{0j}w_{ij}x_{1j} + \ldots + \hat{a}_{ki}\sum_{j=1}^{N}x_{0j}w_{ij}x_{kj} = \sum_{j=1}^{N}x_{0j}w_{ij}P_j.$$

$$\hat{a}_{0i}\sum_{j=1}^{N}x_{1j}w_{ij}x_{0j} + \hat{a}_{1i}\sum_{j=1}^{N}x_{1j}w_{ij}x_{1j} + \ldots + \hat{a}_{ki}\sum_{j=1}^{N}x_{1j}w_{ij}x_{kj} = \sum_{j=1}^{N}x_{1j}w_{ij}P_j.$$

$$\ldots$$

$$\ldots$$

$$\hat{a}_{0i}\sum_{j=1}^{N}x_{kj}w_{ij}x_{0j} + \hat{a}_{1i}\sum_{j=1}^{N}x_{kj}w_{ij}x_{1j} + \ldots + \hat{a}_{ki}\sum_{j=1}^{N}x_{kj}w_{ij}x_{kj} = \sum_{j=1}^{N}x_{kj}w_{ij}P_j.$$

GWR is a computationally demanding procedure since it requires running different regressions for different locations, with potentially big data (a large number of sample properties, and a large number of locations where we estimate separate regressions). But when we perform GWR for valuation purposes, we are really only interested in the pricing model at *one* particular location—that of our target property. For our purposes, it is therefore sufficient to perform a single regression centered on the target property location.

However, it is usually desirable to compute regression equations for other properties in the neighborhood so that we can set our property valuation in the context of a wider valuation map. For example, if the valuation equation for our target property is overly influenced by an unusual transaction that is geographically nearby, we are more likely to be alerted to this distortion if we also compute GWR regression equations for a wider spread of property locations.

We may also require to value several properties in the same geographical area on the same date, e.g., if we are accounting for a property development company. In that case, it is convenient to perform the GWR for the entire set of properties together, as well as for other properties in the data sample.

We will illustrate GWR by using a sample of property prices for residential units listed for sale in around July 2018 to May 2019 in Sante Fe, Rosario, Argentina. This data is taken from the website of properati.com (http://properati.com.ar), which has kindly made it available under a Creative Commons License. The sample data is listed in full in Appendix 1.

One caveat with this data is that the prices are asking prices posted by the potential sellers, and not prices from actual sales transactions. We would not use this data in an actual valuation as we would need to use actual transaction data. But the dataset works fine to help us illustrate GWR. So keeping the caveat in mind, we will proceed to use it in our illustration.

Geographically weighted regression can be performed by specialized software, e.g., the MGWR or GWR4 software (available online). It is also available in add-in packages for general purpose statistical software such as R (current R packages at time of writing are `spgwr` and `mgwrsal`).

We will discuss some implementation details of the GWR algorithm, before proceeding to fit the sample data for our Argentine example.

We will first discuss how to calculate physical distance between two locations when given their respective latitudes and longitudes in decimal degrees (i.e., fractions of a degree are stated as a decimal part of a degree rather than as minutes and seconds). Location data is usually provided in this form.

Secondly, we will discuss different choices for the weighting function, which are based on the distance calculation.

8.5.2.4 Distance

We first discuss some preliminary concepts. In calculating the distance between two locations, we seek the length of the shortest path between them.

A *geodesic* is the shortest path between two points on the Earth's surface.

If we assume that the Earth's surface is approximately flat (a reasonable assumption over a small area), then the geodesic is approximately the straight line connecting the points.

If we treat the Earth as a perfectly round ball, i.e., a sphere, then the geodesic is given by the path along the *great circle* connecting the two points. A great circle is a circle passing through both points, where the circle's centre is the Earth's centre, and the circle's outer rim (circumference) lies on the Earth's surface (i.e., the circle has a radius equal to the Earth's radius).

In actual fact, the Earth is not a perfect sphere, but slightly flatter at the poles than at the Equator. More complicated measurements of distance take into account this irregularity.

In mass appraisal for property valuation, we are typically analyzing a group of properties that are near to each other, within the same neighborhood or city. Over such a small area, the Earth's surface can be assumed to be approximately flat. So the straight-line distance is usually good enough. If we are analyzing properties that are spread out over a wider area, e.g., sheep farms in Australia, then we may prefer a more accurate measure that reflects the Earth's curvature.

Locations are typically described in latitude and longitude, given in degrees, These are *angles*.

It is useful to introduce the concept of *angular distance* between two locations A and B say. We can define this as the *angle* traced out by a rigid rod with one tip stuck into the Earth's centre, and the other tip moving from A to B,

Angles are traditionally measured in *degrees*. If we move the rigid rod in a full circle starting from A and returning to A, then we have moved through 360 degrees (360°). Moving through a right angle is 90° and moving to a position that is diametrically opposite A is 180°.

The *latitude* of a location measures the shortest angular distance in moving to that location from a point on the equator that is due north or due south of that point (or coincident with it if we are on the equator). Points on the equator have a latitude of 0°. The north pole has a latitude of 90°N (N for north). (We could also reach the north pole by moving *south* from the equator and going through 270°. But latitude is the shortest angular distance, so it is 90°N, not 270°S.) Similarly, the south pole has a latitude of 90°S or 90 degrees south of the equator.

In computing with latitudes it is convenient to treat southern latitudes as negative numbers, and northern latitudes as positive ones. We will follow this convention, which is standard.

The *longitude* of a location is the shortest angular distance in moving to that location from a point that is due east or due west (whichever is shorter) on the *Greenwich meridian* (or coincident with it if the point is on the Greenwich meridian). The Greenwich meridian is the geodesic connecting the north and south poles that also passes through the Greenwich observatory near London in the UK. Thus the Greenwich observatory and points due north or south of it have a longitude of 0°. (The north and south poles can be taken as longitude 0° too, though their longitudes are ambiguous).

Santa Fe, Rosario, Argentina has a longitude of approximately 60°W (W stands for "west of the Greenwich meridian"). Singapore has a longitude of approximately 104°E (E for "east of the Greenwich meridian").

In computations, it is convenient to use negative numbers for longitudes that are west of the Greenwich meridian, and to use positive numbers for longitudes that are east of the Greenwich meridian. Thus we would write the longitude of Santa Fe, Rosario, as −60°, and that of Singapore as simply 104°.

In calculations, it is often convenient to measure angles in *radians* rather than degrees.

To define a radian, suppose that we fix one end of a rigid rod of length r and swivel the other end through an arc (part of a circle). Then the angular distance travelled in radians is the length of the arc divided by r. The arc is part of the circumference of a circle with radius r. So the angular distance in radians is the length of the arc (fraction of the circumference) divided by the radius.

The length of the circumference of a circle of radius r is $2\pi r$ where π (the Greek letter "pi") is a standard constant approximately equal to 3.141593.

From this, we can infer that an angular distance of 360° corresponds to 2π radians (one full circumference divided by the radius). Proportionately, an angular distance of 90° corresponds to $\frac{\pi}{2}$ radians, and an angular distance of 180° corresponds to π radians.

In general, an angular distance of X degrees corresponds to an angular distance in radians of:

$$X \times \frac{\pi}{180} \text{ radians.}$$

To illustrate our various distance formulas, let us consider two specific properties in Santa Fe, Rosario. Our target property has a longitude of $-60.68208°$ and a latitude of $-32.92115°$. The comparable property has a longitude of $-60.67475°$, and a latitude of $-32.95144°$.

We will discuss three formulas for distance, that provide progressively more accuracy. These are:

1. the Pythagorean distance formula,
2. the haversine distance formula,
3. the Vincenty inverse formula.

Pythagorean Distance

This is the simplest measure of distance. It assumes that the curvature of the Earth does not significantly affect the distance calculation over the small area examined. So we can assume that the Earth is locally flat.

Let the two locations A and B have latitude $latA$ and $latB$ in degrees respectively and longitudes $longA$ and $longB$ in degrees respectively.

Recall our thought experiment of a rigid rod with one tip fixed at the Earth's center,

Then $\frac{\pi}{180}|latA - latB|$ is the length in radians of the line that we would trace if we start with the tip of our rigid rod at A and move the tip due north or due south (whichever is shorter) to a point that is exactly due east or due west of B, say X. To move from X to B, we further swivel the tip of our rod eastwards or westwards, whichever is shorter, moving through a length of $\frac{\pi}{180}|longA - longB|$ radians.

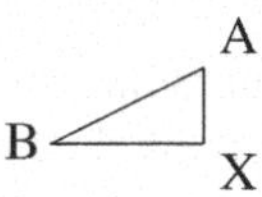

The shortest distance between A and B is the length of the line AB. This is the hypotenuse in the right-angled triangle AXB, whose other two sides are AX and XB with lengths $\frac{\pi}{180}|latA - latB|$ radians and $\frac{\pi}{180}|longA - longB|$ radians respectively.

Therefore, applying Pythagoras' theorem, the length of AB in radians is given by:

$$\sqrt{\left(\frac{\pi}{180}|latA - latB|\right)^2 + \left(\frac{\pi}{180}|longA - longB|\right)^2}$$

$$= \frac{\pi}{180}\sqrt{(|latA - latB|)^2 + (|longA - longB|)^2}.$$

This gives distance in radians or units that are equal to the Earth's radius. To get distance in a standard unit such as metres, we multiply by the Earth's radius in that unit (we can take the radius to be 6,371,007.2 m.)

For our two properties, the calculation is:

$$6{,}371{,}007.2 \times \frac{\pi}{180}\sqrt{(60.68208 - 60.67475)^2 + (32.92115 - 32.95144)^2}$$
$$\approx 3{,}465.$$

This gives us a distance of approximately 3,465 m. or approximately 3.465 km.

Haversine Distance

The haversine distance formula measures the length of the *great circle* connecting the two locations, assuming that the Earth is a perfect sphere (See Sinnott 1984).

We will not go into details of the derivation. Let the latitudes *in radians* of the locations A and B be *latA* radians and *latB* radians respectively. Let the longitudes in radians of locations A and B be *longA* radians and *longB* radians respectively,

Then let:

$$\Delta lat = latB - latA.$$
$$\Delta long = longB - longA.$$

Then the great circle distance in radians d say is given by the following formula:

$$d = 2 \times \arcsin\left(\sqrt{\sin^2\left(\frac{\Delta lat}{2}\right) + \sin^2\left(\frac{\Delta long}{2}\right) \times \cos(latA) \times \cos(latB)}\right). \tag{8.3}$$

The arcsine of X is the angle Y (in radians) for which $\sin(Y) = X$.

To convert d to metres, we multiply by the radius of the Earth (6,371,007.2 m.)

Let us apply this formula to our two locations in Santa Fe, Rosario.

We first convert the latitudes and longitudes to radians. We have:

$$latA = -0.5745824.$$
$$latB = -0.5751112.$$
$$longA = -1.059102.$$
$$longB = -1.0589742.$$

$$\Delta long = 0.0001278785.$$
$$\Delta lat = -0.0005287423.$$

We can compute d to be equal to 0.0005395249 radians.

Multiplying by the Earth's radius 6,371,007.2 m., we get a distance of approximately 3,437 m. or 3.437 km.

Vincenty Inverse Formula

The Earth is not a perfect sphere. It is slightly flatter at the poles than at the equator. A better model is of an *ellipsoid*—an egg-shaped object. Actual measurements show that an ellipsoid model of the Earth's surface at sea-level is very accurate.

The Vincenty inverse formula (see Vincenty 1975) is an iterative procedure that measures distance on the surface of an ellipsoid.[3] The derivation is beyond us, but we can note that it involves projecting points on the ellipsoid to an imaginary sphere called the *auxiliary sphere*. The latitudes on the auxiliary sphere can be derived from the actual latitudes on the ellipsoid. The auxiliary-sphere latitudes are referred to as *reduced latitudes*.

We can use an iterative procedure to jointly calculate the distance on the auxiliary sphere in conjunction with the difference in longitudes on the auxiliary sphere. Using these, we can calculate the distance on the ellipsoid.

Parameters are as follows:

a	radius of the Earth at the equator (equal to 6,378,137.0 m.).
b	radius of the Earth at the poles (equal to 6,356,752.314245 m.).
f	"flattening" of the Earth vs. a perfect sphere, given by $\frac{a-b}{a}$. This equals $\frac{1}{298.257223563}$.
$lat1, lat2$	actual latitudes in radians of the two points (indexed 1 and 2) on the Earth's real (ellipsoid) surface.
L	difference in actual longitudes measured in radians ($lat2 - lat1$).
s	the distance that we seek to estimate: distance between points 1 and 2 along a geodesic on the Earth's real (ellipsoid) surface. It is in the same units as a and b.
α	azimuth of the geodesic at the equator. For our purposes, it is fine to just think of α as a model parameter that is determined by Equation 8.7. But it can be defined as follows: the angle made clockwise between two hypothetical observers standing at the point where the produced geodesic between points 1 and 2 crosses the equator, with one observer facing due North, and the other one facing forward along the geodesic.
U_1, U_2	reduced latitudes for points 1 and 2 respectively (latitudes on the auxiliary sphere) given by: (arctan is the inverse tan function) $U_1 = \arctan((1 - f)\tan(lat1))$ $U_2 = \arctan((1 - f)\tan(lat2))$
λ	difference in the auxiliary-sphere longitudes
σ	angular distance in radians between points 1 and 2 on the auxiliary sphere
σ_m	angular distance in radians on the auxiliary sphere, from the equator to the midpoint of the line joining the two points 1 and 2.

[3]There is also a direct formula that calculates the position of one point, given the position of the other, the distance and some other parameters. The direct formula need not concern us.

We start by estimating λ and σ jointly using an iterative procedure. To start, we set $\lambda = L$ as our starting guess for λ. Then we compute the following expressions in sequence:

$$\sin^2\sigma = (\cos U_2 \sin\lambda)^2 + (\cos U_1 \sin U_2 - \sin U_1 \cos U_2 \cos\lambda)^2. \tag{8.4}$$

$$\cos\sigma = \sin U_1 \sin U_2 + \cos U_1 \cos U_2 \cos\lambda. \tag{8.5}$$

$$\sigma = \arctan\left(\frac{\sin\sigma}{\cos\sigma}\right). \tag{8.6}$$

$$\sin\alpha = \cos U_1 \cos U_2 \frac{\sin\lambda}{\sin\sigma}. \tag{8.7}$$

$$\cos^2\alpha = 1 - \sin^2\alpha. \tag{8.8}$$

$$\cos(2\sigma_m) = \cos\sigma - 2\sin U_1 \frac{\sin U_2}{\cos^2\alpha}. \tag{8.9}$$

$$\text{Let } C = \frac{f}{16}\cos^2\alpha(4 + f(4 - 3\cos^2\alpha)). \tag{8.10}$$

$$\lambda = L + (1 - C) f \sin\alpha(\sigma + C \sin\sigma(\cos(2\sigma_m) + C\cos\sigma(-1 + 2\cos^2(2\sigma_m)))). \tag{8.11}$$

We repeat the sequence of calculations in Equations 8.4 to 8.11. We keep repeating this sequence of calculations, updating λ each time as in Equation 8.11, until the change in λ from the previous iteration is less than some small tolerance limit, such as 10^{-12}.

The iteration may not converge when the two locations are almost at opposite ends of the Earth from each other (antipodes). But since this pathological case is unlikely in our context, we will not discuss it further. (There are other algorithms that can handle such cases. See Karney (2012).)

Once we have got our final values of λ and the other parameters that change during the iteration, we proceed to compute s by going through the following computations in sequence (just once, no need to iterate):

$$\text{Let } u^2 = \cos^2\alpha \times \frac{a^2 - b^2}{b^2}. \tag{8.12}$$

$$\text{Let } A = 1 + \frac{u^2}{16,384}(4,096 + u^2(-768 + u^2(320 - 175u^2))). \tag{8.13}$$

$$\text{Let } B = \frac{u^2}{1,024}(256 + u^2(-128 + u^2(74 - 47u^2))). \tag{8.14}$$

$$\begin{aligned}\text{Let } \Delta\sigma &= B \sin\sigma(\cos(2\sigma_m) + \frac{1}{4}B(\cos\sigma(-1 + 2\cos^2(2\sigma_m)) \\ &- \frac{1}{6}B\cos(2\sigma_m)(-3 + 4\sin^2\sigma)(-3 + 4\cos^2(2\sigma_m)))).\end{aligned} \tag{8.15}$$

$$s = bA(\sigma - \Delta\sigma). \tag{8.16}$$

The algorithm looks daunting, but is easy to program on a computer or programmable scientific calculator.

We run the Vincenty algorithm for the two properties that we have used to illustrate the other distance measures. We will not go through the detailed steps of the calculation. We end up with a measure of the distance that is approximately 3,428 m.

Other Distance Measures

The Vincenty formula is highly accurate, and even the cruder measures give answers that are only a few metres off compared to the Vincenty formula.

All three measures however model distance along a geodesic. But what may be more relevant for valuation purposes is the travelling distance (or travel time) between the locations along the most practical route.

Two properties that are very close to each other along a geodesic may be separated by some impassable barrier such as a mountain, trench or political border.

Conversely, two properties that are more widely separated on the map may be connected by a high-speed, frequent, commuter rail service.

So we may often want more human-scale measures of distance. For example, in Manhattan, where streets are mostly arrayed in a rectangular grid, it is convenient to measure distance between two street addresses in terms of the number of blocks (cross-roads) that need to be traversed to reach one address from the other. This measure extends to many other urban areas where streets are planned in a grid.

More generally, GPS software can compute the distance or travel time between locations along the most practical travel route.

We turn next to the discussion of weighting schemes.

8.5.2.5 Weighting

Recall that GWR applies weighted least squares to perform the regression at each location, where the weights reduce as properties are further away from the regression centre.

We consider the following weighting schemes:

1. Fixed maximum distance
2. K nearest neighbors

3. Gaussian
4. Bisquare.

We proceed to discuss each of these in more detail.

Fixed Maximum Distance

This weighting scheme assigns a weight of 1 to all properties that are within some fixed maximum distance of location i, say D, and 0 otherwise (location i is the location for which we are evaluating the regression).

Formally, suppose that we are evaluating the regression at a particular location i and we are calculating the weight for a sample property whose distance from i is d_{ij}.

Let w_{ij} represent the weight for property j in the regression at location i. Then we have:

$$w_{ij} = \begin{cases} 1 \text{ for } d_{ij} \leq D. \\ 0 \quad \text{otherwise.} \end{cases}$$

The weighting scheme restricts the regression sample to properties that are within D of the location i. Other properties are ignored in the regression estimation.

The weighting scheme has a couple of potential disadvantages.

One is that the map may include a denser concentration of properties in some areas while in other parts, properties may be distributed more sparsely. The weighting scheme would pick up a larger sample when i is in a densely concentrated area, and few or no properties when i is in a sparsely concentrated area.

Secondly, there is a sharp discontinuity in the weights for properties that are close to the border D. For example, suppose that D is 5 km. Then a property that is 4.99 km away would have a weight of 1 and get included, while a property that is 5.01 km away would have a weight of 0 and get dropped.

K nearest neighbors is an alternative scheme that seeks to correct the first of these disadvantages.

K Nearest Neighbors (Adaptive Weighting)

Rather than setting a maximum distance, we could set a maximum number of nearby properties to include in the regression. This scheme is called *adaptive weighting* or K nearest neighbors.

Formally, suppose that we are evaluating the regression at a location i. We choose a parameter K where we want to include exactly K nearby neighbors in our regression estimation. We rank the sample properties in ascending order of their distance from i (that is, nearest first). Then we set the weight to be 1 for the top K properties in the sorted list, and 0 for the others. If rank($d_i j$) is the rank for property j in the sorted list, we have:

$$w_{ij} = \begin{cases} 1 \text{ for rank}(d_{ij}) \leq K. \\ 0 \text{ otherwise.} \end{cases}$$

With adaptive weighting, we would choose the same number of neighbors for every location i, irrespective of whether i is in a sparsely-concentrated or densely-concentrated area.

Gaussian Weights

The two weighting schemes above weight all properties the same within the maximum distance D or the maximum number of neighbors K. For example, suppose that we are using fixed-maximum-distance weighting, we have $D = 5$ km., and we have two sample properties A and B say, where A is at a distance of 4 km from our regression centre i, and B is at a distance of 0.1 km from i. In both cases, the weights are the same (equal to 1), so both properties have equal influence on the regression.

The Gaussian weighting scheme allows weights to decrease continuously as the distance increases.

We introduce a parameter h say, called the *bandwidth*. Its role is somewhat similar to a maximum distance parameter.

Then the weighting formula is as follows (keeping other notation as before):

$$w_{ij} = e^{-\left[\left(\frac{d_{ij}}{h}\right)^2\right]}.$$

Consider the example above of our two properties A and B. Suppose that we are using Gaussian weights with a bandwidth of 5 km.

Then the weight for A (distance 4 km) is:

$$e^{-\left[\left(\frac{4}{5}\right)^2\right]} = 0.5273.$$

The weight for B at a distance of 0.1 km is:

$$e^{-\left[\left(\frac{0.1}{5}\right)^2\right]} = 0.9996.$$

Consider a sample property C that is far away from i, say 20 km. away. We would still include this property in our regression for i, but with a low weight. The weight would be:

$$e^{-\left[\left(\frac{20}{5}\right)^2\right]} \approx 1.13 \times 10^{-7}.$$

There are algorithms that help us select the best bandwidth, but we will not discuss the details. These algorithms are available as part of standard GWR software.

Bisquare Weights

The Gaussian scheme has the disadvantage that non-zero weights are calculated for the entire sample of properties, and so every property is involved in every regression. Then the computer can waste time doing computations for properties with very small weights and very low influence. Very small numbers may also lead to computing errors.

Bisquare weights restrict non-zero weights to only a portion of the sample, but also allow the weights to decrease continuously towards zero as properties get further away.

The bisquare weight formula is as follows:

$$w_{ij} = \begin{cases} \left(1 - \frac{d_{ij}^2}{D^2}\right)^2 & \text{for } d_{ij} \leq D. \\ 0 & \text{otherwise.} \end{cases}$$

where D is a maximum distance, and other notation is as before.

To illustrate, let us repeat our example from earlier—two properties A and B with distances of 4 and 0.1 km respectively from location i. Let D be 5 km.

Then the bisquare weight for A is:

$$\left(1 - \frac{4^2}{5^2}\right)^2 = 0.1296.$$

The bisquare weight for B is:

$$\left(1 - \frac{0.1^2}{5^2}\right)^2 = 0.9992.$$

Notice that if $d_{ij} = D$, the weight becomes zero. Therefore, the weight decays smoothly to zero as distance approaches D.

An adaptive version of the bisquare weight can also be computed, based on K nearest neighbors. Let rank(d_{ij}) be the rank of the distance of property j from location i, where ranks are in ascending order of distance (nearest first). Let D_{iK} be the distance whose rank is exactly K. Therefore D_{iK} is the distance of the K-th nearest property from i, Then the adaptive version of the bisquare weight formula is as follows:

$$w_{ij} = \begin{cases} \left(1 - \frac{d_{ij}^2}{D_{iK}^2}\right)^2 & \text{rank}(d_{ij}) \leq K. \\ 0 & \text{otherwise.} \end{cases}$$

To illustrate, suppose that we have 10 sample properties whose distance from i in km in ascending order is as follows:

$$1, 1.5, 2, 2.5, 3, 3.5, 4, 4.5, 5, 5.5.$$

We choose $K = 8$. Then $D_{iK} = 4.5$.

Say we are calculating the adaptive bisquare weight for the property with distance 3 km. The weight is:

$$\left(1 - \frac{3^2}{4.5^2}\right)^2 = 0.3086.$$

Also consider the weight for the property with distance 5 km. Its weight would be zero (since its distance rank is greater than 8).

8.5.2.6 Running the GWR

We take property no. 139 out of our sample and designate it as our valuation target.

After some experimenting with OLS models, a model which gave a good fit was one with covered area as the only variable, that is,

$$P_j = a_0 + a_1 \text{covered\_area}.$$

We first run regular OLS regression on the whole sample using this model. We get the following regression equation:

$$P_j = 97949.4 + 745.9 \times \text{covered\_area}.$$

Applying this to our target property (covered area = 241 m.), we get:

$$97{,}949.4 + 745.9 \times 241 = \text{US\$}277{,}711.30.$$

We next compute the GWR only at a single location—that of our target property. This has longitude 60.68208°W and latitude 32.92115°S.[4]

We use adaptive bisquare weights based on 20 nearest neighbors.

We get the regression equation:

$$P_j = 113{,}255.27 + 334.54 \times \text{covered\_area}.$$

Applying this to our target property, we get:

$$113{,}255.27 + 334.54 \times 241 = \text{US\$}193{,}879.40$$

[4]I used the spgwr package in R for the GWR runs reported here.

This is lower than our OLS prediction, suggesting that properties at this location have a lower price than the average.[5]

We proceed to run GWR for every location corresponding to a sample property (that is, all the sample properties except the target). We use adaptive bisquare weights based on 20 nearest neighbors.

The distribution of the regression coefficients from the 139 different regressions is as follows:

	Minimum	1st Quartile	Median	3rd Quartile	Maximum
a_{0i} (constant)	−104,736.84	12,530.96	77,954.96	105,019.64	303,120.30
a_{1i} (covered area)	−814.01	651.74	1,138.18	2,319.41	4,473.7

This distribution shows that there is wide variation in the pricing equation for different locations in Santa Fe, Rosario.

We can draw a map of the predicted prices as shown in Fig. 8.2. We also draw a map of the coefficient on covered area Fig. 8.3. (Both maps are drawn after dropping one observation #96 that is far from the others.) The maps show geographical variation in the prices as well as the estimated per-square-meter price.

We turn next to the income approach.

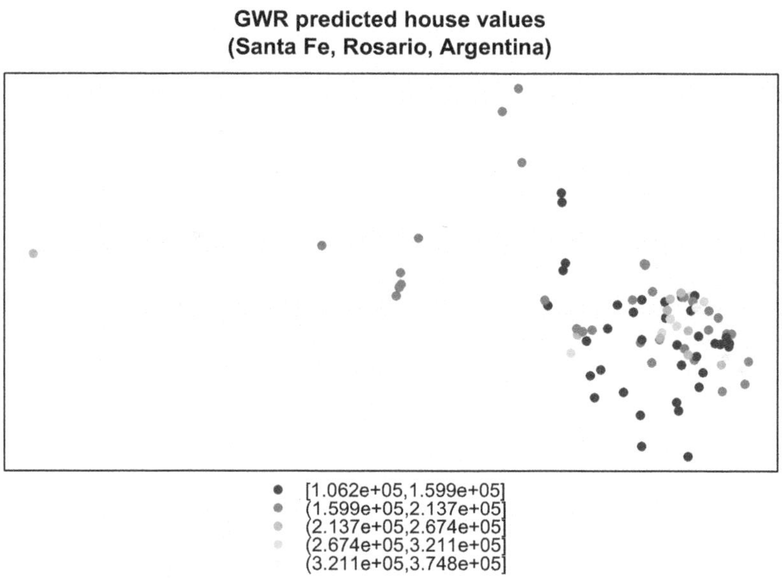

Fig. 8.2 GWR predicted values

[5]Both predictions are significantly higher than the actual listed price of US$125,000. There may be some other price-reducing factor that is not reflected in our data.

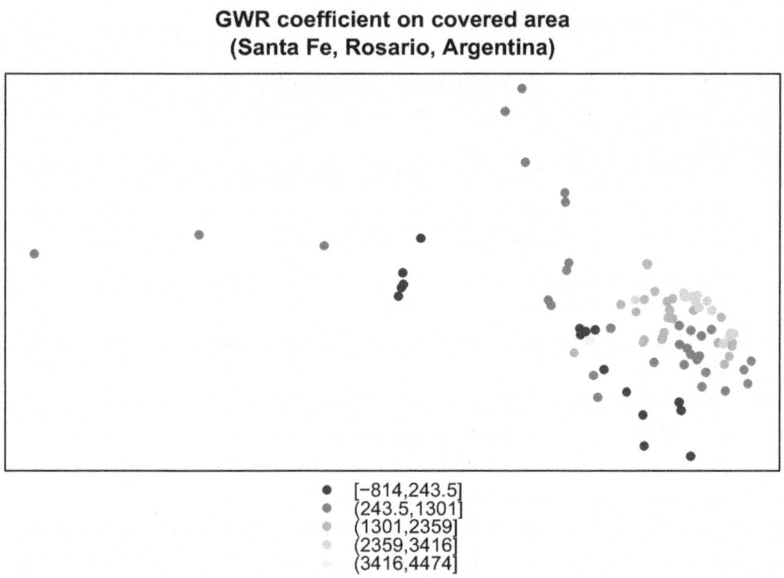

Fig. 8.3 GWR estimated coefficient

8.6 The Income Approach

In the income approach, we capitalize the total income from the property to obtain the fair value.

We would typically use this approach when we do not have a price for the property, but we do have a reliable measure of the income.

There are two main approaches:

1. Direct capitalization
2. Yield capitalization.

Direct capitalization is a ratio-based approach. We apply a ratio-based multiple or rate to convert the rental income to fair value. The ratios used are analogous to P/E and P/S ratios, and are obtained from similar nearby properties for which we have both price and income information.

Yield capitalization uses current income information for the property to project future cashflows, and then discounts these using a property-specific discount rate to arrive at a present value that is our fair value estimate for the property.

We will proceed to discuss each approach in more detail.

8.6.1 Direct Capitalization

Direct capitalization converts a rental income number to a property fair value by either multiplying the income number by a standard multiple, or dividing the income number by a standard rate.

This multiple or rate is usually derived by comparing price to income for nearby similar properties for which both price and income data are available. When we do this, the approach can be considered a hybrid of the market and income approaches.

Less preferably, the multiples or rates could be obtained through an opinion survey of valuation professionals in the area.

We will discuss two standard measures (See Brueggeman and Fisher 2018):

1. Gross income multiple (GIM),
2. Cap (capitalization) rate and cap factor based on *net operating income* (NOI).

8.6.1.1 Gross Income Multiple (GIM)

The gross income multiple is based on the gross annual rental income from the property. Gross here means before subtracting any operating or other expenses.

There are some variations in the income measure used. For example, we could use the actual rental income, reflecting any vacancies. Alternatively, we could use a measure called *potential gross income*, which estimates the income that we would have if there were no vacancies. Another choice could be to apply a standard occupancy rate. Still another choice could be to use standard measures for both occupancy rate and income per unit.

We can write the formula for valuation using GIM as follows:

$$\text{Fair value} = \text{GIM} \times \text{annual rental income}.$$

To estimate the GIM, we would collect information on sale price and annual rental income for a group of similar nearby properties (similar and nearby in relation to the target property being valued).

Then we would calculate the ratio of price to gross income for each of these properties. We would take the median of these as our estimate of the GIM (or the mean if it is not distorted by extremes).

$$GIM = \text{median}\left(\frac{\text{Price}}{\text{Gross annual rental income}}\right).$$

Example (GIM)

We seek to value a commercial office space that we classify as an investment property. We have rented this property out earning annual gross rental income of CU 120,000. The property has an occupancy rate of 80%. Properties of this type have a standard occupancy rate of 90%.

We have the following information about 5 nearby similar office spaces that sold recently (Table 8.2, amounts are in CU).

Table 8.2 GIM example

Record #	Price	Annual gross income	Occupancy rate	Adjusted AGI	GIM
1	1,656,191	141,693	0.88	144,913.3	11.43
2	1,566,613	120,968	0.75	145,161.6	10.79
3	1,464,960	105,390	0.74	128,177.0	11.43
4	1,386,347	131,863	0.87	136,410.0	10.16
5	1,541,126	136,037	0.89	137,565.5	11.20

Since the occupancy rates differ among the various comparable properties, and also deviate from the norm of 90%, we first adjust the annual gross income numbers to reflect an occupancy rate of 90%. The adjusted numbers are in the column labelled "Adjusted AGI" in Table 8.2. We illustrate the calculation for the first record:

$$\frac{141{,}693.3}{0.88} \times 0.9 = 144{,}913.3.$$

The adjusted AGI numbers are more comparable, as they all reflect the same occupancy rate of 90%.

We can proceed to compute the GIM based on the adjusted AGI. This is shown in Table 8.2 in the column labelled GIM.

To illustrate, for the first record, we have:

$$\frac{1{,}656{,}191}{144{,}913.3} \approx 11.43.$$

We use the median GIM for the comparables as our estimated GIM for the target. This is 11.20 (more precisely 11.20285).

To apply this to our target property, we first compute an adjusted AGI for the target property. This is based on 90% occupancy. This works out to:

$$\frac{120{,}000}{0.8} \times 0.9 = CU135{,}000.$$

Then the estimated fair value based on GIM is:

$$135{,}000 \times 11.20285 = CU1{,}512{,}385.$$

Rather than using a multiplier based on gross income, we could equivalently use a rate, sometimes called the gross rental yield. The calculation is simply the reverse of the GIM.

To estimate the gross rental yield from the comparable properties:

$$\text{Gross rental yield} = \text{median}\left(\frac{\text{Gross rental income}}{\text{Price}}\right).$$

To apply the gross rental yield to value the target property:

$$\text{Target fair value} = \frac{\text{Target gross rental income}}{\text{Gross rental yield}}.$$

8.6.1.2 Net Operating Income (NOI)

The GIM is similar to a P/S ratio rather than a P/E ratio. It ignores the fact that the owner may have to incur operating expenses that would reduce their net income from the property and would affect the property value.

The cap rate and cap factor are alternatives to GIM that are based on net operating income rather than gross income.

Before discussing the cap rate and cap factor, we will discuss net operating income (NOI) using an example.

Net operating income (NOI) can be defined as rental income less pre-tax operating expenses that the owner incurs. We ignore expenses that are directly borne by tenants or reimbursed by the tenants.

Here is an example of the calculation:

Rental income at full occupancy	12,000,000
Add: parking fees	100,000
Potential gross income	12,100,000
Less: vacancy losses	2,420,000
Effective gross income	9,680,000
Property tax	1,200,000
Repairs and maintenance	2,000,000
Other administrative costs	100,000
Net operating income	6,380,000

We start with the potential rental and other income assuming that all units are occupied. We call this the *potential gross income*. But the actual occupancy rate is just 80%. We next make adjustments for loss of rental income due to unoccupied units (vacancy losses). This gives us the *effective gross income*. From this, we subtract various pre-tax operating expenses to arrive at net operating income (NOI).

We proceed to discuss the calculation of cap rate. We will revisit this example in demonstrating cap rate.

8.6.1.3 Cap Rate (Cap Factor)

The cap rate (or capitalization rate) is a ratio that we divide into the NOI to get an estimate of fair value. That is,

$$\text{Fair value estimate} = \frac{\text{NOI}}{\text{cap rate}}.$$

Similarly to GIM, we can choose between variants of NOI—actual NOI, standard NOI, NOI adjusted for a standard occupancy rate, etc. Of course, our definition of NOI for the target property should match the definition used in estimating the cap rate from comparable companies.

To estimate the cap rate, we would utilize information on prices and NOI for a group of nearby similar properties (nearby and similar relative to the target property being valued). Alternatively (and less preferred), we can get a cap rate estimate from an opinion survey of experts.

Example (Cap Rate)

Suppose that we are valuing the property for which we calculated NOI in Sect. 8.6.1.2 above (NOI = CU 6.38 million). Let us add the further information that the property tax and administrative expenses are fixed costs (equal to CU 1.3 million in total), while the repair and maintenance expenses of CU 2 million are variable. Recall that the occupancy rate is 80%. Suppose that the standard occupancy rate for such properties is 90%.

We have found a group of 5 nearby similar properties for which we have the data in Table 8.3 (amounts in CU millions):

We calculate an adjusted NOI based on the standard occupancy rate of 90%. This is shown in the column "Adj.NOI" in Table 8.3. Here is the calculation for the second record:

$$\frac{(9.64 - 1.69)}{0.82} \times 0.9 - 1.23 = CU\,7.4956 \text{ million.}$$

We can now calculate the cap rate for the comparable properties. The formula is simply:

$$\text{Cap Rate} = \frac{\text{Adjusted NOI}}{\text{Price}}.$$

The calculation is shown in Table 8.3 in the column labelled "Cap Rate". To illustrate, here is the calculation for the second record:

$$\frac{7.4956}{66} = 0.1136.$$

Table 8.3 Cap rate example (amounts in CU million)

Record #	Price	Effective gross income	Variable costs	Fixed costs	Occupancy rate	NOI	Adj. NOI	Cap rate
1	67	10.64	1.63	1.39	0.90	7.62	7.620000	0.1137313
2	66	9.64	1.69	1.23	0.82	6.72	7.495610	0.1135698
3	63	9.10	1.88	1.20	0.77	6.02	7.238961	0.1149041
4	76	10.00	2.00	1.20	0.78	6.80	8.030769	0.1056680
5	67	10.00	1.56	1.27	0.82	7.17	7.993415	0.1193047

We take the median cap rate from the comparable properties to use in valuing the target property. This is 11.37% (or 0.1137313).

Before applying this to the target property, we calculate the adjusted NOI for the target property:

$$\frac{9.68 - 2}{0.8} \times 0.9 - 1.3 = CU\,7.34 \text{ million.}$$

To calculate the fair value, we divide this by the cap rate:

$$\frac{7.34}{0.1137313} = 64.538.$$

Our estimated fair value for the property is CU 64.538 million.

Rather than using a cap rate, we could equivalently use a multiple. This is called the cap factor. It is simply the reciprocal of the cap rate.

To determine the cap factor from a group of similar companies, we would take:

$$\text{Cap Factor} = \text{median}\left(\frac{\text{Price}}{\text{NOI}}\right).$$

To determine the fair value based on the cap factor, we would take:

$$\text{Fair value} = \text{NOI} \times \text{Cap Factor}.$$

We turn next to yield capitalization.

8.6.2 Yield Capitalization

In yield capitalization, we use an NOI figure as a basis to project free cash flows from the property over its life or a suitable horizon. We then discount these cashflows using a suitable discount rate, getting a present value that serves as our fair value estimate.

This is similar to the discounted cash flow approach in business valuation. In applying the approach to property, we need to be careful that our various parameters are specific to the property rather than the reporting entity (asset-specific rather than entity-specific).

For example, the D/E ratio used in the analysis is not the entity's D/E ratio, but rather the mix of debt and equity in the property investment. For example, if the property is typically funded by a mortgage loan covering 60% of the cost, while 40% is paid upfront by the buyer (equity), then the D/E ratio for the property is 60:40 or 1.5 initially, and will reduce as the mortgage loan gets paid back. Mortgage loans are typically repaid with interest in equal instalments.

Also the cost of equity used in the analysis is not the entity's cost of equity. Rather, it specifically reflects the required return for the equity in the property. If we are using CAPM to determine the cost of equity, then the relevant beta would be the beta of the property, not the beta of the entity's shares.

We will explain yield capitalization using an illustrative example. Let us build on the NOI calculation shown in Sect. 8.6.1.2. We add the following case facts:

- We project the NOI for a five-year horizon. We assume that per-unit gross rental income and expenses would go up by 1% per year over this horizon due to inflation.
- We assume that the occupancy rate for the property would increase from 80% to 90% on a straight-line basis over the 5-year horizon.
- Mortgage rates for this class of property have a fixed interest rate of 6% per year annually compounded. The terms are that the loan covers 60% of the property cost, while the buyer must pay 40% upfront. The loan is repayable in 5 equal annual instalments.
- To estimate the cost of equity for the property, we use the beta for a group of real estate investment trusts (REITs) that invest in a similar class of property. The unlevered beta for the REITs is 1.34.
- The income tax rate is 20%.
- Tax depreciation is on a straight-line basis over 5 years. The tax depreciation exactly matches the capital expenditure required to maintain the property in its current condition.
- The property's terminal value at the end of the horizon is estimated based on a GIM of 8.
- We follow the mid-year convention in evaluating cashflows.
- The risk-free rate is estimated to be a constant 2% p.a. annually compounded. The equity market premium over risk-free rates is 5%.
- Working capital changes are not significant.

The discount rate that we use is called the property mini-WACC, and is based as usual on combining the cost of equity and the cost of debt using the D/E ratio. Although we have assumed constant risk-free rates, the discount rate would change each year, as the D/E ratio changes, affecting both the cost of equity and the mini-WACC. Our discount rates are therefore *forward* rates rather than spot rates.

This setup presents some issues of circular logic. For one thing, the tax depreciation depends on the property value, but is also part of the cashflows used to determine this value. Also the fair-value based D/E ratio, which changes each year, depends on the fair value of the property (which also changes every year), but is also an input in calculating that fair value.

We could use a spreadsheet with circular formulas and iteration turned on. But we can avoid this by making some reasonable simplifications:

1. We can ignore the effect of fair value changes in property on the D/E ratio each year, and calculate it purely based on the pattern of repayments.
2. We can calculate the present value first by ignoring depreciation, and then add the value of the tax savings from depreciation later. This is similar to computing a

tax amortization benefit in intangibles valuation. It is possible to do this because we have made the assumption that depreciation equals capex (a standard and reasonable assumption), so that adding back depreciation and subtracting capex has no impact on free cash flow, meaning that we can ignore both these steps.

We first calculate the loan repayment schedule based on an initial borrowing of 0.6 (60% or our initial debt percentage). Then the beginning balance of the schedule each year gives us the percentage debt in the capital structure at mid-year (assuming that the total property value has stayed approximately constant). From this, we can derive the D/E ratio at mid-year. This is shown in Table 8.4 (numbers rounded).

The units in Table 8.4 can be taken to be proportions of our initial total investment in the property. Thus the initial borrowing is 60% of the initial total investment. After our first payment at the end of Year 1, the amount due has gone down to 49% of the total investment. This is the proportion of debt in the total investment at mid-year in Year 2. At the end of Year 2, after we have paid our second instalment, the proportion we owe has gone down to 38%, which is still the proportion we owe at mid-year in Year 3; and so on.

We can proceed to use these numbers to compute our cost of capital. This changes every year even though we assume constant interest rates. The reason is our changing D/E ratio. The computations for cost of capital are in Table 8.5.

Table 8.4 Loan repayment schedule based on initial borrowing of 0.60

Year	Beginning balance	Interest accrued	Payment	Ending balance
1	0.60	0.04	0.14	0.49
2	0.49	0.03	0.14	0.38
3	0.38	0.02	0.14	0.26
4	0.26	0.02	0.14	0.13
5	0.13	0.01	0.14	0.00

Table 8.5 Mini-WACC computations

Year	1	2	3	4	5
D/C	60.00%	49.36%	38.07%	26.11%	13.44%
D/E	1.50	0.97	0.61	0.35	0.16
Cost of equity k_e					
Risk-free rate	2.00%	2.00%	2.00%	2.00%	2.00%
Equity premium	5.00%	5.00%	5.00%	5.00%	5.00%
Unlevered beta	1.34	1.34	1.34	1.34	1.34
Levered beta	2.95	2.38	2.00	1.72	1.51
Forward k_e	16.74%	13.92%	12.00%	10.59%	9.53%
WACC computation					
Forward k_d	6.00%	6.00%	6.00%	6.00%	6.00%
Forward mini-WACC	9.58%	9.42%	9.26%	9.08%	8.90%

Table 8.6 Projected cashflows (amounts in CU)

Year	0	1	2	3	4	5
Effective gross income	9,680,000	9,899,010	10,244,864	10,596,646	10,954,438	11,318,327
Occupancy rate (year-end)	80.00%	82.00%	84.00%	86.00%	88.00%	90.00%
Occupancy rate (mid-year)		81.00%	83.00%	85.00%	87.00%	89.00%
Property tax (fixed)	1,200,000	1,212,000	1,224,120	1,236,361	1,248,725	1,261,212
Administrative costs (fixed)	100,000	101,000	102,010	103,030	104,060	105,101
Repairs (variable)	2,000,000	2,045,250	2,116,708	2,189,390	2,263,314	2,338,497
EBITDA	6,380,000	6,540,760	6,802,027	7,067,865	7,338,339	7,613,517
Income tax (@20%)	1,276,000	1,308,152	1,360,405	1,413,573	1,467,668	1,522,703
NOPAT (= FCF)	5,104,000	5,232,608	5,441,621	5,654,292	5,870,672	6,090,813
Terminal value (GIM = 8)						90,546,618

In Table 8.5: D/C stands for the debt to capital ratio; we use Hamada's formula to get the levered beta based on the unlevered beta given (that of the REITs); the cost of debt is the interest rate on the mortgage; and our mini-WACC is computed in the usual way from the cost of equity and cost of debt using the D/E ratios that we worked out.

The mini-WACC is a *forward* rate. Also we are discounting cashflows that occur at mid-year. So for example, to discount cashflows for year 4, we would multiply them by the following discounting factor:

$$\frac{1}{(1+9.08\%)^{\frac{1}{2}}(1+9.26\%)(1+9.42\%)(1+9.58\%)}.$$

We would first discount back to the beginning of Year 4 (half a year) using 9.08%, then to the beginning of Year 3 (one year) using 9.26%, then to the beginning of year 2 (one year) using 9.42%, and finally to the beginning of year 1 (one year) using 9.58%.

We proceed to project our cashflows. These are in Table 8.6.

Discounting these cashflows gives us a present value of CU 83,357,013. This is before considering the tax benefit due to depreciation.

The tax savings from depreciation each year are given by:

$$\frac{83{,}357{,}013}{5} \times 20\% = 3{,}334{,}281.$$

The present value of these tax savings over five years works out to CU 13,427,867.

Adding this to the earlier calculation of CU 83,357,013, we get a combined present value of CU 96,784,880.

We turn next to the cost approach.

8.7 The Cost Approach

We explain the cost approach by using an example.

We are valuing a manufacturing plant. The plant cannot be sold in a market. Also it is a cost center, so generates no direct income. Therefore, we use the replacement cost approach to determine fair value.

We start with the estimated outlay needed to build a brand new duplicate of the manufacturing plant. This cost is called the "duplication cost new" (DCN). Our cost estimates are as follows (CU '000):

Materials	10,000
Conversion costs	6,500
Fixed overhead	11,200
Administrative expenses	580
CONSTRUCTION COSTS	28,280
Developer's profit (10%)	2,828
CREATION COSTS	31,108

We now apply a series of adjustments to write down this value to reflect the age and state of our plant. These adjustments are applied sequentially, in the following order:

1. *Excess capital*: an adjustment for the difference between the DCN and the cost of building a plant that has the same functionality but a different more efficient design.
2. *Inutility*: we may be consistently under-using our plant capacity, so if we did have to build a new plant, we could save money by building a smaller one. The amount of our savings thereby is called the inutility penalty.
3. *Physical deterioration*: Our plant has lost value due to wear and tear over the years. We therefore record a further reduction in value to account for this.
4. *Functional obsolescence*: Some legacy parts of our operations may be less efficient than our competitors who have incorporated newer technology in their newer plants. We record a further markdown to account for this.
5. *Economic decline:* Lastly, the entire industry may have suffered a decline in the value of its production capacity, due to a permanent decline in demand for the product. This leads to an industry-wide loss of value that affects both us and our competitors.

We follow this sequence in order. Each step in the sequence is based on the adjusted value after applying the previous step. The particular order of adjustments given here is standard (See for example related cases in Catty 2010).

We proceed to apply the adjustments in our example.

8.7.1 Excess Capital

We estimate that we could rebuild the plant using a different more efficient design that gives us all the same functionality as our existing plant, but is cheaper to build. The required outlay would be as follows (CU ’000):

Materials	9,800
Conversion costs	6,200
Fixed overhead	11,100
Administrative expenses	580
CONSTRUCTION COSTS	27,680
Developer’s profit (10%)	2,768
CREATION COSTS	30,448

We refer to this revised cost estimate as the “replacement cost new” (RCN). The difference between the DCN and RCN is called the excess capital. It is around 2% of the DCN in this case.

The RCN is the starting point for our next adjustment.

8.7.2 Inutility Penalty

Our capacity utilization is just 80% and is not expected to increase in the foreseeable future. Therefore if we rebuilt the plant, we could save money by building a smaller one. These potential savings as a percentage of the RCN are given by the following formula (Catty 2010):

$$\text{Inutility penalty} = 1 - \text{Actual capacity utilization}^{EXP}.$$

EXP (or exponent) is a parameter that reflects the effect of economies of scale. The cost of building a plant with 80% of current capacity will not be 80% of the cost of building the bigger plant. It will be somewhat higher, and this is modelled by including the exponent EXP. The EXP parameter varies from industry to industry. It usually lies in a range between 0.4 and 1.03, and is most commonly equal to 0.6.

In our example, EXP is equal to 0.6. Therefore our inutility penalty is given by:

$$1 - 0.8^{0.6} = 12.53\%.$$

Applying this penalty to our RCN of CU 30,448,000, we get a revised replacement cost estimate of CU 26,632,551. This is the starting point for our next adjustment (physical deterioration).

8.7.3 Physical Deterioration

This adjustment is similar to old-fashioned straight-line depreciation. Our cost estimates so far have all reflected the outlay to build a brand new plant. But our plant is not brand new.

Our plant has completed 6 years of its estimated useful life of 30 years. Assuming that wear and tear occurs at an approximately constant rate through the life, we can assess a decline in value due to physical deterioration using a calculation similar to straight-line depreciation. We have:

$$\text{Physical deterioration} = \frac{\text{Age}}{\text{Life}}.$$

In our case, physical deterioration equals:

$$\frac{6}{30} = 20\%.$$

Applying this to our previous replacement cost estimate of CU 26,632,551, we get a revised replacement cost estimate of CU 21,306,041. This is the starting point for the next adjustment (functional obsolescence).

8.7.4 Functional Obsolescence

Apart from wear and tear, there is a loss of value because our plant may have some inefficient legacy operational features that newer plants have replaced with more modern cost-saving techniques. We cannot do that without replacing our plant. But since we are hypothetically considering exactly this replacement, we account for the fact that if we did so, we would take advantage of newer technology to realize further cost savings.

Our production cost per unit is CU 5. But our engineers estimate that if we had the latest operating features, our cost per unit would come down to CU 4.80, equalling a cost savings of 4%. Applying this to our previous replacement cost estimate of CU 21,306,041, we get a revised replacement cost estimate of CU 20,453,799. This is the starting point for our next adjustment.

8.7.5 Economic Decline

Our industry suffers from chronic overcapacity because of a permanent decline in demand for our product. The extent of this overcapacity is estimated to be 15%. We interpret this as the value of all production facilities in the industry (including ours) being lower by 15% as a result of the weak demand. We therefore apply a

Table 8.7 Summary of the replacement cost calculation

		CU'000
Duplication cost new		31,108
Less: Excess capital	2.12%	30,448
Less: Inutility penalty	12.53%	26,633
Less: Physical deterioration	20%	21,306
Less: Functional obsolescence	4%	20,454
Less: Economic decline	15%	17,386
Less: Income tax savings	20%	13,909

15% penalty to our previous replacement cost estimate. This gives us a final pre-tax replacement cost estimate of CU 17,385,729.

8.7.6 Tax Savings

If we actually spent CU 17,385,730 on a new plant, we would partially offset our cost by reaping tax savings. If our income tax rate is 20%, then the amount of these savings would be 20% × 17,385,730, or CU 3,477,146. After deducting this amount, we are left with our final estimate of the replacement cost which is CU 13,908,583.

8.7.7 Summary

We can sum up the calculations in Table 8.7.

8.8 Concluding Remarks

Several advanced techniques have been proposed for mass appraisal, such as neural networks (see Pagourtzi et al. (2003) for a good overview). In practice, however, cruder individual property appraisal still plays a major role. The reason is that property markets are not very liquid, and we are often valuing large commercial properties that are somewhat unique. So it is difficult to get large datasets of similar properties with recent prices.

This brings our discussion of valuation to a close. In this book, we have covered a range of valuation areas, including financial instruments, enterprise valuation, and property valuation. Hopefully, we have gained useful skills to perform or check fair value measurements in accounting.

Appendix 1: Santa Fe Data

Record #	Date listed	Latitude (deg.)	Longitude (deg.)	Price (US$)	Rooms	Bed rooms	Area (total) (sq.m.)	Area (covered) (sq.m.)
1	2019–02–04	−32.948057	−60.6730157	189,000	4	3	180	170
2	2019–03–30	−32.927457	−60.657118	220,000	2	1	70	65
3	2019–03–30	−32.9671486	−60.6331122	150,000	3	2	85	75
4	2019–03–23	−32.9390948	−60.6387818	161,116	2	1	69	44
5	2019–03–23	−32.9390948	−60.6387818	360,844	3	2	119	93
6	2019–03–23	−32.9552481	−60.6794973	310,000	10	3	250	200
7	2019–01–06	−32.969126	−60.672282	150,000	8	3	130	148
8	2018–12–21	−32.9375627	−60.7335019	180,000	4	3	268	121
9	2019–02–26	−32.9475525	−60.6683317	109,890	2	1	61	49
10	2019–02–26	−32.9514437	−60.6747531	110,000	3	2	50	48
11	2019–01–13	−32.9219113	−60.7563169	260,000	3	2	89	84
12	2019–01–13	−32.9219113	−60.7563169	370,000	4	3	113	107
13	2019–03–22	−32.9424999	−60.660453	120,000	2	1	50	45
14	2019–03–22	−32.9577482	−60.6249568	170,000	2	1	50	45
15	2019–03–22	−32.9377567	−60.6455856	180,000	2	1	50	45
16	2019–03–22	−32.9376165	−60.6431351	250,000	3	2	100	110
17	2019–03–22	−32.9577482	−60.6249568	285,000	3	2	70	65
18	2019–03–22	−32.9495406	−60.6775311	280,000	4	3	96	86
19	2019–04–24	−32.9296119	−60.6819181	130,000	5	2	225	110
20	2019–03–26	−32.9526344	−60.6470245	105,000	2	1	44	39
21	2019–03–26	−32.9514437	−60.6747531	110,000	3	2	50	48
22	2019–01–04	−32.9514437	−60.6747531	110,000	3	2	50	48
23	2019–02–08	−32.9492698	−60.6302742	150,000	6	3	90	90
24	2019–02–28	−32.9475525	−60.6683317	109,890	2	1	61	49
25	2018–12–27	−32.9475525	−60.6683317	109,890	2	1	61	49
26	2018–11–21	−32.9475525	−60.6683317	109,890	2	1	61	49
27	2019–02–10	−32.9378112	−60.6449165	125,000	3	2	63	63
28	2019–03–06	−32.9518793	−60.6582224	145,000	5	2	70	70
29	2019–03–12	−32.9386267	−60.6578084	117,000	3	2	70	60
30	2019–03–08	−32.9475525	−60.6683317	109,890	2	1	61	49
31	2019–03–02	−32.9573156	−60.6417914	180,000	5	3	94	94
32	2019–04–10	−32.895967	−60.694684	230,000	11	2	314	210
33	2019–01–14	−32.9556989	−60.6436165	215,000	4	3	408	180
34	2019–01–23	−32.930382	−60.7321832	145,000	3	2	100	64
35	2018–12–13	−32.9745723	−60.6582126	130,000	4	3	160	117
36	2018–12–13	−32.9745723	−60.6582126	126,000	4	3	117	160

(continued)

Record #	Date listed	Latitude (deg.)	Longitude (deg.)	Price (US$)	Rooms	Bed rooms	Area (total) (sq.m.)	Area (covered) (sq.m.)
37	2019–04–05	−32.9514437	−60.6747531	110,000	3	2	50	48
38	2019–04–05	−32.9604099	−60.6703738	135,000	3	2	70	70
39	2019–04–05	−32.9514437	−60.6747531	110,000	3	2	50	48
40	2019–04–05	−32.9514437	−60.6747531	110,000	3	2	50	48
41	2019–04–05	−32.9514437	−60.6747531	110,000	3	2	50	48
42	2019–04–05	−32.9386987	−60.6606999	175,000	3	2	75	75
43	2019–04–05	−32.9479745	−60.6373458	145,000	4	3	90	90
44	2018–12–20	−32.958779	−60.63344	285,000	3	3	100	90
45	2019–05–04	−32.934963	−60.732601	185,000	6	3	205	220
46	2018–12–14	−32.9514437	−60.6747531	110,000	3	2	50	48
47	2018–12–14	−32.9514437	−60.6747531	110,000	3	2	50	48
48	2019–01–22	−32.9514437	−60.6747531	110,000	3	2	50	48
49	2018–12–15	−32.9421307	−60.6372336	130,000	2	1	64	59
50	2019–02–25	−32.9361013	−60.6546023	195,000	3	2	75	68
51	2019–02–27	−32.9705675	−60.647151	160,000	3	2	72	70
52	2019–01–05	−32.9420025	−60.6428662	114,000	2	1	50	41
53	2019–01–05	−32.9420025	−60.6428662	101,000	2	1	46	39
54	2019–03–28	−32.9514437	−60.6747531	110,000	3	2	50	48
55	2019–02–14	−32.9485205	−60.6759319	189,000	4	3	220	130
56	2019–04–02	−32.9365307	−60.6458201	170,000	6	3	150	80
57	2019–05–08	−32.9401638	−60.6652774	118,537	3	2	63	52
58	2019–05–08	−32.967383	−60.6634225	135,000	5	4	240	180
59	2018–12–19	−32.9514437	−60.6747531	110,000	3	2	50	48
60	2018–12–19	−32.9514437	−60.6747531	110,000	3	2	50	48
61	2018–12–07	−32.8729195	−60.6958289	185,000	3	2	285	140
62	2018–12–07	−32.9622851	−60.673597	105,000	3	2	92	90
63	2019–03–19	−32.948057	−60.6730157	189,000	4	3	180	170
64	2019–02–06	−32.956198	−60.6410681	115,000	2	1	45	40
65	2019–03–15	−32.9657954	−60.6402364	122,000	3	2	69	65
66	2019–04–06	−32.948057	−60.6730157	188,000	5	4	180	170
67	2019–03–25	−32.9562628	−60.631923	430,000	4	3	210	156
68	2018–12–18	−32.9499018	−60.6404869	130,000	6	3	125	100
69	2018–11–29	−32.9475525	−60.6683317	109,890	2	1	61	49
70	2019–01–19	−32.919557	−60.726751	110,000	4	2	220	127
71	2019–01–11	−32.918461	−60.7945885	380,000	3	3	500	400
72	2019–03–21	−32.947681	−60.677774	123,000	6	2	82	82
73	2019–02–23	−32.9475525	−60.6683317	109,890	2	1	61	49
74	2019–02–13	−32.9475525	−60.6683317	109,890	2	1	61	49
75	2019–02–13	−32.9521046	−60.6308888	115,000	2	1	70	60
76	2019–02–13	−32.9475525	−60.6683317	109,890	2	1	61	49

(continued)

Record #	Date listed	Latitude (deg.)	Longitude (deg.)	Price (US$)	Rooms	Bed rooms	Area (total) (sq.m.)	Area (covered) (sq.m.)
77	2019–02–22	−32.951081	−60.6578978	110,000	2	1	54	47
78	2019–03–13	−32.9521298	−60.6354199	105,000	2	1	60	50
79	2018–11–23	−32.9491435	−60.631703	200,000	5	3	115	92
80	2019–02–01	−32.9604952	−60.6272	310,000	7	3	156	234
81	2019–02–01	−32.9537815	−60.6447316	170,000	5	3	118	118
82	2018–12–06	−32.933983	−60.7319772	160,000	4	3	304	149
83	2019–01–25	−32.958157	−60.65474	245,000	8	3	120	120
84	2019–05–09	−32.9874134	−60.6436534	180,000	6	3	234	180
85	2019–05–09	−32.9467686	−60.6470837	250,000	6	3	240	180
86	2019–03–16	−32.973178	−60.6464877	135,000	4	4	80	140
87	2019–03–16	−32.948057	−60.6730157	189,000	4	3	180	170
88	2019–01–29	−32.9475525	−60.6683317	109,890	2	1	61	49
89	2019–02–19	−32.9514437	−60.6747531	110,000	3	2	50	48
90	2019–02–05	−32.9475525	−60.6683317	109,890	2	1	61	49
91	2019–02–05	−32.9514437	−60.6747531	110,000	3	2	50	48
92	2019–02–05	−32.9488766	−60.6516601	300,000	5	3	218	150
93	2019–02–15	−32.9475525	−60.6683317	109,890	2	1	61	49
94	2019–02–15	−32.9083051478	−60.6822508202	160,000	5	2	124	106
95	2019–02–15	−32.9531546	−60.6311278	115,000	3	2	66	58
96	2019–02–15	−31.660511	−60.7147663	115,000	3	2	65	58
97	2019–02–15	−32.9514437	−60.6747531	110,000	3	2	50	48
98	2019–04–27	−32.9622851	−60.673597	105,000	3	2	92	90
99	2019–04–27	−32.8729195	−60.6958289	185,000	3	2	285	140
100	2019–04–27	−32.9745723	−60.6582126	130,000	4	3	160	117
101	2019–01–16	−32.9475525	−60.6683317	109,890	2	1	61	49
102	2019–01–16	−32.9475525	−60.6683317	109,890	2	1	61	49
103	2019–03–29	−32.9272420914	−60.6812232711	130,000	5	3	225	86
104	2019–01–17	−32.9556989	−60.6436165	215,000	4	3	408	180
105	2019–01–17	−32.9556989	−60.6436165	215,000	4	3	408	180
106	2019–01–17	−32.9556989	−60.6436165	215,000	4	3	408	180
107	2018–11–22	−32.9372818	−60.6416956	100,500	2	1	46	41
108	2018–11–22	−32.9404725	−60.6866171	105,000	3	2	110	60
109	2019–02–12	−32.9475525	−60.6683317	109,890	2	1	61	49
110	2019–02–02	−32.924509	−60.845791	219,000	3	2	500	120
111	2019–02–02	−32.9514437	−60.6747531	110,000	3	2	50	48
112	2019–01–18	−32.939335	−60.6507576	108,000	2	1	45	45
113	2019–03–01	−32.9648192	−60.6260124	110,000	2	1	52	52
114	2019–03–01	−32.8801463	−60.7009001	135,000	3	2	300	200
115	2019–03–01	−32.9482716	−60.6436795	220,000	6	3	150	150
116	2018–11–15	−32.9054072	−60.6825	108,000	3	1	51	51
117	2019–03–20	−32.951028	−60.652426	175,000	3	2	80	75

(continued)

Record #	Date listed	Latitude (deg.)	Longitude (deg.)	Price (US$)	Rooms	Bed rooms	Area (total) (sq.m.)	Area (covered) (sq.m.)
118	2019–01–10	−32.9475525	−60.6683317	109,890	2	1	61	49
119	2019–01–10	−32.9514437	−60.6747531	110,000	3	2	50	48
120	2019–01–10	−32.9523916	−60.6337085	140,000	2	2	82	72
121	2019–01–10	−32.9514437	−60.6747531	110,000	3	2	50	48
122	2019–01–10	−32.958157	−60.65474	268,000	4	3	112	100
123	2019–05–07	−32.9391419	−60.6422601	210,000	5	2	81	75
124	2019–05–03	−32.9842198	−60.657834	140,000	6	2	200	200
125	2018–12–05	−32.9278904758	−60.6568473556	200,000	2	1	50	45
126	2018–12–05	−32.9588372	−60.6456409	115,000	2	1	63	63
127	2018–12–05	−32.9276565	−60.6567785	200,000	2	1	55	50
128	2018–12–05	−32.9442426	−60.6505388	185,000	3	1	50	50
129	2018–12–05	−32.9612386	−60.6390377	135,000	3	2	70	70
130	2018–12–05	−32.9383725	−60.6491233	340,000	3	2	100	100
131	2018–12–05	−32.9410577	−60.641195	386,000	4	3	125	125
132	2018–11–24	−32.9445701712	−60.649090899	360,000	4	3	244	161
133	2019–04–29	−32.9404405	−60.6866712	105,000	3	2	110	60
134	2019–04–29	−32.9419243	−60.6499991	165,000	3	2	110	95
135	2019–04–29	−32.9502053	−60.6319071	139,000	3	2	74	68
136	2019–04–29	−32.9505544	−60.6521605	325,000	4	3	165	115
137	2019–04–29	−32.958157	−60.65474	249,000	4	3	112	100
138	2019–04–29	−32.9387754	−60.6875807	195,000	5	4	150	120
139	2019–05–10	−32.921149	−60.68208	125,000	5	3	241	241
140	2019–03–09	−32.9442143	−60.6344314	298,000	4	2	85	85

Exercises

(Monetary units are in CU unless otherwise mentioned).

8.1 Euclidean Norm
Refer to the data in Table 8.1. Recalculate using weights the Euclidean norm for all the properties in the table (relative to the target property) using area, age, and a True/False variable indicating a sale in 2019. Use a weight of 0.8 on area, 2 on age, and 1 on the True/False variable.

8.2 Minkowski p-Norm
Refer to the data in Table 8.1. Recalculate the Minkowski p-norm for the properties in the sample (relative to the target property), setting $p = 3$. The variables included are area, age and "sold in 2019" (True/False).

8.3 Distance Formulas
Calculate the Pythagorean distance and the haversine distance for the following pairs of properties from Appendix 1.

(a) #140, #10.
(b) #96, #124.
(c) #57, #42.

8.4 Weight Formulas
For each of the pairs in 8.3, assuming that the first item of the pair is the centre of a particular GWR regression, compute:

(i) A Gaussian weight with bandwidth 5 km.
(ii) A bisquare weight with fixed maximum distance 5 km.

Repeat your calculations for the Pythagorean and Haversine distances.

8.5 Income Approach
Refer to the example in Sect. 8.6.2. We made some assumptions to avoid iteration. Re-do the example, this time allowing iteration, i.e.:

- Do not estimate the tax savings from depreciation separately. Include depreciation in the calculation allowing circular logic.
- Re-calculate the property value each year in your spreadsheet, and allow the D/E ratio to reflect the re-calculated property value. This again involves iteration, as the property value depends on the D/E ratio.

8.6 Programming
Write a C/C++ function to calculate Vincenty distance, when given the latitude and longitude of two positions in radians.

References

Brueggeman, W., & Fisher, J. (2018). *Real estate finance and investments*. New York: McGraw-Hill Education.

Brunsdon, C., Fotheringham, A., & Charlton, M. (1996). Geographically weighted regression: A method for exploring spatial non-stationarity. *Geographical Analysis, 28*, 281–298.

Catty, J. (Ed.). (2010). *Wiley guide to fair value under IFRS* (1st ed.). Hoboken: Wiley.

Karney, C. (2012). Algorithms for geodesics, arXiv:1109.4448.

Pagourtzi, E., Assimakopoulos, V., Hatzichristos, T., & French, N. (2003). Real estate appraisal: A review of valuation methods. *Journal of Property Investment and Finance, 21*(4), 383–401.

Sinnott, R. (1984). Virtues of the haversine. *Sky and Telescope, 68*, 159.

Vincenty, T. (1975). Direct and inverse solutions of geodesics on the ellipsoid with application of nested equations. *Survey Review, XXII*, 88–93.

C/C++ Programming Tutorial

A

A.1 Introduction

This tutorial introduces a minimal subset of C/C++ that should be sufficient to complete the optional progamming exercises in this book.

The programs here run from the command line—the Command Prompt application in Windows, or the Terminal application in MacOS X or other flavors of UNIX. The discussion here assumes some basic knowledge of how to use the command line. You should know at a minimum how to start and exit the command line application, and how to list files and folders (`dir` on Windows, and `ls` on MacOS X or other UNIX systems).

You should also know how to parse file pathnames on your system (for example, "C:\Files\test.cpp" on Windows which means that the file test.cpp is in the top-level folder "My Files" which is on the drive labelled "C". On MacOS X we could have "/home/myname/test.cpp" which means that test.cpp is in the folder "myname" which is in the enclosing top-level folder "home".)

C/C++ is a commonly used computer programming language. C++ is an extra layer on top of an older language called C. We will not use this extra layer except for the routines for reading and writing to the computer screen (input-output or I/O).

C/C++ is a *compiled* language. This means that programming proceeds in two steps.

First, we write the *source* program in C/C++. This is in a plain text file with the filename ending in the extension .cpp (e.g., test.cpp).

Second, we *compile* the source program by running a compiler such as g++. If using g++, we could type in a command such as the following at the command prompt:

```
g++ test.cpp -o test.exe
```


S. Lynn, *Valuation for Accountants*, Springer Texts in Business and Economics,
https://doi.org/10.1007/978-981-15-0357-3

This command would read the source program test.cpp and create an *executable* file (a set of machine-readable instructions) called test.exe. We can directly run the file test.exe by entering its name at the command prompt:

```
test.exe
```

On some UNIX platforms such as MacOS X, we may need to first set the user permissions to make the file runnable, by issuing the following command at the command prompt:

```
chmod u+x test.exe
```

We may also need to specify the path when running the executable, as follows:

```
./test.exe
```

where . is UNIX shorthand for the current directory (folder). This is because UNIX systems are often configured not to look for executables in the current directory unless this directory is specifically indicated when calling the executable.

A.2 Getting the C/C++ Compiler

While any C/C++ compiler should work fine with our programs, it is recommended that you get the GNU C/C++ compiler `gcc` (or its near-equivalent Clang). These work similarly on all major platforms. We will assume the GNU C/C++ compiler in the examples that follow.

To get the GNU C/C++ compiler for Windows, you can install mingw (minimalist GNU for Windows), currently available at http://www.mingw.org. An alternative is Cygwin, which is currently available at http://www.cygwin.com.

To install the `gcc` compiler on Mac OS X (actually Clang), you would install the command line tools for XCode, from the Apple developer website at http://developer.apple.com.

On other UNIX-based systems such as Linux, the GNU compiler or equivalent is typically a standard part of the platform and is likely to be pre-installed. If not pre-installed, it should be easy to install using the standard package installation process. Check your system documentation.

You can also install gcc (actually Clang) on a smartphone running Android by installing the "termux" app, which produces a UNIX command prompt. Once installed, you can use the following command to install `gcc`:

```
pkg install clang
```

It is also desirable on Termux to install a user-friendly text editor such as nano on Termux to edit programs (`pkg install nano`).

A.3 Program Format

All the programs in our exercises follow a consistent format. They ask the user to input various parameters for some model, say a binomial lattice model for option valuation. Then they run the model with these parameters. Finally they print out the model output, say the option value.

All the action takes place at the *command prompt*. So to run these programs, open a command prompt window in Windows, or run the Terminal app in MacOS X (or Linux etc.).

To illustrate the basic format of a program, we will start with a simple program that does nothing. Let us call this program `donothing.cpp`.

A.3.1 The #include Directive

The opening lines of the program are calls to include various standard C source files in our program so that we can use the standard routines defined in these files. We will consistently include two standard files: iostream, which defines the standard C++ I/O routines, and "math.h" which defines several math functions (in plain C) that we will use in our programs.

To include a standard C/C++ source file, we use the invocation:

```
#include <... >
```

Task

Try to write out the commands to include iostream and math.h, before looking at the solution given below:

Solution

```
#include <iostream>
#include <math.h>
```

A.3.2 The Program Body

C programs are built up out of *functions*. A function has a standard format as follows:

```
Type_Of_Return_Value name_of_function (list_of_inputs){

    C/C++ statement_ending_in_semicolon;
    C/C++ statement_ending_in_semicolon;
    ...
}
```

Every runnable program must have a function called `main`. By convention, this function returns a value of type "int" or integer (a positive or negative whole number).

Task
Create and compile a program donothing.cpp with our standard headers followed by an empty `main` function (the input list is blank and there are no C/C++ statements in the body). This must be a plain text file. So do not use a word-processor like MS Word to create the file. Use a text editor like Notepad on Windows or TextEdit on the Mac. After saving, compile and check that your program works by running the executable donothing.exe.

Be careful that C/C++ is *case-sensitive*. This means that "main" is not the same as "Main" or "mAin" or "MAIN".

Solution (donothing.cpp)

```
#include <iostream>
#include <math.h>

int main(){
}
```

Compiler Command

```
g++ donothing.cpp -o donothing.exe
```

A.3.3 Comments

Comments are memos to the human reader (you, the programmer) that are ignored by the compiler.

Comments in C are enclosed within the symbols /* ... */.

In addition, C++ allows comments that start with the symbol // and run to the end of the current line.

Task
Edit donothing.cpp to include C- and C++-style comments that say "This program does nothing". You can put them anywhere in the program.

Solution (donothing.cpp)

```
#include <iostream>
#include <math.h>

// This program does nothing

int main(){
/* This program
   does
   nothing */
}
```

A.4 Printing Text to the Screen

Strings of text are enclosed in double inverted commas (double quotes) as in “hello”. These are called *strings* in computer programming jargon.

The C++ command to print a string to the screen is:

```
std::cout «...
```

The prefix `std` signifies that cout is a command that is defined in the standard namespace (“`std`”). This is to avoid any conflict in case cout is defined somewhere else in your program.

The items to be printed to the screen are separated by the symbol “«”. You can remember this by thinking of an open mouth spitting out something (output).

The items to be printed to the screen could include strings, variables (to be discussed soon), mathematical expressions (to be discussed later), and a special command to signify end of line: std::endl.

For example, if we have a variable named x and we want to print out “The value of x is: ” followed by the value of x, followed by a new line, we would include the C++ statement:

```
std::cout << ``The value of x is: ''
                    << x << std::endl;
```

Do not forget the semicolon. In the body of a function, every C/C++ statement must end with a semicolon.

Task

Create and run a program called `helloworld.cpp` (executable helloworld.exe) that prints the text “Hello World!” followed by a new line.

Solution (helloworld.cpp)

```
#include <iostream>
#include <math.h>

int main(){
  std::cout << "Hello world!" << std::endl;
}
```

A.5 Variables

A variable is an item that can take on different values in the course of a program.

In C/C++, although a variable can take on different values, the values must all be of the same *type*, for example whole number or decimal. We need to declare the type of a variable before we use that variable.

We will just consider two types in our minimal subset of C/C++ (there are many others):

`int`	an integer, a whole number which could be positive or negative, e.g., -1, 2, 3, 0, 500 are all integers.
`double`	a decimal, e.g., 7.89, 0.1453, -1.0, or -1.859.

To declare the type of a variable, we type int or double followed by the name of the variable and ending of course in a semicolon.

For example, to declare an integer called x, we type

```
int x;
```

To declare a double named y, we type

```
double y;
```

We can declare multiple variables of the same type by separating the variable names with commas.

Thus to declare two integers z and a in the same statement, we type:

```
int z,a;
```

A.5.1 Assigning Values to Variables

To set a variable equal to a number (or another variable), we use the equals sign "=".

For example, to set the variable x to be equal to 1, we type:

```
x = 1;
```

This assigns the value 1 to the variable x. We can think of this as shorthand for the natural-language command:

SET x TO BE EQUAL TO 1.

The order is important. The command `1 = x` is wrong. The variable to be assigned to (x) is always on the left hand side, and the value to be assigned (1) is always on the right hand side.

To set the variable y to be equal to the variable z (that is, the value currently stored in the variable z), we type:

```
y = z;
```

A.6 Keyboard Input

To input a number from the keyboard, we use the std::cin command.

The format is:

```
std::cin >> variable_name;
```

where `variable_name` is the variable in which the inputed value would be stored.

For example, to read in some number into a variable named x, we would type:

```
std::cin >> x;
```

You can remember the symbol » as a mouth that is closing to ingest something (input).

Task

Write a program called `readnumber.cpp` that:

1. Asks the user to input a number. (Hint: use cout.)
2. Reads the number into a variable called x. (Hint: Don't forget the variable declaration).
3. Print out "The number you typed is:" followed by the number.

Solution (readnumber.cpp)

```
#include <iostream>
#include <math.h>

int main(){
   int x;
   std::cout << "Input a number: ";
   std::cin >> x;
   std::cout << "The number you entered is: " << x <<
std::endl;
}
```

A.7 Mathematics

Common mathematical operations are as follows:

$+$	addition, e.g., $a + b$.
$-$	subtraction, e.g., $a - b$.
$*$	multiplication, e.g., $a * b$ means $a \times b$.
/	division, e.g., a/b.
%	$x\%y$ (x modulo y) gives the remainder when x is divided by y.
pow(a, b)	a to the power of b (a^b).
exp(a)	e to the power of a (e^a).
log(a)	Natural logarithm of a ($\ln(a)$).
sqrt(a)	Square root of a ($\sqrt{a}$).
sin(a)	Sine of a.
cos(a)	Cosine of a.
tan(a)	Tangent of a.
asin(a)	Arcsine of a.
atan(a)	Arctangent of a.
`M_PI`	The standard constant π.

We can also group expressions using parentheses (...) as in standard algebra. In a complex expression, operations are evaluated in the same order as in standard algebra, that is, first items grouped in parentheses, then exponents (powers and roots), then multiplication and division, then addition and subtraction. We can remember this using the mnemonic PEMDAS.

Examples

`a = b + c`	replaces a with the sum of b and c.
`a = a + 1`	replaces a with its original value plus 1.
`a = pow(a,2)`	replaces a with its original value squared.

Task

Write a program findpv.cpp that finds the present value of some amount A after n years at an APR rate r based on compounding k times per year (n and k can be restricted to be integers).

Your program should first request values for A,n,r and k, and then calculate the present value, and finally print out the present value.

Solution (findpv.cpp)

```
#include <iostream>
#include <math.h>
```

```
int main(){
  double A,r,pv;
  int n,k;

  std::cout << "Input future amount: ";
  std::cin >> A;
  std::cout << "Input time to maturity in years: ";
  std::cin >> n;
  std::cout << "Input APR discount rate (as a decimal): ";
  std::cin >> r;
  std::cout << "Number of compounding periods per year: ";
  std::cin >> k;

  pv = A / pow (1 + r/k, n*k);
  std::cout << "Present value is " << pv << std::endl;
}
```

We could also directly include the present value expression in the final std::cout statement, in which case we would not need the variable pv. This would look like:

```
std::cout << "Present value is "
          << A / pow (1 + r/k, n*k)
          << std::endl;
```

Task

Write a program findpvcontinuous.cpp that finds the present value of A after n years compounded at a continuously compounded rate rc. (Hint: copy the previous program to a new file named findpvcontinuous.cpp and then make a few changes).

Solution (findpvcontinuous.cpp)

```
#include <iostream>
#include <math.h>

int main(){
  double A,rc,pv;
  int n;

  std::cout << "Input future amount: ";
  std::cin >> A;
  std::cout << "Input time to maturity in years: ";
  std::cin >> n;
  std::cout << "Input continuously compounded discount
               rate"
            << " (as a decimal): ";
```

```
  std::cin >> rc;

  pv = A/exp(rc*n);
  std::cout << pv << std::endl;
}
```

Task

Write a program ratorc.cpp that finds the continuously compounded rate rc that corresponds to a given annually compounded rate ra. Ask the user for the annually compounded rate, then do the conversion and report the equivalent continuously compounded rate.

Solution (ratorc.cpp)

```
#include <iostream>
#include <math.h>

int main(){
  double ra, rc;

  std::cout << "Input annually compounded rate: ";
  std::cin >> ra;
  rc = log(1 + ra);
  std::cout << "The equivalent continuously
                compounded rate is : "
            << rc << std::endl;
}
```

A.8 Conditionals

We may want a program to branch in different directions depending on source condition. We can use an if statement to achieve this. This is of the form:

```
if (...){
...
}
else if (...){
...
}
...
else {
...
}
```

The above is a skeleton of a program that first checks if some condition is true: the condition in the parentheses following if. If the condition is true, the program follows the instructions within the braces ... that follows the initial if (...) statement.

If the statement is not true, we can have zero or more else if statements that test for some other conditions, and execute the instructions that follow if those conditions are true.

We can also finally have zero or one else ... blocks that perform the default action if none of the above conditions are true.

Conditions can be stated in the following forms:

$a == b$	tests if a equals b.
	Not the same as $a = b$.
$a <= b$	tests if a is less than or equal to b.
$a < b$	tests if a is less than b.
$a >= b$	tests if a is greater than or equal to b.
$a > b$	tests if a is greater than b.
$a! = b$	tests if a is not equal to b.

We can also join together logical conditions using "&&" (and), or "||" (or).

For example, we can read the following:

```
if (a >= 1 && a <= 5)}
```

as: "If (a is greater than or equal to 1) AND (a is less than or equal to 5)" (in other words, a lies between 1 and 5).

Example

```
if (x == 1){
    std::cout << 1 << std::endl;
}
else if (x == 2) {
    std::cout << 2 << std::endl;
}
else{
    std::cout << "Some other number" << std::endl;
}
```

We can nest if ... else loops inside each other, as in:

```
if (...){
 if (...) {
   ...
 }
}
```

Task

Write a program `optionvalue.cpp` that finds the value of an option on a share at the exercise date given the strike price K, the share price at the expiry date St, and a variable isput that equals 1 if the option is a put and 0 if it is a call.

Your program should first ask the user to input the parameters, then calculate and output the option value at exercise. Recall that for a call, the option value is given by the higher of $St - K$ and 0. For a put, the option value is given by the higher of $K - St$ and zero.

Solution (optionvalue.cpp)

```
#include <iostream>
#include <math.h>

int main(){
  double K, St, optionvalue;
  int isput;

  std::cout << "Input strike price: ";
  std::cin >> K;
  std::cout << "Input share price at option expiry: ";
  std::cin >> St;
  std::cout << "Input 1 for put, 0 (or anything else)
                 for call: ";
  std::cin >> isput;

  if (isput == 1){ // put
    if (K > St){
      optionvalue = K - St;
    }
    else {
      optionvalue = 0;
    }
  }
  else { // call
    if (St > K){
      optionvalue = St - K;
    }
    else {
      optionvalue = 0;
    }
  }
```

```
    std::cout << "The option value at expiry is: "
              << optionvalue << std::endl;
}
```

A.9 Loops

One of the most useful devices in a program is a *loop*—a routine that runs a sequence of instructions multiple times. There are a number of looping commands in C/C++, but for our purposes, it is sufficient to consider one—the `for` loop. This is of the form:

```
for (initial_condition; loop_condition; change_each_step){
    commands_to_be_repeated
}
```

Here initial_condition is the starting point of the loop, usually setting a counter or index equal to some starting value such as zero or 1.

The loop will keep repeating while the second condition, the loop_condition is true. Usually this is a condition that the counter is less than or less than or equal to some maximum stopping value. When the counter reaches that value, the loop stops running.

The change_each_step is some action that takes place each time the loop is run. For example, the counter could increase by 1.

Here is a simple example loop that runs 10 times and prints out the numbers from 1 to 10:

```
for (ctr = 1; ctr <= 10; ctr=ctr+1){
    std::cout << ctr << std::endl;
}
```

One convenient shorthand that C/C++ allows is to replace the statement `x=x+1` with the statement `x++`. Similarly, we can replace `x=x-1` with `x-`.

So we can rewrite the loop above as:

```
for (ctr = 1; ctr <= 10; ctr++){
    std::cout << ctr << std::endl;
}
```

Task

Write a program `pvannuity.cpp` that finds the present value of an annuity for 10 years that is CU 10 in the first year, and increases by a fixed amount of CU 0.80 each subsequent year (i.e., CU 10 in Year 1, CU 10.80 in Year 2, ...) The forward discount rate is 6% in year 1, and increases by 10 basis points each subsequent year (i.e., we discount by 6% from year 1 to year 0, by 6.1% from year 2 to year 1, by 6.2% from year 3 to year 2 ...).

Solution (pvannuity.cpp)

```
#include <iostream>
#include <math.h>

int main (){

  double amount, discountrate , discountfactor , pvannuity;
  int ctr;

  amount = 10.0;
  discountrate=0.06;
  discountfactor = 1/(1+discountrate);
  pvannuity = amount*discountfactor;

  for (ctr=2; ctr<=10; ctr++){
    amount = amount+0.80;
    discountrate = discountrate+0.001;
    discountfactor = discountfactor*1/(1+discountrate);
    pvannuity = pvannuity + amount*discountfactor;
  }

  std::cout << "Present value of the annuity is: "
            << pvannuity << std::endl;
}
```

Loops can be nested inside other loops. The following task implements this.

Task

A binomial lattice for option valuation starts from an initial share price S_0, then at the first step branches to an up step $S_u = S_0 \times u$ or a down step $S_d = S_0 \times d$. We continue the process by adding up and down branches to each subsequent price, where the up step involves multiplication by the up factor u and the down step involves multiplication by the down factor d, until we reach the option expiry date.

Write a program `binomialprices.cpp` that asks for the initial price S0, the number of steps to expiry n, the up factor u, and the down factor d.

Given this information, print out the prices at each step as follows:

Step 0: S0
Step 1: $S0 \times u$ $S0 \times d$
Step 2: $S0 \times u \times u$ $S0 \times u \times d$ $S0 \times d \times d$
...

Solution (binomialprices.cpp)

```
#include <iostream>
#include <math.h>

int main(){
  double S0, startprice ,u,d;
  int n,ctr1 ,ctr2;

  std::cout << "Input initial share price: ";
  std::cin >> S0;
  std::cout << "Input up step factor: ";
  std::cin >> u;
  std::cout << "Input down step factor: ";
  std::cin >> d;
  std::cout << "Input number of steps: ";
  std::cin >> n;

  std::cout << S0 << std::endl;

  startprice = S0*u;
  // first price in the next line

  for (ctr1 = 1; ctr1 <= n; ctr1++){

    // print first price in the line
    S0 = startprice;
    std::cout << S0 << " ";

    // each subsequent price is the previous price times d/u
    for (ctr2 = 1; ctr2 <= ctr1; ctr2++){
      S0=S0*d/u;
      std::cout << S0 << " ";
    }
    std::cout << std::endl;

    // update startprice for the next line
    startprice = startprice*u;
  }
}
```

Two useful commands help us to break out of a loop early. These are:

```
break;
```

which exits the loop completely when encountered; and:

```
next;
```

which jumps immediately to the next round of the loop, ignoring any remaining commands in the current round.

These commands would typically be used inside an `if ...` block.

A.10 Arrays

An array is a list of items of a particular type (like int or double). We can refer to the n'th item in an array called say arry as arry[n]. Array indices start from 0.

To declare an array, we use the format:

```
type arrayname [maximum_index_of_items_in_array];
```

For example, to declare an array called arry with 5 items that are integers, we have:

```
int arry[4];
```

To assign a value to an item in an array, we simply use:

```
arrayname[index] = value;
```

For example, to assign the value 3 to arry[2], we have:

```
arry[2]=3;
```

Arrays can also be two-dimensional (or more). We can think of a two-dimensional array as a table or matrix in which the first index refers to the row number and the second to the column number.

For a two-dimensional array called arry2d with 3×3 items of type `double`, the format to declare the array would be:

```
double arry2d [2][2];
```

To assign the value 3.5 to the 1st row (index 0) and the 2nd column (index 1), we would have:

```
arry2d[0][1] = 3.5;
```

Task

Write a program arry.cpp that creates an array with 5 items. Fill the array with the numbers from 5 to 10 in order using a loop. Print out the array with items separated by spaces.

Solution (arry.cpp)

```
#include <iostream>
#include <math.h>

int main(){
   int arry[4],ctr;

   for (ctr=5; ctr<=10; ctr++){
      arry[ctr-5]=ctr;
      std::cout << arry[ctr-5] << " ";
   }
   std::cout << std::endl;
}
```

Task

Rewrite `binomialprices.cpp` using a two-dimensional array of prices (copy the original to a new file `binomialprices2.cpp` and then make changes). You can declare the array using some large number of rows and columns say 100×100.

Solution (binomialprices2.cpp)

```
#include <iostream>
#include <math.h>

int main(){
   double S0[100][100],u,d;
   int n,ctr1,ctr2;

   std::cout << "Input initial share price: ";
   std::cin >> S0[0][0];
   std::cout << "Input up step factor: ";
   std::cin >> u;
   std::cout << "Input down step factor: ";
   std::cin >> d;
   std::cout << "Input number of steps: ";
   std::cin >> n;

   std::cout << S0[0][0] << std::endl;

   for (ctr1 = 1; ctr1 <= n; ctr1++){

      // print first price in the line
      S0[ctr1][0]=S0[ctr1-1][0]*u;
```

```
    std::cout << S0[ctr1][0] << " ";

    // each subsequent price is the previous price times d/u
    for (ctr2 = 1; ctr2 <= ctr1; ctr2++){
      S0[ctr1][ctr2]=S0[ctr1][ctr2-1]*d/u;
      std::cout << S0[ctr1][ctr2] << " ";
    }
    std::cout << std::endl;
  }
}
```

A.11 Functions

Apart from main(), we can create other functions. We can then call these functions with a given set of inputs.

The function should be declared before we create it, similarly to how we declare variables. For example, suppose that we want to create a function called factorial, which finds the factorial of a given integer greater than 1. It takes an integer greater than 1 as an input and returns the factorial of that integer.

The statement to return a value from a function is as follows:

```
return value_to_be_returned;
```

We declare the function outside any other function, following the #include commands, as follows:

```
int factorial (int x);
```

We can then create the function as follows:

```
int factorial (int x){
    int retval, ctr;
    retval=1;

    for (ctr=1; ctr<=x; ctr++){
        retval = retval*ctr;
    }
    return retval;
}
```

We can call the function from another function such as main():

```
int main(){
 int y;

 std::cout << "Input a whole number greater than 1: ";
 std::cin >> y;
```

```
    std::cout << "The factorial of "
              << y << " is " << factorial(y)
              << std::endl;
}
```

In the main() function above, it would have been perfectly fine to use x instead of y to hold the input value. This is inspite of the fact that we have another x inside the factorial() function. The compiler knows to treat these as two different variables. In technical terms, each x lives only inside the particular function where it is defined.

Task

Rewrite findpv.cpp (use a new program findpv2.cpp) to use a function presentvalue that finds the present value of a cashflow A at time n discounted at rate r with discounting k times per year.

Solution (findpv2.cpp)

```
#include <iostream>
#include <math.h>

double presentvalue (double A, int n, double r, int k);

double presentvalue (double A, int n, double r, int k){
  return A / pow (1 + r/k, n*k);
}

int main(){
  double A,r;
  int n,k;

  std::cout << "Input future amount: ";
  std::cin >> A;
  std::cout << "Input time to maturity in years: ";
  std::cin >> n;
  std::cout << "Input APR discount rate (as a decimal): ";
  std::cin >> r;
  std::cout << "Number of compounding periods per year: ";
  std::cin >> k;

  std::cout << "Present value is "
            << presentvalue (A,n,r,k) << std::endl;
}
```

A.12 Advanced Topics

The tasks in this section include a number of functions. It is convenient to enter all these functions in the same file, that you could call say "myfunctions.cpp". You can include a temporary main() function to call your functions after attempting each to test if your functions work.

A.12.1 The Standard Normal CDF

For many of our applications, we may wish to generate the standard normal cumulative distribution function, for which we use the notation $\Phi(z)$ in this book. The function $\Phi(z)$ gives the probability that a random variable following a normal curve with mean 0 and standard deviation 1 (standard normal) is less than or equal to the number z.

We can derive the normal CDF using a related function available in C/C++ called the "error function" and written erf(x). We have the relationship:

$$\Phi(z) = \frac{1}{2}\left(1 + \operatorname{erf}\left(\frac{z}{\sqrt{2}}\right)\right)$$

Task
Write a C/C++ function `double phi (double z)` that gives the standard normal CDF.

Solution (phi)

```
#include <iostream>
#include <math.h>

double phi (double z);

double phi (double z){
  return 0.5*(1 + erf(z/sqrt(2)));
}
```

Task
Write a function `double normCDF (double x, double mu, double sigma)` that gives the probability that some normally-distributed variable is less than z, where the variable is distributed normally with mean mu and standard deviation sigma. Hint: Use the fact that a normally distributed variable x with mean μ and standard deviation σ can be transformed to a standard normal variable Z (mean 0, standard deviation 1) as follows:

$$Z = \frac{X - \mu}{\sigma}.$$

It is convenient to call the previous function phi(...) in your answer. To do this easily, type the normCDF function in the same file where you typed phi.

Solution (normCDF)

```
double normcdf (double x, double mu, double sigma);

double normcdf (double x, double mu, double sigma){
  return phi ( (x - mu)/sigma );
}
```

A.12.2 The Inverse Normal CDF

We may also wish to generate some number z such that $\Phi(z)$ equals some value say p. We can define the function that finds z given p as the inverse standard normal CDF, and write it as $\Phi^{-1}(p)$.

We can implement the standard normal CDF function in C/C++ using an approximation correct to at least 3 decimal places that works as follows, if p is greater than 0.5. (Formula source: Abramowitz and Stegun 1964)

$$\Phi^{-1}(p) = t - \frac{c_0 + c_1 t + c_2 t^2}{1 + d_1 t + d_2 t^2 + d_3 t^3},$$

where:

$$t = \sqrt{\ln \frac{1}{(1-p)^2}}.$$

$$c_0 = 2.515517.$$

$$c_1 = 0.802853.$$

$$c_2 = 0.010328.$$

$$d_1 = 1.432788.$$

$$d_2 = 0.189269.$$

$$d_3 = 0.001308.$$

If p is less than 0.5, we can use the fact that the normal curve is symmetric. So for example $\Phi(-1.96) = 0.025$, while $\Phi(1.96) = 0.975 = 1 - 0.025$ (the region to the right of 1.96 is the mirror image of the region to the left of -1.96, and has the same area). So if we are given p = 0.025, we can use the formula above to find $\Phi^{-1}(0.975) = 1.96$, and then stick a minus sign in front of the result to get -1.96.

Task

Write a function `double invphi (double p)` that finds $z = \Phi^{-1}(p)$ using the approximation given above. (If you get stuck trying to figure out how to deal with cases where $p < 0.5$, try writing a program that only handles $p \geq 0.5$. Then you can peek at the solution below to see one way to modify your program to handle the general case.)

Solution (invphi)

```
double invphi (double p);

double invphi (double p){
  double t, c0, c1, c2, d1, d2, d3, retval;

  if (p > 0.5){
    retval = 1;
  }
  else {
    retval = -1;
    p = 1-p;
  }

  t = sqrt(log(1/pow(1-p,2)));
  c0 = 2.515517;
  c1 = 0.802853;
  c2 = 0.010328;
  d1 = 1.432788;
  d2 = 0.189269;
  d3 = 0.001308;


  retval = retval*(
    t - (c0 + c1*t + c2*pow(t,2))/
    (1+d1*t+d2*pow(t,2)+d3*pow(t,3)));

  return retval;
}
```

Task

Write a function `double invnormcdf (double p, double mu, double sigma)` that finds a number x such that a random number from a normal distribution with mean mu and standard deviation sigma has a probability equal to p of being less than or equal to x. You can call the previous function invphi, in which case, you would type invnormcdf in the same file as you used for invphi.

Solution (invnormcdf)

```
double invnormcdf (double p, double mu, double sigma);

double invnormcdf (double p, double mu, double sigma){
  return invphi(p)*sigma + mu;
}
```

A.12.3 Rounding

We can round a given double x to zero decimal places by using the function `round(x)`. For example:

```
round(3.6) // gives 4.0.
```

To round x to say two decimal places, we can multiply x by 100 and then round the result, and then finally divide by 100 to get the desired number.

For example, if $x = 1.23456$, and we want to round to two decimal places, we use:

```
round(x*100)/100   // gives 1.23 for x=1.23456.
```

Similarly, to round to four decimal places, we multiply by 10,000 (10^4), round, and then divide by 10,000.

```
round(x*10000)/10000 // gives 1.2346 for x=1.23456.
```

Task

Write a function `double roundn (double x, int n)` that rounds a given double to n decimal places. (Hint: Use 10^n).

Solution (roundn)

```
double roundn(double x, int n);

double roundn(double x, int n){
  return round (x * pow(10,n)) / pow (10,n);
}
```

A.12.4 Random Numbers

We may wish to generate random numbers, for example in Monte Carlo simulation. The C function to generate a random number is `rand()`. This gives a randomly generated positive integer (usually a very large integer).

By default, the random number generator would give us exactly the same sequence of numbers every time we run our program, which somewhat defeats the purpose. To vary the sequence, we would change the "seed", a parameter which the random number generator uses in determining its output. The seed is also a positive integer.

To change the seed, we use the command `srand (seed)`. For example to change the seed to 64, we would use `srand (64)`. In programs that generate random numbers, it is a good idea to reset the seed at or near the start of your program, before generating any random numbers. It is possible to set srand() to use the current system time as the seed, which guarantees a fresh random number every time the program is run. But we will restrict ourselves to the cruder device of asking the user to input some seed.

```
int seed;
std::cout << "Input a seed for the random number generator: ";
std::cin >> seed;
```

What if we want random numbers that are between say 0 and 100? We can use the modulus operator "%" to do this. Taking `x % 101` would find the remainder from dividing a number by 101. This remainder would be a number between 0 and 100. So to get a random number between 0 and 100, we would use:

```
rand() % 101;
```

How about if we wanted a random number between say 100 and 200? We could take the random number modulus 101 (`rand()%101`) and add the starting 100 to it. In general, to find numbers between a and $a+x$, where a and x are both integers, we can take:

```
a + ( rand() % (x+1) ).
```

What if we wanted our random numbers to be decimals? In particular, we may want to generate decimals between 0 and 1 (to model random probabilities for example).

To generate a random decimal between zero and 1 with 4 decimal places, we would use `(rand()%10001)/10000.0`. This first generates a random integer between 0 and 10,000, and then divides by 10,000 to get a decimal between 0 and 1. When dividing by 10,000, we should be careful to write it as 10000.0 to indicate that we are dividing by a double, not an integer. Otherwise the program would give the result as an integer, which would always be 0.

We are often interested in generating random numbers that follow a standard normal distribution. How could we do this? One way is to first generate a random probability as described above. Then we could use our `invphi(p)` function to find a number z such that $\Phi(z)$ equals the random probability.

Task

Write a function `double simstdnorm()` that simulates a random number drawn from a standard normal distribution. Create your function in the same file as contains invphi, so that you can call on this function. Your function can assume that srand() is already set.

Solution

```
double simstdnorm();
```

```
  double simstdnorm(){
    return invphi((rand()%10001)/10000.0);
}
```

Task

Write a function `double simnorm(double mu, double sigma)` that simulates a random number drawn from a normal distribution with mean mu and standard deviation sigma. Create your function in the same file as contains invnormcdf, so that you can call on this function. Your function can assume that srand() is already set.

Solution

```
double simnorm(double mu, double sigma);

double simnorm(double mu, double sigma){
    return invnormcdf((rand()%10001)/10000.0, mu, sigma);
}
```

Task

The Black-Scholes equation assumes the following:

Share prices $S_{0+\Delta t}$ at some incremental future step in time Δt years have the following risk-neutral probability distribution:

$$\ln\left(\frac{S_{0+\Delta t}}{S_0}\right) = \ln S_{0+\Delta t} - \ln S_0 \sim N\left(\left(r - \frac{\sigma^2}{2}\right) \times \Delta t, \sigma \times \sqrt{\Delta t}\right).$$

That is, the natural logarithm of the ratio of the future price $S_{0+\Delta t}$ at time Δt to the price today S_0 has a risk-neutral distribution that is normal (Bell curve) with mean equal to $(r_c - \frac{\sigma^2}{2}) \times \Delta t$, and standard deviation equal to $\sigma \times \sqrt{\Delta t}$. Here r_c is the risk-free rate, assumed constant, and σ is the volatility parameter.

The same distribution holds for relative prices at additional increments of Δt. Thus,

$$\ln\left(\frac{S_{\Delta t+\Delta t}}{S_{\Delta t}}\right), \ln\left(\frac{S_{\Delta t+\Delta t+\Delta t}}{S_{\Delta t+\Delta t}}\right), \ldots \sim N\left(\left(r - \frac{\sigma^2}{2}\right) \times \Delta t, \sigma \times \sqrt{\Delta t}\right).$$

where S_x is the price at some time x years from today.

We can therefore simplify our notation by defining Δs as follows:

$$\Delta s = \ln\left(\frac{S_{x+\Delta t}}{S_x}\right) = \ln(S_{x+\Delta t}) - \ln(S_x).$$

where S_x is the price at any future time x years from today.

We can summarize our exposition so far as:

$$\Delta s \sim N\left(\left(r - \frac{\sigma^2}{2}\right) \times \Delta t, \sigma \times \sqrt{\Delta t}\right).$$

Write a function `double simdeltas(double rc, double sigma, double deltat)` that simulates one instance of Δs given r_c = rc, σ = sigma, and Δt = deltat. Your function can call simnorm.

Solution (simdeltas)

```
double simdeltas(double rc, double sigma, double deltat);

double simdeltas(double rc, double sigma, double deltat){
  return simnorm((rc - pow(sigma,2)/2)*deltat, sigma*sqrt(deltat));
}
```

A.12.5 Your Own #include File

If you have typed in the various functions in this section in a file named say "myfunctions.cpp", you can make them available to your programs written in other files (in the same folder) by including the following line together with other #include commands at the beginning of your file.

```
#include "myfunctions.cpp"
```

Depending on your system, you may need to give the full path of the file e.g., "C:\...\myfunctions.cpp" on Windows. One quirk is that \has special meaning to the C compiler, so we have to represent a literal backslash by putting two backslashes in sequence. To type \, enter it as \\. For example the path C:\myhome \myfile.cpp would be written as follows in a C program:

```
C:\\myhome\\myfile.cpp
```

You should make sure that the included file myfunctions.cpp does not include any main() function. If you have included a temporary main() function to test your functions, you should delete this main() function before including myfunctions.cpp in other programs.

Task

Write a program test.cpp that includes your function file containing the simdeltas function. Write a main() function that calls simdeltas to simulate and print out a price history of 100 daily prices. Remember to set the random number seed at the beginning of your program. The inputs to your program are the starting share price S0, the risk-free rate rc, and the volatility parameter sigma. Recall that Δt for a day is $\frac{1.0}{365.0}$ years (keep the decimal points in this expression so that C/C++ treats this as a double not an int).

Solution (test.cpp)

```
#include <iostream>
#include <math.h>
#include "myfunctions.cpp"

int main(){
  int seed, ctr;
  double mynormsim[100], rc, sigma, S0;

  std::cout << "input random number seed: ";
  std::cin >> seed;
  std::cout << "input risk-free rate (rc): ";
  std::cin >> rc;
  std::cout << "input starting share price (S0): ";
  std::cin >> S0;
  std::cout << "input volatility (sigma): ";
  std::cin >> sigma;

  srand(seed);
  mynormsim[0]=S0;
  for (ctr=1; ctr<100; ctr++){
    mynormsim[ctr]=mynormsim[ctr-1]*exp(simdeltas(rc, sigma,
                    1.0/365.0));
    std::cout << mynormsim[ctr] << std::endl;
  }
}
```

A.13 Learning More

The C/C++ covered in the tutorial so far is sufficient to do any of the programming exercises in this book. But it does not go far enough to enable us to implement all the models covered in our text. To do that, we would need to cover at least two more programming topics for which we do not have space—date/time operations, and the implementation of a solver function.

A more detailed C/C++ tutorial and reference is Prata (2011). A good tutorial on using C++ in quantitative finance is Joshi (2008).

Quantlib is an extensive open-source library of C++ functions for quantitative finance that can be found at http://www.quantlib.org. (It requires considerably more advanced knowledge of both C and C++ than what we can provide here.)

Financial Math Refresher B

B.1 Learning Outcomes

After finishing this appendix, you will be able to:

1. Explain exponential function and natural logarithm computations.
2. Apply APR compound interest rates to find future values and present values.
3. Derive and apply the formulas for future value and present value based on continuous compounding.
4. Convert between continuous and discrete (non-continuous) interest rates.

B.2 Euler's Number

Consider the expression $\left(1+\frac{1}{n}\right)^n$ for some $n \geq 1$.

As n gets larger and larger, this expression gets closer and closer to a constant known as Euler's number.

Euler's number is written as e, and is approximately equal to 2.7182818...

Exercise 1. Try evaluating the expression $\left(1+\frac{1}{n}\right)^n$ for n=10, n=1,000, n=10,000, n=100,000, n=1,000,000 ...

n	$(1+\frac{1}{n})^n$
10	2.593742
1000	2.716924
10000	2.718146
100000	2.718268
1000000	2.718280

S. Lynn, *Valuation for Accountants*, Springer Texts in Business and Economics,
https://doi.org/10.1007/978-981-15-0357-3

B.3 The Exponential Function

Definition 1 (exponential of x or $\exp(x)$). The exponential function $\exp(x)$ for any number x is given by:

$$\exp(x) = e^x.$$

Your calculator might show it as the EXP button or the e^y button. In Excel,use =EXP(x)

Exercise 2 (Exponentials drill). Find e^2, $\exp(2)$, e^{-1}, $\exp(0)$.

Answer:

$$e^2 = \exp(2) = 7.3891.$$

$$e^{-1} = (1/e) = 0.3679.$$

Definition 2 (a^{-b}). For any numbers a, b, we have:

$$a^{-b} = \frac{1}{a^b}.$$

$$\exp(0) = 1$$

Definition 3 (a^0). For any number a, we have:

$$a^0 = 1.$$

B.4 Natural Logarithms

Definition 4 (Natural logarithm of x or $\ln(x)$). If $e^y = x$ then y is called the natural logarithm of x.

Your calculator may show it as the LN button. In Excel, use =LN(x).

Exercise 3 (Logarithms drill). Find $\ln(1)$, $\ln(e)$, $\ln(2)$, $\ln(1{,}000{,}000)$, $\ln(-10)$, $\ln(0.5)$.

Answer:

$$\ln(1) = 0.$$

This follows because $e^0 = 1$.

$$\ln(e) = 1.$$

This follows because $e^1 = e$.

$$\ln(2) = 0.69315.$$

$$\ln(1{,}000{,}000) = 13.8155$$

Notice how very large numbers have relatively small logarithms. This is often convenient in drawing graphs. By using a *logarithmic scale*, we can fit large and small numbers in the same graph.

$$\ln(-10) \text{ is not defined.}$$

There is no real number x such that $e^x = -10$. The log of a negative number does not exist.

$$\ln(0.5) = -0.69315.$$

Notice that this is the negative of $\ln(2)$. Why?
Why Is $\ln(0.5) = -\ln(2)$?

Proof.

$$0.5 = \frac{1}{2}$$

This equals $\frac{e^{\ln(1)}}{e^{\ln(2)}}$.
This equals $e^{\ln(1)-\ln(2)}$.
(recalling index arithmetic from your secondary school maths)
Therefore, $\ln(0.5) = \ln(1) - \ln(2) = 0 - \ln(2)$.
By similar logic, for any positive number a, $\ln(1/a) = -ln(a)$.

B.5 Logarithm Arithmetic

$$\ln(xy) = \ln(x) + \ln(y).$$

Exercise 4 (Theorem on logs). Prove that:

$$\ln(x/y) = \ln(x) - \ln(y). \tag{B.1}$$

$$\ln(x^y) = y\ln(x) \tag{B.2}$$

Proof.

Equation B.1

Take for example $\ln(3/2)$.

This can be written as: $\ln\left(3 \times \frac{1}{2}\right)$.

This equals: $\ln(3) + \ln(0.5)$,

which is the same as: $\ln(3) - \ln(2)$.

By similar logic, the result holds if we replace 3 and 2 by any positive numbers.

Equation B.2

Take for example $\ln(3^4)$.

This can be written as: $\ln(3 \times 3 \times 3 \times 3)$ (multiplying three by itself 4 times).

This equals: $\ln(3) + \ln(3) + \ln(3) + \ln(3)$

which is the same as: $4 \times \ln(3)$.

By similar logic, the result holds if we replace 3 by any positive number and 4 by any natural number.

The result holds for any power, not just natural numbers. We can prove this using index arithmetic, noting that for any [real] numbers a, b, c, x, y:

$$(a^b)^c = a^{b \times c} \Rightarrow \left(e^{\ln(x)}\right)^y = e^{\ln(x) \times y}.$$

B.6 APR Interest Rates

Definition 5 (APR or annual percentage rate convention). The annual percentage rate convention for calculating compound interest is as follows: The future value A_t at the end of t years of a principal amount P earning compound interest at a rate r per year, where the interest is compounded n times every year, is:

$$A_t = P \times \left(1 + \frac{r}{n}\right)^{t \times n}$$

Exercise 5 (Practice Drill). You lend CU39,247 at an interest rate of 3.83% compounded monthly, with principal and interest due at the end of 30 years. How much interest will you earn over that period?

Answer:

$$39{,}247 \times \left(1 + \frac{0.0383}{12}\right)^{12\times 30} - 39{,}247 = 84352.35$$

The interest rate is always stated as a rate *per year*.

B.7 APR Discount Rates

Definition 6 (APR present value). The present value A_0 of some amount P to be received after t years discounted at a rate r is:

$$A_0 = \frac{P}{\left(1 + \frac{r}{n}\right)^{t\times n}}$$

Exercise 6 (Practice Drill). You face a risk-free opportunity to get CU97,387 at the end of 6 years. You analyze the interest rates on government bonds, and estimate that if the government offered a similar instrument with just one payment after 6 years, it would pay interest at 1.89 percent compounded semi-annually (every half-year). How much would you pay today for the risk-free investment?

Answer:

$$A_0 = 97{,}387 \Big/ \left(1 + \frac{0.0189}{2}\right)^{6\times 2} = 86{,}993$$

B.8 Continuous Compounding at 100 Percent

Exercise 7. What is the future value of CU1 after one year if it is compounded *continuously* at a rate of 100 percent? (Hint: recall the definition of e.)

Answer:

The value is e.

Consider for example CU1 compounded 1000 times per year at a rate of 100%. The future value after 1 year is: $\left(1 + \frac{100\%}{1000}\right)^{1000}$.

As we keep increasing the frequency, to say $n = 100{,}000$ or $1{,}000{,}000$ times per year, the future value changes to: $\left(1 + \frac{100\%}{n}\right)^{n}$.

This expression approaches e as n gets larger and larger (more frequent compounding). Therefore with the most frequent compounding possible (continuous), the value would be e.

B.9 Continuous Compounding at 5 Percent

Theorem 1. *The continuously compounded future value of CU1 after one year at an interest rate of 5 percent is given by* $e^{0.05}$.

Proof *(Sketch of proof).* Let's take $e \approx (1 + 0.0001)^{10,000}$.

We can take CU 1 compounded continuously at 5% to approximately equal: $\left(1 + \frac{0.05}{500}\right)^{500}$ or $(1 + 0.0001)^{10,000 \times 0.05}$ or $e^{0.05}$ (using our approximate expression for e).

The approximation gets better and better as we increase the compounding frequency in the first equation.

B.10 Continuous Compounding for *t* Years

Exercise 8. You are investing CU30,000 for 6 years at a continuously compounded rate of 3.067 percent. How much will you get on maturity?

Answer:

The amount would be:

$$30{,}000 \times \left(e^{0.03067} \times e^{0.03067} \times e^{0.03067} \times e^{0.03067} \times e^{0.03067} \times e^{0.03067}\right)$$
$$= 30{,}000 \times \left(e^{0.03067}\right)^6$$
$$= 30{,}000 \times e^{0.03067 \times 6} = 36{,}061.20.$$

In general, the future value of CU Y earning compound interest at continuously compounded interest rate r_c for t years is:

$$Ye^{r_c t}.$$

B.11 Continuous Discounting for *t* Years

Exercise 9. You want to buy an instrument that will pay you a total of CU30,000 after 8 years, with no interim payments. If your required return is 5.4% continuously compounded, how much will you pay for the instrument?

Answer:

Let the amount be X. Then

$$X \times e^{0.054 \times 8} = 30{,}000.$$

Therefore,

$$X = 30{,}000 \Big/ e^{0.054 \times 8} = 19{,}476.28.$$

In general, the present value of CU Y discounted from year t to year 0 at continuously compounded interest rate r_c is:

$$Ye^{-r_c t} \text{ or } \frac{Y}{e^{r_c t}}.$$

Exercise 10. The monthly compounded interest rate is 6.95 percent. What is the equivalent continuously compounded rate? (Hint: Find the rate that gives the same present value for some fixed period, say 1 year).

Answer:
Let the required rate be r_c. Then:

$$e^{r_c} = \left(1 + \frac{0.0695}{12}\right)^{12}$$

Taking natural logarithms on both sides:

$$r_c = 12 \ln \left(1 + \frac{0.0695}{12}\right) = 6.93\%$$

Exercise 11. The monthly compounded interest rate is 6.95 percent. What is the equivalent semi-annually compounded rate?

Answer: Let the required rate be r_s. Equate future values of CU1 after 6 months.

$$\left(1 + \frac{0.0695}{12}\right)^6 = \left(1 + \frac{r_s}{2}\right) = 1.035257$$

Therefore,

$$r_s = (1.035257 - 1) \times 2 = 7.0514\%$$

Exercise 12. The continuously compounded interest rate is 3.26%. What is the rate compounded every 187 days? (Hint: that is, $\frac{365}{187}$ times per year).

Answer: Let the required number be r. Equating future values after one year,

$$e^{0.0326} = \left(1 + \frac{r}{\frac{365}{187}}\right)^{\frac{365}{187}}$$

Rearranging, we get

$$r = \left(e^{0.0326 \times \frac{187}{365}} - 1\right) \times \frac{365}{187} = 3.287\%.$$

References

Abramowitz, M., & Stegun, I. A. (1964). *Handbook of Mathematical Functions with Formulas, Graphs, and Mathematical Tables* (9th dover printing, 10th GPO printing edition). New York: Dover.

Joshi, M. (2008). *C++ design patterns and derivatives pricing*. Cambridge, UK: Cambridge University Press.

Prata, S. (2011). *C++ primer plus* (6th ed.). New Jersey: Pearson Education.

Index

S. Lynn, *Valuation for Accountants*, Springer Texts in Business and Economics,
https://doi.org/10.1007/978-981-15-0357-3

The manufacturer's authorised representative in the EU is Springer Nature Customer Service Centre GmbH, Europaplatz 3, 69115 Heidelberg, Germany. If you have any concerns regarding our products, please contact ProductSafety@springernature.com

Printed and bound by CPI Group (UK) Ltd, Croydon, CR0 4YY
25/09/2026
02222898-0015